they see it. The media tend to place these catch phases in the forefront of their reports to shock and catch the attention of viewers. This may pique the interest of subsequent killers to create a final statement to further establish their infamy, media attention and transcendence.

The glorification of infamy

The publicity and obsessive focus on the perpetrators of multiple murder run the gamut from Jeffery Dahmer gracing the cover of *People* magazine to the terrible affront to decency that the magazine exhibited by choosing Dahmer as one of the "100 Most Intriguing People of the 20th Century" (Fox and Levin, 2005, p. 6). This public fascination extends to reality-based television dramas and films that cast handsome stars in the role of the vicious killer. More obscure niches in the comic book and trading card industries even print works that portray the actual crimes committed by some of these real-life killers (ibid.). In addition, artwork completed by serial killer John Wayne Gacy and mass killer Richard Speck has achieved what has been called an inflated commercial value (ibid.). One might argue that it is not artistic talent that places a morbid sense of value on their work, but rather society's fascination with their crimes and celebrity. Real-life crime and infamous characters generate revenue.

The impact of celebrating murderers

"Making monsters into celebrities only teach our youngsters – especially alienated and marginalized teenagers – a lesson about how to get attention" (Fox and Levin, 2005, p. 13). Some outcast kids may be inspired by prior, well-publicized shootings and crave similar anti-hero celebrity status for themselves. Similarly, this craving for celebrity is noted among captured serial killers who boast about more killings than they actually committed (or at least, more killings than can be proven legally). These criminals perceive their transgressions purely as a number game – and the one with the most kills achieves greatest notoriety. The media unwittingly – and arguably with disregard for the consequences of doing so – play into the killers' egos.

The *copycat phenomenon* is a result of this quest for power and infamy. The prospect of heightened media attention can influence the killer's plans in the timing of an attack, the location and the method of killing (Fox and Levin, 2005). Typically, the greatest effect is produced when a copycat mass murder takes place within a relatively short window of time after extensive media attention given to a prior type of killing (ibid.). Copycat killers mirror the prior incident fairly closely. This type of emulation was clearly demonstrated in the Virginia Tech massacre by Cho's use of weapons and his fatigue attire; however, Cho's killing spree was not in close proximity time-wise to the Columbine shooting – it was actually just over seven years later. The Columbine event took place when Cho was 15 years old, which perhaps may have been a critical time in his identity development. As stated earlier, Cho's fixation with Harris and Klebold began to appear in some of his writing assignments at school shortly after the news coverage of Columbine. Overall, "the copycat phenomenon" tends to be strongest when a particular incident or particular criminal receives substantial media attention (p. 213).

Craving attention

The lack of any crystallized, positive self-concept may be a precipitant for an individual who craves affirmation through notoriety, to fantasize about, plan and commit mass or serial murder. Such fantasy allows perpetrators to see "themselves as a somebody, a person who should have a place in the world and who can act to change what might be wrong in the world" (Tonso, 2009, p. 1277).

On August 5, 2009, George Sodini (48 years old) walked into an LA Fitness Center that he frequented near Pittsburgh, Pennsylvania, and opened fire on a women's aerobics class. Sodini killed four people, including himself, and badly injured nine others. Before Sodini carried out the LA Fitness massacre, he left references on his blog speculating about the public's reaction to his plans. He states that "probably 99% of the people who know me well don't even think I was this crazy" (NYPOST.com, August 6, 2009, Blog Full Text Source). Sodini also states that "any of the 'Practice Papers' left on my coffee table I used or the notes in my gym bag can be published freely. Maybe all this will shed insight on why some people just cannot make things happen in their life, which can potentially benefit others" (ibid.). Sodini actually seemed to think that by randomly shooting and killing innocent people, he is doing good for society. Moreover, he also ruminates on his dismal life to offer justification for homicide. By contrast, Sodini also reflects on the fact that people will judge him. He concludes that society's judgment really does not matter, since he plans on being dead.

During his 20-year battle with the IRS, Joseph Stack perhaps saw himself as a "lone wolf (extremist)" and the more he was going on his own in protest, the more his own belief system intensified (Levin, in CNN: Special Investigations Unit, April 18, 2010). Evidenced by both his final actions and his final words, Stack's revenge fantasy might have included himself in the role of the common man, engaged in a high-stakes game on an uneven-playing field, forced to both compete and lose, yet willing to take his own life (along with others) to "light the fuse" to an uprising for the people – a real "folk hero" of sorts (ibid.).

In a video from March 15, 1999, Eric Harris and Dylan Klebold discuss their hope that the videos they are making will one day be shown all over the world, when their "masterpiece" is done. Dylan proclaims: "Directors will be fighting over this story" (Shepard, 1999b; Video Tape Transcripts, A Columbine Site). The boys speculate whether Steven Spielberg or Quentin Tarantino should direct the film (ibid.). Their desire for fame did come about as they imagined. Klebold and Harris's photo appeared on the cover of *Time Magazine* under the headline "The Monsters Next Door" (Fox and Levin, 2005, p. 13).

Adult readers indeed may have viewed the boys as monsters, but some young teens instead may have seen them as celebrities and anti-heroes (Fox and Levin, 2005). Seung Hui Cho, who later became the Virginia Tech shooter, was known to have openly admired Klebold and Harris.

Before Columbine, research suggested that school shooters "drew upon cultural scripts drawn from the popular media, particularly film and video games – such as the *Basketball Diaries, Natural Born Killers,* or '*Mortal Combat*' – that glorify the violent male as an alluring anti-hero" (Newman and Fox, 2009, pp. 1294–1295). "However, after Columbine, it seems clear that the tragedy has itself become a script" (ibid.). The perpetrators become antisocial icons. They are admired by social outcasts for their "defiance in the name of upending conformist social pecking orders (i.e., athletes, rich kids, or other popular teens)" (ibid.).

This consciousness was the case for Seung Hui Cho. Cho was a complete outcast; he had no friends, no social life and no interest in spending time with people (Dupue, in the Virginia Tech Review Panel Report, 2007). Cho saw himself as invisible and he was utterly incompetent at fitting in. His college suite-mates reported taking him to a few parties, where "he would always end up sitting in the corner by himself" (p. 42). Cho's self-identification as a "question mark" (ibid.) implies that he was aware of his social incompetence and was an enigma even to himself. His attempt to disguise himself in class only drew more attention to himself. Despite all the protestations of "invisibility" Cho, in fact, craved recognition – either as a published author, or when that didn't work out, as a vengeful mass murderer (Dupue, in the Virginia Tech Review Panel Report, 2007, Appendix M, p. 5).

Cho was scheduled to graduate in early May (Levin and Madfis, 2009). He had not yet secured a job or managed to adapt to other pressures of early adulthood (ibid.). Cho's impending eviction of sorts from his contained life on the university campus may have been his final straw (ibid.).

Thus, the fantasy began and Cho rationalized a plan to kill those who were destined to achieve what he could not (Dupue, in the Virginia Tech Review Panel Report, 2007). To do so, he demonized his peers as frivolous spenders of their parents' money and partygoers who lived lives of gluttony. Cho vowed to put an end to their debauchery and assure his place in history. He was compelled to replicate the Columbine boys, even outdo them. Like Klebold and Harris, Cho was "desperate to make his fellow students take notice of him" (Levin and Madfis, 2009, p. 1238), so much so that on the afternoon of April 16, 2007, in the midst of his killing spree, Cho took a break long enough to get to the post office and mail carefully crafted videotapes, photos of himself and a manifesto to NBC News. These materials depicted Cho as a dangerous and powerful person holding guns and knives in a threatening "V" formation, dressed in combat fatigues and ranting over his mistreatment. The media and the world were left with plenty to ponder and to study, adding to Cho's infamy.

Discussion and conclusion

By examining the personal histories of numerous multiple murderers, a common theme of developmental interruption emerges. From a psychological perspective, most killers exhibit severe abnormalities in their psychological and social development. These developmental difficulties predispose the individual to interpersonal difficulties. The psychological perspective highlights the killers' transcendent fantasies and imagined results. These fantasies provide the fractured person with a new self-image that resolves, transforms or otherwise alters the meaning of the mass killing.

From a sociological perspective, killers develop and experience their fantasies within discernible social contexts. The cognitive constructs they develop are always directed to others or devised in light of others, real or imaginary. For this reason, the sociological concept of the *self* is a useful tool for analyzing the killers-to-others relationship, as Athens's (1995) work does so well.

Yet, the power of psychological explanations and interpretations of mass killers can also be seen as a critique of the deviance perspective.

Since its inception in the 1960s (Becker, 1963), labeling theory in particular has tended toward a behaviorist view of the impact of the label on the actor. The label can shape the actor's behavior through the process of *secondary deviance* (Lemert, 1967) by which the actor's motivation to break rules is a direct result of the label, not the etiology of the original act. Becker (1963) went so far as to focus moral attention on the actor as a "victim" of often immoral and unfair labeling practices. The documents reviewed in this chapter, however, offer a different take. Much of the activity that leads up to mass killing, including the killing itself, is the active result of the killers trying to negate, deflect, nullify and contradict labels applied to them by peers, teachers, administrators and a range of agents of social control. Kotarba (1984) refers to this process as the *subversion of* labeling by which the actor attempts to avoid the label and its consequences, especially on self-identity.

Thus, a reasonable approach to a scholarly understanding of mass killers requires an acceptance of a very complex interplay between social contexts and preconditions and psychological processing of those contexts and preconditions, in particular kinds of situations. The etiology of mass killing may have social corollaries and accouterments, but it surely lies deeper than the moral judgments of others. The fantasies described in this chapter are much more than mirror reflections of the worldviews of significant – or even generalized – others. Further, psychological processes do not operate in a sociocultural vacuum. This complex interplay is made more visible and analytically relevant given both the increasing role played by the media in this formula and our increasingly sophisticated ability to understand the media.

References

Altheide, D. (2004) "Consuming Terrorism", *Symbolic Interaction*, 27 (3), 289–308.

—— (2009) "The Columbine Shootings and the Discourse of Fear", *American Behavioral Scientist*, 52, 1354–1370.

Altheide, D. and R. Snow (1979) *Media Logic* (Beverly Hills, CA: Sage).

Athens, L. (1995) "Dramatic Self-change", *The Sociological Quarterly*, 36, 571–586.

—— (1997) *Violent Criminal Acts and Actors Revisited* (Urbana, IL: University of Illinois Press).

Becker, H. (1963) *Outsiders* (New York: Glencoe).

Cullin, D. (2004) "The Depressive and the Psychopath: At Last We Know Why the Columbine Killers Did It", *Slate*, http://www.slate.com/id/2099203/, date accessed March 1, 2011.

Fox, J. A. and J. Levin (2005) *Extreme Killing: Understanding Serial and Mass Murder* (Thousand Oaks, CA: Sage).

FOXNews.com (2010) "Pilot Crashes into Texas Building in Apparent Anti-IRS Suicide", http://www.foxnews.com/us/2010/02/18/pilot-crashes-texas-building-apparent-anti-irs-suicide, date accessed April 28, 2010.

Frymer, B. (2009) "The Media Spectacle of Columbine: Alienated Youth as an Object of Fear", *American Behavioral Scientist*, 52 (10), 1387–1404.

Giroux, H. A. (2009) *Youth in a Suspect Society: Democracy or Disposability* (New York: Palgrave Macmillan).

Goffman, E. (1963) *Behavior in Public Places* (New York: Simon & Schuster).

Healy, R. (2006) "The Columbine Papers: What Their Parents Knew", *Time, http://www.nytimes.com/2010/06/17/us/17bishop.html*, date accessed December 15, 2009.

Hickey, E. W. (2010) *Serial Murderers and Their Victims,* 5th edn. (Belmont, CA: Wadsworth).

—— (2013) *Serial Murderers and Their Victims,* 6th edn. (Belmont, CA: Wadsworth).

Hightower, S. (1991). "Killer May Have Had Vendetta against Women", Associated Press, Retrieved from Lexis/Nexis, date accessed January 15, 2010.

Holmes, R. M. and S. T. Holmes (2001) *Mass Murder in the United States* (Upper Saddle River, NJ: Prentice Hall).

Kimmel, M. S. and M. Mahler (2003) "Adolescent Masculinity, Homophobia, and Violence", *American Behavioral Scientist*, 46, 1439–1458.

Klein, J. (2006) "Cultural Capital and High School Bullies: How Social Inequality Impacts School Violence", *Men and Masculinities*, 9, 53–75.

Kotarba, J. A. (1984) "One More for the Road: The Subversion of Labeling in the Tavern Subculture", in J. D. Douglas (ed.) *The Sociology of Deviance* (Boston: Allyn and Bacon).

Larkin, R. (2007) *Comprehending Columbine* (Philadelphia, PA: Temple University Press).

—— (2009) "The Columbine Legacy: Rampage Shooting as Political Acts", *American Behavioral Scientist*, 52, 1309–1326.

Lemert, E. (1967) *Human Deviance, Social Problems and Social Control* (Englewood Cliffs, NJ: Prentice-Hall).

Levin, B. (2010) In CNN: Special Investigations Unit. "Death and Taxes: Joe Stack's Attack on the IRS", http://www.archives.cnn.com/TRANSCRIPTS/1004/18/siu.01.html, date accessed April 25, 2010.

Levin, J. and E. Madfis (2009) "Mass Murder at School and Cumulative Strain", *American Behavioral Scientist*, 52 (9), 1227–1245.

Madfis, E. and T. Arford (2008) "Investigating Precipitating Factors in Mass Murder: Do 'Last Straws' Get to the Bottom of Rampage Killing or Merely Scratch the Surface?", paper presented at the "Conference of the Eastern Sociological Society", New York

Michaud, S. and H. Aynesworth (1983) *The Only Living Witness* (New York: W. W. Norton).

Newman, K. and C. Fox (2009) "Repeat Tragedy: Rampage Shootings in American High School and College Settings, 2002–2008", *American Behavioral Science*, 52, 1287–1308.

Newman, K., C. Fox, W. Roth, J. Mehta and D. Harding (2004) *Rampage: The Social Roots of School Shootings* (New York: Basic Books).

Ramsland, K. (2005) *Inside the Minds of Mass Murderers: Why They Kill* (Westport, CT: Praeger).

Rhodes, R. (1999) *Why They Kill: The Discoveries of a Maverick Criminologist* (New York: Alfred A. Knopf).

Rudd, M., A. Berman, T. Joiner Jr., M. Nock, M. Silverman, M. Mandrusiak et al. (2006) "Warning Signs for Suicide: Theory, Research, and Clinical Applications", *Suicide and Life-Threatening Behavior*, 36 (3), 255–262.

Shepard, C. (1999a) A Columbine Site, http://acolumbinesite.com/eric/writing/journal.html, date accessed October 10, 2009.

—— (1999b) A Columbine Site, http://acolumbinesite.com/media.html, date accessed October 10, 2009.

Tonso, K. (2009) "Violent Masculinities as Tropes for School Shooters: The Montreal Massacre, the Columbine Attack and Rethinking Schools", *American Behavioral Scientist*, 52, 1266–1285.

Virginia Tech Review Panel Report (2007) "Mass Killings at Virginia Tech April 16, 2007", http://www.vtreviewpanel.org/report/index.html, date accessed January 28, 2010.

Vossekuil, B., R. Fein, M. Reddy, R. Borum and W. Modzeleski (2004) *The Final Report and Findings of the Safe School Initiative: Implications for the Prevention of School Attacks in the United States* (Washington DC US Secret Service and US Department of Education).

Part III

Doing Deviance between Teaching and Research

13

The Didactic Relevance of the Death of Deviance Debate

Susan Day and Joseph A. Kotarba

Introduction

The purpose of this chapter is to explore the implications of the "death of deviance" debate for the teaching of deviance and related courses. There are two separate yet related phenomena at play here that deserve discussion. On the one hand, as the various chapters in this book illustrate, the "death of deviance" debate can be quite theoretical with policy implications. The issue is whether "deviance", as a conceptual framework, leads to powerful explanations for certain types of social behavior. Critics of deviance argue two things. First, contemporary structural and/or social psychological theories can explain these behaviors without resorting to the moralistic, sometimes journalistic, often romantic and unfortunately politically biased baggage that the idea of deviance carries with it (Gouldner, 1975). Second, the emasculation of traditional deviance theory has been facilitated by the overwhelming popularity of labeling theory, which has effectively removed deviance as a dependent variable (Sumner, 1994). On the other hand, we need to address the implications of this theoretical debate for teaching sociological approaches to understanding moral and rule-related behavior.

While the death of deviance debate continues, one fact of academic life cannot be ignored: undergraduate and graduate courses in deviance and related areas remain among sociology's most popular offerings (Goode, 2004). These other courses include social problems, social pathology and criminology, among others. Furthermore, standard courses such as introductory sociology, the sociology of health, the sociology of mental health and social psychology commonly contain instructional units or reading material on deviance. Since healthy enrollments in today's competitive world of higher education are sacred among cash-strapped college and university administrators, department leaders must continue to offer these courses. The question then becomes: how can our course offerings and content reflect the issues and intellectual integrity of the debate without destroying our curriculum and its overall value to our students?

This chapter is a display and summary of an ongoing conversation between two scholars who both teach deviance, but in very different ways. Their conversations reflect contrasting paradigms in sociology as well as contrasting empirical topics to which deviance theory is applied. Susan begins with a Mertonian/anomie theory approach to deviance, whereas Joe takes more of a symbolic interactionist/postmodernist approach. Susan's approach lends itself to the design and implementation of conventional, free-standing deviant behavior and criminology courses, with an emphasis on combining multiple viewpoints into a perspective that overlooks their divergent assumptions. Joe's approach lends itself to the embedding of ideas and notions of rule-related and morally tinged behavior in the discussion of topics ranging from health behavior and recreational drug use to popular music and youth cultures. This chapter contributes to the death of deviance debate by comparing and contrasting these two somewhat outlying paradigmatic positions though the death of deviance debate to date has largely been among adherents of the more middling theoretical positions of social constructivism and critical theory (Goode, 2004). We argue that having all four major paradigms represented in the death of deviance debate mirrors the desirable policy of teaching four paradigms in undergraduate and graduate sociology courses: consensus, conflict, interactionist and postmodernist theory (Kotarba and Johnson, 2002).

Finally, we discuss the value of even bringing the debate into the classroom. Is the death of deviance debate one of those particularistic, in-house, intellectually technical issues that would only serve to confuse students, especially undergraduate students, who are struggling to understand *the* sociological perspective on social life? Or, is the death of deviance debate a dramatic case study of the ultimate reality of social theory, that is, theory is not truth but *merely* a way of asking questions about the social world with suggestions for where and how to find the answers?

Structural thoughts on deviance

Although Joe and Susan are in the same professional age cohort, their professional training and theoretical influences are different. As an undergraduate student in the late 1960s, Susan's theoretical grounding in deviance was in the anomie/strain tradition, beginning with Durkheim, and extending through Merton, Albert K. Cohen and Richard Cloward and Lloyd Ohlin. Unlike Joe whose graduate training was riddled with constructivism, subjectivism and the somewhat mystical side of existential phenomenology, Susan viewed sociology as a science. Accordingly, she understood labeling theory as an adjunct to structural explanations of deviance. She just never saw the labeling approach as a complete sociological explanation. She did indeed see labeling theory as a valuable supplement to the structural approaches she used in numerous social problems courses she taught while working on her PhD at the University of Kansas, specifically, Thomas Scheff's *Being Mentally Ill* (1966). Despite the attraction of Scheff's repudiation of the medicalization of mental illness, Susan's master's level deviance courses emphasized the anomie perspective as the definitive sociological explanation for deviance. A key feature of the anomie/strain perspective was a critique of American society in general, particularly Merton's rather Marxian notion that the most-valued aspects of the society (freedom, competition and high aspirations) were the source of the most condemned aspects of society (deviance, crime and delinquency). Far from locating the source of deviance in families and immigrant groups, as was the focus from earlier social disorganization theory, anomie theory found the source of deviance in the class structure and the unequal opportunities created by the class structure. This aspect of the anomie perspective makes it core sociology in the Marx-Weber-Durkheim structural tradition, but also provides a significant reason for the decline of anomie/strain theory: it argued that higher rates of deviance, crime and delinquency were to be found in the lower classes.

A second major feature of that era's structural explanations for the higher rates of deviance found in the lower classes was the impact of middle-class standards on working and lower class children. This point of view noted the impact of teachers' strongly held bias for middle-class skills and attitudes (e.g., gratification deferral, control of private property and high aspirations) organized in the "middle class measuring rod", against which working-class males were measured and found unable to "measure up", thus making academic and occupational success less likely (Cohen, 1955).

In many ways, the decline of popularity of anomie/strain theory can be linked to the decline of liberalism and the rise of radicalism among sociologists in America and Europe during the politically fervent 1960s. The critics argued that while anomie theory offered a critique of society, it nevertheless located deviance specifically in the lower classes. The critics charged liberal sociologists with "blaming the victim" (Ryan, 1971). Perhaps just as damning was the close policy association between Cloward and Ohlin's (1960) theoretical perspective and the ameliorative neighborhood programs of the Great Society, associated with President Lyndon Johnson. While liberals saw such programs as a way to change inner cities, radicals asserted that the reforms did not go far enough or were simply window dressing.

In addition, a number of perspectives emerged in the sociology of crime and deviance, some seemingly more radical (e.g., Quinney, 1970) because they located the source of deviance in the formal labeling aspects of the oppressive government, and others simply more aggressively liberal (Scheff, 1966; Schur, 1971), who located the labeling process in both formal and informal processes conducted by *agents of social control*. Control theory (Hirschi, 1969; Nettler, 1974) must also be seen as offering an attractive and accessible alternative to anomie theory by providing the source of deviance in the individual's orientation to his family and social groups, and direct refutations of aspects of anomie theory offered by some theorists (Matza, 1964; Kornhauser, 1978) must be seen as a factor contributing to the decline of the anomie perspective.

The disappearance of anomie/strain theory from all but introductory texts and deviance/crime readers during the 1970s and 1980s was remediated in the 1990s with the rise of "champions" for the theoretical perspective: Steven Messner and Richard Rosenfeld (2006) for anomie theory and Ronald Akers (2009) for learning theory. Messner and Rosenfeld returned to Merton's emphasis on the American Dream and extended the anomie analysis to explain middle- and upper-class crime. In so doing, they dealt with assertions of inappropriate class bias. Any discussion of the American Dream is particularly meaningful to current students, who understand the notion, but are told that the possibility of their achieving the American Dream is less likely than previous generations.

Finally, it must also be said that a major reason for the decline of anomie/strain theory in the latter part of the 20th century was the tendency of sociologists to emphasize the differences in their perspectives or to combine a variety of perspectives together (e.g., Hirschi and Gottfredson, 1990; Sampson and Laub, 1995). Criminology is more interdisciplinary and much more social psychological than before, and deviance theorists still like to apply techniques of neutralization (Sykes and Matza, 1957) to groups of people they study, as well. Susan argues that a number of these and other perspectives are compatible with anomie theory at the structural level of analysis as interpreted by Merton and Cohen. This assertion provides the basis for our later agreement on strategies for teaching deviance in the university curriculum.

Teaching the structural aspects of deviance

Structural explanations of deviance, whether based upon anomie theory or some other perspective, have at their core an inherent problem in the classroom: from whose perspective is any particular behavior called deviant? Put differently, the very essence and social location of deviant behavior was made theoretically and methodologically problematic by the emergence of labeling and social control theory. Early structural theorists assumed that widely held cultural standards emerged from the "majority," which was typically, if loosely, defined as upper- and middle-class society, and that segment of the population defined what was deviant and what was not. But the proliferation of counter-culture behaviors (e.g., recreational drug use, open marketing of pornography and premarital and extramarital sexual behavior) – or at least the awareness of these behaviors – once perceived as rare or exotic are now increasingly seen commonplace. Other behaviors (e.g., delinquency and under-age drinking) once seen as serious are now redefined as part of maturation.

Other forms of behavior once considered deviant in classroom lectures and general societal discussion have come to be redefined as "illness". Labeling theory has sparked the examination of the medicalization of deviance, that is, the movement to redefine deviants as "patients" who should not be blamed for their conditions. Some of these conditions are increasingly treated with drugs (e.g., eating disorders, depression, learning disorders and many forms of emotional disturbance), whereas other formerly deviant behaviors are now increasingly seen as commonplace behaviors in our culture (e.g., homosexuality, membership in religious cults and sects and political extremism). While it may be the case that no one wants his or her child to partake of these behaviors, some people and many students frequently challenge the label of deviant when applied to the behaviors listed earlier, with the question, "Who are you to say that is deviant?"

The best answer Susan has found to this question comes straight from the perspective that emerged out of the work of conflict theorists such as Quinney in the 1970s. Behavior is deviant if defined as deviant – a simple labeling statement – but certain kinds of behaviors and certain kinds of people are more likely to be defined as deviant (a more sophisticated labeling perspective) because of their social position, or status. Their behavior is seen as deviant because that behavior, when known, more than occasionally results in a formal punishment of incarceration, citation or arrest, or an informal but powerful punishment of shunning, physical attack, bullying, quarantine or hospitalization. In other words, the discussion moves from a structural explanation of deviance (What is it about social organization that encourages this behavior?) to an answer at the intersection of structure and interaction (certain people are more likely to be defined as deviant because their behavior is more likely to be observed, adjudicated and punished).

Once this hurdle is vaulted, assuming a safe landing, a professor has the opportunity – but not the necessity – to offer a powerful critique of American society and a predictive discussion of the future of the world next century by exposing the basic perspective in Merton's 1938 article. Beginning with the notion that the American Dream carries within it the seeds of its own destruction, which allows paying proper homage to Marx, the professor can begin to discuss how powerful groups in the society have the ability to define behaviors as deviant (cocaine use) or not (wearing religious symbols as fashion items). At this point, a structural discussion can begin which emphasizes the role power and wealth play in the creation of deviant categories. Moreover, a perspective that combines structural elements with interactionism (Erikson, 1966) can be advanced.

This approach to deviance allows the professor to integrate theories, discussing their complementary areas of intersection, an approach that Susan believes is the way to make the subject relevant and to demonstrate that sociology offers more complete and complex understandings. For too long, sociologists have emphasized their differences, particularly in their teaching. Structural-functionalism is made to seem radically different from conflict theory, when their similarities could just as easily be noted. (Both analyze at the macro level; both focus on institutions.) The "natural" sciences do not emphasize their theoretical differences in their undergraduate courses and students come away from those courses thinking that those scientists know something, whereas students often think sociologists are just debating their opinions.

In addition to demonstrating that sociology and sociologists actually *know* – that is, can explain – a great deal, an emphasis on integrating perspectives can move sociology away from having to discuss the more extreme or dramatic forms of deviance. Since *Silence of the Lambs*, students have been increasingly interested in serial killers. Sociologists cannot completely explain why serial killers do what they do, but we can explain the function a discussion of serial killers has for a society that needs to divert attention from economic failures in a capitalist system or totalitarian behaviors in a purported democratic representative form of government. We can also discuss sexual behaviors that are criminalized in the United States (prostitution, adultery) as deviance defined by more powerful groups rather than emerging from personal failure. The same is true of other forms of deviance more common to the lower classes. Gambling, street hustling, gangs of all kinds (motorcycle, territorial) and even burglary and car theft can be seen through a lens emphasizing the resources poured into a criminal justice system that bears down most heavily on behaviors most common to the lower classes and gives relative short shrift to the behaviors more common to the upper middle and upper classes (stock manipulations, real estate fraud and all the stock market behaviors leading to the 2008 crash and recession). We can also show the social movements that seek to counter these upper-class behaviors, the counter-labeling efforts or even the "subversion of labeling" activities (Kotarba, 1984) and we can show that they sometimes succeed!

Finally, of course, an integrated perspective allows professors to take on the most difficult of topics in the United States: capital punishment. Student comments reflect the sentiment in favor of capital punishment that is common at the national level, which has changed from opposition to capital punishment in the 1960s to support for the punishment today (Saad, 2005). But when students learn that capital sentences are given to lower class men of color at rates disproportionate to their numbers in society, and when they understand (1) opportunity differentials and (2) criminal justice system process inequities, they often change their ideas about capital punishment. Put more accurately, female students often change their ideas because, like their female counterparts in the larger society, they often reject capital punishment as a "fitting" punishment; support for capital punishment is far greater among males in the United States.

In summary, a traditional and purely structural assessment of deviance fails in class because there is less agreement about many kinds of deviance definitions (drug use, homosexuality, delinquency) that are popular subjects in structural analysis. On the other hand, students agree that homicide, theft and sexual assault, to name the obvious, are deviant as well as criminal –without, of course, understanding the legal processes by which some killings, coveting of one's neighbor's goods and unwelcomed sexual advances come to be labeled criminal and other are not. Yet the structural view of traditional criminal deviance can be made if the professor incorporates a view that emphasizes the power aspects of criminal and deviance definitions that are congruent with structural definitions. Why are poor people more likely to be defined as deviant? Because they have less opportunity to succeed through "conventional" means and their unconventional means have been criminalized by the more powerful elements in the society.

These ideas illustrate the strength in analysis generated over many years by writers whose goal has been to develop powerful *theories* of deviant behavior. On the one hand, these theories fit the traditional sociological mandate of elevating our analysis to the level of theory. On the other hand, these theories should be useful to professionals and students alike for whom the very notion of *deviance* is real and worthy of study. Thus, deviance is still relevant to the curriculum if the paradigmatic bases of the debate are clearly presented and differentiated. The many theories maintaining currency in deviance and criminology courses, perhaps ironically, are representative of a discipline that is, in our postmodern era, increasingly fragmented itself. Deviance is a useful tool for differentiated competing sub-disciplines in sociology. It is also valuable for teaching specialized courses in social control (e.g., criminology and social problems). Finally, deviance should remain in the curriculum because students like the perspective and the topics it attracts.

Interactionist thoughts on deviance

Joe was a member of the intellectual milieu raised on labeling theory. As an undergraduate student at Illinois State University in the mid-1960s, he was taught the foundation of deviance theory. Some of the bricks were structural, like Merton's anomie theory, whereas others were early versions of what would come to be known as constructivist/interactionist theory. Joe and his fellow students were taught that there were two specific and early constructivist/interactionist ideas that were seminal to the later emergence of labeling theory. The first was Frank Tannenbaum's (1938) insightful notion of *tagging*. Tannenbaum was a criminologist who argued that the local community can inadvertently force certain boys down the path of delinquency. There can be a progression of conflict between the juvenile delinquent and the larger community. A snow-balling effect takes place as the delinquent increasingly sees himself in the negative terms with which the community tags him. The second was Alfred R. Lindesmith's (1947) study of opiate addiction, which found that addiction occurs at the point in the life of the addict when others – that is, other users – help him associate withdrawal symptoms with the absence of the drug.

The lasting point of these early studies, as Susan noted earlier, is that the interactionally and symbolically based definition of deviance can be analyzed quite separately from the behavior or alleged behavior in question. This analytical observation resonated well with students for at least one major reason; it fit well with the more general criticism of mainstream, Parsonian sociology students were learning about in many of their other courses (e.g., theory, the family and social problems). This sociological insight, however, was a necessary but probably not sufficient trigger for labeling theory and the energy, momentum and thoughtfulness it brought to the sociological enterprise in general and students in particular. For Joe and his peers, that trigger was Becker's *Outsiders* (1963). Let's look at this through a bit of autobiography.

In 1969, Joe was finishing his BA at Illinois State University. To that point, deviance was simply another substantive course to fill out a schedule, along with complex organizations, the family and social psychology. Although we were taught that there was theoretical foment growing in the discipline, and that labeling theory was in the forefront to the critique of mainstream sociology, we did not see labeling theory as a telling critique against mainstream sociology. The relativism that permeates early labeling theory still seemed relevant only to bad behavior. Put differently, we were not taught that the juvenile delinquent behavior discussed by Tannenbaum was not bad per se; we were simply taught how this bad behavior was processed by their system. We still pretty much assumed that everyone "knew" that deviant behavior could be easily equated with criminal and/or delinquent behavior. When we read *Outsiders* in 1968, our whole perception and sense of deviance really changed. Instead of illustrating the travails of *true* deviants like delinquents, heroin users and criminals, Becker wrote about the way labeling takes place among regular, normal people like us – middle-class college students. We saw ourselves in at least three parts of the book. The first was Becker's (1963) somewhat structural discussion of moral entrepreneurs, adults if you will, who through the power of legislation and the judicial system, go around magically and somewhat arbitrarily denoting the things poor and otherwise disadvantaged people do as wrong. Agents of social control were much like the parents back home with whom we argued when visiting for Thanksgiving or Christmas. Becker rallied us to see how the negative designation of our new and experimental lifestyles – marijuana smoking in particular – was wrong, and capricious at best.

264 *Susan Day and Joseph A. Kotarba*

The second feature of the *Outsiders* that caught our eye was the forceful statement Becker made about the morality of deviance. This version of labeling theory fit well with our increasing commitment to civil rights, the anti-war movement and equality issues in general. Becker made it clear that it is not bad people necessarily who engage in deviant behavior, but it may be bad people who do the labeling. These are the same bad people who beat up peaceful hippie activists and murdered community activists like the Black Panthers. Becker (1963) again rallied us to see how smoking marijuana specifically, and other lifestyle experiments in general, need not be seen as bad. Becker made us college students see ourselves as victims, "more sinned against than sinning" (p. 76). As members of what would come to be known as the "Baby Boomer Generation", we appreciated the removal of personal responsibility for what we chose to do.

The third feature of the *Outsiders* that caught our eye was the *psychological* tone of the book. Again, as baby boomers living in or near the edge of the counter-cultural revolution, we seemed to be obsessed with ourselves. We experimented with various religions, alternative lifestyles and unconventional relationships (see also Roszak, 1969). We tried meditation and read Khahil Gibran religiously. Becker told us that that, for better or for worse, our sense of self was largely shaped by the people we respect, listen to or have to listen to – *significant others*, as he put it. Some unfortunate people in society – poor people and people of color in particular – were subject to autocratic labeling and often abusive labeling. As members of the privileged classes, we believed we could manage the self-labeling process by, among other things, selecting the significant others who defined who we were.

When Joe began graduate work for a Master's degree at Arizona State University in 1971, sociology was undergoing a radical change. Instead of studying the social world and devising ways to save it, he and his classmates spent increasing time and thought studying sociology itself. They read all the politically radical attacks on Talcott Parsons, then the premier mainstream theorist in the discipline, for taking much too conservative a stance toward problems in American society. They also read Blumer's symbolic interactionist critiques of structuralism, as Blumer called the study of the processes by which society is created through interaction and the meaning resources available in culture. Symbolic interactionism (SI) was a very attractive alternative to traditional, structuralist, and statistical sociology, especially to young scholars in the field. SI was comfortably close to the psychological view of the life most students enjoyed. SI was also conducive to qualitative research methods, which helped turn sociology into an adventure by which we could discover the otherwise hidden and mysterious corners of the social world.

One of the more valuable features of symbolic interaction we learned in graduate school was the way it served as a theoretical and philosophical home to labeling theory. Labeling theory emerged as a powerful game plan for operationalizing the exciting ideas in the more general symbolic interaction platform – especially for those young scholars who were not very interested in criminology and delinquency but in the evolving social problems of race, gender and war. Yet, it fit our lifestyles as well as our ways of thinking. As Joe Kotarba (1980) summarized in his review essay on labeling theory,

> Labeling theory was also a product of the times. The late 1950s and early 1960s were marked by growing social ferment. The Civil Rights movement, student dissent, and the growing awareness of poverty amongst plenty resulted in a shift of sympathy, especially among academics, to those people presumed to be oppressed by the more powerful "rule makers" and "rule enforcers"...This position of being a rebel within the system influenced the temperament and tone for much of the work of the labeling perspective. The world of deviance, with all its romantic establishments, was studied in depth, as dictated by the tenets of symbolic Interactionism. (pp. 88–89)

In conclusion, symbolic interactionism and its intellectual protégé, labeling theory, were exciting ways of doing sociology. To some degree, we wanted to relive the intellectual adventures of the generation that preceded us: the Beat Generation. Perhaps the most colorful description of the interactionist/labeling project was provided by one of its harshest critics, Alvin Gouldner (1962):

> This group of Chicagoans finds itself at home in the world of hip, Norman Mailer, drug addicts, jazz musicians, cab drivers, prostitutes, night people, drifters, grafters, and skidders, the cool cats and their kicks. To be fully appreciated, this stream of work cannot be seen solely in terms of the categories conventionally employed in sociological analysis. It has also to be seen from the viewpoint of the literary critic, a style or genre...it prefers the offbeat to the familiar, the vivid ethnographic detail to the dull taxonomy, the sensuously expressive to dry analysis, naturalistic observation to formal questionnaires (p. 209).

Thus, labeling theory was never seriously positioned to compete head-on with structuralist theories of deviance. Labeling theory followed the interests of labeling theorists: in the different rather than the deviant, the odd rather than the dangerous, the mysterious rather than the forbidden.

Teaching the constructivist aspects of deviance

Susan and Joe agree that the sociology of deviance is a valuable intellectual and pedagogical tool, for several reasons. Organizing behavioral expectations in terms of social rules provides a visible matrix of social order that is observable, analyzable and, for instructional purposes, demonstrable in the classroom. Our students, as common-sense members of society, "see" problematic behavior in terms we sociologists would recognize as *deviance*. Organizing our analysis of problematic social phenomena as deviance, as people of common sense see them, helps make our work relevant to both social policy formation and the meaning-needs of people of common sense.

To appreciate the value of labeling theory as a tool in the sociology of deviance enterprise – and the teaching of deviance – we must step back and see labeling theory as a feature of the symbolic interaction paradigm. There are two very important substantive topics in symbolic interactionist inquiry whose understanding is enhanced by a framing as deviance, and one in particular by an application of labeling theory. Both deal directly with issues of *morality* in everyday life.

Health and illness

The first topic is health and illness, and Joe's graduate training in the sociology of health shaped his thinking on this issue. His master's project at Arizona State University was on the chronic pain experience and acupuncture (Kotarba, 1975). He was interested in the various ways people who suffer from intractable pain seek various sources of meaning-in-culture to both make sense of their dilemma and to control if not eliminate the problem. Labeling theory suggested the value of analyzing the ways people with chronic pain's search for meaning and/or a cure as a social process. From an interactionist perspective, people seek meanings all the time to make sense of everyday life, especially everyday life's problems. Embodied problems that interfere with the routine and efficient living of everyday life, such as pain and disability, are among the most urgent. The primary reason people in pain visit physicians – and other healers – is to make sense of their pain, and to obtain meaning that will hopefully lead to pain management if not cure. Unfortunately, meanings for pain given by frustrated health care professionals are often pejorative meanings that function as labels that often do more harm than good (Kotarba, 1983).

Labeling theory was a useful analytical tool that helped Joe make sense of the common experience among people with chronic pain of shame and guilt for suffering. These feelings were commonly the result of others' critical definitions of self in terms of the sufferers' alleged inability to cope with pain without complaining, their search for meaning and cure outside of mainstream Western medicine and so forth. These others included significant people such as spouses and parents, but also professionals such as orthopedic surgeons, clinical psychologists, neurologists and psychologists. Erving Goffman's (1963) writing on *stigma* provided a useful concept for understanding the negative consequence of labels such as "malingerer" and "psychosomatic patient".

In making sense of the power of the medical establishment to control the pain industry, Eliot Freidson's (1975) interactionist analysis of the process by which doctors define (i.e., diagnose) problems as relativistic and situational phenomenon placed medical work squarely in the middle of the labeling model. The concept of *agent of social control* provided a nice model for understanding the work of the doctor sociologically. Doctors, like criminal agents of social control, are empowered by society to have the first and last say over what is illness and what are the legitimate ways of treating it. If the doctor decides that the patient's claims of illness are illegitimate, he is empowered to label that patient as deviant (e.g., hypochondriac, psychosomatic or malingerer) and punish the patient accordingly (e.g., deny the patient access to prescription drugs and hospital care).

The debate between labeling theorists and structuralist theorists – such as Talcott Parsons (1951) who argued that there is such a real thing as illness, which the doctor correctly manages through his training and expertise – provides Joe with a way to examine contrasting sociological models of modern medicine. Thus, Joe uses labeling theory to help undergraduate and graduate students in his sociology of health courses understand the *processes* by which sick people, their healers, their significant others and others try to make sense of illness in order to manage it. As Eliot Freidson (1975) and many other interactionists have noted, symptoms and the people presenting symptoms have no intrinsic social or medical meanings. The essence of formal and informal heath care is the search for meaning, and one of the primary ways it is applied is through labeling. A person in pain has either a slipped disc or arthritis, and the orthopedic surgeon or the rheumatologist gets to make the call – hopefully, but not necessarily, with good data! Morality emerges in terms of blame, competence and consequence. This argument is exactly the rationale for Susan's use of labeling theory for understanding the mental illness management enterprise.

Popular culture

The second topic is popular culture. This is a topic in which Joe has become increasingly interested, especially in terms of popular music and the subcultures and social scenes that evolve in and around it. Popular culture in general, and popular music in particular, serve as mechanisms by which people of common sense, especially young people, invoke, create, apply, negotiate and violate *morality* in everyday life. The everyday life perspective on deviance is predicated on the common observation that morality is pervasive in everyday life. Following Jack Douglas's (1970) writings on the essence of the American social order, morality refers to the way people create social order as a practical accomplishment and deal with social order issues through a reliance on their sense of values and right and wrong. The fact that people *see* morality all around them is, as mentioned earlier, a good reason to consider the power of deviance theory to explain the way people use that morality. In terms of culture in general, Pino (2009) has shown how music critics, over time, have invoked heavily moralistic labels or tropes to de-value music: "Debates concerning musical taste are embedded within larger debates regarding culture, notions of right and wrong, and the like" (p. 40).

To illustrate these points for students in his graduate and undergrad-uate courses on the sociology of popular music, Joe assigns an essay he wrote several years ago on a heavy metal band called Gwar (Kotarba, 1994). Gwar is a heavily costumed, theatrically oriented band that plays purposefully terrible and terribly loud music. Their shtick is to try to be as irreverent and outrageous as possible, to the great joy and apprecia-tion of their largely 15- to 18-year-old male audience. An ethnographic as well as autobiographical experience of Gwar led Joe to witness firsthand the everyday management of morality in a setting and within a popula-tion one might not expect to see a strong and effective morality play. We present here excerpts from this essay written several years ago:

> I must confess...I am intrigued by GWAR. I have seen them twice in live performance...The pretext for my presence at GWAR is the

fact that I am conducting sociological research on various aspects of rock and roll, specifically focusing on adolescents and heavy metal rock. The genesis of my intellectual interest in this rock genre can be traced at least as far back as 1986, when I conducted a study of adolescent rock music styles (e.g., punkers, headbangers, preppies and hippies)...

But, I especially like GWAR. In a way... perhaps in somewhat of a sick way... they represent an essence of the rock music experience: rock artists pandering to their youthful audience, drawing clear cultural boundaries between the kids performing back flips before them and the adult world of parents, police officers, ("Private Parts") Jesse Helms type good ol' boy moralists, and others. An especially clear boundary is drawn between adolescent boys – the visible majority of fans – and women... busty women, bimbo women, women to be abused and women to abuse you.

GWAR is great adolescent camp. They remind me so much of Fright Night at AstroWorld during the Halloween season, the fun of being scared by an extraterrestrial-cum-gothic version of Freddy Kruger. A number of kids have described them to me as a '90s version of KISS, but I prefer to compare them to the prehistoric/futuristic creatures on the He-Man and She-Ra cartoon programs. But the gore is essential to GWAR's shtick. I just love the way the kids leave the stage diving pit after a song/skit, strutting around like a bunch of West Texas high school football players at halftime on a hot Friday evening, wearing their version of the red badge of courage. The kings of the party are those who have accumulated the greatest amount of "blood" on their t-shirts... did you ever wonder why the kids at a GWAR concert prefer white t-shirts to the traditional black concert t-shirts worn at other heavy metal/speed metal shows? Yet, although Freddy Kruger seems quite content torturing his teen-aged victims a bit before snuffing them out, GWAR would rather eat their victims, caring less whether these victims are alive or dead at dinner time.

The kids love GWAR as much as I do. They refer to GWAR as an example of "hard core" music, as opposed to "cheese rock" stuff, you know, the kinds of junk girls like, like Bon-ugh-Jovi! The music, however, is mainstream metal drone. The lyrics, except for an occasional "Fuck" word, are predictably beyond audible comprehension. But, the message is clear: it's youthful rebellion gone completely out of control.

When I first saw GWAR...I got a chance to go backstage and talk to the ensemble. It was one of those great experiences when conducting something I call the sociology of rock and roll – subsidized by the Texas taxpayer, no less! I got to see all the high-pressure pumps used to jet colored water through some unsuspecting gnome's brain when one of the Galactic Warriors slices his head with a six-foot hatchet. I got to see all the elaborate costuming and make-up. And, I got to see the members of the cast as "artists". They reassured me they were not proposing or condoning abuse of women when the Galactic Warriors hacked some transvested bimbo's breasts off with an eight-foot hatchet. The bimbo in question represented groupies and other sleaze in the world of rock who ask for, no, virtually demand abuse by their foolish, unliberated behavior. Yes, they reassured me, the skit in which one Galactic Warrior sticks another in the bottom with a huge hypodermic needle is not an endorsement of drugs, but a parody of drugs and their sad users. I'm not totally sure I agree, but that's the script.

Well, I decided to take my twelve year-old son to my second GWAR experience... Like many middle-aged, middle class dads today, I want him to grow up just the way I did, or at least the way I want to remember growing up. Don't get me wrong, I gave it all quite some thought. After all, the youngest fans I remembered from the Numbers concert were eleven years-old, but of course my kid is mature, gifted, and anxious for new learning experiences and all those other good things all college professors want to believe about their kids. I cooled out my wife by insisting that it was all good fun, a lot like KISS, probably no worse than the upcoming Ninja Turtles rock and roll concert to which I am taking my whole family (including nine year-old daughter and five year-old son), and I would make sure he wears his little foam rubber earplugs. Why not, I wear mine! The fact that the show was to start at 6:00 p.m. on a Sunday evening provided me the argument that I wouldn't even have to keep Chris out too late before a school day. I won.

What I predicted to be one of those heart-warming father-son bonding experiences turned out to be just that, but an awful lot more from a sociological perspective. For being at the show with a twelve year-old kid provided me with a lot of insight into the place GWAR holds in the world of rock, and the place rock holds today in society. The bottom line: rock music can mess with virtually any of society's sacred cows, but as is the case with all forms of culture, society maintains boundaries or limits beyond which those cultural forms that threaten the most essential and most sacred possessions are banished. GWAR, like Robert Mapplethorpe and faceless old men lurching around playgrounds, fucks with our kids. Jesse Helms doesn't like it, parents don't like it, and as I learned that Sunday evening, working class, heavily ethnic, common, everyday, head-banging teenagers don't like it after some point either.

Let me start from the beginning. When we arrived at the parking lot that evening, I was admittedly a bit freaked out. There were dozens of kids hanging around the lot, some skin heads with no hair, some punks with red and green hair. This was a veritable laboratory for a sociologist studying youth culture, but an ominous unknown for a parent with a first-born male in tow. Nevertheless, everybody was cool. All kinds of kids came up to us to ask Chris if he knew a lot about GWAR, and quite a few kids flipped us a "thumbs up" from a distance.

Once inside and waiting for the warm-up act (Agony Column – your basic neo-satanic, sweat-metal band) to begin, I approached two young boys, who appeared to be about eleven or twelve years old, to talk rock and roll. They had their white, just purchased GWAR t-shirts on, and they fit my desire to interview the youngest kids present. As I led them to a corner of the large hall to get as far away as possible from the two Marshall speaker towers, two sixteen or seventeen year old kids, a Hispanic-looking boy in a black King Diamond t-shirt and a very pretty Anglo girl, ran up to me, and the girl asked anxiously, "Where are you taking my brother?" After I accounted for my legitimacy, we all had a nice talk about Satanism in rock, rock venues in Houston, etc. The older sister's demeanor, however, was most notable here, showing concern for her little brother's welfare as a little boy, while playing "chaperone" for him paradoxically at a GWAR concert. She, in other words, set boundaries on what is OK and what is not OK for her little brother.

I took Chris backstage before the GWAR set, and he had a ball, scouting out all the technology, false faces and stuff. He even got his picture taken with the band. During their performance, I put Chris up on a chair towards the side of the stage so he could see over the stage divers and slam dancers, at least until a security officer told me to get him down. I agreed with the officer's reasoning that we all didn't need any potential projectiles near the stage.

Chris loved just about everything from that moment on ... the action, the non-stop combat, etc. I was quite relieved when Chris viewed the five foot plastic penis as hilarious, and we left it at that. But a strange thing occurred just before we left, which was unfortunately just before the twenty foot dinosaur came on stage, we later learned. GWAR did a skit on missing children. Three large posters representing the pictures of missing kids placed on milk cartons were marched on stage. At first, I thought that GWAR was simply doing parody on the largely phony missing children's phenomenon, and the fact that most missing children are really in the possession of parents passed my mind. Yet, the audience was a bit more subdued during this skit, as everyone's attention seemed to be glued to the stage to see what would happen next. Sure enough, the band leader screamed out to the audience something like: "Parents, do you know where your children are? Well, let me tell you, they are in Antarctica where GWAR is performing sodomy on them." Uh, oh. No visible response from an audience still watching to see what was going to happen next. Sure enough, they brought a small casket-like container on stage from which GWAR removed what appeared to be the decaying body of a young child. It was clearly not designed to appear like a doll, but like a dead kid, about two or two and a half feet long. The crowd was really still and quiet as GWAR proceeded to abuse the child, cracking open its head to remove its brains for consumption, and so forth.

I didn't like it, but then again I am a parent. As Chris and I left a bit later, his first question to me out in the parking lot was: "What were they doing to that kid?" It was a serious question. GWAR was doing something bad or wrong that hit close to home to a kid not all that much more than two and a half feet long himself. But, then again, he's just a kid who probably shouldn't have been there in the first place...or so mom would later say.

I got a chance to talk to several fans out in the parking lot before we left, and I was most interested in asking them about the missing child skit. From skin head to punks to ordinary white t-shirted kids, I got the following kinds of responses: "It was gross...not that cool...GWAR gets carried away with their shit." I didn't get a lot of articulate assessments, but it was clear that that skit didn't go over well with a crowd of teenagers most of us (adults) assume are pretty emotionally cold if not ruthless. Thankfully, we're wrong.

I was a bit uncomfortable driving home. It was pretty easy talking about and explaining to Chris what all the skits were about – except for the missing child skit. How could I explain that away, how could I account for that truly scary experience – remembering that kids today see much of GWAR's kind of shtick on cable TV anyway? Why was I, a liberated dad who doesn't believe in censoring much from his kids, lost for words?

The next day I called one of the more articulate and interesting teenagers I met the previous night and I asked him for his reaction to the skit. He told me that at first he thought it "might have been funny", but when he got home he later thought that "it sucked...you don't fuck with little kids like that". All this from a kid who is no wimp, a kid who has seen his share of King Diamond and Butthole Surfer concerts – and probably a bit of violence in the neighborhood or at home.

I still love GWAR. I just wish I had the chance to talk to the band after the concert about the skit. My guess is that they put the skit together for its shock effect, nothing more. The sociological irony in all this, of course, is that the wise city fathers in Charlotte, North Carolina, arrested GWAR's lead singer just the previous week on an obscenity charge, for prancing around stage with a five foot plastic penis hanging out. Obviously, the city fathers believe they were protecting the moral boundaries of Charlotte by their actions. Too bad they don't realize that the scruffy kids out in the audience are the true agents of (rock 'n' roll) social control. Even if only through the relative silence during the skit and their negative evaluations afterwards, the teenagers end up themselves acknowledging and protecting one of the core values in American society: you don't fuck with little kids. Is this a great country, or what?.

This little essay, perhaps more than any other assigned reading, elicits great class discussion. Almost regardless of gender, ethnicity or musical persuasion, students seem to understand and generally agree with the kids at the concert. For them, the risks to and appropriate protection of young children is an everyday-life reality. Some of them have been abused by adults themselves, and many of them have younger siblings for whom protection is called for almost instinctively. Their morality includes criteria for separating fun and fantasy from real risk and danger.

The point here is that Joe does not teach free-standing courses in deviance. He does, however, inject deviance theory in general and interactionist theory in particular when trying to unpack social phenomena involving right versus wrong, normalcy versus abnormalcy, but especially morality versus immorality. And without question, our students know of or even experience innumerable examples of these phenomena in their own everyday lives.

The value of teaching deviance

Susan's and Joe's many years of teaching sociology is solid evidence for sustaining and nurturing the sociology of deviance. In terms of formal courses in deviance, Susan has argued that deviance is still relevant to the curriculum if the paradigmatic bases of the debate are clearly presented. The seemingly increasing fragmentation in the areas of deviance theory may simply reflect the increasing theoretical, if not paradigmatic, fragmentation in the discipline of sociology. Deviance can, therefore, help illustrate the dynamics of this more general fragmentation by utilizing research and analysis from commonsensically interesting and policy-relevant social phenomena. As long as we continue to teach specialized courses in social control (e.g., criminology and social problems), we should invoke formidable theories to make this instruction intellectually legitimate. Finally, deviance should remain in the curriculum because students like the perspective and the topics it attracts. Continuing to teach deviance will remind us that our overall university instruction should be relevant to our students' needs and interests.

Joe has argued that symbolic interactionist theory in general and labeling theory in particular can and should be embedded in other basic and substantive courses when relevant and useful. For example, labeling theory is a useful tool for exploring any social phenomenon that involves experiences of shame or guilt. This application illustrates labeling theory's intellectual and theoretical affiliation with social psychology. Labeling theory is a crucial resource in courses on health and mental health for helping understand the intricacies of diagnosis, treatment, evaluation and prognosis. Similarly, labeling theory can be a useful tool for unpacking sociological theories of culture. Howard Becker's (1980) work on the concept of *art world,* for example, includes a discussion of the role members of those worlds wherein they function as what Joe would humbly refer to as "agents of artistic taste control".

Susan and Joe agree that deviance theory of all varieties should be included in instructional units on quantitative and qualitative methods (e.g., Prus, 2005); the history of social thought; the history of the discipline of sociology; social psychology (e.g., self and identity issues); and the analysis of social policy issues (e.g., Gusfield's [1967] work on *moral entrepreneurs*). Labeling theory in particular is a great resource when examining ethics and human subjects in research (e.g., Klockars and O'Connor, 1979). Finally, all sociological theories of deviance are relevant in any class discussion of morality.

References

Akers, R. (2009) *Social Learning and Social Structure: A General Theory of Crime and Deviance* (New Brunswick: Transaction).

Becker, H. S. (1980) *Art Worlds* (Chicago: University of Chicago Press).

—— (1963) *Outsiders* (New York: Free Press).

Cloward, R. and L. Ohlin (1960) *Delinquency and Opportunity* (Glencoe: Free Press).

Cohen, A. K. (1955) *Delinquent Boys* (New York: Free Press).

Erikson, K. T. (1966) *Wayward Puritans: A study in the Sociology of Deviance* (Boston: Allyn and Bacon).

Freidson, E. (1975) *Profession of Medicine: A Study of the Sociology of Applied Knowledge* (New York: Free Press).

Goffman, E. (1963) *Stigma*. New York: Simon and Schuster.

Goode, E. (2004) "Is the Sociology of Deviance Still Relevant?" *The American Sociologist*, Winter, 46–57.

Goffman, E. (1963) *Stigma* (New York: Simon and Schuster).

Gottfredson, M. R. and T. Hirschi (1990) *A General Theory of Crime* (Stanford: Stanford University Press).

Gouldner, A. (1962) "Anti-Minotaur: The Myth of the Value-Free Sociology", *Social Problems*, 9, 199–213.

—— (1975), *For Sociology: Renewal and Critique in Sociology Today* (London: Pelican).

Gusfield, J. (1967) *Moral Entrepreneurs* (Chicago: University of Chicago Press).

Hirschi, T. (1969) *Causes of Delinquency* (Berkeley and Los Angeles: University of California Press).

Klockars, C. B. and F. W. O'Connor (1979) *Deviance and Decency* (Beverly Hills, CA: Sage).

Kornhauser, Ruth (1978) *Social Sources of Delinquency* (Chicago: University of Chicago Press).

Kotarba, J. A. (1975) "American Acupuncturists: The New Entrepreneurs of Hope", *Urban Life*, 4, 149–178.

—— (1980) "Labelling Theory and Everyday Deviance", in J. D. Douglas (eds.) *Introduction to the Sociologies of Everyday Life* (Boston: Allyn & Bacon).

—— (1983) "Perceptions of Death, Belief Systems, and the Process of Coping with Chronic Pain", *Social Science and Medicine*, 17, 681–689.

—— (1984) "One More for the Road: The Subversion of Labeling in the Tavern Subculture", in J. D. Douglas (ed.) *The Sociology of Deviance* (Boston: Allyn and Bacon. Reprinted in Herm Smith (1994) *Strategies of Social Research*, 3rd edn. [New York: Henry Holt]).

—— (1994) "You Don't Fuck with Little Kids", paper presented at the annual meeting of the Society for the Study of Symbolic Interaction, Los Angeles, CA.

Kotarba, J. A. and J. M. Johnson (eds.) (2002) *Postmodern Existential Sociology* (Walnut Creek, CA: Alta Mira).

Lindesmith, A. R. (1947) *Opiate Addiction* (Bloomington, IN: Principia Press).

Matza, D. (1964) *Delinquency and Drift* (New York: John Wiley & Sons)

Messner, S. F. and R. Rosenfeld (2006) *Crime and the American Dream*, 4th edn. (Belmont, CA: Wadsworth).

Nettler, G. (1974) *Explaining Crime* (New York: McGraw Hill).

Parsons, T. (1951) *The Social System* (Glencoe, Ill.: Free Press).

Pino, N. (2009) "Music as Evil: Deviance and Metaculture in Classical Music", *Music & Arts in Action*, 2, 37–55.

Prus, R. (2005) "Terrorism, Tyranny, and Religious Extremism as Collective Activity: Beyond the Deviant, Psychological, and Power Mystiques", *The American Sociologist*, 36, 47–74.

Quinney, R. (1970) *The Social Reality of Crime* (Boston: Little, Brown).

Roszak, T. (1969) *The Making of a Counter Culture: Reflections on the Technocratic Society and Its Youthful Opposition* (Berkeley, CA: University of California Press).

Ryan, W. (1971) *Blaming the Victim* (New York: Vintage).

Saad, L. (2005) "Support for Death Penalty Steady at 64%", *Gallup*, http://www.gallup.com/poll/20350/Support-Death-Penalty-Steady-64.aspx#2, date accessed December 8, 2005.

Sampson, R. and J. Laub (1995) *Crime in the Making: Pathways and Turning Points through Life* (Cambridge, MA: Harvard University Press).

Scheff, T. (1966) *Being Mentally Ill: A Sociological Theory* (Hawthorne, NY: Aldine).

Schur, E. (1971) *Labeling Deviant Behavior* (New York: Harper & Row).

Sumner, C. (1994) *The Sociology of Deviance: An Obituary* (New York: Continuum Press).

Sykes, G. and D. Matza (1957) "Techniques of Neutralization: A Theory of Delinquency", *American Sociological Review*, 22, 664–670.

Tannenbaum, F. (1938) *Crime and the Community* (New York: Columbia University Press).

14

"Deviance" Is for Undergrads, "Social Control" Is for Grad Students

Michael Dellwing

Something odd is happening: an argument against abstract pronouncements on the presence of deviance has spawned abstract pronouncements on the death of deviance. The insight that deviance is not an objective category, but rather a locally negotiated definition of the situation, was, as so often happens, first taken too far to have consequences arguments of this sort cannot have. Then, the insight was forgotten the moment these arguments were made, and all the abstract stances eschewed for the local definitions of the situation returned to create an abstract scientific definition of the situation: the "death of deviance".

Interactionists questioned the classical perspective that deviance is an objective category, instead shifting attention to social processes in which actions and people gain an ascription of "deviance" in concrete interactions (Becker, 1963; Erikson, 1966; Kitsuse, 1962; Schur, 1980; Spector and Kitsuse, 2001 [1977]). To interactionists, this has always been merely an instance of our general point that meanings are products of interactional processes, constructed in situ (though also situated) rather than being pre-existing, pre-given objective entities. Then, in large part based on this shift, the term "deviance" was argued to be discredited, ideologically loaded with pre-deobjectified meaning, creating a wide category that "in truth" did not exist. This is not only a mangled argument, it is also controlling in a global way that is not suited to a sociology of the local (Fine, 2010) such as interactionism. Not only do deobjectifying arguments have no global consequences of this sort, as Stanley Fish (1989, p. 324) reminds us, pragmatists are also ill-advised to make global pronouncements of this sort expecting that others should now "control their talk" because of it. Deviance is a definition of the situation arising in concrete situations; all that an ethnographically informed interactionism is suited for is being curious where, when and how these definitions arise. That means researching their *concrete* uses in *concrete* contexts, not extrapo-lating any abstract "rules" or "structures" of its use in the form of "devi-ance is used whenever A is the case", or "the presence of X generally leads to the situation being defined as 'deviant'". As a sociology of the local, any such generalizing, abstract statements overstep the bounds of ethno-graphic work. Ethnographic statements can only note that deviance seems to have been used in certain contexts and may be there as a resource for the taking in similar contexts as well, but it cannot limit its use or claim that some objective boundary in "the world" limits its use. There are, Rorty (1982, p. 165) reminds us, "no wholesale constraints derived from the nature of objects, or of the mind, or of language, but only those retail constraints provided by the remarks of our fellow inquirers".

Thus, we can gather from the criticisms brought forward against devi-ance that the term is concretely used in certain surroundings, but less in others. Specifically, there is much use of the term in intro classes for undergraduate students. There is decidedly less use in professional journals, and there is some use in everyday life, but much less than more specific, concrete definitions of the situation (such as, "vagrancy" or the like). To turn these empirical insights into general pronounce-ments is problematic at best: as far as interactionists are concerned, we can show how things are used, but we can neither proclaim that they are used correctly or falsely, nor how they *should* be in the future, and most decidedly cannot pronounce that we found (i.e., invented) deep-seated, hidden structures of use that show how actors themselves don't know why they do what they do. What we can note is that there seems to be a tendency to use the term in contact with novices, that it is not deemed useful in professional journals within sociology, and that there is a tendency to use it in a rough "us versus them" context in everyday life. Though some sociologists may find that modesty disconcerting, interactionist deobjectification should preclude us from "scientifically knowing" what the "right uses" or the "true reasons for use" are.

While this has long been argued in the sociology of deviance, this chapter argues the same basic point for its evil twin, the "death of deviance". Deviance is not a thing but a tool, and all that interactionists can do is note ethnographically what it is used for. Any pronunciation on its abstract "function" or abstract "value" overstates the interactionist insight.

Deobjectification of deviance

As formulated by Herbert Blumer (1969), interactionists hold that mean-ings are not inherent in objects, but products of intersubjective processes in concrete contexts. People negotiate meanings in actual situations, and as situations and contexts change, negotiated meanings change along with them. There is no static meaning available that exists apart from this *active* process (cp. also Prus, 1996, 1997; Dellwing and Prus, 2011): Meanings do not arise from abstract categories, pre-set and pre-decided, making them subject to a continuous and insurmountable contingency and chaos (Shalin, 1986). Rather than representations of a world "out there", or of representations of "clear norms," pragmatists and interactionists thus see definitions as ways of "puzzle-solving" (Rorty 1982, p. 193). They are moves in a game to organize and reorganize a specific, concrete situation in order to cope with it. These situations are fixed with specific contexts and aims. Writes Shalin (1986, pp. 12–13): "'The definition of the situation is equivalent to the determination of the vague', wrote [William I., M.D.] Thomas; before the definition sets in, 'the situation is quite undetermined,' but as the definition unfolds, 'the situation becomes definite'" (Thomas and Znaniecki, 1966, pp. 240, 23–244). *How* it is fixed, that is, organized is always entangled with what exactly it is people need to cope with, who defines it as a situation that needs to be coped with (rather than, say, ignored, "normalized" in interactionist-speak – technically also a way to cope), and who prevail in conflicts over what to cope with and how. Beginning in the 1950s and elaborated in the 1960s and 1970s, the sociology of deviance started to apply this perspective to the field, treating deviance as a definition *of* the situation to be achieved *in* a situation rather than as an "objective fact" to be "found". Interactionist scholars hold, accordingly, that deviance is not the "recognition" of an objective quality, but rather, as Howard Becker (1963) famously tells us, a socially ascribed (and negotiated) meaning that is subject to the flow of situated action. That meant opposition to the formulation that deviance can be defined objectively as behavior in breach of norms and rules (Kitsuse, 1962; Erikson, 1966; Spector and Kitsuse, 2001 [1977]) and eschewing the generalizing talk of social norm structures "determining" anything.

This was much misunderstood, and this is not the place to discuss these misunderstandings (but see Dellwing [2011b] for a more elaborate argument): this does *not* mean that deviance is a "control agency's decision" independent of the actor whose action is so labeled in an "attack" on her/his public face (a stance Akers [1968] famously criticized interactionists for). Neither does "local definition" mean that deviance is determined by "local" rules instead of more general (i.e., "societal") ones (even though early formulations often watered down this basic point in unfortunate formulations, compare Becker's [1963] infamous table and the criticism in Spector and Kitsuse, 2001 [1977]). The core anti-foundationalist point of interactionist sociology is that meaning is not "structurally" given on any level, and thus rules do not define and determine deviance, neither globally nor locally (cp. Spector and Kitsuse, 2001 [1977] ; Dellwing, 2011a). Rules are the public front-stage, a vocabulary of negotiation *with* which deviance is *argued*, but it is this local argument in a "thickly peopled" situation (Strauss, 1993, p. 25), not the normative talk used to produce it, that allows deviance definitions to emerge as products of these social processes. This emergence of deviance is entangled with the emergence of object meanings for behaviors and norms, also negotiated in this process: It is only when norms are *interpreted* to be applicable on *interpreted* behavior in *interpreted* contexts that deviance is ascribed (cp. Dellwing, 2010, 2011). These thickly peopled situations of plural interpretation are thicklyconflictual, and any recourse to abstract "norms" to untangle these conflictual situations are thinly veiled attempts to take sides in them and refusal to analyze them in their complex interactional detail. Scholarship in an interactionist attitude thus rejects the idea that norms help us much in debating deviance and replaces the classical recourse to norms with an insistence on the need for thick ethnographic descriptions of the multiperspectival nature of situations and the actions therein. Taking simplified recourses to "norms" and thinking we've solved anything by parroting everyday strategies to *legitimize* the ascription of a deviant status accomplishes nothing, but glosses over what happened in a contingent and chaotic social situation. To analyze this situation, it is the scientist's task to empirically gauge the way *actual* participants in *concrete* situations *make use* of these categories to "do things together" (Becker, 1986) in "joint action" (Blumer, 1969) with shared "definitions of the situation" (McHugh, 1968; Stebbins, 1967). There is, simply put, no such "thing" as deviance apart from the situational and local ascriptions people *actually* engage in, and engage in, for reasons, with goals and in contexts.

Deviance and its critics

This reorientation spawned both the call for the abandonment of "deviance" as a category as well as arguments for its retention. Both are, as I get to later, odd; but before I get there, I discuss the arguments that give rise to both, which in turn give rise to this volume.

After the deobjectifying shift, the deviance concept has been under criticism from at least three distinct, but related lines. There is the classical (i.e., first out the gate) criticism by Sumner (1994), who states that deviance is an ideological concept of control that is no longer able to do its job after deviance was de-objectified. The second criticism is also at home in the "critical" spectrum and finds that the continued use of a term coined in a structural-functionalist, and thereby also moralist, sociology obscures the very achievement that its deobjectification had sought to achieve: the objectivism still dormant in it makes it politically incorrect. The final criticism comes from a less oppositional quarter: it is the statement that the term was a social scientific invention to unify something that in the world does not come with this unity and is therefore too wide and too unclear.

Ideologically useless

In 1994, Colin Sumner published a much-noted book in which he issued a death certificate for the sociology of deviance. According to his own version of history, he was 20 years late: It died, he states, in the middle of the 1970s, killed by the throes of its interactionist transformation. Until that point, objectivist deviance was a classification that provided sociological support for an ideological process of exclusion that took the deviants to be really deviant and the conformists to be real conformists. It delivered a taxonomy of disorder, a scientifically legitimized story of how these disorders came about and expert recommendations on how to curb it. In short, the field ordered deviance by taxonomy, etiology and prevention, took an expert role to assist the side of order and thus took part in a political game on the side of those who were concerned or irritated, while they appeared "not to understand that they are participants in a play at all" (Rock, 1979, p. 55). The transformation, Sumner notes, ruptures the clear moral-political utility the concept had before. The old way was oriented to the needs of the powerful, Sumner states in familiar hegemony-analyzing fashion; with this aim, it was "a rational, liberal-minded attempt to make the society of the powerful more economic, more predictable, more humane and less chaotic" (Sumner, 1994, p. 301). Now, the "new" sociology of deviance is used rather the exact other way around, to provide support to the "underdog" (Becker, 1968; Akers, 1968 and others, but see, especially, Liazos, 1972) rather than the controllers, to question the categories that used to be just there. The new train wins its support in the 1960s for precisely that reason: it is a tool to attack the establishment with (Goode, 2004b, p. 50).

The argument that the deobjectification of deviance killed the concept is not merely made by critics. Conservatives have echoed it, bemoaning the loss of the black-and-white terminology for moral control. The main protagonist of this charge is Anne Hendershott (2002), who bemoans the destigmatization of deviance in academic discourse in a book published by Encounter (a company associated with the conservative think tank *American Enterprise Institute*), calling for a return to the status quo before the interactionist and postmodern formulations of deviance "relativized" the field. This new "relativism", Hendershott charges, kills off a concept that had served to show people what was immoral and dangerous (cp. Goode, 2004b, p. 48). She thus argues for the exact "ideological use value" that both Sumner and her saw lost, albeit both see this change from a different vantage point.

Goode notes the importance of understanding the exact nature of Sumner's argument: it is neither about the analytical usefulness of the field in general nor about the empirical presence of the field in current research. "In Sumner's scheme of things, the death of the sociology of deviance is not about numbers; it is not about citations or enrollments or publications. Sumner's argument is about the ideological role of the field and its collapse as a justification for and a rationalization of social control" (Goode, 2002, p. 111). It is a certain *characterization* of the field, namely: *his*, that died (p. 110). A local sociology would hold that nothing else is possible.

Politically incorrect

Sumner's argument comes from a critical perspective, but not all proponents of such a perspective formulate the same criticism of the term "deviance". Calling an action "deviant" picks up the exclusionary moment inherent in the term and objectifies it, other critics argue, even when it is done within the frame of a constructionist perspective. Thus, the retention of the term leaves remnants of objectivism in the debate, which they argue should be expunged completely by changing the terminology to "social control". This argument is related to the first, though it is not identical: here, it is the continued use of the term deviance that threatens the critical thrust of the new perspective.

Liazos (1972) had formulated his criticism within this frame when he charged the "new sociology of deviance" with reproducing the categories of "nuts, sluts and preverts [*sic*]" by analyzing how these categories (and *exactly* these categories taken from everyday stigmatizations) are reproduced. A second criticism thus enters the discussion: even though the new sociology of deviance had left the assumption of objectivity in these categories behind, it had retained the classifications, the social stigmatizations that led to some groups being marked deviant (and others not), through *using the term*. The retention of the term means the implicit retention of this focus, and thus, the new deviance scholars reproduced stigmatizations while either just "pretending" to be on the side of the "underdogs" or not knowing what they were really doing.

Especially members of stigmatized groups have argued against the retention of the term on this basis, stating they did not want to appear as examples, of constructions or otherwise, in textbooks on "deviance" (Best, 2004a). On that basis, the concept can be seen as "politically incorrect" (cp. Goode, 2004a, p. 506), and *especially* within a constructionist paradigm that should know better. The continued use of the category transports the exclusionary motive after all, the critics assert. On this basis, Mariana Valverde (2000, p. 1802) can consider deviance to be "a concept (that) has been thoroughly discredited but that nonetheless refuses to make a graceful exit from curricula".

Analytically too wide and no longer vital

The third line of criticism against the term deviance is not "critical" in its classical sense, even though elements from the first two remain notable in it. The main protagonist of the third, and perhaps current, line is Joel Best. Best states that deviance is not dead, but it is also not especially vital in professional academic debates. His argument has two lines, one empirical, one analytical. Empirically, Best notes that publication activity that utilizes the term has declined. Analytically, he thinks that this decline is due to the term's attempt to subsume massively different phenomena under the same heading.

The empirical argument Best (2004a) makes is that there are fewer and fewer publications using the word "deviance" in professional journals: after examining the *American Journal of Sociology*, the *American Sociological Review*, and *Social Forces*, Best notes that there is a steady decline since the middle 1970s, exactly the time for which Sumner issued the death certificate. If there is vitality to the concept, it is to be found in university courses, usually introductory in nature. However, a plentitude of courses, Best asserts, does not yet a successful concept make. Rather, to ascertain the vitality of the term, only professional articles can count as a measure that the field is vital and active for professional sociologists.

For Best, this empirical decline of professional attention, gathered as ethnographic information on the *in situ* use of the term, is not the final point. He goes on to see it only as a measure of something *deeper*: it is, to him, a sign of the decreasing *analytical* vitality of the perspective. This attempt to create a common concept for everything that irritates people has tried to gather too many marbles in the same bag: "the term's appeal lay in its promise to reveal similarities in phenomena that were usually considered to be very different" (p. 10), which includes the "big four": crime, mental illness, drugs and sex (p. 34), in the hope that "all rule-breaking behaviors might share important qualities" (p. 14). The only thing in common, Best asserts, is that they are all actions that others react to in irritated ways, judging and balking at it (p. 16) – but not much else (p. 34). It is this slim commonality that makes the concept analytically thin as well: "Generalizing concepts are most powerful when the instances they encompass are most similar; the more diverse the phenomena covered, the fewer the similarities they share, the simpler the general patterns that can be identified and the weaker the predictions that can be made" (p. 85). Since there is not much in the way of similarity to be found here, all that "deviance" is – all it *was* – was an attempt to unify very divergent phenomena under a "grand theoretical scheme" (p. 14) appropriate for structural-functionalism, but inappropriate for as plural and open a perspective as interactionism.

All these three death certificates list the new deviance's emphasis of contingency, plurality, heterogeneity and uncertainty as at least accomplices in its demise. All three betray the new deviance sociologists' anti-objectivist thrust.

Abstractions upon abstractions

The three criticisms explicated earlier overextend the interactionist insight by thinking of deobjectification and the resistance to abstraction as an objective, abstract argument. As a consequence, they engage in abstract evaluations of the term "deviance". Even when, as in Best's case, they talk about concrete utilization of the term in real life, they still abstract their findings to an argument that the term *itself* is "too wide" to encompass the (objectively?) "vastly different" phenomena it collects – as if these phenomena *wanted* to be called anything above and beyond what happens in actual definitional behavior.

Again, the basic, and rather simple, interactionist point is that meanings are social products that arise not in discourses, structures, power relations or any other abstract blueprint that controls everyday life, but in interactive processes in *everyday life itself*. They are *live* as much as they are used in concrete situations, and those uses are not mere epiphenomena of an abstract magical realm, a world hidden behind the veil (a world that, in many perspectives, scientists are responsible for figuring out to then tell the inhabitants of everyday life how to "really" use it). The ethnographic temperament that pervades interactionist scholarship maintains that "abstractions...are abominations upon the land"

(Lofland, 1976): nothing exists in the abstract, and meanings are inter-subjective achievements in situations that come with contexts and aims, both enmeshed in other meaning-ascriptions that occur alongside any meaning ascription currently under study. These situations are "thickly peopled" (Strauss, 1993, p. 25) and require a sensitivity for their contingency and chaos (Shalin, 1986). Interactionist scholarship values abstractions as helpful definitions of the situation that participants *work with* to achieve things, but not as representational vocabularies that get at the way the world is "really" ordered. If this insight is taken to its conclusion, then the statement that abstractions are tools used in everyday life to cope with situations cannot mean that they are "false"; for that to be true, the idea of a "true description" would have to make sense first, which, to interactionists and postmoderns alike, it does not.

> In everyday practice, it is impossible to act without naming and categorizing that toward which we act (in the very act of acting). To think otherwise is to "make the mistake of thinking that by telling people that there is something that they have never been able to do—leave the realm of practice for a realm more general and abstract—you take something away from them; but of course you can't take away a capacity no one has ever had". (Dellwing, 2011b, p. 668, citation from Fish, 1989, pp. 26–27).

Interactionist–pragmatist thought does not take away abstractions that had once existed, but is an argument about the interactionally emergent nature of abstractions and their *uses.*

The fact that we now have a new explanation of how we got our beliefs...does not free us from other beliefs or cause us to doubt them. These consequences would follow only if I also believed in the possibility of a method independent of belief by which the truth...could be determined; but if I believed that, I wouldn't be an anti-foundationalist at all. (Fish, 1989, p. 324).

So this is the problem with the attempts to derive consequences from the interactionist argument: "If pragmatism is true it has nothing to say to us; no politics follows from it or is blocked by it," as Fish notes (p. 419).

Things are not called "deviant" because they "really are" deviant: rather, things "really are" deviant locally because they are successfully described as deviant in a situation, and that achievement happens in a (local) context and with (local) aims. The "new" sociologists of deviance made rule-breaches problematic through questioning their existence as *abstracts*. They held that deviance, like all definitions of the situation, is an *in vivo* code, not a structural one. Their mantra is that all definitions are local; all attempts to fix them abstractly are so much *voodoo*, Lofland's "abominations upon the land". As Charles Edgley notes, it is not that this perspective denies order; rather, it "makes order fully situational" (in Fine, 2010, p. 358).

The insight that meanings are not objective does not mean that they are not fixed, and in fact, a situation cannot unfold if definitions are not fixed momentarily in them. And this is where pragmatists and postmoderns part: postmoderns, as well as critical scholars, scorn "invented abstractions" as they show that the high rhetoric and idealist aspirations transported through them are shown to be unfulfilled. Pragmatists, on the other hand, give any invented abstraction such as, in Fish's (1994, p. xx) case, the law "passing and even high marks because it works" (when it does). Their deconstruction does not kill them; it just shows how they come about in situations: That they are not "in the world" in the strong sense does not mean that they do not exist; it merely means that they are constantly made and remade, used and re-used in concrete circumstances. The same goes for deviance: that deviance is a product of an interactional process does not lead to any abstract pronouncements on deviance. It does not make it "ideologically useless", as no abstract uses are predetermined anywhere; it does not make it politically incorrect, as that is an ascription (in fact, a deviance ascription!) as well that comes up to attack specific kinds of deviance ascription.

That "ideological actors" – read: state control agencies – have found the new approach useless is then far too sweeping a statement. It is true that the institutions of law enforcement cannot but deny the interactionist *(labeling)* approach to crime when it comes to public communication of their action. However, this denial should not be over-interpreted. The constructionist perspective disturbs the front-stage justification of law enforcement (and any kind of public claims of deviance) as it questions the objectivity of it, which the institutions (and anyone making charges in everyday life) need to depersonalize the reaction. This is the purpose of the objectification: without the objectification that comes with depersonalization, the control activity would not be legally covered control, but an assault. Critical perspectives have always claimed that control is in fact an assault; they must do so, as their purpose, *when* they criticize control agencies, is to delegitimize these control activities. When they are not engaged in that purpose, for example, when the critical actors see deviance in *their* ranks, it will be "outrageous" and "treacherous" again, objectified as it must to hold their group together and legitimize exclusionary actions within their own group. Definitions remain entangled with purposes, and thus to think the institutions to be solidly permeated by a denial of constructionist perspectives is ridiculous.

In many ways, deviance constructionism perfectly catches their internal talk about their activities: law enforcement officers, lawyers, judges and their associates are constructing, and quite openly so, when they are in the process of negotiating plea bargains, deliberating what to pursue further and for what reason and what the political frames and likely outcomes of one decision over another may be (cp. Posner, 1990; Lautmann, 2011). However, the public face of these deliberations must again be presented in the form of impersonal applications of the objective rule, as the public face must wash these creative human activities from the process. Thus, there is some room to overstate the claims of distance between the practitioners of control and the constructionist approach. It is, as everything is, *occasional*. In some situations, one will steadfastly argue objective meanings. In another, one will critically, and perhaps even deconstructively, play with it. The same people engage in both. As Fish (1998, p. 427) notes,

> You had better be ... a literalist when you argue a case or talk to your dean or bargain with a car dealer or give directions to someone trying to get to your house. Ruth Anna Putnam criticizes philosophers "who lead one life in their studies and another outside" and argues for a philosophy "that enables us to lead one life, to be as consistent as possible". I suppose that one could achieve that consistency but I'm not sure how human it would be and I suspect that the result would be something akin to insanity.

Within the sociology of social problems, constructionists have been blamed for apparent contradictions in their talk at different times, with different aims in the same texts: on the one hand, they oppose objectifications when it comes to problems (only "claims"); on the other hand, objectifications abound, such as the necessary assumption that "claims" exist and that there is a "public" to be swayed by it (Gubrium, 1993, p. 96). Some have seen this is a theoretical problem: Woolgar and Pawluch (1985) called it "ontological gerrymandering". Within the debate, it was seen as an inconsistency to be smoothened. However, following Fish, this inconsistency is part of the normal operation of the everyday world. Different situations are differently objectified. Breaking down objectifications in everyday life is called "criticism"; when social scientists do it, it is sometimes called "deconstruction", but the movement is always an everyday life one, even if in some cases they sport more complex rhetoric than in others.

That deviance is not "really" an objective category also does not make the category "too wide", as there is no abstract category except when it produced, "fixed" in a concrete instance of use, and then it is so produced because it is supposed to *do something*. If that works, then it obviously was not too wide: It did its job. While Joel Best notes that the term is not generally in use in public debates, which rather turn to more specific terms such as "violence", "drugs", "immorality" and the like, asking if anyone is arrested and prosecuted or even chastised much for "deviancy". Joe Kotarba et al. (2011) find instances of the use of "deviance" in everyday life, for example, by the Iranian government in their criticism of rap musicians. This is both true: there are uses of the term in everyday life, and at the same time, most public irritations are supported with more specific claims. But that misses the heart of the matter. Deviance as a concept is found useful, found to have value – obviously, as it would not be used if it didn't.

Deviance is a tool that is used because it is connected to expectations that it will do a job, *when* it is so expected. Other terms could be used for the same job. It seems to find more practitioners who find value in using it in intro classes than in professional journal articles. The problem, for interactionists, is not to decide on such value, to *pronounce* on the term deviance ex cathedra (or ex libris, or ex anything). In a pluralist field, no one has that authority. There is no abstract term "deviance", no abstract concept, no abstract functions or uses of it, no abstract meaning to be lost or regained. Fighting over the *term* is always the fight over a *concrete use* of the term in a *concrete context*; there is nothing more abstract to say. If we start from here, we can analyze not if "deviance" is useful in any larger sense but how it is used and *what is done with it*.

The uses of deviance

There is no abstract reason why social processes of negotiating irritation and reaction should be analyzed with the term "deviance". Ethnography has no generalized, abstract pronouncements on deviance to make. It can only gauge how the term is actually used, what for, with what success. Humanly made categories are not frozen once made: categories are abstractions used in concrete contexts, and they are used differently between contexts when goals and contexts change. The categorizations have to be continuously updated in the light of the current context, where they will be interpreted and thus always necessarily adapted.

Categories and concepts are not things (in any abstract sense), they are rather *things-in-the world* in the Blumerian sense that they become objects only when interpreted, and differentially, fluctuatingly so. These interpretations are always in a situation, and so are we, as Fish (1980, p. 272) notes: "We are never not in a situation. Because we are never not in a situation, we are never not in the act of interpreting". As categories are not things and our task is not to mirror the descriptions the world has already laid out for us (James, 1995 [1907]), this is not something done "for the sake of pure knowledge" – whatever that may be – but for a purpose, which means that when a category of this sort is constructed in a certain moment, *something is done with this category at that moment*. You cannot talk without fixing meanings. The *ethnographic* debate is not about what deviance *can* do in the abstract, but about *what it practically does* (in the practical world, what it can do and what it does so are the same thing, as the "world of potentials" is another beyond-the-veil abstraction again).

The contributions that do make their argument on deviance based on actual utilization in everyday life (Best, 2004a, 2004b; Schur, 1980) concede that there *are* uses that are observable: there is much activity in curricula – there are many deviance classes – but little innovative scholarship at the top ranks of sociology. That Best does not see this as a sign of vitality seems curious. For one, it is a presumption that professional use is worth more than class use, which has a whiff of "real sociologists" versus "teachers of intro classes" to it. But the analytical point he makes is more curious still: that this shows the lack of analytical vitality because *there is nothing generalizing to say* about these diverse phenomena. Of course, this comes from Best's commendable and correct interactionist opposition to generalizing things to say. At the same time, however, it is itself a generalizing thing to say: it implies that there are objective differences between these phenomena that the term is not able to grasp, a literalist, literal formalist position.

Deviance is, indeed, a term known in everyday life. The term does come up, and even when it doesn't, members *do* connect the different categories of irritation in everyday life, when these different "objective facts" of irritation are taken as a unit, as can be seen when "immorality" is argued to be a precursor to crime, disobedience in a child a precursor to a gang career, drug use a precursor to violence or sexual license a precursor to the downfall of society. There *is* a common categorization in everyday life between these phenomena, and though "deviance" is rarely used (though it can be found), the term catches that simple phenomenon: people in the world claim different sorts of irritating and outrageous behavior and they objectify it and connect the different forms. That justifies "deviance" as a term for noting the construction by members even if it is not an *in vivo* code (though it sometimes is). If there is a term used to encompass all of these ("divergent") phenomena, it cannot fail because these instances "really have nothing in common." It is rather a sign that, in a specific context, it is *used* practically, precisely *in order to construct them as a common category* (i.e., to fix the situation so that they appear as a common category).

These everyday life irritations are also argued and legitimized completely objectivistically. Violence, drug use and immorality are completely objective facts for those who charge it, not contingent and contextual constructions. No charge, no insult, no irritation, no pain could be expressed without fixing situations and holding on to that fixation; no change in behavior could be demanded, no shame or exclusion producible without giving reasons. This necessity is used cynically permanently: people pretend to be outraged, claim rule-violations that do not touch them, exploit situations that can be successfully portrayed as revolting. This, however, works only because people take these fixations seriously in everyday life and act with them. Everyday life is, as we have already noted, permeated by the necessity to objectify its categories. When irritation and outrage are communicated, the legitimizing basis claimed for them is the breach of rules of conduct (Fish, 1994; Dellwing, 2009, 2011b). Those who make charges do so in a fixed way: those who have to legitimize irritations do so by anchoring them in the facticity of the reasons for the irritation, the facticity of the rules broken and the facticity of the connection between the two. To describe this as an "ideology", as Sumner does when he separates the old from the new, or as an objectivism to be exorcized, as the proponents of the political incorrectness of "deviance" tend to do, misunderstands the direction of an anti-foundationalist perspective.

Deviance is for undergrads, social control is for grad students

Goode and Best note that when you put their results together, "deviance" is not in high use any longer in the flagship journals of sociology, but that it is in high – and possibly growing – use in introductory classes. While Hendershott (2002, p. 47) had noted that no one wanted to teach deviance classes any longer, Goode quickly eschews the assertion: "more departments today are offering a course in deviance during any given semester than was true 30 years ago, and about the same number of students are taking the course per semester for a given department". Best (2004b, p. 485) concedes that deviance classes are aplenty, but finds that "there is little or no intellectual coherence to these courses". This empirical insight, combined with the apparently existing fixation of "deviance" as an "everything that irritates us" category in everyday life, can be used to note what is done with the concept in the academic world, what it is used for, what it achieves – in concrete instances, not as an abstract function.[1] In the academic world, we can note, it is often used precisely as a *tool* to teach deobjectification of deviance through reference to the everyday objectifying connotation the term has. Thus, "deviance" is a hook to get sociological novices into a reformulation that is so entrenched, perhaps normalized, in professional sociology that it has stopped being a contentious issue in its higher echelon journals: Deviance is thus a tool used to do a job that needs doing in courses, but not in journals, as only neophytes have to be pried away from their everyday self-evident moralism to become decent sociologists (at least in the situation of being sociological analysts of deviance, and for that purpose alone).

Interesting to us, beyond any argument on abstract utility, is this differential use: teachers seem to think they need it, practitioners not so much (anymore).[2] It is quite plausible, and can be validated with the experience of the author and numerous colleagues, that "deviance" is used as a bridge. It is exactly its objectivist everyday life connotation that lets practitioners use "deviance" as a teaching tool: *"Deviance" is a bridgehead used to bring (constructionist) sociological questions and interests to those who do not hold them yet.* Best (2004a, p. 85) notes: "Some sociologists abandoned deviance for other, livelier, yet still related, fields of study, such as social problems or criminology. Research conducted under these headings could circumvent much of the controversy attached to the study of deviance". It is, however, exactly that controversy that leads people to use the heading for their teaching. David Altheide noted that it is a good term for eliciting student interest (Kotarba et al., 2011). To keep using

---

[1] Here lies the distinction between functionalism and pragmatism. Both will look toward what is done with things, but functionalists attempt to locate the functions within these things, *sui generis*: pragmatism looks for them in open social processes in which these elements can, but need not be used, and when they are used, can be used for many different things.

[2] Though, of course, there are different stories here as well. Goode finds continued use of the term when he searches a wider database of publications and does not limit himself to the flagship journals that tend to not be very constructionist at all.

that term seems to be a piece of advice that need not be given. Once it is used to teach students to use another tactic (deobjectification), teachers are then able to move on to fields such as social control.

That professional, that is, flagship journal talk, has seen most of it in the 1970s and less before and after indicates the development of the constructionist paradigm in the sociology of deviance is now only logical: It comes up in professional literature when the profession has to be "taught", that is, taken from the objectivist understanding to the constructionist one, just as students have to; however, in the discipline, that happened once. Now, naturally not everyone in sociology shares the perspective, but everyone working within the discipline knows of it. The profession no longer has to be socialized into it, no longer has to be taught; that was done once, and the effects are here to stay. In the flagship journals, which moved back to methodologically rigorous, but insightless positivist sociology, the constructionist point was no longer invited. In other journals, the wider fray Goode targeted, there is more, and here, the constructionist point is sometimes still made with "deviance", and the classical literature is still cited, giving the term some use value *on these occasions*. On the other hand, neophytes do have to be taught anew every new generation, every new freshman year: and thus, while the professional mechanism has ebbed, the teaching mechanism continues to thrive.

The term "deviance" allows practitioners to collect their everyday moralism about everything from not cleaning up your room to mass murder and take it for the exact point Best made connects them: that they are moralized, objectified as forms of rule-breaking so that reactions can be justified with them. This everyday-life moralism makes not just for a common point to start from, from which teachers can then introduce more sociologically interesting questions and slowly un-teach the moralism of everyday life at least for purposes, *occasions*, of doing sociology. It also makes for an interesting way to move students toward the point of socially negotiated, constructed, produced worlds, to show how rules are used in situations, how divergence from rule and behavior is interpreted and negotiated. It can use this clarity of everyday-life justifications to make the didactic point that, reflecting on these situations and the conflicts in them, they are not as clear as has to be claimed when one is in the situation. It can thus ready the students for more specific courses on medicalization, social control, "disease mongering", punitive expansion and whatever else sociologists will then want to do more specifically.

The job described here is one that practitioners seem to currently do with the term "deviance", but other terms as well could do the job. All of this is an argument that could well do without the term "deviance". As I already noted, a pragmatist treatment of the matter has little justification to focus on specific terms, much less to "strongly define" them or "make them clear" or whatever else it is that strict theorists and positivist empiricist do with terms. All we can note is what's done with it and hope that this job keeps being done, with whatever term that gets it done.

References

Adler, P. A. and P. Adler (2006) "The Deviance Society", *Deviant Behavior*, 27, 129–148.

Akers, R. L. (1968) "Problems in the Sociology of Deviance: Social Definitions and Behavior", *Social Forces*, 4, 455–465.

Becker, H. (1963) *Outsiders: Studies in the Sociology of Deviance* (New York: Free Press of Glencoe).

—— (1986) *Doing Things Together* (Evanston: Northwestern University Press).

Best, J. (2004a) *Deviance: Career of a Concept* (Belmont, CA: Wadsworth).

—— (2004b) "Deviant Behavior May Be Alive, but Is It Intellectually Lively?", *Deviant Behavior*, 25, 483–492.

Blumer, H. (1969) *Symbolic Interactionism: Perspective and Method* (Englewood Cliffs, NJ: Prentice Hall).

Dellwing, M. (2008) "Reste. Die Befreiung des Labeling Approach von der Befreiung", *Kriminologisches Journal*, 38, 161–172.

—— (2009) "Ein Kreis mit fünf Sanktionen", Österreichische *Zeitschrift für Soziologie*, 34, 43–61.

—— (2010a). Das interaktionistische Dreieck. Monatsschrift für Kriminologie und Strafrechtsreform 92, 3

—— (2011a) "Langeweile mit der Eindeutigkeit", in H. Peters and M. Dellwing (eds.) *Langweiliges Verbrechen. Warum KriminologInnen den Umgang mit Kriminalität interessanter finden als Kriminalität* (Wiesbaden: Springer).

—— (2011b) "Truth in Labeling: Are Descriptions All We Have?", *Deviant Behavior*, 32, 653–675.

Dellwing, M. and R. Prus (2011) *Einführung in die interaktionistische Ethnografie* (Wiesbaden: Springer).

Dotter, D. (2004) *Creating Deviance: An Interactionist Approach* (Walnut Creek, CA: AltaMira Press).

Erikson, K. T. (1966) *Wayward Puritans: A Study in the Sociology of Deviance* (Upper Saddle River: Pearson).

Fine, G. A. (2010) "The Sociology of the Local: Action and Its Publics", *Sociological Theory*, 28, 355–376.

Fish, S. (1980) *Is There a Text in This Class? The Authority of Interpretive Communities* (Cambridge: Oxford University Press).

—— (1989) *Doing What Comes Naturally* (Durham: Duke University Press).

—— (1994) *There's No Such Thing As Free Speech, and It's A Good Thing, Too* (Durham: Duke University Press).

—— (1998) "Truth and Toilets", in M. Dickstein (ed.) *The Revival of Pragmatism* (Durham: Duke University Press).

Goffman, E. (1967) *Interaction Ritual* (New York: Doubleday).
—— (1986) *Stigma: Notes on the Management of Spoiled Identity* (New York: Basic Books).
Goode, E. (2002) "Does the Death of the Sociology of Deviance Make Sense?", *American Sociologist*, 33, 107–118.
—— (2003) "The MacGuffin that Refuses to Die: An Investigation into the Condition of the Sociology of Deviance", *Deviant Behavior*, 24, 507–533.
—— (2004a) "The 'Death' MacGuffin Redux: Comments on Best", *Deviant Behavior*, 25, 493–509.
—— (2004b) "Is the Sociology of Deviance Still Relevant?", *American Sociologist*, 35, 46–57.
Gubrium, J. F. (1993) "For a Cautious Naturalism", in J. A. Holstein and G. Miller (eds.) *Perspectives on social problems* (New York: Aldine de Gruyter).
Gusfield, J. (1986) *Symbolic Crusade* (Urbana: Illini).
Hendershott, A. (2002) *The Politics of Deviance* (San Francisco: Encounter Books).
James, W. (1995 [1907]) *Pragmatism: A New Name for Some Old Ways of Thinking* (New York: Longman Green).
Jenkins, P. (1998) *Moral Panic: Changing Concepts of the Child Molester in Modern America* (New Haven: Yale University Press).
Kitsuse, J. I. (1962) "Societal Reaction to Deviant Behavior: Problems of Theory and Method", *Social Problems*, 9, 247–256.
Kotarba, J., D. Altheide, J. Best and A. Groenemeyer (2011) "Death of Deviance: A Panel Debate", paper presented at "Everyday Life, Ethnography and Social Control" at the 2nd European Conference of the Society for the Study of Symbolic Interaction, Kassel, Germany, July 21–24.
Lautmann, R. (2011) *Justiz–Die stille Gewalt* (Wiesbaden: Springer).
Liazos, A. (1972) "The Poverty of the Sociology of Deviance: Nuts, Sluts and Preverts", *Social Problems*, 20, 103–120.
Lofland, J. (1976) *Doing Social Life* (New York: John Wiley & Sons).
McHugh, P. (1968) *Defining the Situation: The Organization of Meaning in Social Interaction* (Indianapolis).
Posner, R. A. (1990) *The Problems of Jurisprudence* (Cambridge, MA: Harvard University Press).
Prus, R. (1996) *Symbolic Interaction and Ethnographic Research: Intersubjectivity and the Study of Human Lived Experience* (New York: SUNY Press.)
(1997) *Subcultural Mosaics and Intersubjective Realities: An Ethnographic Research Agenda for Pragmatizing the Social Sciences* (New York: SUNY Press).
—— (2011) "Generating, Intensifying, and Redirecting Emotionality: Conceptual and Ethnographic Implications of Aristotle's Rhetoric1", paper presented at the conference "Emotions and Everyday Life", University of Lodz, Lodz, Poland. June 15–17.
Rock, P. (1979) "The Sociology of Crime, Symbolic Interactionism and Qualities of Radical Criminology", in D. Downes and P. Rock (eds.) *Deviant Interpretations* (Oxford: Martin Robertson).
Rorty, R. (1982) *Consequences of Pragmatism* (Minneapolis: Minnesota University Press).
Schur, E. (1980) *The Politics of Deviance: Stigma Contests and the Uses of Power* (Eaglewood Cliffs: Spectrum).

Shalin, D. N. (1986) "Pragmatism and Social Interactionism", *American Sociological Review*, 51, 9–29.

Spector, M. and J. I. Kitsuse (2001 [1977]) *Constructing Social Problems* (Piscataway: Transaction).

Stebbins, R. (1967). "A Theory of the Definition of the Situation". *Canadian Review of Sociology and Anthropology* 4, 148–164.

Strauss, A. (1993). *Continual Permutations of Action* (New York: De Gruyter).

Sumner, C. (1994) *The Sociology of Deviance: An Obituary* (Detroit: Open University Press).

Thomas, W. and F. Znaniecki (1966). *The Polish Peasant in Europe and America* (Chicago: University of Chicago Press).

Valverde, M. (2000) "Review of Joel Best: Controlling Vice", *Journal of American History*, 86, 1802–1803.

Woolgar, S. and D. Pawluch (1985) "Ontological Gerrymandering: The Anatomy of Social Problems Explanations", *Social Problems*, 32, 214–227.

15
Deviance and Social Justice
Nathan W. Pino

Introduction

This chapter is an attempt to elucidate how research and teaching on the sociology of deviance can contribute to a more just society. Research in deviance and criminology has the capacity to both promote and hinder social justice, but I write here to support the former from a sociological perspective. While mainstream academic criminology tends to have a narrow focus and rigidly holds to an atheoretical empirical approach increasingly removed from its sociological roots, studying and teaching deviance within a social justice framework and a sociological perspective can help maintain the vitality of the sociology of deviance. The sociology of deviance has generated a large number of ideas, concepts and theories that are used in other concentration areas within sociology, such as medical sociology, race, ethnicity, gender studies, criminology, social problems and collective behavior, among others (Goode, 2004), and it is important to make use of these ideas to inform research and teaching that can advance the discipline and promote social justice.

In what follows I define social justice and discuss how scholars have attempted to conceptualize and advocate for social justice through their work. I then discuss the limits of mainstream academic criminology in terms of seeking social justice and argue against the idea that the sociology of deviance is six feet underground. Next, I discuss how my research on international police reform efforts and extreme forms of violence are informed by a concern for social justice. Finally, I conclude explaining how I try to inspire students to link deviance and crime with social justice concerns by engaging in critical thinking and challenging taken-for-granted assumptions about social phenomena.

Social justice and deviance

Scholars in numerous disciplines explore social justice as a concept, but there is no consensus on what constitutes social justice and social scientists have not elucidated sufficiently the empirical measures that can determine whether or not social justice is being realized (Richie, 2011). Beth Richie (2011) provides the following broad conceptualization of social justice, describing it as:

> a signifier of a range of conditions that would expand opportunity for those who have been constrained by their social position or lack of access to institutional privileges. This includes creating a set of circumstances where disadvantaged groups or individuals who experience injustice are compensated for their plight. It means using a methodological approach that takes our understanding of social problems into account and links individual pathology and social deviance to the role of institutions and the state in creating disadvantage. Social justice, in this sense, incorporates a range of macro variables (such as race, class and gender) and takes on a corrective role in responding to the social inequality that results from institutionalized forms of domination by restoring rights, creating opportunity, and strengthening the social position of those who suffer the most in contemporary society because of structural racism, persistent sexism and exploitation of poor people. (p. 213)

On the basis of a comprehensive examination across the vast spectrum of critical criminology, Arrigo (1999) found that theorists ranging from structural Marxists to postmodernists differ on whether to focus on the macro or micro level of analysis, to take a modernist or postmodern approach or to focus on structure or agency. However, these critical criminologists appear to reach a convergence of opinion on five broad points regarding social justice (pp. 256–261). First, they value social justice needs over criminal justice demands, placing priority on the interests, needs and rights of individuals and citizen groups while focusing on issues such as economics, race, gender and sexual orientation. Second, critical theorists place great importance on power, its social nature and how it is used to harmfully exploit and oppress others. Third, the source(s) of crime are linked directly to the criminal justice system and how it operates. Individual and social responsibility for crime are both emphasized, and in the sociological tradition the actions of individuals, including criminal actions, are seen as best understood by examining political, economic, ideological and other conditions giving rise to the behavior of criminals and the criminal justice agencies and agents. Fourth, they seek to create a just society in the sense that people, particularly those who are voiceless or underrepresented in decision making, are no longer criminalized, stigmatized or devalued based on their individual or group differences and can freely represent themselves and reclaim their voices throughout the criminal justice system. Finally, these theorists promote social change, agreeing that social change is healthy for society and is needed in order to realize a more just society. As Arrigo elaborates,

> Society benefits because no one group can unleash indefinite, indiscriminate, and unchecked power against other groups or citizens without eventually succumbing to the evolving will of the people. Members benefit because they are active contributors in the process of creating and reexamining the extent to which their unique life experiences are reflected in the unfolding script that is justice. (p. 260)

Sokoloff and Burgess-Proctor (2011) urge scholars of crime and deviance to view inequality in terms of the intersection of race, class and gender, understanding that the effects of these forces as a whole are greater than the sum of their individual effects. Within this intersection we can analyze how a variety of groups are marginalized in society, including religious minorities and atheists, immigrants and lesbian, gay, bisexual, and transgendered (LGBT) persons in addition to other sexual minorities and gender-nonconforming individuals. When stratification increases, it can lead to the creation of more disvalued characteristics by those in positions of power. Therefore deviance can easily be considered a human rights issue.

Liazos (1972) was (and still is) correct to write that we should concentrate on power and its implications for deviance more vociferously. He pointed out that deviance textbooks of the time would not discuss governmental, corporate and other forms of elite deviance, but had no problem ascribing the deviant label to addicts, prostitutes, homosexuals, the mentally ill and political radicals. Therefore, the study of deviance was more about "nuts, sluts, and preverts [*sic*]" than about institutionalized forms of deviance perpetuated by corporations and governments, which cause far more societal harm than street criminals. By focusing more on street criminals, the mentally ill, sex workers and sexual minorities and calling them "deviant," even if it was from a sympathetic view, sociologists were further marginalizing their subjects and acting as tools of the elite. Instead of seeing prisoners as individuals with defective personalities, Liazos argued that they should be described as political prisoners, because political and social conditions (e.g., capitalism, institutional racism) led to their imprisonment.

Erich Goode (2003), however, makes the following counterargument:

Norms have existed in human societies for as long as humans have existed, and non-normative behavior, beliefs, and physical conditions, likewise, have existed for equally as long, which means that for this stretch of time, the people who have enacted this behavior, held these beliefs, and possessed these traits have, in turn, been criticized, reviled, condemned, shunned, socially isolated, punished, and scorned. Negative reactions to such acts, beliefs, and conditions represent a trans-historical, trans-cultural phenomenon, constituting an analytic concept that points to a powerful, significant sociological process. Again, this process is a fundamental element in all social relations. If we don't refer to this process as "deviance", what do we call it? It's there, it's real, it's important, it is in need of investigation. Is Liazos seriously suggesting that we ignore it? (pp. 518–519)

If we are attempting to advance social justice through a study of crime and deviance, we should examine the processes of norm construction and promotion, the "deviance" of both the elite and those they marginalize, how people resist the labels placed upon them and the implications of all of these activities for social justice. For example, if we decide to redefine deviance narrowly and avoid examining sexual minorities in terms of how they are marginalized and treated as deviant by those in power – or by anyone else attempting to uphold traditional heteronormative scripts – simply because we wish it were not true or because we are afraid to stigmatize sexual minorities further, we might actually be marginalizing these groups more by ignoring their voices and the stigma they face. By ignoring the powerful forces at work in various social institutions to oppress LGBT persons (e.g., criminal justice processes, educational institutions, housing, employment), and by not studying empirically how the intersection of race, class and gender affects how sexual minorities are criminalized (and which ones are criminalized more than others), we are saying that their suffering is not an important area of inquiry, and we may not fully understand how to effectively fight against the marginalization (see Mogul et al., 2012). Traditional notions of morality are often rooted in norms concerning gender and sexuality, and a focus on social justice should lead to developing a critical eye toward elites and the harms they cause as well as a concern for all of those who are unjustly treated and how different groups are, for various reasons, defined as deviant or marginalized in other ways.

The complexities of deviance, including the marginalization of various minority groups and the attempts of those labeled deviant to resist, could be reflected in the way in which scholars seeking social justice might conceptualize deviance. Heckert and Heckert (2002) provided a broader conceptualization by developing a typology consisting of four types of deviance based on both normative and relativist conceptions of deviance: negative deviance, deviance admiration, rate busting and positive deviance. Negative deviance refers to under-conforming deviant behavior that elicits a negative reaction from groups and is the kind of deviance typically discussed in the field, such as violent crimes. Deviance admiration, on the other hand, is under-conforming behavior that elicits positive reactions from others. Examples include the glorification of certain outlaws, gangsters, serial killers and other criminals (ibid.), but can also include those who support or celebrate marginalized groups out of a concern for social justice. Rate busting involves the stigmatization of over-conformity. For example, an overly achieving individual can be called a "nerd" or "dork" for going beyond what is expected among a group of teenagers in a high school (p. 461). Finally, positive deviance refers to over-conformity that elicits a positive response from groups. Examples might include Nobel Prize winners.

Scholars interested in doing so can pursue the advancement of social justice through a critical sociology of deviance and criminology "formed around a broad vision of social injury" (Michalowski, 2010, p. 9). If we seek to engage in a normative approach focused on social justice, we should also be committed to research that seeks to reveal objective causes of social injuries utilizing both quantitative and qualitative methods in order to improve our effectiveness at combating such injuries. This also means that we should remain skeptical, critical and unwilling to stubbornly hold on to our orthodoxies when the evidence dismantles them. Working toward social justice also requires engaging in scholarship oriented toward collectively defined interests rather than self-absorbed and individualistic pursuits. These collectively defined interests, however, must not be based on a paternalistic or ethnocentric view that one knows what is best for everyone else. Rather, scholars in their research and activism roles should highlight human agency, the ability of marginalized groups to organize and resist and ensure that "marginalized groups are the center of analysis, organizing and social change" (Sokoloff and Burgess-Proctor, 2011, p. 238).

In addition to studying the intersection of race, class and gender as a way to both understand and promote social justice in various ways, we should examine this intersection within the context of neoliberal globalization and how global-level forces shape and are shaped by local-, regional- and national-level phenomena. The movement across and within borders of people, cultural scripts, economic and political models, capital and goods and services, as a consequence of imperialism, neocolonialism and other various actions of transnational corporations, governments and international non-governmental organizations influences how people are marginalized and how they can resist this marginalization. A post-colonial perspective that sees crime and deviance as categories contextualized through the ideologies and practices of colonial states and how colonized peoples resist can be helpful here, particularly when racialized and gendered constructs are linked with the colonial and post-colonial (Cunneen, 2011; also see Agozino, 2003).

Mainstream academic criminology is less able to tackle issues of social justice as things currently stand because it has been depoliticized and replaced with a pragmatic cynicism that engenders a refusal to think beyond established ideas in the discipline (Richie, 2011; Winlow and Atkinson, 2013; Young, 2011). Mainstream criminology should be more mindful of the contributions of critical theories and interactionist perspectives to the study of crime and deviant behavior in general in part because these perspectives can help us examine critically taken-for-granted assumptions within academia and in the larger society in a way that promotes reflexive, critical thinking and can engender a commitment to social justice. The "death of deviance" argument attempts to take these contributions away from us, but the ability to unfasten the world to show divergent definitions of the situation can be useful for understanding the world and seeking social justice.

Another challenge, however, is that much of the work on social justice will remain rhetorical unless more attempts are made to broadly operationalize social justice (Richie, 2011). Empirical research oriented toward social justice must be grounded in theory, intellectualism and evidence-based research. Unfortunately, intellectual abstract theorization in criminology, particularly American criminology, is generally eschewed in favor of a strictly empirical approach that sees theory as redundant or simply an add-on that rarely plays a central role in the analysis (Winlow and Atkinson, 2013; Young, 2011). However, as Winlow and Atkinson (2013) remind us,

> Just as an analysis of capitalism that focuses purely on workers, employers and tradable commodities misses out the fundamental truth of a self-sustaining global capitalist system that has a reality beyond the material, so criminological work that seeks to jettison abstract analysis and get back to the hard work of empirical research misses out on a fundamental truth of crime causation. In both cases, ideology resides in the attempt to cover up the "real abstraction" with a faux-reality of good old straightforward empirical analysis. (p. 14)

It is imperative that evidence-based research informs collective action in part because misinformed activism can lead to actions that cause further harm. For example, in preparation for the 2006 World Cup a diverse collection of activist groups sought to prevent organized crime syndicates from trafficking young women from developing countries to engage in sex work, but their efforts actually led to increased punitive actions by governments against the women they sought to protect. Verifiable data on human trafficking are limited at best, and yet organizations of various stripes claimed arbitrary and likely inflated trafficking figures in order to bring attention to the problem, creating a moral panic fueled by sensational media reports that allowed governments to further criminalize sex workers, many of whom, according to research wherein sex workers were interviewed, entered into such work on their own volition (Milivojevic and Pickering, 2008). As a result, there was a law enforcement crackdown in Germany leading to over 100 arrests, around 25 percent of which were made on immigration violations against minority female non-sex workers who for various reasons just wanted to attend the World Cup. Gendered immigration enforcement under the guise of anti-trafficking enforcement was allowed to occur thanks in part to the actions of well-meaning activists that helped engender the moral panic based upon wildly inflated human trafficking numbers. "'Protective measures' that prevent women from exercising their agency further narrow women's options and restrict rather than promote women's rights" (p. 38).

Research on marginalized groups such as the urban underclass and sex workers ought to involve those being researched. Researchers could walk the streets of the neighborhoods of interest, interviewing the residents in person rather than relying on data-gathering companies to do the leg-work for them (see Young, 2011). For example, as Milivojevic and

Pickering (2008) point out, ethnographic research that involves actually speaking with sex workers reveals a more complex and nuanced picture of the sex trade than we often see depicted in the news media and in some academic and activist circles. The voices of those being studied must be heard, and where appropriate those being studied should also be part of the research planning and design process to ensure a more ethical and informed process. It should also go without saying that the activities of activists should involve local ownership, involving and, where possible, being led by the groups the activists are supporting, with researchers and outside activists acting only in a facilitative role. Otherwise, in the name of doing good, researchers and activists may engage in "othering". As Young (2011) explains, othering involves contrasting, distancing and separating oneself from those he or she studies. Well-meaning liberal scholars and activists can engage in othering in such a way that the subjects are seen as determined creatures who can be improved through intervention. The othered group members are seen as different because they live in deficient circumstances, but they would be the same as us if the deficit were repaired. The idea is that we would simply need to educate them and improve their material circumstances so that they can be just like us.

Research that seeks social justice

At this point I demonstrate how a commitment to social justice is reflected in my research on global issues regarding police reform efforts and extreme forms of violence.

International police reform efforts

My research on Western-led police reform efforts in developing countries (see Ellison and Pino, 2012; Pino, 2009; Pino and Wiatrowski, 2006) critically examines these efforts in part by demonstrating that "democratic" police reforms, despite their rhetoric, are often not democratic or committed to human rights, and must be placed within the context of a neoliberal-led globalization that politically and economically marginalizes a significant proportion of the world's population and increases feelings of insecurity as well as the likelihood that people engage in vigilantism. Scholars in this area, particularly from the United States, generally assume good intensions from donors even though it is a grave error to do so. While much is written on recipient resistance to implementing Western human rights and other norms, we must recognize that donors do not always forward plans that uphold these norms, either. In some cases Western-led reforms actually undermine those norms, as in the case when most resources are spent on the war on drugs or terrorism rather than on strengthening local police capacity to interact and build trust with the public.

Donor countries in the West are also increasingly failing to uphold their own stated norms and the rule of law in their own countries. In the name of security, we see Western countries removing legal and privacy protections for the accused, cracking down on social movements and working with private actors to gather information on their own citizens without a warrant. One example involves the recent release of documents in the United States demonstrating that the FBI, the Department of Homeland Security and local police coordinated with large banks, other private actors and universities to violently crack down on the Occupy Wall Street protests in the fall of 2011 (Wolf, 2012). In a nutshell, we cannot expect donors to be committed to promoting human rights abroad if they are actively undermining them back home.

My research in Trinidad and Tobago reflects these concerns (Pino, 2009). On the basis of interviews with national non-governmental organizations (NGOs), smaller community based organizations (CBOs) and members of the Trinidad and Tobago Police Service and Ministry of National Security, I found that foreign-led police reform efforts were top-down, did not involve civil society groups to any significant extent and did not result in any changes in police behavior or organization. Police reformers did not appear to take the adequate amount of time to learn from or work with the local population and based reforms on those that occurred in Northern Ireland rather than tailoring a program specifically to the needs and concerns of those in Trinidad and Tobago. Agreements between the US government and the government of Trinidad and Tobago tend to benefit the donor more than the recipient. For example, ship rider agreements were signed that allow US law enforcement to engage in hot pursuit and board ships suspected of shipping drugs in Trinidad and Tobago's territorial waters, but Trinidad and Tobago law enforcement are not able to conduct the same kinds of operations in US territorial waters (Griffith, 2000).

What we are witnessing is not inevitable because social movements and civil society groups can and have challenged the neoliberal order in numerous ways. In terms of fighting for social justice, we could borrow from the sociology of development literature and realize the importance of civil society participation and local ownership for successful and sustainable security sector reform efforts. Civil society might be able to stop or mitigate anti-democratic actions by both donors and by elites in recipient countries. Security sector reform could be seen as a long-term effort that requires genuine local ownership and the full inclusion of women and other minority groups; the placing of process over outcome; mutual capacity building based on already existing local strengths and equal emphases on security and human rights from the beginning of the process. Donors can avoid paternalism and learn at least as much from recipients as recipients learn from donors, increasing legitimacy and, thanks to the use of local knowledge, the chances for the development of sustainable reforms. Security sector reform should therefore compliment rather than hinder economic and political development activities.

Civil society groups and other non-state security actors can play an important role in all of these activities in a way that promotes the genuine inclusion and full participation of those who are most affected by reform efforts. Research activities that include civil society groups and their local knowledge such as the work I conducted in Trinidad also have the potential to lead to sustainable reform efforts that can promote social justice. It must be said, however, that civil society groups and social movement organizations have been attempting to promote more local ownership in reform efforts for decades. For example, in 1987, the Development Group for Alternative Policies submitted a report to the US House of Representatives criticizing the Caribbean Basin Initiative, which was a pre-NAFTA trade agreement. Their criticism was based on six principles that can be used to promote social justice in a post-colonial context. These six principles include (1) *self-determination* to shape Caribbean development policies within rather than from outside the region; (2) *participation* of the Caribbean people in the definition and implementation of policies; (3) *self-reliance* to build local structures and capacities that reduce dependence; (4) *regionalism* for strengthening cooperation rather than competition between countries in the region and to strengthen regional organizations; (5) *equity* in the distribution of opportunities, resources, burdens and benefits of development; and 6) *sustainability* for the long-term preservation of a secure and healthy resource base, economic relations and local human capacity (Development Group for Alternative Policies, 1987, p. 6).

Violence

Criminological research generally focuses on street crimes. In most cases, researchers examine only the criminal aspects of subcultures such as youth gangs, and theories of violence such as those focusing on low impulse control or the routine activities of social life cannot come close to explaining the violence committed or ordered by those in power. The following quote from Young (2011) is instructive:

> The lens of orthodox criminology not only distorts, it leaves out. It has a narrow focus which leaves out much more than it sees. These omissions are of as great an interest as the inclusions. In particular it omits all those acts and activities which would suggest that there are wider structural forces involved in the generation of social harms. Let us take violence as an example; it omits the violence of war, of genocide, of injuries at work, of corporate malfeasance, of the state, of torture, it largely ignores the violence of imprisonment, of police brutality and until recently it ignored domestic violence. Indeed it ignores the vast majority of violence in our society. (p. 189)

That being said, it is still important to discuss how violent street crimes could be reduced if more attention was paid to issues of social justice. For example, although there are a few exceptions, countries with more economic inequality and underdevelopment tend to have higher murder rates, and both victims and perpetrators of murder are more likely to be members of marginalized populations – such as the poor and minority ethnic groups – and live in impoverished urban areas (UNODC, 2011). The victims of corporate and governmental violence also tend to be from marginalized populations. A concern for social justice compels us not to neglect the massive amounts of killing committed by corporations, militaries, private mercenaries, police and other governmental and private agents. Wilful killing occurs when corporations knowingly make unsafe products, pollute and create unsafe working conditions, and when hospitals and medical workers deny life-saving care or engage in various forms of medical malpractice that knowingly lead to death.

My research with an anthropologist, Robert Shanafelt, has revealed that different forms of violence are more similar than mainstream criminologists tend to reveal. Atrocities against marginalized people committed by serial killers or in war, for example, often involve torture, rape, the belittling of depersonalized victims before killing them and the keeping of trophies such as the body parts of victims (Shanafelt and Pino, 2012). However, while serial offending is almost always committed by individual offenders that develop pathological belief systems and fantasies over time, police torture and atrocities committed during times of war and political oppression are often conducted by "normal" men trained to engage in extreme forms of violence and depersonalization in normalized group settings. That being said, all of these forms of killing involve social learning and the development of ideologies and personas that allow a person to engage in these behaviors; and these ideologies are shaped by larger structural economic, political, educational and cultural forces that support patriarchy, the idea that violence is a way to solve problems and the dehumanization and othering of marginalized groups (ibid.). Fighting for social justice can therefore not only reduce the inequalities and prejudiced attitudes that can engender violence but also alert us to the crimes of the powerful that cause more financial harm and deaths than street criminals are capable of committing.

Teaching the sociology of deviance within a social justice framework

I teach undergraduate classes in deviant behavior and juvenile delinquency. In both classes I challenge students to think critically and to challenge their own taken-for-granted assumptions; and I take time to explain how research findings have compelled me to change the way I think about a number of issues. Students are exposed to the ways deviance and delinquency are socially constructed and tied to other social institutions (e.g., schools and religious institutions) and harmful forces, driving problems such as inequality and heterosexism. The processes involved in treating the mentally ill as deviant persons, for example, are in part influenced by the medicalization of deviance. Powerful institutions in the United States, such as the pharmaceutical and health insurance industries, promote norms (and in turn economic and political policies) that individualize social problems and prevent our ability to see how psychological distress is primarily caused by social forces driving inequalities in education and employment (Mirowski and Ross, 2003). I assign reflection papers in my undergraduate courses, and I am pleased to see that many of my students, most of whom are not sociology majors, appreciate the sociological perspective and how it compels them to see the world around them differently. Rather than "beating the students over the head" with the concept of social justice, which can easily lead to a backlash from students coming from both liberal and conservative political backgrounds, I find it more effective to promote critical thinking and to challenge the assumptions students assert during class discussion, even if I agree with what the student is saying. Social change begins when citizens ask more questions. As researchers we must also be sure to think critically and, when the data compel us to do so, be willing to challenge our taken-for-granted assumptions.

In conclusion, the sociology of deviance need not be dead if we concentrate on issues of social justice, and how social institutions, including the mass media, promote definitions of deviance that compliment other institutionalized methods of marginalization. We can also examine how these structural forces impact and are impacted by social interaction at the micro level of analysis. A concern for social justice helps point out these social problems and links them to economic and political marginalization and keeps the sociology of deviance vibrant and alive whether one studies the deviance of the powerful or the powerless.

References

Agozino, B. (2003) *Counter-Colonial Criminology: A Critique of Imperialist Reason* (London: Pluto Press).

Arrigo, B. A. (1999) "In Search of Social Justice: Toward an Integrative and Critical (Criminological) Theory", in B. A. Arrigo (ed.) *Social Justice/Criminal Justice: The Maturation of Critical Theory in Law, Crime and Deviance* (Belmont, CA: Wadsworth).

Cunneen, Chris (2011) "Postcolonial Perspectives for Criminology", in M. Bosworth and C. Hoyle (eds.) *What Is Criminology?* (Oxford: Oxford University Press).

Development Group for Alternative Policies (1987) *The Caribbean Basin Initiative: Caribbean Views. Report of a Congressional Study Mission on the Caribbean Basin Initiative, September 18–19, 1987 to the Committee of Foreign Affairs, US House of Representatives.* Washington DC: US Government Printing Office, http://www.developmentgap.org/americas/index.html.

Ellison, G. and N.W. Pino. (2012). *Globalization, Police Reform and Development: Doing it the Western Way?* New York: Palgrave Macmillan.

Goode, E. (2003) "The Macguffin that Refuses to Die: An Investigation into the Conditions of the Sociology of Deviance", *Deviant Behavior*, 24, (6), 507–533.

——(2004) "Is the Sociology of Deviance Still Relevant?", *The American Sociologist*, Winter, 46–57.

Griffith, I. L. (2000) *The Political Economy of Drugs in the Caribbean* (New York: St. Martin's Press).

Heckert, A. and D. M. Heckert (2002) "A New Typology of Deviance: Integrating Normative and Reactivist Definitions of Deviance", *Deviant Behavior*, 23, 449–479.

Liazos, A. (1972) "The Poverty of the Sociology of Deviance: Nuts, Sluts and Preverts", *Social Problems*, 20 (1), 103–120.

Michalowski, R. (2010) "Keynote Address: Critical Criminology for a Global Age", *Western Criminology Review*, 11 (1), 3–10.

Milivojevic, S. and S. Pickering (2008) "Football and Sex: The 2006 World Cup and Sex Trafficking", *Temida*, 11 (2), 21–47.

Mirowski, J. and C. E. Ross (2003) *Social Causes of Psychological Distress* (Piscataway, NJ: Transaction).

Mogul, J., A. Ritchie and K. Whitlock (2012) *Queer (In)Justice: The Criminalization of LGBT People in the United States* (Boston: Beacon Press).

Pino, N.W. (2009). "Developing Democratic Policing in the Caribbean: The Case of Trinidad and Tobago." *Caribbean Journal of Criminology and Public Safety*. 14:1&2, pp. 214–258.

Pino, N. W. and M. D. Wiatrowski. (2006). *Democratic Policing in Transitional and Developing Countries*. Aldershot, UK: Ashgate.

Richie, B. (2011) "Criminology and Social Justice: Expanding the Intellectual Commitment", in M. Bosworth and C. Hoyle (eds.) *What Is Criminology?* (Oxford: Oxford University Press).

Shanafelt, R. and N. W. Pino (2012) "Evil and the Common Life: Toward a Wider Perspective on Serial Offending and Atrocities", in S. Winlow and R. Atkinson (eds.) *New Directions in Crime and Deviancy* (New York: Routledge).

Sokoloff, N. J. and A. Burgess-Proctor (2011) "Remembering Criminology's 'Forgotten Theme': Seeking Justice in US Crime Policy Using an Intersectional Approach", in M. Bosworth and C. Hoyle (eds.) *What Is Criminology?* (Oxford: Oxford University Press).

United Nations Office on Drugs and Crime (UNODC) (2011) *2011 Global Study on Homicide: Trends, Context, Data* (Vienna: UNODC).

Winlow, S. and R. Atkinson (2013) "Introduction", in S. Winlow and R. Atkinson (eds.) *New Directions in Crime and Deviancy* (New York: Routledge).

Wolf, N. (2012) "Revealed: How the FBI Coordinated the Crackdown on Occupy", *The Guardian*, http://www.guardian.co.uk/commentisfree/2012/dec/29/fbi-co-ordinated-crackdown-occupy, date accessed December 29, 2012.

Young, J. (2011) *The Criminological Imagination* (Cambridge, UK: Polity Press).

Index

Printed and bound by CPI Group (UK) Ltd, Croydon, CR0 4YY

Critical Criminological Perspectives

The Palgrave *Critical Criminological Perspectives* book series aims to showcase the importance of critical criminological thinking when examining problems of crime, social harm and criminal and social justice. Critical perspectives have been instrumental in creating new research agendas and areas of criminological interest. By challenging state defined concepts of crime and rejecting positive analyses of criminality, critical criminological approaches continually push the boundaries and scope of criminology, creating new areas of focus and developing new ways of thinking about, and responding to, issues of social concern at local, national and global levels. Recent years have witnessed a flourishing of critical criminological narratives and this series seeks to capture the original and innovative ways that these discourses are engaging with contemporary issues of crime and justice.

Series editors:

Professor Reece Walters
Faculty of Law, Queensland University of Technology, Australia

Dr. Deborah Drake
Department of Social Policy and Criminology, The Open University, UK

Titles include:

Kerry Carrington, Matthew Ball, Erin O'Brien, Juan Tauri
CRIME, JUSTICE AND SOCIAL DEMOCRACY
International Perspectives

Claire Cohen
MALE RAPE IS A FEMINIST ISSUE
Feminism, Governmentality and Male Rape

Melissa Dearey
MAKING SENSE OF EVIL
An Interdisciplinary Approach

Michael Dellwing
THE DEATH AND RESURRECTION OF DEVIANCE
Current Ideas and Research

Deborah Drake
PRISONS, PUNISHMENT AND THE PURSUIT OF SECURITY

Margaret Malloch, William Munro (*editors*)
CRIME, CRITIQUE AND UTOPIA

Erin O'Brien, Sharon Hayes and Belinda Carpenter
THE POLITICS OF SEX TRAFFICKING
A Moral Geography

Maggi O'Neill and Lizzie Seal (*editors*)
TRANSGRESSIVE IMAGINATIONS
Crime, Deviance and Culture

Diane Westerhuis, Reece Walters, Tanya Wyatt (*editors*)
EMERGING ISSUES IN GREEN CRIMINOLOGY
Exploring Power, Justice and Harm

Tanya Wyatt
WILDLIFE TRAFFICKING
A Deconstruction of the Crime, the Victims, and the Offenders

Critical Criminological Perspectives
Series Standing Order ISBN 9780–230–36045–7 hardback
(outside North America only)

You can receive future titles in this series as they are published by placing a standing order. Please contact your bookseller or, in case of difficulty, write to us at the address below with your name and address, the title of the series and the ISBN quoted above.

Customer Services Department, Macmillan Distribution Ltd, Houndmills, Basingstoke, Hampshire RG21 6XS, England

The Death and Resurrection of Deviance

Current Ideas and Research

Edited by

Michael Dellwing
Kassel University, Germany

Joseph A. Kotarba
Texas State University, USA

Nathan W. Pino
Texas State University, USA

First published 2014 by
PALGRAVE MACMILLAN

Palgrave Macmillan in the UK is an imprint of Macmillan Publishers Limited, registered in England, company number 785998, of Houndmills, Basingstoke, Hampshire RG21 6XS.

Palgrave Macmillan in the US is a division of St Martin's Press LLC, 175 Fifth Avenue, New York, NY 10010.

Palgrave Macmillan is the global academic imprint of the above companies and has companies and representatives throughout the world.

Palgrave® and Macmillan® are registered trademarks in the United States, the United Kingdom, Europe and other countries

ISBN: 978–1–137–30379–0

This book is printed on paper suitable for recycling and made from fully managed and sustained forest sources. Logging, pulping and manufacturing processes are expected to conform to the environmental regulations of the country of origin.

A catalogue record for this book is available from the British Library.

A catalog record for this book is available from the Library of Congress.

Contents

Notes on Contributors

Peter and Patricia A. Adler are retired professors of sociology at the University of Denver and University of Colorado, respectively. Their research interests revolve around symbolic interactionism, ethnographic practices, deviant behavior, sociology of childhood, sociology of sport and microsociologies. From 1986 to 1994, they served as editors of *Journal of Contemporary Ethnography*. In 2006–2007, they were co-presidents of the Midwest Sociological Society. In 2010, they were honored with the George H. Mead Award for Lifetime Achievement from the Society for the Study of Symbolic Interaction.

Joel Best is a professor of sociology and criminal justice at the University of Delaware. He is a former president of the Society for the Study of Social Problems and a former editor of the journal *Social Problems*. He has written several books about deviance and social problems, including *Organizing Deviance* (with David F. Luckenbill, 2nd edn., 1994), *Threatened Children* (1990), *Controlling Vice* (1998), *Random Violence* (1999) and *Deviance: Career of a Concept* (2004). His most recent books are *The Student Loan Mess: How Good Intentions Created a Trillion-Dollar Problem* (with Eric Best, 2014) and *Kids Gone Wild: From Rainbow Parties to Sexting, Understanding the Hype over Teen Sex* (with Kathleen A. Bogle, 2014).

Michael Ian Borer is an associate professor in the Department of Sociology at the University of Nevada, Las Vegas. His specializations include urban and community sociology, culture, religion and qualitative methods. He is the editor of *The Varieties of Urban Experience: The American City and the Practice of Culture* (2006) and the author of *Faithful to Fenway: Believing in Boston, Baseball, and America's Most Beloved Ballpark* (2008). His work has been published in *City & Community*, the *Journal of Popular Culture*, *Religion & American Culture*, *Social Psychology Quarterly*, *Symbolic Interaction* and the *Journal of Religion & Media*, among other journals and books. Dr. Borer served as the vice president of the Society for the Study of Symbolic Interaction in 2011–2012. He is the recipient of the 2011 Maines Narrative Research Award – granted by the Ethnography Division of the National Communications Association – for his article "From Collective Memory to Collective Imagination: Time, Place, and Urban Redevelopment", published in *Symbolic Interaction* (2010).

Scott Wm. Bowman is an associate professor in the School of Criminal Justice at Texas State University. He received his PhD in justice studies from Arizona State University. His doctoral work focused on racial and socioeconomic inequalities. His current teaching and research interests include race and crime, socioeconomic status and crime, hip-hop culture and positive youth development and juvenile justice.

Jessica Autumn Brown is an assistant professor of sociology at the University of Houston. She received her PhD from the University of Wisconsin. She conducts research in the areas of gender, immigration, race and ethnicity, citizenship and transnational sociology. This project is an outgrowth of her doctoral research, which was funded by a 2006–2007 grant from the German Academic Exchange Service (DAAD). Her current projects focus on citizenship education in U.S. public schools with large populations of first and second-generation American students, and deviance framings of undocumented immigrants in U.S. presidential debate discourse.

Michael J. Coyle is an associate professor of Political Science at California State University, Chico. His areas of specialization include social justice, crime and justice theory, and discourse analysis. Dr. Coyle received his B.A. in Religious Studies from Arizona State University, his M.T.S. in American Studies from Harvard University, and his Ph.D. in Justice Studies from Arizona State University. His most recent book is *Talking Criminal Justice: Language and the Just Society* (2013).

Susan Day is a professor of sociology at Texas State University. She has also served as chair since 1998. She received her PhD from the University of Kansas. She teaches undergraduate and graduate courses in deviance, criminology and social control, as well as introduction to sociology. Her teaching philosophy focuses on the application of classic sociological theories to understand contemporary society. She is the recipient of numerous awards for teaching, including the president's Excellence Award at Texas State.

Michael Dellwing is a lecturer in the Department of Social Sciences at Kassel University. His research interests include the sociology of psychiatry, everyday life sociology and television studies. A collection of pieces on law and deviance, *Recht als Interaktion* (Law as Interaction), is forthcoming. English publications include "Truth in Labeling" (in *Deviant Behavior*, 2011), "Little Dramas of Discomposure" (in *Symbolic Interaction*, 2012) and "Addiction Diagnoses as Involvement Controls" (in *Reset*, 2013). He is the editor, with Heinz Bude, of a German collection of Herbert Blumer's works (2013) and of the German edition of Howard Becker's *Outsiders* (2014) and also the author, with Robert Prus, of an introduction to ethnography, *Einführung in die interaktionistische Ethnografie* (An Introduction to Interactionist Ethnography) (2012).

Daniel Dotter is a professor of criminal justice at Grambling State University, where he teaches courses in criminology, deviant behavior and media and crime, among other subjects. He received his PhD in sociology from Virginia Polytechnic Institute and State University. His research and writing focus on the areas of social deviance and cultural criminology. In addition to publishing numerous articles and book chapters, he has authored the monograph *Creating Deviance: An Interactionist Approach* (2004). He is currently working on a book titled *Whispers in the Dark: Conspiracy Culture as Extreme Deviance*.

Lori L. Fazzino is a doctoral candidate in the Department of Sociology at the University of Nevada, Las Vegas. She specializes in culture, religion, social movements and deviance, and her dissertation explores the individual and collective construction of irreligious morality among non-believers living in Las Vegas. Her work on evangelical deconversion is forthcoming in the *Journal of Contemporary Religion*. Lori is the recipient of the 2014 James Frye Graduate Student Research Award.

Erich Goode is Professor Emeritus in sociology at Stony Brook University. In addition to Stony Brook, he taught for nearly four decades at half a dozen universities, including the Universities of North Carolina, Maryland and New York, and he has written dozens of academic journal articles as well as articles in newspapers and literary and popular magazines, edited seven anthologies and published eleven books, including *Deviant Behavior* (10th edn, 2015), *Drugs in American Society* (9th edn, 2015) and *Justifiable Conduct* (2013). He is presently editing the *Wiley Handbook on Deviance*.

Mohammad Abdel Haq is a visiting instructor in the Department of Sociology at California State University, Fullerton. As a self-identified atheist, he is very interested in understanding the collective consciousness that exists within the atheist community. Mohammad was awarded the Carlene Nelson Scholarship in Sociology and he received an Honorable Mention by the Sally Casanova Pre-Doctoral program as recognitions of his strong dedication to the sociological field. His other research interests lie in the sociology of religion, education, collective behavior and deviance.

Mark Horsley is a senior lecturer in criminology at the University of the West of England (UWE) in Bristol, United Kingdom. His research interests include social and criminological theory, consumer culture, the debt industry, international finance and corporate crime. He completed his PhD in June 2013 at the University of Teesside with a semi-ethnographic research project into socio-cultural motivations for consumer borrowing. Before taking up his current post at UWE, Mark taught various aspects of criminology and sociology at York, Sunderland, Northumbria, West of Scotland and Leeds Metropolitan Universities.

Joseph A. Kotarba is a professor of sociology and the director of the Center for Social Inquiry at Texas State University. He received his doctorate from the University of California at San Diego. Current projects include a study of the culture of translational scientific research at the University of Texas Medical Branch in Galveston, Texas (funded by the National Institutes of Health) and the development of a sociological model of the pop music song. He is the recipient of the Society for the Study of Symbolic Interaction's George Herbert Mead Award for Lifetime Achievement and the Mentor's Excellence Award. His most recent books are *Baby Boomer Rock & Roll Fans: The Music Never Ends* (2013) and *The Present and Future of Symbolic Interactionism* (co-edited with Andrea Salvini and Bryce Merrill, 2012).

Jennifer Lynn Murray is an assistant professor in the Department of Criminology at Indiana State University. Her research focus is on mass and serial murder. She has lectured about her work in the United States, the United Kingdom and Europe. She has also analyzed, consulted and been interviewed nationally and internationally on numerous murder cases. She is an expert commentator on several episodes for the Investigation Discovery Channel's (ID) Television Series *Evil Kin*. She recently taught a course at Scotland's Stirling University comparing US and British mass killings with regard to prevalence, gun laws, health care and bullying.

Robin D. Perrin received his doctorate in sociology from Washington State University in 1989. Following his doctoral studies, he worked as an assistant professor of sociology at Seattle Pacific University in Seattle, Washington. Currently he is professor of sociology at Pepperdine University in Malibu, California. Perrin's research interests and publications are in the areas of family violence, deviance theory, the social construction of social problems and the sociology of religion. He is the co-author of three books: *Social Deviance: Being, Behaving, and*

Branding (with David Ward and Tim Carter, 1991), *Child Maltreatment: An Introduction* (with Cindy Miller-Perrin, 1999) and *Family Violence across the Lifespan* (with Ola Barnett and Cindy Miller-Perrin, 1997). He is also the author or co-author of numerous articles on a variety of topics including family violence, deviance theory and the sociology of religion. At Pepperdine, Professor Perrin teaches introduction to sociology, introductory statistics, deviant behavior and social control and sociology of religion. He is the 2004 recipient of Pepperdine's Howard A. White Award for Teaching Excellence.

Nathan W. Pino is a professor of sociology at Texas State University, where he conducts research on international policing and police reform, violence and the attitudes and behaviors of college students. In addition to numerous academic journal articles, he is author (with Robert Shanafelt) of *Rethinking Serial Murder, Spree Killing, and Atrocities: Beyond the Usual Distinctions* (forthcoming). He is also the author (with Graham Ellison) of *Globalization, Police Reform, and Development: Doing It the Western Way?* (2012) and the editor (with Michael D. Wiatrowski) of *Democratic Policing in Transitional and Developing Countries* (2008).

J. Patrick Williams is associate professor of sociology at Nanyang Technological University, Singapore. Much of his research has focused on the experiential and cultural implications of identifying as a member of a subcultural group. That research has been published in *Deviant Behavior, Journal of Contemporary Ethnography, Justice Quarterly, Social Problems, Symbolic Interaction* and elsewhere. He has published several books, including *Authenticity in Culture, Self and Society* (2009) and *Subcultural Theory: Traditions and Concepts* (2011).

Introduction
Tales of Death and Deviance

Michael Dellwing, Joseph A. Kotarba, and Nathan W. Pino

"Deviance" is one of the most easily recognizable terms in sociology. It has long been a central subfield of the discipline. Introductory classes widely teach the subject, and a plethora of deviance textbooks introduce mostly undergraduates to the concept and, through it, to the profession at large. At the same time, deviance has become a contested category in the past few years. Some sociologists have proclaimed the "death of deviance," (Sumner, 1994) noting that the abundance of introductory classes is not synonymous with a vibrant field of research (Best, 2004a, 2004b, and in this volume). They further claim that the concept has run its course, done in by the pluralistic, open, and interpretive approaches that have conquered at least the qualitative arm of the discipline. Interactionist and postmodern approaches in particular, the argument goes, have no more use for a concept so firmly rooted in an orderly picture of the world. The concept of deviance is a holdover from structural-functional sociology and from a time when sociologists believed in things like abstract norms, even in clear and holistic norms that envelop and thus create and sustain an entire society.

The structural-functional model offers precisely the kind of static and structural universe that interactionists sought to unravel, a world of normality and abnormality where a single word like "deviance" can indicate the abnormal. With the pluralistic world denoted by interactionist and postmodern sociology, there is no normal any longer, not in any general sense and not in a "normal for you, but not for me" sense of split-up, divergent static realms. Normal is more deeply contextual than just "normal in reference to a group's norms." Normal is a local ascription that arises in a specific and situational contest, unfettered by any abstract system (cf. Prus, 1996, 1997; Dellwing, 2011).

We would like to thank Maike Simmank for her assistance in creating this volume.

1

Deviance as a concept seems a child of this static universe, and yet interactionist sociology has steadfastly held on to the term. The reason is, at least in part, historical: the sociology of deviance was one of the main catalysts creating a position of influence for symbolic interactionists in the discipline of sociology. Howard Becker's *Outsiders* (1963) is one of the classics in the literature on deviance, and the classics in the sociology of deviance are by and large interactionist works. Other most-cited deviance texts are Howard Becker's *The Other Side* (1964), Kai Erikson's *Wayward Puritans* (1966) and "Notes on the Sociology of Deviance" (1961), Jack Douglas's *Deviance and Respectability* (1970), Douglas and Fran Waksler's *The Sociology of Deviance* (1982), Paul Rock and Mary McIntosh's *Deviance and Social Control* (1974), Edwin Schur's *The Politics of Deviance* (1980), Peter Conrad and Joseph Schneider's *Deviance and Medicalization* (1980), Joseph Gusfield's *Symbolic Crusade* (1986) and Spitzer and Denzin's *The Mental Patient* (1968). The list continues into the near-present with Patricia and Peter Adler's *Constructions of Deviance* (2012) and David Downes and Paul Rock's *Understanding Deviance* (2007). This is a much abbreviated list that does not include most works on social problems (Blumer, 1971; Spector and Kitsuse, 2001 [1977]) and the literature on moral panics (e.g., Cohen, 1972), most of which are deeply integrated into the deviance debate.

It is precisely this body of work that established interactionist sociology's prominence, while simultaneously being credited with the destruction of the concept. These constructionist and interpretivist authors insist that there is no such thing as abstract deviance: deviance is, in the famous words of Howard Becker (1963: 9–10), only behavior that is labeled as deviant. The quoted works therefore do not analyze what deviance is, or how it comes about and how it can be prevented. They, by and large, tend to take no position on defending normality or the current moral order. Rather, they analyze how a person or a behavior comes to be known or defined as deviant in local contexts and enterprises both in the life-worlds of the participants studied as well as in the works that these researchers wrote about them.

Noting this disconnect, however, provides exceedingly weak grounds for the critics of deviance to assail the term. It is a given that deviance is a construction, not an objective thing. It may even be a given, at least within this school, that deviance is not a stable construction, as it is formed differently in different interaction contexts. This is nothing especially groundbreaking or threatening to the sociological endeavor. All social meanings are constructed; if that were sufficient as an argument for the death of *whatever*, all terms would have to be abandoned. The *whatever* of this particular demise encapsulates every category possible. But "whatever" is not a useful reaction to this old insight, and the argument is not sufficient (Dellwing, 2011). Constructions are neither arbitrary nor abstractly prestructured; interactionists insist especially that they are products of interactive processes that can be studied, and those in which different social orders can be discovered without reifying these orders. Deviance is no exception.

We can note that the proliferation of university deviance courses is a consequence of this openness, not an opposition to it: these classes take up a field in which every student has opinions – about what is true and good and right and just – and shows these opinions to be reproductions of socially shared narratives, usually façade moralizations with little connection to concrete action that cover up contextual constructions of reality that are much more complicated than the easy answer you give to an ethics question. In addition, these easy answers are often deeply entangled with hierarchies, exclusions, and oppressions that many students would rather not know of, let alone admit. Sociology classes make them admit them and tear down the façade. Deviance courses are often the first that disabuse students of the notion that their moral opinions are truly – or singly – their own, dispossess them of taking the side of that which is established as "normal" in everyday life and media narratives as a matter of course. For many students, deviance is therefore the gateway drug to this kind of sociological unraveling of the settled and lazy positions of abstract morality they have come to learn (and have seen used excessively) in school, at home and in the media. It is the first in a long line of courses in which assumptions about societal normalities and seemingly self-evident truths are historicized, contextualized and analyzed to reveal their hidden dynamics.

Deviance, in other words, is a course that seeks to *destroy* the taken-for-granted categorization of behavior and people as "deviant." Therefore, it is *especially* the pluralistic sociology championed by interpretivists of all shades to which deviance introduces students. Interpretivism is not the bane of deviance, it is the reason for its vitality as a course.

As Best argues (in this volume as well), the vitality and usefulness of a subject as a part of the curriculum in sociology does not mean that it is also a viable analytical concept. This particular critique of deviance is that it is alive in courses, but dead in serious research, and that for much of the same reasons, it is alive in the curriculum. As a teaching tool, deviance is useful because it picks up students where they are, with their everyday unreflected reproduction of moral normality through judgments they consider innocent opinions, in order to guide them toward an understanding of their social underpinnings. In research, it is exactly this position – where, in everyday life, "we are" – that is now rather useless after the interpretivist turn. In the abstract tradition, there was an abstract thing called deviance, opposite an abstract thing called conformity, a remnant of a sociology that aimed to name everything as if it were unquestioningly there. This sociological holism did not just disregard the lived reality of those studied (especially when they found themselves on the fringes and the receiving end of the "deviance" label), it was often *proud* to supersede that reality for the chance at an abstract pronunciation.

However, research is not about setting boundaries between conformity and deviance any longer. It can no longer supersede these with the arrogance of the professor who professes to "know" conformity from deviance. The stronger argument concerning the disconnect that arises between deviance's death at the hands of interpretivists and the continued use of the concept by interpretivists is, therefore, lodged more deeply inside the approach. Interactionists, especially those in the ethnographic tradition, study the lived reality of people. This approach compels us to find the meanings that the participants in social inter-actions create for themselves, the meanings that become their reality as they act on them and on their basis (Thomas and Thomas, 1928; Blumer, 1969). These are plural and often surprising. In the contextual tradition, deviance may still be around, but as a category in the lived reality of the people we study, and in what they *do* with that category: The research, then, is about where the people *researched* put them. From this follows, then, that "deviance" runs the risk of being a life-less structural-functionalist monster, a Frankenstein operationalization, if it is not a category people use to order their world. But that border is as devoid of stability as those invented by enlightened professors of the structural-functional tradition. The interpretivist position, following Becker, analyzes the *situational* uses of border maintenance, and when the people we research differentiate deviance from non-deviance, that border changes in different contexts and in different situations for the same people. The mess that results can be ordered in analysis, but "conformity" and "deviance" may be a naïve and simplistic attempt at ordering it.

And yet, this is too easy. First, deviance came into the public vocabu-lary *because* it was initially an analytic category; the people under study use it because they have learned it from sociology, back when soci-ology reproduced the simple and naïve moralism of those it studied. Then, the popularity of the deviance class made the term one of the few sociological concepts to gain entry into everyday life parlance. The term is used in its life-world sense because of us. Second, not all categories developed by sociologists are lifeless monsters as long as they capture something that is relevant and understandable in the life-world of those we study. Many categories may not be *in vivo* categories, that is, may not be categories used and even named in the everyday life of those whose reality we analyze, but they may still have utility to highlight the processes that those we study engage in; "construction of reality" is one clear example of this. Regardless of how situational, shifting and fluid people's border maintenance operations are, that is, how different the things that they identify as scandalously different in different contexts are, they do draw these lines clearly *within* these contexts, and these lines have hard and often harsh consequences for the people involved. Even if the term is not used, deviance ascriptions are an everyday occurrence: they are exclusions that the actors involved legitimize with normative underpinnings, and they refer to social idealisms to differentiate violence from justice. A sociological analysis that takes its interpretivism seriously will refrain from supporting these judgments about legitimacy and can marvel at the double pluralism of the way these are used: for one, there is a wide pluralism of legitimization tropes, besides a wide pluralism of often very different instances in which the same trope can be used successfully by participants in the social situations we study. If we can find this sort of border maintenance operation, and "construction of deviance" helps us understand it, then deviance may have a place in the discipline still. The question thus remains: does deviance have analytic utility that does not simply override and ignore the life-worlds of the people we study and reintroduce old phantoms of stable worlds we put to rest long ago?

In assembling the present book, we sought to give prominent authors space to debate these questions. What resulted was a lively discussion that picks up the debate on the term "deviance" and challenges its utility as well as our thinking about society with the help of the term. The first section of the book focuses squarely on the "death of deviance" debate itself. We start, fittingly, with Erich Goode, who evaluates The "meaning and validity of the death of deviance claim," followed by Patricia and Peter Adler, who analyze the "critical role of deviance in society," demonstrating how deviance labeling remains one of the major practices with which we order our life-worlds. Joel Best provides a critical response to the comparative optimism of the first two chapters, noting that there is a "deviance bubble" – the term was first interestingly used, then overused, and is now on the verge of bursting, if that has not already happened. Mark Horsley examines the intersection between sociology and criminology in "The 'Death of Deviance' and Stagnation of 20th Century Criminology," arguing that the "death of deviance" transformed criminology to a discipline focused on representation and political portrayal, and analyzes how the sociology of deviance made a return to a more sociological criminology. Patrick Williams provides a transitional piece, "Subcultures and Deviance," where he looks at the connection between subcultures and deviance, two terms that have both been embattled in recent sociology, but that provide much material to analyze and support one another.

In the second section, we discuss the productive uses of the deviance concept in various fields of sociological inquiry. This topical segment is kicked off by Daniel Dotter, who is interested in the status of deviance in conspiracy theories in "Debating the Death of Deviance: Transgressing Extremes in Conspiracy Narratives." Religion turns out to be of major interest to our contributors, who find strong tendencies to socially control "deviant religion." Robin Perrin tills this field in his piece on "Religious Deviance," while Lori Fazzino, Michael Borer and Mohammed Haq look at the increasing deviantization of atheism in contemporary United States in "The New Moral Entrepreneurs: Atheist Activism as Scripted and Performed Political Deviance." Scott Bowman comes to the deviance debate with a different take: rather than survey the viability of the term, he differentiates what we could call "normal deviance" from formally punished behavior in schools, bemoaning the "death of deviance" and the formalization of social control in education. Jessica Brown looks at Germany in "For These People It Is Almost Too Late: German Citizenship Education, Islam and the Construction of Normativity and Deviance" to survey the role of deviance constructions of the "alien" in citizenship classes; and Jennifer Murray compares psychological and sociological/deviance approaches to understanding the role media play in the construction of serial killer narratives.

In the third section of the volume, we turn to the consequences of the death of deviance argument and of deviance as a category for teaching and research. Susan Day and Joseph Kotarba, in "The Didactic Relevance of the Death of Deviance Debate," ask what the "death of deviance" means to sociological instruction. Michael Dellwing treads a similar path in "'Deviance' Is for Undergrads, 'Social Control' Is for Grad Students" by noting that deviance, as a sociological concept, is useful to start undergraduates out on sociology. Nathan Pino, in "Deviance and Social Justice," brings the discussion around to practical matters of political appraisal when he questions the connection between deviance and social justice.

The chapters in this volume as a whole debate the vitality of deviance as a concept and as a field of study. Does deviance deserve a resurrection? Has it ever passed away? If anything, scholarship over the past few decades has opened up new possibilities for deviance research and theorizing in a way that can help bridge disciplines that often seem to be drifting further and further apart, including criminology, medical sociology and the sociologies of immigration, belief systems, education and sexuality, to name a few. Deviance scholarship can speak to the effects on lived experiences of accelerated globalization and other rapid forms of social change that deepen inequalities while both bringing people together and taking them apart in numerous ways and to varying degrees.

References

Adler, P. A. and P. Adler (2012) Constructions of Deviance (Belmont, CA: Wadsworth).

Becker, H. S. (1963) Outsiders: Studies in the Sociology of Deviance (New York: Free Press).

—— (ed.) (1964) The Other Side: Perspectives on Deviance (New York: Free Press).

Best, J. (2004a) Deviance: Career of a Concept (Belmont, CA: Thompson Wadsworth).

—— (2004b) "Deviance May Be Alive but Is It Intellectually Lively? A Reaction to Goode", *Deviant Behavior*, 25, 483–492.

Blumer, Herbert (1969). Symbolic Interactionism: Perspective and Method (Berkeley, CA: University of California Press).

Cohen, S. (1972) Folk Devils and Moral Panics: The Creation of the Mods and the Rockers (New York: MacGibbon and Kee).

Conrad, P. and J. Schneider (1980) Deviance and Medicalization (St. Louis: Mosby).

Dellwing, M. (2011) "Truth in Labeling: Are Descriptions All We Have?", Deviant Behavior, 32, 653–675.

Douglas, J. D. (1970) *Deviance and Respectability: The Social Construction of Moral Meanings* (New York: Basic Books).

Douglas, J. D. and F. C. Waksler (1982) The Sociology of Deviance: An Introduction (Boston: Little, Brown).

Downes D. and P. Rock (2007) Understanding Deviance, 5th edn (Oxford: Oxford University Press).

Erikson, K. T. (1961) "Notes on the Sociology of Deviance", Social Problems, 9, 307–314.

—— (1966) Wayward Puritans: A Study in the Sociology of Deviance (New York: John Wiley & Sons).

Gusfield, J. (1986) Symbolic Crusade (Urbana: Illini).

Prus, R. (1996) *Symbolic Interaction and Ethnographic Research: Intersubjectivity and the Study of Human Lived Experience* (Albany, NY: State University of New York Press).

——(1997) *Subcultural Mosaics and Intersubjective Realities: An Ethnographic Research Agenda for Pragmatizing the Social Sciences* (Albany: State University of New York Press).

Rock, P. and M. McIntosh (1974) Deviance and Social Control (London: Tavistock).

Schur, E. M. (1980) The Politics of Deviance: Stigma Contests and the Uses of Power (Englewood Cliffs, NJ: Prentice-Hall).

Spector, M. and J. I. Kitsuse (2001 [1977]) Constructing Social Problems (Piscataway: Transaction).

Spitzer, S. P. and N. K. Denzin (1968) *The Mental Patient: Studies in the Sociology of Deviance* (New York: McGraw-Hill).

Sumner, C. (1994) The Sociology of Deviance: An Obituary (Buckingham: Open University Press).

Thomas, W. I. and D. S. Thomas (1928) The Child in America: Behavior Problems and Programs (New York: Knopf).

Part I
The Death of Deviance?

1
The Meaning and Validity of the Death of Deviance Claim

Erich Goode

Introduction

Even patently untrue assertions, especially those that are ideologically appealing, if accepted as valid among certain circles, need to be falsified. But before empirical falsification comes conceptual clarification. "Define your terms", said Voltaire, in the *Dictionnaire Philosophique* (1764), "or we shall never understand one another". In 2007, then President Bill Clinton took Voltaire's warning to heart by brilliantly ducking a question about his sexual indiscretions with a White House aide. "It depends", he replied jesuitically, "on what the meaning of *is* is". Such definitional evasions aside, before we investigate a given sphere of inquiry, we need to delineate and define the concepts we use. This admonition applies to no endeavor more forcefully than investigating the "death of deviance" claim.

Conceptualizing deviance

Deviance can be anything that violates a society's, or a social collectivity's, normative structure. All sociological notions of deviance presuppose an audience, real or hypothesized, abstractly normative or operationally reactive. Most discussions, however, focus exclusively on behavior rather than beliefs or characteristics. The study of deviance is fundamentally two independent but interlocking enterprises. When sociologists investigate normative violations and the censure that violators are

---

I am grateful to Nachman Ben-Yehuda for helpful discussions of this chapter's topic as well as comments on an earlier version of this chapter, and the publishers of the half-dozen works from which I borrowed and adapted my own material.

likely to receive, they adopt one of two distinctly different perspectives or approaches, and thus engage in two contrasting endeavors.

When we conceptualize deviance, the questions we should ask ourselves initially are these: *What is our mission? What is to be explained?* Our answers place us in one or another camp, which sociologists refer to as *positivism* (or explanatory theory) and *constructionism*. We can regard these two approaches as "master visions". They might seem contradictory but in fact they complement one another, constituting two sides of the same coin.

Although all positivist or explanatory theorists know that deviance and crime are defined by socially and legally constructed norms and laws, the focus of their analysis is such that they perforce consider their subject's qualities as objectively real. To seek a cause is to assume that a phenomenon has a common thread, a distinctive or singular feature that *permits* a causal explanation. The answer to the "What is to be explained?" question is that it is the *deviant behavior, beliefs or conditions themselves* that must be explained. *Deviance is conceived of as a type of behavior* – not exclusively a way of *looking* at behavior. What causes "deviance" to come about or take place in a certain time, locale or setting is our guiding concern. The positivist is likely to ask: What kind of person would do or believe such a thing? What social arrangements, settings or factors make such behaviors (or beliefs) more likely? What causes the crime rate to be so high in one place, so much lower in another? These are the sorts of questions positivists who study deviance and crime ask, and they center on the guiding question: *Why do they do it?* Because deviance possesses a pre-given or indwelling trait, we are led to the inevitable question: "Why?"

In contrast, the approach we call *constructionism* or "social constructionism" answers the "What is to be explained?" question by saying that it is *thinking about* and *reacting to* rule-violators that is crucial. This approach argues that it is the *rules*, the *norms, reactions to* and the *cultural representations of* certain behavior, beliefs or conditions that need to be looked at and illuminated. In other words, constructionism is curious about how and why something comes to be *regarded as* or *judged to be* deviant in the first place, what is *thought, made of, said about* and *done about* it. How are phenomena generally, and deviant phenomena specifically, *conceptualized, defined, represented, reacted to* and *dealt with*? How are certain actions *conceptualized* and how do they *come to be regarded* or *deemed* as "crime", "prostitution", "treachery" or "incest"? How are certain beliefs judged *as* "heresy", "blasphemy", "godlessness", "disloyalty" "treachery"? The constructionist is more interested in issues that have to do with thinking, talking, writing about, narrating or reacting to such actions than in why deviant behavior, beliefs or traits take place, occur or exist in the first place. To the constructionist, deviant behavior, beliefs and traits "exist" – *as a social category* – because they are conceptualized and reacted to in a certain way. The constructionist does not take the conceptualization of an act, a belief, a condition, for granted; instead, it is *how something is regarded and dealt with* that must be accounted for, not the origin of the occurrence of the behavior, the beliefs or the conditions. That is, positivists take norms and rules for granted; constructionists are interested in how rules are made and applied. Constructionism simultaneously hugely expands and narrowly focuses deviance inquiries on extra-normativity.

Delineating the "deviance is dead" notion

We can divide up the pie of the critiques of the death of deviance in many ways, but perhaps the most basic and fundamental division is between evaluations based on the argument that the sociology of deviance is not merely dead, it is stillborn – it was never alive – because it is an invalid, unviable, sterile notion to begin with, as opposed to the view that, at one time, deviance may have had some currency, traction or validity, but has outlived its usefulness. In 1972, Alexander Liazos penned the first full-blown, detailed and emphatic "stillborn" critique of the deviance sub-discipline – the "nuts, sluts, and deviated preverts [*sic*]" argument. Sociologists of deviance back then, he claimed, concentrated on condemned and stigmatized behavior and people, thereby ignoring "the unethical, illegal and destructive actions of powerful individuals, groups and institutions in our society" (p. 111). Corporate crime steals vastly more money from the public pocket and physically imperils the lives of ordinary citizens than is true of the sneak thief, the bank robber and the mugger. What's *really and truly* deviant – and what sociologists of deviance should pay attention to, Liazos argued – is oppression, exploitation, racism, sexism and imperialism, and not prostitution, mental disorder, child molestation or rape. The enterprise of studying deviance was never valid to begin with because it has ignored what's most important about normative violations: wrongful actions by fat cats that cause harm to the rest of us. The problem with Liazos's argument is that sociologists do not *define* deviance by harm, nor is it even, primarily, *about* harm – it is about behavior, beliefs and conditions that elicit censure, condemnation, stigma and punishment. If objectively harmful actions do not call forth censure, that in itself would be interesting and noteworthy; if harmless acts do, that too is worth studying. However ideologically satisfying pulling monstrously and calamitously injurious actions inflicted by putative villains into the tent of deviance may be, their harm is not what imparts to them a specifically deviant tenor; it is their desecration of a valuative system and the consequent nega-tive reactions of audiences – overlapping but not identical universes. Investigations of harm are not the primary mission of the sociology of deviance; harmful actions are not what we are charged to investigate. Of course, harm is one of the many *factors* that determine how *audiences* decide that acts and beliefs are wrongful – but it is not the only one.

Do the "deviance is dead" claimants assert that *deviance itself* is dead? Or that, over time, *the sociology of deviance* died – as any "obituary" would indicate? Or that the field of the sociology of deviance has *declined* – not died – in its influence and centrality – less important and innovative, let's say, than it was in its heyday? Or that the sociology of deviance is no longer as theoretically *creative* or *innovative* as it once was, say, *in comparison with* other fields of sociology? Or even in comparison with the field of sociology generally?

Let's examine each formulation in turn.

Is deviance dead?

Sociologists define deviance as the violation of a social norm, the departure from an accepted standard. It is possible that James Ford was the first academic to use the term "deviance", or some equivalent – specifically, "deviation" – in 1936. Ford was a classic social pathologist (Mills, 1943), and his meaning of the term is now regarded as archaic. Establishing and enforcing norms represents one of the many arms of social control, which is, according to Jack Gibbs (1989, pp. 55 and 400), sociology's "central notion". In using this definition, sociologists imply no taint of condemnation, stigma, pathology, dysfunctionality, instability, criminality, amorality, immanent evil or a departure from psychiatric normalcy or a threat to the stability of the society; these are empirical questions to be investigated, not an assumed component of the definition.

It is true that throughout the entire stretch of human existence, norms, *some* species of norms – norms of one kind or another – have existed, have been ubiquitous, and they are likewise violated in every institutional sphere in every society throughout history. And reactions to these normative violations, real or imagined, are also enacted every-where. Actors hardly ever *refer to* what they recognize as "deviance" when they punish, shun or condemn persons they regard as wrong-doers, but this is irrelevant; it seems an appropriate sociological term for behavior that calls forth such reactions. True, it was not until the 20th century that sociologists invented the term, *deviance*, but if we do not *call* what we're investigating "deviance" – what *should* we call it? Norms are the bone and sinew of culture, social structure and everyday life where such breaches of what's considered right are commonly enacted, and they do not, upon discovery, always (perhaps not even usually) result in censure. Moreover, this process of chastisement is sociologically patterned according to rank, privilege, race, sex and gender, age, friend-ship networks and situational contingencies. But the *endeavor* of social control is implicit in all norms. These assertions do not imply or rest on the essentialistic, universal, indwelling nature of deviance: they simply make an empirical observation about the consequences of normative violations. *What it is* that generates these censorious reactions is vari-able and relative. But normative violations occur everywhere, and so do reactions to them, though the cause and consequences of the violations themselves are social, cultural and situational – in a word, *constructed*.

The death of the sociology of deviance?

What of the claim that "deviance is dead"? Colin Sumner (1994) and Ann Hendershott (2002) indicate that it is the *sociology* of deviance – not deviance itself – that has died. What do these observers mean by their claim? Does it mean that the *enterprise* of studying deviance has expired? Sumner dismisses courses, students and the publication of books devoted to deviance, texts included, as a measure of viability. Researchers still work in the field, he admits, textbooks are still written and published under its rubric and students still enroll in courses with the title "deviance" or some such equivalent – but he doesn't care. In contrast, Hendershott does care; these manifestations constitute her pivotal indicators. What do these indicators say?

Literally every one of the current editions of the first 30 introduc-tory sociology textbooks whose title and table of contents I located included a chapter on deviance – variously entitled "Deviance, Crime, and Social Control", "Deviance and Norms", "Deviant Behavior and Social Control", "Deviance and Conformity", "Deviance and Crime" and, simply, "Deviance" – and though, as we all know, passing fashion strongly influences the college textbook market, the subject is clearly foundational for the field of sociology generally. And most departments of sociology offer courses in the sociology of deviance, undergraduates still enroll in these courses and textbooks on deviance written by sociologists still bear titles such as *Deviant Behavior* and *Sociology of Deviant Behavior.* Moreover, more than half a dozen deviance textbooks have stood the test of time; their authors have revised them and their publishers have continued to issue new editions, some, with new co-authors, while others, text-readers, updated every few years, contain new material alongside the classic readings. And scholars still write and publish advanced research monographs with "deviant" and "deviance" in their titles. Moreover, the field still produces a mountain of academic journal articles with these terms in the titles. *Deviant Behavior*, the field's flagship journal, was founded in 1970, and is still issued – closing in on half a century beyond the field's predicted demise. All of this indicates that the enterprise of the sociology of deviance field is strong, vibrant and continually in the process of undergoing revision – in short, anything but "dead" or stagnant.

In *The Sociology of Deviance: An Obituary*, British criminologist Colin Sumner (1994, p. vii) – like Liazos, a radical and a Marxist – proclaimed that, by the 1970s, the sociology of deviance, though once useful, had "died". During the era in which he wrote his book, two decades subsequent to its putative demise, the field, he argued, had become "barren", "a graveyard" – and his book, a message chiseled onto the headstone of its buried corpse (p. ix). The study of deviance is no longer an intellectual pursuit with a pulse, and has not been for, now, close to four decades. Its practitioners have abandoned the intellectual territory and research program once laid out by its pioneers. Over the years, "combatants ... have completely demolished the terrain", which, he says, is now "barren, fruitless, full of empty trenches and craters, littered with unexploded mines and eerily silent ... It is now time to drop arms and show respect for the dead" (p. ix).

What exactly is the nature of Sumner's claim? What do his eloquent but overwrought and fanciful metaphors refer to? A close reading of Sumner's thesis reveals that he does not mean what he alleges. In fact, his argument is not about the death of an academic specialty at all. Instead, it is a theory about the origin and function of that discipline, and the argument that the field no longer serves its original purpose. Its collapse, says Sumner, was brought on by its inability to serve its prior ideological function. In other words, Sumner is not putting forth an empirically testable hypothesis. Instead, he is guilty of a bait-and-switch scam in which metaphor and rhetoric substitute for data and analysis.

Here is Sumner's argument. It starts with the assumption that the ruling elite follows the ideas and research of the academy very closely and makes conspiratorial use of these ideas to maintain hegemony. Social control, Sumner argues, is buttressed by theories generated by intellectuals and academics. Until the late 19th century, the powers that be made use of the concept of "degeneracy" to keep troublemakers in line and maintain control over the masses. But with the dawn of the modern age and the birth of a correspondingly more sophisticated and diverse public, a simple characterization of wrongdoers as degenerates became less and less plausible – hence, less effective as an instrument of social control. "Degeneracy" came to lack the ring of truth; moral absolutism no longer worked. The masters and rulers needed a more flexible instrument of domination. In Sumner's scheme of things, the death of the sociology of deviance is not about citations or enrollments or publications but about the ideological role of the field and its collapse as a justification for and a rationalization of social control, about maintaining hegemony. In this reconfiguration, says Sumner (1994, p. 301), a field of study was born: the sociology of deviance. In other words, deviance studies was born to serve as ideology; it served, he argues, as a "rational, liberal-minded attempt to make the society of the powerful more economic, more predictable, more humane and less chaotic".

At the opposite side of the ideological spectrum from radicals Liazos and Sumner, conservative sociologist Anne Hendershott reiterated Sumner's *dies irae* for the field by approvingly repeating the query a colleague put to her when he incredulously challenged her suggestion that a course in deviance be taught in their department. "Why would anyone want to teach a course on deviance?" he asked. "No one wants to teach about a discipline that died a generation ago" (Hendershott, 2002, p. 1). Hendershott, unlike Sumner, places a great deal of stock in courses and textbooks to measure signs of vitality, but she agrees with the "death" judgment. How did enrollments fare when the "death" argument was in full swing? In a prior publication (Goode, 2003), I contacted the relevant parties in 34 sociology departments (the chair, director of undergraduate studies, departmental secretary) for information on the offerings and enrollments of deviance courses; representatives of 19 responded with the information. The enrollment figures stretched back to 1977 and ended a year after Hendershott's polemic and hence are entirely relevant to the claims of our two critics. In the former year, for five departments, total enrollments were just over 1,000; in the latter year, for 12, just over 3,000. In the former year, we see a mean enrollment of 202 per course; in the latter, 260. (In the United States, college enrollments totaled 11.5 million in 1977, 16.6 million in 2003, and 21.6 million in 2012.) Clearly, during the era when the "death" claims were in full throttle, somebody was taking deviance courses – and somebody was *teaching* them – negating the utterance of Hendershott's sock-puppet spokesperson. As with the academic study of deviance, university *teaching* of the subject remains alive and well.

The *decline* of the sociology of deviance?

At the 2011 York Deviancy Conference, presenters delivered 175 papers on multiple aspects of deviance; their abstracts filled 70 pages of 11-point type. The conference was truly international, with presenters from, and teaching at universities located, all over the globe – the United Kingdom, the United States, Canada and the West Indies, Greece, Mexico and Argentina, Oslo, Stockholm, Copenhagen and Helsinki, Barcelona and Lisbon, Armenia, Poland, Cyprus, South Africa, India, Tasmania, Queensland and Melbourne. This conference and the background of its speakers give pie-in-the-face testimony to the fact that rather than being "dead", research on deviance is flourishing, conducted worldwide. Moreover, the York papers tell us that the deviance concept has become extremely diverse, having transmogrified into something far broader than the narrow notion that its critics stereotypically imagine it to be. The conference also reminds us that what is practiced in the United States under the banner of the sociology of deviance may be more uniform than its cousins elsewhere in the world. The American version of the sociology of deviance is more pragmatic, more policy-oriented and perhaps more aligned with criminology and the field of criminal justice, while the international version is more theoretical, free-wheeling, open, diverse and politically attuned, but it is ubiquitously the sociology of deviance. Today, world-wide, the enterprise of the sociology of deviance seems to be booming, and especially in some nations where it was previously unknown.

Both Sumner's and Hendershott's arguments fall into the "outlived its usefulness" rather than the "stillborn" line of attack. And Best (2004, p. 84) dismisses courses and texts, indicating that they represent "only minimal signs of life". Early in the 21st century, Best holds, deviance "has come to occupy an insecure, perhaps even precarious place in sociology". The idea of deviance "no longer plays nearly as prominent a role in sociologists' thinking as it once did" (p. ix).

The title of their article notwithstanding, Miller et al. (2001) and Best (2004) do not endorse the "death" claim but *do* make a related and altogether gloomy contention: that the sociology of deviance is "not thriving", that it has substantially declined in influence since the salad years of the 1960s and 1970s. Unlike Sumner and Hendershott, who produce no, or only anecdotal, evidence, Miller et al. (2001), along with Best (2004, pp. x–xi), do offer evidence: the work of oft-cited deviance authors and the recency of their published works, and citations using "deviance" and "deviant" sociology's most prestigious journals, respectively. Presumably, such indicators measure the vitality, centrality and influence of the field – a reasonable supposition.

Elsewhere (Goode, 2004), I conducted a search of my own and came up with findings that qualify but do not contradict those of these researchers. At my request, a colleague (Nachman Ben-Yehuda) counted the 1,600-plus articles published in academic journals with "deviance" in the title that were indexed in the *Social Science Citation Index*. In the 1950s, there were, not surprisingly, very few: only 0.3 per year. In the 1960s, 12.9; in the 1970s, 40.4 per year; and in the 1980s, the peak decade, 52.8. Clearly, by the 1970s, the field had become hugely important in sociology, and its influence grew into the 1980s; it had become an intellectual phenomenon of note. In the 1990s, the count slumped a bit, to 42.3. And in the four years between 2000 and 2003, another slight yearly decline, to 35.3. Electronic indicators for the 2000s are all over the map, but consider the fact that between 2004 and 2012, the Web of Science citation reference count approximately doubled for both "deviance" and "deviant" from 151 to 289, and from 277 to 551, respectively. In 2013, I conducted a book count for the New York University library for volumes with "deviance" and "deviant" in their titles. I did *not* count titles that pointed to deviance-related, deviance-sounding or deviance-included topics. My results for recent book-length publications produced a remarkable finding: 20 such volumes in the 1960s, 79 in the 1970s, 57 for the 1980s, 58 for the 1990s and 59 for 2000–2009. But remarkably, 2010–2012, a period of three years, produced 35 titles, or 10.5 annually – the highest within-decade average, and significantly higher than the 7.9 for the 1970s. Whatever is happening in the world of book publishing for the study of deviance, it indicates exactly the *opposite* of a "death" or a "decline".

What we see is that in the 1980s, a decade *after* the 1970s, which Sumner selects as the era of the field's demise, the number of articles on deviance grew enormously since that decade was the actual heyday of the sociology of deviance, with over 50 articles per year indexed in the *Social Science Citation Index*. Even more embarrassing for Sumner's thesis, more such articles appeared in the 1990s than in the 1970s, indicating that his "obituary" was more than two decades premature. And in the 20th century, the field seems to be going strong with respect to articles, and, even more telling, for books, the first few years of the second decade of the 2000s represents the field's pinnacle. Again, these data do not directly address the Sumner thesis, though he doesn't make it clear how his demise claim can or could be operationalized or manifested, but these counts do address Hendershott's and Best's theses. Clearly, the field of the sociology of deviance is not "dead" in the sense that no one conducts or publishes the research results within its parameters; nor, more importantly, since the 1970s, has it declined in importance – but according to some measures, its importance increased after 2010. At the very least, its purported decline is far more complex than these critics have it.

Has the sociology of deviance declined in intellectual vitality?

Miller et al.'s (2001) second test of the declining theoretical and intellectual vitality of the sociology of deviance – the fact that the most often cited works under its rubric tend to have been written more than a generation ago – is the fact that only two of 31 of the most often cited works in deviance were published later than 1975; this would appear to be convincing evidence that the discipline is theoretically dormant. Upon closer inspection, however, this measure founders on the shoals of the brute force of numbers. With the exception of the natural sciences, where genuine discoveries are made and old paradigms are demolished, often never to return, in practically any field, a small number of foundational works are routinely cited in a substantial proportion of its publications. It is extremely difficult for any recent work to break into the charmed circle of the 31 most often cited works in the field. This is especially the case for a field, like deviance, that stands next to a much larger field – criminology – whose works attract close to half of the citations in its publications. Why?

The fact is it is much more difficult for a single work to become as influential or as foundational as was once the case. Because of the number and variety of publications in the field, over time, citations become increasingly dispersed to a wider range of works. In the field of deviance studies, in the 1960s and 1970s – and before – it was possible to publish work that was regarded as innovative and original, work that came to be cited by a substantial number of practitioners. Into the 1980s and 1990s, that became increasingly difficult.

Today, it is virtually impossible to become another Becker – let alone another Durkheim – in the sociology of deviance. If he were working today in the sociology of deviance, even Howard S. Becker could not be another Becker. This has virtually nothing to do with the decreasing intellectual vitality of the sociology of deviance. The fact is it is increasingly difficult to produce a work that is regarded as making an original contribution to the field. I am not arguing that the theoretical work produced during the 1960s and 1970s was not original, or that it was less original than the work produced today. Indeed, that earlier work was enormously innovative in that it represented a sharp break from established, traditional perspectives, and, if we are to judge by citations, in its time, produced a powerful impact on the field. But originality is relative, bound by time and place, as these pioneers would agree. And today, it is more difficult even to conceive of ideas that would both represent a sharp break with current approaches and would be embraced by a major sector of the field in the same way that the earlier writings did.

I am convinced that the field of the sociology of deviance is not as theoretically innovative as it once was, but Miller et al. (2001) have not made a convincing case. Of these tests, surely citations to works outside of deviance studies *per se* are fatally flawed, and for two reasons. First, Miller et al. (2001) base their argument on a time line, that is, that the sociology of deviance is declining in vitality. However, the number of references to studies in this field to the work of criminologists does not refer to changes over time at all. It is entirely possible that in the decades prior to the 1990s, more than half the references in the sociology of deviance were also to works by non-deviance specialists. In fact, it is even possible that the percentage was higher in earlier decades because the community of deviance specialists was smaller then and consequently, the body of work from which its members could draw was correspondingly smaller. Miller et al.'s test of the vitality of the sociology of deviance hinges on the number of its practitioners, especially in comparison to the field of criminology. The introductory criminology course is now a stepping-stone to a possible career, whereas the sociology of deviance is quite a small field, and taking a course in it is not a path to a job of any kind.

These researchers never answer the nagging question: Is the tendency of the field to cite early, pioneering works more true for the sociology of deviance than for most other fields? We do not know, because Miller et al. do not make any comparisons. It is entirely possible that the sociology of deviance has declined in theoretical originality, innovativeness and the production of foundational works that chart new territory and attract new adherents. But as compared with what other disciplines? And disciplines of what size? It would have been more convincing had Miller et al. compared deviance with fields such as the sociology of education, medicine and occupations. Has deviance been less innovative over time than they have? If so, why? What are the factors, variables or conditions that produced this stagnation? Miller et al. never explain. Randall Collins (2001) argues that the social sciences generally "won't become high-consensus, rapid-discovery science". In this respect, the sociology of deviance is no different from all the social sciences, a point that is glossed over in Miller et al.'s argument.

Most observers agree that that fewer influential "big" ideas are being generated within the ranks of deviance studies. As we saw, the field is riven into two camps. This distinction between the essentialist/positivist and the constructionist positions serves to distinguish fundamentally different and distinct enterprises. One major portion of the researchers in the field engages in an enterprise not essentially different from that of positivistic criminologists – hence the reliance on citations from that field. In this first or positivist mode, the "deviance" of a given form of behavior is assumed, taken for granted, or in the background. What is sought is an explanation for why some people engage in it, or why it is more common under certain conditions than others. This enterprise is criminology's domain. Given that field's greater size and prestige, as well as the greater clarity in the etiology of higher-consensus street crimes than for most forms of deviance, it should come as no surprise that positivistic theories of non-normative behavior are more likely to grow out of criminology than deviance studies. Hence, it is unlikely that a deviance specialist will generate a theoretical framework accounting for non-normative behavior that will be cited by a major proportion of the field's researchers and authors. In fact, nearly all of Miller et al.'s (2001) most often cited works that are in the positivistic vein were written by criminologists, relatively few of whom pursue constructionist lines of inquiry. In short, what is conceptualized from outside the field as "deviance" lacks theoretical coherence. Hence, we need new measures of innovativeness, not based on the perspective's divergence. Much work by the field's specialists is never tagged as "deviance" and yet such research resonates within and beyond its compass.

Obliteration by incorporation

Consider the debate over the supposed intellectual decline of the parent of the sociology of deviance – sociology itself. It is no secret that the entire field of sociology is not as fashionable as it was in the 1960s and 1970s. Joel Best (2001) argues that sociology's academic prestige has always been low, in part because it has been guilty of "giving it away", that is, generating subfields and major concepts that have been reconstituted as, or incorporated into, other fields. One need only cite demography and criminology, Best says, to name entire fields that owe their origin to sociology, not to mention public opinion polling and concepts such as social mobility, charisma, the self-fulfilling prophecy, status symbol, role model, peer group and significant other, to appreciate the fact that sociology has been a "wellspring for ideas that have spread widely and have proven to have considerable utility" for practitioners in other fields (p. 111). In this respect, the field of sociology has triumphed over the fickleness of academic fad by spawning influential intellectual progeny.

The same applies to deviance studies. An immense number of fields have adopted the deviance concept, transformed it, adapted it, renamed it and used it in ways that are parallel to the way it was intended to be used by Howard Becker (1963) and the other social constructionists. In his discussion of citation patterns, Robert Merton (1979) refers to "obliteration by incorporation". In a given field, or in related fields, Merton argues, some ideas, once innovative, have become so taken for granted that it is no longer appreciated how original they once were – hence, an "obliteration of the source of ideas, methods, or findings by their incorporation in currently accepted knowledge". At a certain period in its history, the sociology of deviance generated or highlighted a host of interesting ideas, concepts and theories that seeped out into, and influenced, allied fields, eventually becoming incorporated into their practitioners' thinking about how the social world works. These concepts include stigma (which has influenced disability and transgender studies); anomie (social theory and sociology generally); the contingencies of labeling (ethnic studies); social disorganization (criminology); the social construction of non-hegemonic definitions of reality (postmodernism); the sociology of the underdog (queer theory); the outsider or "the other" (postcolonialist studies); the medicalization of deviance (the sociology of medicine); deviance neutralization (autoethnography and narrative studies); and moral panics (collective behavior, criminology, social problems and communication studies). The sociology of deviance did not necessarily originate these concepts, but it did help catapult them onto the academic and intellectual map, and whether directly or indirectly its discussions served to plant seeds that bore fruit in other disciplines.

Consider the work of Mitch Duneier, author of *Sidewalk* (1999). Duneier adapts Becker's "outsider" concept by investigating men (and a few women) who live lives on the margin of conventional society, who, like Becker's jazz musicians and marijuana smokers, maintain their dignity and self-respect in spite of the fact that many of the people who swirl through their lives look down their noses at them and consider them deviants. There's an echo of Goffman's *Asylums* (1961) in *Sidewalk* when we see Duneier's street people trying to work out a place to urinate, or Goffman's *Stigma* (1963), specifically the stigma of tribe, race,and nation, when Duneier himself felt that, at Hakim's table, African Americans were welcome, but he was not. Merton's concept of retreatism is echoed when many of Duneier's (1999, pp. 353, 20 and 61) subjects and informants adopt what he calls the "fuck it" or "I don't give a fuck" attitude.

Virtually any discussion of the war on illicit drugs, by its very nature, incorporates concepts – such as marginalization and stigma – that were given a prominent place in the pioneering work of Becker, Goffman and their peers. Hence, when Philippe Bourgois (1995) discusses adaptations inner city Latino residents make to political and economic marginality, he's fusing conflict theory, social disorganization, differential association, and labeling theory, all gleaned from classic perspectives on deviance.

In discussing how the urban homosexual subculture was generated by the stigmatized, marginalized and "othered" status of gays, Jeffrey Escoffier (1998) draws on Mary McIntosh's (1968) discussion of the homosexual role, John Gagnon and William Simon's (1973, pp. 19–26) delineation of sexual scripts and Kenneth Plummer's (1975) treatment of labeling and sexual stigma.

When William Julius Wilson (1996) discusses the disappearance of middle class and working class role models in the inner city, he's using deviance concepts, articulated by David Harvey and others (2008), taking their cue from David Matza (1971), in referring to *poverty and disrepute*; in fact, poverty and deviance share in – and, together, mutually reinforce – disrepute.

Sociology is shot through with the deviance concept, but the field's practitioners are less likely to *call* something "deviant" than they were in the past. Deviance is not as likely to be crystallized out, pointed to, and referred self-consciously as the organizing principle of what's going on, but the fact is, that *is* what's going on. Clearly, the deviance concept is still relevant, but today, in some quarters, it's not as likely to be directly referred to as *deviance*.

Labeling theory: constructionism in action

Labeling theory specifically left two legacies to the contemporary study of deviance. The first, its "major" mode, was its constructionist vision.

Other, earlier approaches were careful to point out that deviance and crime were a matter of violating rules, norms, and laws, which are socially constructed and vary somewhat historically and culturally. But labeling theory stressed and highlighted this point more forcefully; unlike the other perspectives, its analysis pivoted on this conceptualization. Indeed, it went further and emphasized that definitions of wrongdoing vary not only from society to society but from one *category* or *social context* to another. This remains a basic and crucial assumption in all sociological work on deviance. The second legacy of labeling theory, its "minor" mode (which, unfortunately, critics stress as its main point), is its argument about the causal mechanism of deviance: being labeled as a wrongdoing inevitably or usually leads to the strengthening of a deviant identity and hence an escalation in the seriousness and frequency of deviant behavior. This argument is as often wrong as it is right; its lack of empirical verification should not negate the perspective's "major" mode or constructionist legacy.

Labeling theory's influence declined sharply since its heyday roughly from the mid-1960s to the mid-1970s. At that time, it was the most influential and most frequently cited perspective in the study of deviance. This was especially so among the field's younger scholars and researchers, who yearned for a fresh, unconventional and radically different way of looking at deviance. The perspective was widely and vigorously attacked, and many of these criticisms stuck. Eventually, much of the field recognized and emphasized its flaws and moved on to other perspectives, or sharply modified or adapted interactionist or labeling insights. Today, no single approach or paradigm dominates the field in the way that the Chicago School did in the 1920s or labeling theory circa 1970. What we see today is diversity, fragmentation and theoretical dissensus. While the practitioners of a variety of perspectives attacked labeling theory for its inadequacies, no single perspective has managed to succeed in attracting a majority following in the field. In spite of the criticisms, the labeling school left a legacy to the field that even its critics make use of, albeit, for the most part, implicitly. Today it is clear that while, as a total approach to deviance, labeling *theory* is incomplete, labeling *processes* take place in all deviance and deserve a prominent place in its study.

By the 2000s, the insights of labeling theory became so taken for granted and densely interwoven into the conventional wisdom of criminology and the sociology of deviance that it provided a case of "obliteration by incorporation" (Merton, 1979). In other words, "the central strands of the perspective live on in cognate areas of inquiry"

(Grattet, 2011b, p. 186). Ongoing research has demonstrated that the consequences of negative labeling tend to be long-lasting and often dire. Matsueda's (1992) study of troublesome boys revealed that parental definitions ("informal social control") often resulted in self-conceptions that increased the likelihood of these boys' further delinquencies (Grattet, 2011a, p. 124). Work on mental disorder by Bruce Link and his associates (1989) "has also been a fertile area" for demonstrating the baleful impact of stigma and deviance labeling. Working with a "modified labeling theory", Link uncovered how mental illness processing agencies' "perceptions of patient dangerousness" as well as their putting social distance between themselves and the patient are likely to make the condition more serious. Sampson and Laub (1997) have advanced the hypothesis of "cumulative disadvantage", which refers to the consequences of repeating and increasing seriousness of involvement in criminal sanctioning over the life course (Grattet, 2011a, p. 124). Their contention is that there is only "one theoretical position in criminology that is inherently developmental in nature – labeling theory" (Sampson and Laub, 1997, p. 3). This cumulative disadvantage represents a kind of "snowballing effect" which increasingly "mortgages" the offender's future, especially when negative evaluations in the realms of school and employment further reduce their life chances. For instance, convicted felons face increasingly difficult conditions for reintegrating into civil society, disenfranchising them and making the choice of further criminal activity increasingly attractive; negative labeling by work settings, marriage and family dynamics all make desistance increasingly difficult (Petersilia, 2003; Uggen and Manza, 2006; Western, 2006). A criminal record has a powerful chilling effect on the likelihood of employment outcomes for the offender. Pager (2007, p. 32) introduces the concept of "negative credentials" to stress this process; these are the "official markers that restrict access and opportunity rather than enabling them". As Grattet (2011a, 2011b) argues, recent research powerfully argues for the ongoing influence of the labeling/interactionist tradition in the study of crime and deviance. And at this writing, police "stop and frisk" policies for questionable suspects remain a hotly debated topic, impacting on thousands of lives in communities everywhere. And last, when deans and chairs decide which courses should be offered and which should be deleted from a department's catalogue, it is possible that they may base their decision on a fallacious assumption – namely, that deviance is "dead" and "no one wants to teach it any more" – and excise it from the departmental curriculum, a sad development, since, in my experience, there are few courses with more takeaway value.

Conclusion

Any sociologist contemplating a description of the extent and scope of deviance must consider the realms in which normative violations occur. Such a consideration inevitably runs into the issue of numbers as well as seriousness. How many people are judged to be on the wrong side of the norms, and how serious are these violations? In other words, as a criterion that enables us to select topics on specific forms of deviance, we have to consider how many people we are talking about and how much of a violation has taken place. Textbooks that discuss deviance in general are likely to include chapters on alcohol and drug abuse, sexual violations, criminal behavior, economic malfeasances, deviant beliefs, deviant physical characteristics and mental disorder. The inclusion of these topics for discussion, again, makes sense by virtue of the fact that they are relatively common and are regarded as relatively serious normative violations. Critics who call for a discussion of very different topics usually fail to consider one or the other or both of these topics. An instructor or author who complains that sociologists of deviance typically trot out a "freak of the week" for discussion – and offers alternative candidates – must contend with these two considerations.

The subject of deviance is foundational for sociology. It spells out processes, issues and subjects that are essential for any consideration of how society works. Deviance is neither marginal nor trivial for an understanding of the social order. It is central to everything we see and experience in the social world, from the economic to the religious realm, from birth to death and from the intimacy of a love affair to the public proclamations made on the soap box and the drama of the television and movie screen. Without an understanding of deviance, we cannot comprehend social relations, social interaction, the workings of the community, or, indeed, what we call the human spark. To simplify the matter, "deviance is us", and it will remain "us" forever.

It is likely that much the same fate that befell sociology generally has also befallen the sociology of deviance. The field lacks a central theoretical core, there are no intellectual assumptions that tie its practitioners into a coherent community and the disagreements among researchers concerning its legitimate subject matter are profound. In fact, for the sociology of deviance, the positivist-constructionist split may very well have been fatal to the coherence of the discipline. And just as in the academy generally, sociology lacks prestige, among sociologists, deviance specialists lack prestige. It is possible our low prestige is a "courtesy stigma", that is, it stems in part from the fact that we are tainted by the stigma of our subjects. Consider Liazos's (1972) contemptuous subtitle, "nuts, sluts, and preverts", an obvious aspersion on some of the people we study – and hence, the researchers who study them. But at the same time, an enormous amount of research continues to be conducted under the banner of the sociology of deviance, undergraduates continue to take and become interested in the course, textbooks on the subject continue to be published and continue to sell at least modestly well, monographs and journal articles are written – the study of deviance is clearly a lively enterprise.

As a qualification to some of the measures I've used, consider the fact that the electronic conveyance of written material has increasingly replaced paper facsimiles. The number of paid subscriptions to the American Society of Criminology's flagship journal, *Criminology*, declined in the past decade from 4,200 to 3,800. The decline is not due to an academic decline in the field but to the conversion by many libraries to electronic materials. Clearly, at the present time, the academic and intellectual worlds are undergoing a significant transition to different ways of reading, apprehending, and measuring the materials that practitioners and researchers use, as new ways become adopted and old ways become obsolete.

It is true that fewer new, earth-shattering theoretical breakthroughs have been made from within the field recently, and that much of the field's impetus stems from a field that used to be conjoined with the sociology of deviance, that is, criminology. It is possible that this is inherent in the very nature of the deviance concept, that is, once the insight is made that stigma and labeling take place, few further major theoretical developments are possible. Or it is possible that the field has simply fallen victim to the vagaries of passing trends. None of this, however, adds up to the bumper-sticker slogan "the sociology of deviance is dead". As small, underfunded marginal fields go, the health of the sociology of deviance is surprisingly good. Its representatives say, with Mark Twain, that the reports of its death are "greatly exaggerated".

References

Becker, H. S. (1963) *Outsiders: Studies in the Sociology of Deviance* (New York: Free Press).

Best, J. (2001) "Giving It Away: Ironies of Sociology's Place in Academia", *The American Sociologist*, 32, 107–113.

—— (2004) *Deviance: Career of a Concept* (Belmont, CA: Thompson Wadsworth).

Bourgois, P. (1995) *In Search of Respect: Selling Crack in El Barrio* (Cambridge: Cambridge University Press).

Collins, R. (2001) "Why the Social Sciences Won't Become High-Consensus, Rapid-Discovery Science", in S. Cole (ed.) *What's Wrong with Sociology?* (Edison, NJ: Transaction Books).

Duneier, M. (1999) *Sidewalk* (New York: Farrar, Straus & Giroux).

Escoffier, J. (1998) *American Homo: Community and Perversity* (Berkeley: University of California Press).

Ford, J. (1936) *Social Deviation* (New York: Macmillan).

Gagnon, J. H. and William Simon (1973) *Sexual Conduct: The Social Sources of Human Sexuality* (Chicago: Aldine).

Gibbs, J. P. (1989) *Control: Sociology's Central Notion* (Urbana: University of Illinois Press).

Goffman, E. (1961) *Asylums: Essays on the Social Situation of Mental Patients and Other Inmates* (Garden City, NY: Doubleday Anchor).

—— (1963) *Stigma: Notes on the Management of Spoiled Identity* (Englewood Cliffs, NJ: Prentice Hall/Spectrum).

Goode, E. (2003) "The MacGuffin That Refuses to Die: An Investigation into the Condition of the Sociology of Deviance", *Deviant Behavior*, 24 (November–December), 507–533.

—— (2004) "Is the Sociology of Deviance Still Relevant?", *The American Sociologist*, 35 (Winter), 46–57.

Grattet, R. (2011a) "Labeling Theory", in C. D. Bryant (ed.) *The Routledge Handbook of Deviant Behavior* (London and New York: Routledge).

—— (2011b) "Societal Reactions to Deviance", *Annual Review of Sociology*, 37, 185–204.

Harvey, D. (2008) "Poverty and Disrepute", in G. Ritzer (ed.) *Encyclopedia of Sociology* (Cambridge and Boston: Blackwell).

Hendershott, A. (2002) *The Politics of Deviance* (San Francisco: Encounter Books).

Liazos, A. (1972) "The Poverty of the Sociology of Deviance: Nuts, Sluts, and Preverts", *Social Problems*, 20 (Summer), 103–120.

Link, B. G., F. T. Cullen, E. Struening, P. Shrout and B. P. Dohrenwend (1989) "A Modified Labeling Theory Approach to Mental Disorders: An Empirical Assessment", *American Sociological Review*, 54 (June), 400–423.

Matsueda, R. L. (1992) "Reflected Appraisals, Parental Labeling, and Delinquency: Specifying a Symbolic Interactionist Theory", *American Journal of Sociology*, 97 (May), 1577–1611.

Matza, D. (1971) "Poverty and Disrepute", in R. K. Merton and R. Nisbet (eds.) *Contemporary Social Problems*, 3rd ed. (New York: Harcourt Brace Jovanovich).

McIntosh, M. (1968) "The Homosexual Role", *Social Problems*, 16 (Fall), 182–192.

Merton, R. K. (1979) "Foreword", in E. Garfield (ed.) *Citation Indexing: Its Theory and Application in Science, Technology, and Humanities* (New York: John Wiley & Sons).

Miller, J. M., R. A. Wright and D. Dannels (2001) "Is Deviance 'Dead'? The Decline of a Sociological Specialization", *The American Sociologist*, 31 (Fall), 43–59.

Mills, C. W. (1943) "The Professional Ideology of Social Pathologists", *American Journal of Sociology*, 46 (September), 165–180.

Pager, D. (2007) *Marked: Race, Crime, and Finding Work in an Era of Mass Incarceration* (Chicago: University of Chicago Press).

Petersilia, J. (2003) *When Prisoners Come Home: Parole and Prisoner Reentry* (New York: Oxford University Press).

Plummer, K. (1975) *Sexual Stigma: An Interactionist Account* (London: Routledge & Kegan Paul).

Sampson, R. J. and J. H. Laub (1997) "A Life-Course Theory of Cumulative Disadvantage and the Stability of Delinquency", in T. P. Thornberry (ed.) *Developmental Theories of Crime and Delinquency* (New Brunswick, NJ: Transaction).

Sumner, C. (1994) *The Sociology of Deviance: An Obituary* (Buckingham, UK: Open University Press).

Uggen, C. and J. Manza (2006) *Locked Out: Felon Disenfranchisement and American Democracy* (New York: Oxford University Press).

Western, B. (2006) *Punishment and Inequality in America* (New York: Russell Sage Foundation Press).

Wilson, W. J. (1996) *When Work Disappears: The World of the New Urban Poor* (New York: Alfred Knopf).

2
The Critical Role of Deviance in Society

Patricia A. Adler and Peter Adler

It has been nearly two decades since Sumner (1994) rang the death knell for the sociology of deviance. Several notable scholars, in particular, have debated the vibrancy of the field – from the liveliness of its empirical and theoretical contributions to its interest to students, scholars and publishers (Ben-Yehuda, 1990, 1994, 2006; Best, 2004a, 2004b; Goode, 2002a, 2003, 2004, 2005; Hendershott, 2002; Liazos, 1972). We believe in the continuing vitality of the intellectual and empirical contributions of the field of deviance in the early 21st century. There are many reasons to make such a claim.

Here we are, almost 20 years after Sumner's proclamations, textbooks in their tenth (and beyond) editions still doing well, and newer ones cropping up on the horizon (see, e.g., Curra, 2011; Dotter, 2004; Goode, 2002b; Hall, 2012; Jacobs, 2002; Pontell and Rosoff, 2011; Prus and Grills, 2003; Terrell and Meier, 2001; Vandenburgh, 2004; Weitzer, 2002). Our courses are filled and a seemingly endless number of empirical cases have arisen that solidify our strong stance about how social power creates new categories of deviants. Goode reminds us that interest in deviance is high, although Best argues that enrollments are not an accurate measure of vitality. When we began teaching the course (to over 1,000 students a year) in the 1980s, students were mostly attracted to the deviant (exotic) aspects of the curriculum. During the 1990s, students' purpose became geared more toward pre-law enforcement. The 2000s and 2010s, however, have witnessed a healthy mix of the two groups. As Erikson (1966) noted, ever since the earliest years of American settlement, the discovery, apprehension and punishment of deviants have held a central place in the public interest. We *do* think that the continued popularity of the courses and the research to support them are signs of deviance's continued contributions to sociology.

We are no more theoretically bereft than any of our counterparts. Theoretical and conceptual advancements come in increments. Heckert and Heckert (2002) augmented positive and negative typologies of deviance with analysis about the relation of deviation to the norms and how it is socially received. They constructed a matrix integrating normative expectations (whether deviance "flips out" into nonconformism or "flips in" into overconformism) with society's collective evaluation of that deviation. This enabled them to offer conceptual insight into why some instances of overconformism are negatively received and some types of underconformism are positively received. In subsequent works they examined the relationship between their matrix of deviance types and Tittle and Patternoster's (2000) ten middle-class norms (Heckert and Heckert, 2004), and between high achievers (positive deviants and rate-busters) and techniques of neutralization theory, advancing their contributions to positive deviance by connecting this to the traditional categories of neutralization along with two new ones: guilt and shame (Schoenberger et al., 2012). Although it is rare that we witness the kind of Kuhnian (1962) revolutions that paradigmatically change our disciplines, one new meta-narrative, still in its infancy, is the cultural studies or postmodern theory of deviance, which focuses on the social creation and historical context for the generation of meaning (Dotter, 2004; Foucault, 1977).

Building on the interactionist perspective, Dotter (2004) focuses on the creation and contestation of stigma by importing concepts from the metaphor of film. He argues that stigmas are conferred in screenplay scenarios in three interactive layers. The first layer is the deviant event, involving acts, actors, normative definitions and societal reaction. The second layer involves media reconstruction, where media, law enforcement and other audiences offer interpretations of the deviant event. The third layer is the stigma movie, where mediated reconstructions become ideologized as social control narratives. Deviance, defined and applied, becomes a commodified cultural representation that is consumed through the celebrity-drenched popular culture and mediated through modern power structures. At the levels of individual concepts, process and structural models and broad theories, conceptualization about deviance remains strong. Studies abound, grants are received, dissertations are produced and the area remains one of the core foundations of sociology.

Deviance is all around us. It is ubiquitous. Now, more than ever, we see a barrage of case studies that stretch our imaginations of how far deviance can go, how far beyond the evolving limits of human (in)capacity this technologically advanced, warp speed society can take us. Our own research on self-injury (see Adler and Adler, 2011) is a case in point. The more involved we got with this group, the more "normalized" their behavior seemed. When we first began the study, we were asked, "Who are these kooks?" "Why would people do that to themselves?" Many thought that these cutters, burners and branders were pre-suicidal, but our research showed that this behavior is an increasingly common coping mechanism for dealing with typical feelings of teen angst, with situations of powerlessness and with anger or fear coupled with frustration. Be it tattoos, cigarettes, new drugs, creative forms of sex or multibillion dollar fraud widely perpetrated, people incorporate these new forms of behavior into their repertoire and accept (or reject) the creativity of the human soul for expanding the boundaries of normative behavior. As Frank Zappa, a cultural icon from the 1960s said, "Without deviation from the norm, progress is not possible". This is heady stuff and speaks to the heart of the sociological enterprise. Deviance is not marginal, it is central to what we do.

We invite you to conduct exit interviews with your undergraduate sociology majors. Invariably, when you ask them what concepts they remember, they'll tell you Merton's (1938) five modes of adaptation, Sykes and Matza's (1957) techniques of neutralization, Becker's (1953) stages of becoming a marijuana user, Hirschi's (1969) elements of control theory, or Goffman's (1963) dichotomy of the discredited and discreditable. They'll remember their most favorite books, such as Anderson and Snow's *Down on Their Luck* (1993), Sanders's *Marks of Mischief* (1988), Ehrenreich's *Nickel and Dimed* (2001), the public ethnographies of Anderson's *Streetwise* (1990), *Code of the Streets* (1999), Duneier's *Sidewalk* (1999), Newman's *No Shame in Their Game* (1999), and Best's enlightening expose, *Threatened Children* (1990), or our own insider account of drug smugglers, *Wheeling and Dealing* (1985). Even recently, award-winning works by Adler and Adler (*The Tender Cut*, 2011), Altheide (*Creating Fear*, 2002), Hays (*Flat Broke with Children*, 2003), Goffman (*On the Run*, 2014), Pager (*The Mark of a Criminal Record*, 2002) and Venkatesh (*Off the Books: The Underground Economy of the Urban Poor*, 2006; *Gang Leader for a Day*, 2008) speak to the elements of deviance in one way or another. People continue to be mesmerized by the proliferation of crime dramas on television. All highlight, legitimize, denigrate or celebrate deviant behavior in one form or another. Clearly, deviance is percolating in the public mind.

One of the hallmarks of any society is its changing definitions of deviance, with fluctuations occurring up and down over time and variations existing between groups. As sociologists have long known and Moynihan (1993) and Krauthammer (1993) re-articulated, all societies change the boundaries around what is considered deviant, defining it "down" when they have more deviance than they can handle, and defining it "up" when they want to point to problematic issues. Matthews and Wacker (2002) discussed the way ideas move from deviance into the core as they start on the fringe, moving first to the edge, then to the realm of the cool, into the "next big thing", and finally becoming social convention. This is one of the dynamics that so fascinate sociologists: the deviance-making and -unmaking process.

We see no need to re-hash completely the arguments our distinguished colleagues have advanced. Rather, we would like to take this space to focus on another aspect of the sociology of deviance: its centrality to society, and hence, to sociology. There can be no mistake that the empirical world around us is filled with deviance and deviance-makers. We live in what we might call a "deviance society". We highlight several of the recent trends here.

The political society

Deviance has been, and continues to be, a vitally insightful concept for understanding the mechanisms by which society operates. It plays an integral part in Quinney's (1975) model of the conflictual society, where groups vie for dominance over each other. Deviance has always been a key vehicle through which struggles for power and legitimacy are enacted. By defining the other side as deviant, moral entrepreneurial and advocacy parties stigmatize and disempower each other. At the same time, by doing so, they elevate their own status and power. These are sometimes legal, but more often ideological contests. Deviance is a key element in forging a system of social stratification, with some groups buoyed by pushing others down. As Tuggle and Holmes (1997, p. 79) wrote, "Status conflicts and the resultant condemnation of a behavior characteristic of a particular status category symbolically enhance the status of the abstinent through the degradation of the participatory". Deviance is thus a fundamental force at the core of society, not merely at the fringes.

We have witnessed the extreme politicization and fragmentation of American society. In the 21st century, each presidential contest has been billed as the "election of a lifetime", with animus between the two main political parties escalating progressively. We have become accustomed to a continuingly ugly contestation over ideological paradigms, with each side trying to gain power by representing the other as deviant, immoral liars. Our country is divided into "red" and "blue" Americas, with the greatest polarization in a half-century or more. Families torn apart again and again, with men and women splitting between Republicans and Democrats. The Supreme Court's *Citizens United* ruling enabled enormous amounts of money to be raised and spent through the unlimited contributions to Super PACs (Political Action Committees), and billionaires flexed their newly enriched bank accounts to pour hundreds of millions of dollars into campaigns. At the same time, acrimony and negative campaigning ascended to ever-new highs, with facts and fact-checking thrown out the window. Radio and television news programming was fragmented by the rise of "opinion news", where right- and left-wing talk show ideologues pushed the extremes of their constituents further from the center. Political accusations further split mainstream and cable television and the print media into liberal and conservative camps. Dirty tricks were elevated to a new level. Bogus news reports, memos, documents and records emerged, with accusations of bias abundant. Journalists were accused of passively accepting political press releases and responded by moving into an era of rabid fact-checking, as politicians seemed impervious to the accuracy of their statements. The government was caught making secret payments to journalists to support their policies at the same time that they were embracing fake reporters and jailing real ones. Campaign corruption abounded with a series of revelations about the actions of various politicians who sought illegally to trade cash for favors. The cost of elections rose to billions of dollars, further isolating the top one percent of the country from everyone else.

Our tradition as a free-speech society was first challenged by the Bush administration, which labeled any dissenting opinion as a deviant assault on patriotism and an undermining of the war effort. People wishing to attend Republican campaign rallies had to sign "loyalty cards" to be admitted to the events. Republican politicians taking moderate stands were replaced by more radical conservatives, as the right-wing of the party coalesced with conservative and evangelical Christians to solidify an alliance that would dictate national and international medical and family policy and judicial appointments. The separation of church and state, long a bedrock of the American Constitution, was also cast as deviant, with fights over religious doctrine, stone tablets in courthouses, church involvement in political fundraising and lobbying and religious organizations' receipt of governmental charity funds.

Conservative politico-religious-family groups proposed that radio and television be more tightly policed against affronts to decency by the federal government, calling for offenders to be pursued through a "criminal process". Libraries once again banned and destroyed books from high school curricula on the basis of curse words, pagan references or homosexual themes, and conservative groups forced the recall of popular children's shows and diversity efforts, accusing them of encouraging gay lifestyles. Legislation such as the "Family Entertainment and Copyright Act" was passed allowing "family-friendly" companies to sell filter technology that cleans up DVDs of Hollywood movies without permission or input from the films' authors and copyright holders.

During the Bush era we saw the growth and strengthening of civil religion in America. Deviance was "defined up" so that the behaviors formerly considered acceptable became regarded as treasonous. Politicians challenged the faith of people opposing Bush's judicial nominees. Catholic priests refused communion to pro-choice politicians, labeling them heretics. Pastors excommunicated church members who wouldn't vote for their candidates. Pharmacists refused to fill prescriptions for birth control and morning after pills on religious grounds, and hospitals have refused to offer legally prescribed post-rape contraception, counseling and medication. All of these political issues became re-cast as moral, and hence deviance issues. At the same time, corporations got into the election business, with CEOs including notices in employees' paychecks saying that if they didn't vote for their candidates, they might find themselves out of a job.

At the same time there was a return to McCarthyist purges and the invocation of Holocaust metaphors to inflame and radicalize public sentiment. Ward Churchill, a formerly little-known University of Colorado professor, was jeopardized for comparing the victims of the 9/11 crisis to "little Eichmanns". In the resulting controversy, faculty members were required to sign loyalty oaths to the Constitution of the United States and the state of Colorado, or face losing their jobs. The leader of the conservative group, Focus on the Family, called the Supreme Court Justices more dangerous to this country than terrorists because of their decision in *Roe vs. Wade*, comparing the deaths of unborn babies caused by this ruling to the Holocaust.

Despite the presence of a centrist president elected in 2008 who promised to transcend the division of American into "red" and "blue" states and who reached out the hand of friendship to the Arab world, we have seen a strong rise of uncivil discourse. At President Obama's 2009 State of the Union address to a joint session of Congress, Joe Wilson, a South Carolina member of the House of Representatives interrupted by shouting, "You lie!" from within the congressional chamber, as he became incensed over Obama's (ultimately accurate) denial that his health care proposal would mandate coverage for undocumented immigrants. Old-time veterans decried this as rude, but Wilson's campaign coffers swelled immediately. This lesson was not lost on his colleagues.

Campaign stump speeches and televised addresses have become nastier and dirtier, filled with "red meat rhetoric", a term that refers to the type of ammunition politicians can feed their supporters that will arouse and enflame them, like throwing meat into the cage of a hungry lion. Sarah Palin rose to prominence as the 2008 Republican Vice-Presidential candidate on it by simplifying complicated ideas into political shorthand in ways that fired up her party's already committed followers. The success that met her partisan politics, as she threw derisive zingers at candidate Obama while avoiding outlining any policies of her own, helped legitimate and spread this type of rhetoric nationally. Fanning the flames of this rhetoric was Fox News on the right and MSNBC on the left, feeding partisan news presentations, commentary and editorials, which were then parroted back by their viewers, including Supreme Court members.

During the early years of Obama's tenure, Democrats followed his lead and adopted more of a civil, centrist line, but Republicans seized political advantage (and capitalized on their great strength) by using the attack mode and cultivating their attack machine. Right-wing media personalities such as Glenn Beck, Rush Limbaugh, Sean Hannity, and (later) Sarah Palin spewed forth a shameless ocean of unfounded allegations, untruths and danger messages, branding people, their ideas and their actions as deviant. Sean Hannity proclaimed Obama as associated with the 1960s radical group, the Weather Underground, and Glen Beck called the Egyptian uprising "orchestrated by the Marxist Communists and the Muslim Brotherhood". A coterie of right-wing journalists spearheaded by Donald Trump fomented the "birther" movement, promulgating the false allegation that President Obama is a Muslim born outside the United States. He followed this up in 2012 by offering $5,000,000 if Obama would produce his high school and college transcripts, alleging that he was admitted to schools on the basis of affirmative admission, not on his own merits. On Sarah Palin's Fox News Network syndicated show, she made a gun sights map and put a rifle crosshairs over the district of US representative Gabrielle Giffords in 2011, potentially encouraging the actions of a gun-toting lunatic who subsequently put a bullet through her brain.

Following the success of these highly influential journalists, Republican politicians used similarly uncivil discourse and tactics for the 2012 election cycle. The Tea Party movement, born in reaction against Obama's health care bill of 2009, possibly the progenitors of uncivil discourse, took to hanging the president in effigy at their rallies. They set a hard line and pulled the Republican party to the right, drumming out moderate Republicans and droving others to avoid seeking re-election. The erosion of the political middle in America has been exacerbated by the electoral process, in which candidates for office are selected by their own parties, and therefore play to their base rather to the center upon whom they have to draw for actual election. But the rhetoric of deviance has become so strong and so standard that followers have become inured to it and have a tendency to reinforce the ingroup-outgroup bias, overly attributing truth and value to the statements of their own and disvaluing the remarks of outsiders, even when confronted with factual evidence to the contrary. In short, red meat rhetoric labeling others as deviant has become an established and hugely successful electoral strategy in America. Celebrity media pundits use this tactic to attract attention, score points and promote their viewpoint, as even negative publicity is good because it sells. At a not-distant time in the past, the rhetoric of moral high ground was the norm and parties scrambled to portray themselves as reasonable, altruistic and trustworthy. This has become supplanted by screaming and hurling the deviant label, no matter how ludicrous it might appear or how thinly grounded in fact.

The election of 2012 saw a host of social issues, formerly defined as deviant, rise and become political fodder. Gay marriage became a contentious issue, with Democrats and Republicans pitted against each other in their party platforms. Following the 2012 election, ten states had permitted such unions, with Maine, Maryland and Washington voting by referendum to allow it. Court battles over gay marriage as a civil rights issue moved up the ranks. Medical marijuana became legalized in many states, with legalized recreational marijuana referendums passing in Colorado and Washington. Racial intermarriage, once frowned upon, increased greatly, as the country began to deal with increasing numbers of bi-racial and multi-racial citizens. Illegal immigration remained an unsolved and polarizing issue as the numbers of Hispanics swelled in the country, gaining political power. Gun control remained problematic, with mass shootings abounding and politicians constrained by the powerful gun lobby. Concealed carry permits were expanded, and access to purchasing guns in venues that skirted investigation continued relatively unchecked.

At stake in all of these issues was the ability to define behavior, and those who practice it, as deviant. This heightens the critical role of deviance in society, illustrating a growing paradigm that uses definitions of deviance to disempower and control people who dissent from the majority opinion. In a society with heightened moralism, heightened radicalism and heightened polarization, deviance is the mechanism of disempowerment and control.

Moral panics

In an afterword to his 2004 article, Goode mentions the concept of moral panics as thriving. We have been infused with a spate of moral panics coming in successive waves. Many followed the pattern of one dramatic incident followed by a flurry of copycatters that led to national hysteria and over-reaction. The 1999 Columbine shooting set off a chain of school shootings by young people. Our country felt overwhelmed by these incidents, and we searched our national soul for their cause. In an effort to prevent these, we installed metal detectors in schools, padlocked exit doors, brought in dogs to sniff student lockers and installed cameras in schools and adjacent areas. Students' joking comments were taken seriously, their private online and hard-copy diaries were searched and they were subjected to harsh sanctions. These applications of the deviant label were prompted not only by administrators' fear of violence on their campuses, but also by their fear of parental and community lawsuits. Student riots on college campuses spread in similar fashion, with alcohol- or sport-generated riots often following athletic events, the weekend closure of bars and semester's end. Cars were smashed and overturned, couches burned, students teargassed and clashes between students and police turned into violent confrontations. College administrators cracked down, labeling rioters as criminals, posted police and bystander photos and videos on websites and asked for help in identifying participants. As wave followed wave, students were arrested, charged, expelled and fined, cast out from their campus communities.

The most notable panic that gripped America followed the 9/11 terrorist attacks. This event mushroomed into an aftermath of terror-related panics generated around anthrax, foreigners, flying and, for many, even leaving the country. Strains in relations with our neighbors to the North and South appeared, as politicians tried to secure the country's borders. Common American foods such as French fries were named as deviant, as was any country or person who tried to connect the bombings to American foreign policy. God was invoked and, driven by national unity and fear, Congress passed the Patriot Act, despite the protests of civil liberties groups. Racial profiling, once outlawed and condemned, came back into acceptance. Hundreds of foreigners were detained indefinitely in military prisons, many of them subjected to various degrees of humiliation and torture. These abusive behaviors, often in violation of international laws and the Geneva Convention, were facilitated by defining the detainees as deviant, as "other" and as sub-human. Part-time reservist soldiers, under prodding from military police, brutalized their captives, becoming themselves deviant.

Our country was also subject to a variety of drug-related moral panics. Musto (1999) has noted that drug use and enforcement trends seem to cycle periodically, swinging back and forth between states of relative permissiveness and prohibition. Following the lax 1960s and 1970s, the 1980s and 1990s brought "crackdowns". Large-scale fears erupted, especially over crack cocaine and ecstasy, leading to overwrought citizens and factually exaggerated assertions (Reinarman and Levine, 1997). In fear, consumers sought other, potentially more dangerous, drugs such as methamphetamine and ice in place of the former, heroin and HCL cocaine in place of the latter. Law enforcement officials turned a war on drugs into a war on inner-city residents, a war on people of color and a war on immigrants. Alcohol also took its share of the spotlight, with cases of drinking deaths on college campuses leading administrators to legislate new rules on rushing, hazing, private parties and underage drinking. Fears were fueled by media portrayals of students on spring breaks engaging in excessive drinking and wanton sex. Applications declined at identified "party" schools, as parents feared for their children's lives and three-strike policies were reduced to two-strikes.

We also went through cycles of food and body panics with some periodic regularity, as new and dangerous foods were identified only to be re-cast a few years later as beneficial. We have seen the rise and fall of cholesterol-laden foods, carbohydrates, proteins, grains, trans-fats, fiber, sugar, anti-oxidants and various additives. Both the foods and the people who ate them were labeled deviant. We were cast as a "supersized", obese nation, but then told that a little fat could make us live longer. Anorexia and bulimia blossomed, becoming one of our largest cultural exports. Cosmetic surgery continued to climb. These food and body panics cycled and contradicted each other in such a way that our whole nation ultimately became very confused about what was deviant and wrong, and what was current scientific thinking.

Ownership of deviance

Controlling the ability to define deviance is a valuable asset in our society, and we have witnessed a fervent interdisciplinary struggle between sociology, psychology, criminology and medicine over the ownership of deviance as a social problem. These struggles begin with establishing dominance over the ability to label phenomena. Goode (2002a) and Best (2004a) alerted us to the propensity for criminology to steal the domain of deviance from sociology.

This was possible because sociology serves as a "parent" discipline, spawning substantive spin-offs (women's studies, ethnic studies, gerontology) that still overlap considerably with us, their generating area. This has led to domain contests between the original and the breakaway fields. As criminology arose, it portioned off a chunk of our subject matter. When one looks at the relationship between crime and deviance there is clearly an area within each that stands apart from the other, but there is also a sizeable area of common ground. Through its more narrow focus, its practical application, its self-presentation as a quantitative science and its tie-ins to the world of grant funding, criminology has generated a vibrancy and prestige that has attracted large numbers of students, practitioners and policymakers. It has seized the area of overlap as its own as well, leaving only, for practical purposes, the domain of non-criminal deviance to the field of sociology. Sociological contributions to the field of crime, law and deviance are, and continue to be, rich. Yet, as Goode noted, when criminology split from deviance it adopted a positivist paradigm and left behind the social constructionist perspective. Although the latter is a vital approach and introduces powerful insights on relativity into a world governed too often by absolutes, its very relativism makes it fuzzy. Criminologists, with their self-report surveys and statistics, have gained greater legitimacy, resources and adherents.

In reality, however, psychology and psychiatry have made the most successful encroachments into the domain of sociological deviance. Armed with their profession's official guide, the *Diagnostic Statistical Manual* (DSM-5), practitioners have defined various socially deviant behaviors as emotional and mental illnesses. Has the Internet become too popular? Psychiatrists have created the "Internet addiction disorder", and Cincinnati police have charged a woman with neglecting her children because of it. Also new to the manual are "caffeine-induced anxiety disorder", "inhalant abuse disorder", "telephone scatologia" (making heavy breathing phone calls), "body dysmorphic disorder" (sufferers become fixated on perceived physical flaws to the point where their obsession interferes with daily functioning), "road rage disorder" (for people who cut us off and give other drivers the finger),[1] "compulsive hoarding" (practitioners have excessive clutter, difficulty categorizing, organizing, making decisions about and throwing away possessions and fears about needing items that could be thrown away) and "chronic procrastination" ("arousal procrastinators" put off for the last-minute rush while "avoiders" put off out of fear of failure or success).

Some of the nation's top psychiatrists have advocated the creation of an entirely new category of mental illness that could profoundly alter the practice of psychiatry and result in tens of thousands of families being diagnosed with a psychiatric disorder. Doctors in the American Psychiatric Association recommended a category called "relational disorders" for the DSM-5. Unlike every previous psychiatric diagnosis, this disorder identified sickness in groups of individuals and in the relationships between them. Here, individuals might be "healthy" except when it comes to certain relationships. This category incorporated couples who constantly quarreled, parents and children who clashed and troubled relationships between siblings. Its application could quickly become extended to troubled relationships between managers and workers or even troubled relationships between individuals and the state. Even terrorism could be re-defined as a form of "social pathology".

We have already seen the success with which other common forms of mood and behavior have been defined as psychiatric problems and labeled not only as deviant, but as "sick". We are no longer permitted to be excessively sad. People who are sad are diagnosed as depressed. When this alternates with being very happy, we label people bipolar. When they have too much energy, they can't sit still and concentrate, or when children fidget in the classroom, jiggle their feet excessively while sitting in their chairs, or don't line up neatly in a row, they are diagnosed as having ADD (attention deficit disorder) or ADHD (attention deficit hyperactivity disorder).

After diagnosis comes the struggle over the treatment of deviance. Psychologists and psychiatrists move from creating new categories of disease to launching systematic studies of them. If these can be successfully studied and affirmed, doctors can offer private outpatient and

---

[1] J. Leo, (n.d.) "Having a Rough Day? No, a Mental Disorder", *The Daily Camera*.

clinical inpatient therapy. Drugs can be prescribed to "manage" or "cure" them. This brings the pharmaceutical industry into the picture, followed quickly by the insurance companies.

Conrad and Schneider (1980) first alerted us to the growing trend toward the medicalization of deviance, but we now face the rising medicalization of our society. At no previous time in history have people taken so many legally prescribed drugs. With too much energy and not enough concentration, people find themselves on Ritalin or Adderall, even at the age of four and five. Teachers press parents to medicate their children as a way of controlling unruly students. A host of antidepressants starting with Prozac have invaded American life. Some make people so speedy they can't sleep well and lose their appetite, or in the newest scourge, develop erectile dysfunction, necessitating taking other medications in a "cocktail" fashion to control the side effects.

This paradigm fundamentally removes the volition and responsibility for deviant behavior and moves it into the disease category. It is surrounded and supported by pharmaceutical companies, therapists and professional associations that lobby for the ownership and control of deviance. At stake are enormous financial benefits, domain expansion, power and prestige. Vastly complex social issues and behavior are being re-defined as psychological, biological and chemical problems that can be solved by medication. Psychiatrists are inventing brain disorders as a backdoor way to fix social problems. We sociologists have apparently been doing a very poor job in defending our turf from all of these encroachments.

The deviant cyberworld

The rise and spread of the World Wide Web has had dramatic effects on deviance in our society in three ways.

Illicit markets

First, a range of deviance has been made available over the Web to people who would not ordinarily have access to it. People with hidden identities or in remote locations can access illicit markets who would not otherwise be able to locate them, finding deviant goods and services to buy, sell or trade. For example, all sorts of stolen items are offered for sale on the Internet through both normal channels such as eBay and through other, deviant sites. Many of these are not traceable to their source, such as electronics, stamps, coins, art and gemstones or jewelry. Youngsters have become criminals with rationalizations as creative as

Cressey's (1953) embezzlers 60 years ago, pirating items that are copied and sold illegally, a problem plaguing the entertainment industry, including CDs, DVDs, movies, television shows, music, concerts and pilfered cable television service/boxes. We have seen a rise in the flow of pharmaceuticals from one country to another, where American buyers are able to obtain drugs from Canada, Mexico, the offshore Caribbean or other locations, with or without a prescription, and to buy unlimited amounts of drugs such as painkillers from illicit "drug mills". People are also able to get intoxicating substances that are banned in the United States, such as "herbal" ecstasy, steroids and hosts of others that may be legal in some places but not everywhere.

International markets can be found on the Internet for pornography, sexual services, underage liaisons, prostitution, tearooms, sex slaves, immigrant brides, illegal immigrant smuggling and various types of people. Teenage boys' fantasies of naked women are now replaced with hardcore videos of every conceivable sex act readily available. Interested purchasers can find illegal adoptions, surrogate mothers, egg donors, organ donors, organ thieves, nationally forbidden animals, endangered species and illegal gambling.

The ease with which people can disguise their postings, responses, identities and popping up and disappearing at a moment's notice makes this medium much easier for criminals with technical expertise to navigate, hiding their trails from the law and/or operating outside of national jurisdictions.

Internet fraud

Second, the Web is a source for the easy transmission of fraud, with individuals and groups having new ways to access unsuspecting users. Many offers, posing as either deviant or legitimate exchanges, turn out to be scams where victims are fleeced. Some of these involve stocks, where sellers offer securities for sale that turn out to be bogus. Other stock frauds involve people offering fake accounts of their securities' successes, where they use fictitious names to send optimistic or pessimistic messages to investing chat rooms about stocks, hailing or bemoaning these companies. In reality, these scammers buy or sell the stocks they intend to manipulate right before they post, and then unload after they have sent the price up or down.

Travel scams abound on the Web as well, with offers of free trips abundant. Prospective participants are notified of free trips that then turn out to have hidden costs such as fees to "reserve" their trips, to pay the agents or to buy required memberships. Some pay the fees, never get the trips and are unable to get their money back. Other "card mill scams" sell bogus travel agency credentials purportedly enabling buyers to get travel agent discounts on transportation and lodging, at a time when both airlines and hotels have begun to tighten up on the availability of such discounts for legitimate travel agents while training their employees to weed out fake travel agents. Finally, people use online auctions to offer purportedly expiring frequent flyer miles or tickets purchased under someone else's name, which then turn out to be non-transferable.[2]

Identity theft has risen to stellar proportions, with hackers downloading credit and debit card numbers from banks, credit reference companies, Western Union financial transfers and such vendors as Amazon, eBay, Microsoft and VISA. "Phishing", a form of online fraud in which victims disclose account passwords and other data in response to e-mails that seem to come from legitimate business, has prospered, targeting users of a number of sites, especially eBay.[3] Beyond this we have seen the rise of "pharming", where experienced hackers are able to redirect people from a legitimate site to a bogus site without users even knowing it. Instead of ordering a sweater from their favorite online clothing site, people may be giving away their credit card numbers to crooks. For example, good Samaritans wanting to offer charitable aid to victims of the Indian Ocean Tsunami and Hurricane Katrina were notably "phished" and "pharmed", being duped into making donations to fake charities and logging on to fake Websites capable of depositing spyware on their computers that stole their credit cards and other identity markers.[4] Scammers' sophistication had increased so exponentially between the December 2004 tsunami and the August 2005 hurricane that the speed and volume of bogus sites (including KatrinaHelp.com, KatrinaDonations.com, KatrinaRelief.com and KatrinaReliefFund. com) of Katrina vastly outnumbered the Indian Ocean relief swindles. E-mail "hurricane news updates" also lured users to Web sites capable of infecting computers with a virus that allows hackers to gain control of their machines.[5] Internet sellers were also fleeced by purported buyers

---

[2] D. C. Johnston (2000) "Practical Traveler; A Boom Market in Travel Scams", *The New York Times*, September 10; H. Eldeson (2002) "The Pop-Up Ed Says You've Won a Vacation. Then Come the Bills", *The New York Times*, August 25.

[3] I. Austen (2005) "On EBay, E-Mail Phishers Find a Well-Stocked Pond", *The New York Times*, March 7, Section C, p. 1.

[4] T. Zeller, Jr. (2005) "Asia's Deadly Waves: Swindle; F.B.I. Warns of Internet Frauds That Capitalize on Tsunami", *The New York Times*, January 6, Section A, p. 14.

[5] T. Zeller, Jr. (2005) "After the Storm, the Swindlers", *The New York Times*, September 8.

offering counterfeit cashier's checks to purchase items for sale online, typically overpaying for the goods and asking for the difference to be sent back before the victim or the bank realizes that the check is a fake.[6] Customers of companies like eBay, with its online auction business and its heavy dependence on e-mail, are particularly vulnerable to not only these kinds of scams, but also to fraudulent product and sales offers more generally. EBay does little to police participants who trade under its auspices, and the average reported loss ranged in the area of $400.

Finally, "advance fee" fraud artists work "419" (named after a section of the Nigerian legal code) schemes. Here, con artists allegedly hailing from Nigeria and other West African countries, sometimes operating out of Europe, send e-mails from far-off lands offering fabulous riches to people who will help them recover some lost fortune. It might be $25 million spirited away during the fall of an obscure African regime, or $400 million in oil lucre skimmed off the top by the son of a wealthy (now often deceased) oil executive who has fallen from power. All they ask is a helping hand (ideally your bank account) and a meager amount as fees, and perhaps a quarter of the money is promised to the unsuspecting dupe. These operations have netted millions of dollars, even luring people into foreign countries where they are supposed to meet their prospective business partners, only to find themselves robbed or kidnapped.

Internet communities

Third, the Web has provided a place where previously non-existing deviant subcultures can flourish. People involved in what might otherwise be solitary forms of deviance, such as sexual asphyxiates, self-injurers, anorectics and bulimics, computer hackers, depressives, pedophiles and others, now have the opportunity to go online and find international cyber communities populated 24/7 by a host of others like them. These websites offer chatrooms, newsgroups, e-mail discussion lists and message boards for individuals to post where they can seek the advice and cyber company of others. Some, such as the "proana" (anorexia) and "promia" (bulimia) sites, explicitly state that they reinforce and support the deviant behavior, regarding this as a lifestyle choice (Force, 2005). Others, such as many self-injury sites, purport to help users desist from their deviance, but may actually end up reinforcing it by providing a supportive and accepting community where

---

[6] S. Stellen (2003) "Online Sellers Fall Victim to Counterfeit Cashier's Checks", *The New York Times*, May 15.

individuals can go when they feel misunderstood and rejected by the outside world.

Whether the sites aim to reinforce or discourage the deviance, nearly all tend to serve several unintended functions that have significant consequences for participants. First, they transmit knowledge of a practical and ideological sort among people, enabling them to more effectively engage in and legitimate the behavior. This helps people learn new variants of their activities, how to carry them out, how to obtain medical or legal services, and how to deal with outsiders. Second, they tend to be leveling, bringing people together into a common discourse regardless of their age, gender, marital status, ethnicity or socio-economic status (although users do need a computer, and most have high-speed Internet access). Third, they bridge huge spans of geographic distance, putting Americans in contact with English-speaking people from the United Kingdom, Australia, New Zealand, Canada and all over the world.

These interactions, regularly conducted among a range of regular and moderate users as well as periodic posters and "lurkers" (those who read but do not post), forge deviant communities. Participants develop ties to them by virtue of the support and acceptance they offer, especially to individuals who are lonely or semi-isolated. People unable to find "real" friends "FTF" (face-to-face) may come to rely on these cyber communities and cyber relationships, interacting with members for years and even traveling large distances to meet each other. They may, then, take the place of core friendships. In this way, if in no other, they reinforce continuing participation in the deviance as a way of maintaining membership. The stronger and more frequent these bonds, the greater effect they have on strengthening members' deviant identities. Deviant cyber communities thus provide a space and mechanism for deviance to grow and thrive in a way that it has not previously had.

Social networking

The Internet, or as some have recently taken to calling it, "the Cloud", has rapidly evolved, spreading dramatically around the world, generating significant and multi-faceted effects. Everyone is aware of the role of social networking in fomenting and organizing the wave of revolutionary protests and uprisings in North Africa and the Middle East that have toppled some governments and threaten to unseat or dramatically change more. The penetration of this technology through computers, cell phones and tablets has been dramatic. People communicate with one another instantly in this "microwave generation", emailing, blogging, Facebooking, texting, tweeting and tumbling.

Depending on one's perspective, the technology of the Internet can be seen as a force of deviance for or against social change; it has shown usefulness as a weapon against as well as a vehicle for oppression. On the one hand, we have seen these protest movements emboldened, organized, strategized and spread via the Internet. Recognizing this, many governments have cracked down, trying to control their subjects' access to various sites and information.

Yet, the Internet can also serve as a tool of repression. In 2010, China got into a heated dispute with Google when the company refused to allow Chinese censorship of its content in the way other search engines, businesses and governments had permitted. Google accused the Chinese government of deviance, claiming it had hacked into the accounts of human rights activists, stolen software code or otherwise enforced censorship and subjugation. This standoff, with the Chinese accusing Google of causing civil unrest and allowing treasonous content, was won by the Chinese, with Beijing holding their political firewall and Google losing their China-based service. China's aim here was not just the elimination of the free speech and virtual free assembly inherent to the Internet, but by promulgating numerous cyber-attacks against US businesses, the Pentagon and other government agencies, to turn the Internet into a weapon that could be used to combat democrats and democratic societies.

At the same time as the Cloud serves as deviant dissidents and deviant tyrants, it also provides a platform for slinging deviant labels on a smaller scale. The blogosphere is only loosely regulated at best, and people post things about public figures there that might never have surfaced in print or in the mainstream media. For example, in covering the Egyptian uprising in February of 2011, CBS "60 Minutes" journalist Lara Logan was sexually assaulted and beaten in the crush of a Tahrir Square mob. When the news of the attack broke, it took only minutes before people decided to hinge the story on the blond reporter's looks or to slam her, suggesting she was trying to outdo CNN reporter Anderson Cooper who got roughed up in Cairo earlier. Blogging for *LA Weekly*, Simone Wilson attacked her as a war zone "It girl", calling attention to Logan's "shocking good looks and ballsy knack for pushing her way to the heart of the action". Describing her as a "gutsy stunner", Wilson suggested, "It's not like she deserved it, but well, she is hot, right?" She also included in her column salacious reports about Logan's alleged sex life and reprinted a quote from *Mofo Politics* that said, "OMG if I were her captors and there were no sanctions for doing so? I would totally rape her". At the same time, Nir Rosen, a fellow at the New York University

Center for Law and Security, promptly whined to Twitter that Logan was a major war monger who got what she deserved and that "it's always wrong, that's obvious, but I'm rolling my eyes at all the attention she'll get", adding, "She's so bad that I ran out of sympathy for her". He soon backpedaled, deleting several of his most offensive posts and tweeting, "I apologize and take it back. joking with friends got out of line when i didnt want to back down. forgot twitter is not exactly private". In his apology (which didn't save his fellowship), he noted that he "resented" Logan because she "defended American imperial adventures" and claimed that she got so much attention for her assault only because she was white and famous.

Some have called the anonymity of online posting and blogging responsible for creating a deviant "culture of sadism". They suggest that its false sense of intimacy brings out the worst in people, encouraging shallow, funny, contrarian and cynical commentaries. We may have to ask ourselves if the technology of the Cloud amplifies everything, base instincts as well as good ones. Similarly, does its immediacy encourage hastiness of judgment? Does this technology dampen empathy and exonerate foul expression? We could probably agree that it has created a space for the global posting of sentiments that would elsewhere be labeled as deviant and likely censored before they destructively hit the airwaves.

The rise of cyber-bullying

Just as schools began to crack down on face-to-face bullying in the wake of the Columbine school shooting, bullying has taken on a new form online. In what was just the first incident of many, 13-year-old Megan Meiers committed suicide after being cyber-bullied on the social network, MySpace. From a small town in Missouri, Megan had been so badly teased and so unhappy, in seventh grade, that her parents pulled her from public school and moved her to the local Catholic grade school where she made friends. The process also resulted in the disintegration of a best friendship she had with a neighborhood friend, as the two quarreled and split apart. Angry at the distress caused to her daughter, Lori Drew (the mother of this neighborhood ex-friend) retaliated by creating a fictitious MySpace profile of a teenage boy, "Josh Evans", who courted Megan through the online venue and became her "boyfriend". They chatted daily for six weeks, during which time "Josh" pumped Megan for information about her friends. One day he told her that he'd heard she was a bad friend and that he was dumping her. Desperate to know who had told Josh she was mean, Megan kept typing the names of people she knew, which he then posted, accompanied by the mean things Megan had allegedly said about them. As she guessed names, some of those teens fired back responses. The effect was an online "pile-on". The final message of the evening pushed Megan over the edge when "Josh" wrote: "The world would be a better off place without you". When Megan broke down sobbing at the family computer, her parents made her log off and go to her room. Twenty minutes later they found her hanging by a belt in her closet. It took six weeks before they found out that "Josh" was fake and that the whole thing was a hoax perpetrated by Mrs. Drew to "mess with Megan". Police have said that although the prank was mean-spirited, Mrs. Drew broke no law. This was but the first incident of many such acts of cruelty.

Anonymous cyber sites are prevalent on the Cloud. From GirlsAsk-Guys.com to Quora to WordPress, Inout Queryspace, PostSecret, Pligg, Formspring.me and many more, boards have sprung up where people can post questions without disclosing their identities. Some of these can be set up to automatically link to users' Facebook or MySpace pages, so that when you anonymously post a question the replies come to your page. Many of these are used by teens, "tweens", and 20s-somethings to ask questions about what people think of them. The replies are often mean-spirited and insulting, available for all to see. Although many of these posts seek affirmation, they usually draw the opposite. Yet people continue to be drawn to these venues to seek the sociability they can't attain face-to-face. If these things happened in school or other adult-monitored venues, such deviant behavior would likely be sanctioned, with possible mediation to follow. But in the Cloud, a Lord of the Flies, Wild West frontier ethos prevails, and people are free to act in the basest ways. This suggests that the pseudo-intimacy created in cyber-space promotes the rise of cruelty, and that the norms of civility in this era of technology seem to have evaporated, leaving deviance to reign supreme.

Conclusion

Deviance is one of the core concepts of sociology, cutting across and being integrated into our major theories and substantive fields. When we think of deviance, we refer not only to attitudes, behavior and conditions that lie outside the margins of acceptability, but also to the very norms that cast them out, to the power structures of how folkways, mores and laws are created, and to the way that social control is attempted and achieved. Deviance is involved in key processes by which social order is maintained, as affirmations and re-affirmations of collective sentiment enhance social solidarity and stability. Deviance is also critically engaged in the dynamics of social change, as ideas and behavior move around and go in and out of currency. Finally, it is central to the hierarchy of social stratification, as it enables individuals and groups to raise themselves up and strike down their adversaries. It represents a paradigm by which definitions of deviance are used to disempower and control people who dissent from the majority opinion. In a society with heightened moralism, heightened radicalism and heightened polarization, deviance is the mechanism of disempowerment and control.

Deviance can represent both a serious and a light-hearted concept, can be found in both the social health and social ills of society, and, despite disciplinary turf wars, can be approached from both positivistic and constructionist perspectives. It has always been, and will always be, one of our most encompassing sociological tools.

References

Adler, P. A. (1985) *Wheeling and Dealing: Ethnography of an Upper-Level Drug Dealing and Smuggling Community* (New York: Columbia University Press).

Adler, P. A. and P. Adler (2011) *The Tender Cut: Inside the Hidden World of Self-Injury* (New York: New York University Press).

Altheide, D. (2002) *Creating Fear* (New York: Aldine).

Anderson, E. (1990) *Streetwise* (Chicago: University of Chicago Press).

—— (1999) *Code of the Streets* (New York: W. W. Norton).

Becker, H. S. (1953) "On Becoming a Marijuana User", *American Journal of Sociology*, 59, 235–252.

Ben-Yehuda, N. (1990) *The Politics and Morality of Deviance* (Albany: State University of New York Press).

—— (1994) *Moral Panics: The Social Construction of Deviance* (England: Blackwell).

—— (2006) "Contextualizing Deviance within Social Change and Stability, Morality, and Power", *Sociological Spectrum*, 26, 559–580.

Best, J. (1990) *Threatened Children* (Chicago: University of Chicago Press).

—— (2004a) *Deviance: Career of a Concept* (Belmont, CA: Thomson Wadsworth).

—— (2004b) "Deviance May Be Alive but Is It Intellectually Lively?: A Reaction to Goode", *Deviant Behavior*, 25, 483–492.

Conrad, P. and J. Schneider (1980) *Deviance and Medicalization* (St. Louis: Mosby).

Cressey, D. (1953) *Other People's Money* (New York: Free Press).

Curra, J. (2011) *The Relativity of Deviance*, 2nd edn. (Thousand Oaks, CA: Pine Forge Press).

Dotter, D. (2004) *Creating Deviance* (Walnut Creek, CA: Alta Mira).

Duneier, M. (1999) *Sidewalk* (New York: Farrar, Strauss, and Giroux).

Ehrenreich, B. (2001) *Nickel and Dimed* (New York: Henry Holt).

Erikson, K. (1966) *Wayward Puritans* (New York: Wiley).

Force, W. R. (2005) "There Are No Victims Here: Determination vs. Disorder in Pro-Anorexia", paper presented at the annual *Couch-Stone Symposium of the Society for the Study of Symbolic Interaction* (Boulder, CO).

Foucault, M. (ed.) (1977) *Language, Counter-Memory, Practice: Selected Essays and Interviews* (Ithaca, NY: Cornell University Press).

Goffman, A. (2014) *On the Run: Fugitive Life in an American City* (Chicago: University of Chicago Press).

Goffman, E. (1963) *Stigma* (Englewood Cliffs, NJ: Prentice Hall).

—— (2004) "The 'Death' MacGuffin Redux: Comments on Best", *Deviant Behavior*, 25, 493–509.

—— (2005) *Deviant Behavior*, 7th edn. (Upper Saddle River, NJ: Prentice Hall).

Goode, E. (2002a) *Deviance in Everyday Life* (Prospect Heights, IL: Waveland Press).

—— (2002b) "Does the Death of the Sociology of Deviance Make Sense?", *The American Sociologist*, 33, 107–118.

—— (2003) "The MacGuffin That Refuses to Die: An Investigation into the Condition of the Sociology of Deviance", *Deviant Behavior*, 24, 507–533.

Hall, S. (2012) *Theorizing Crime and Deviance* (Thousand Oaks, CA: Sage).

Hays, S. (2003) *Flat Broke with Children* (New York: Oxford University Press).

Heckert, A. and D. M. Heckert (2002) "A New Typology of Deviance: Integrating Normative and Reactivist Definitions of Deviance", *Deviant Behavior*, 23, 449–479.

—— (2004) "Using an Integrated Typology of Deviance to Analyze Ten Common Norms of the U.S. Middle-Class", *The Sociological Quarterly*, 45, 209–228.

Hendershott, A. (2002) *The Politics of Deviance* (San Francisco: Encounter Books).

Hirschi, T. (1969) *Causes of Delinquency* (Berkeley: University of California Press).

Jacobs, B. (2002) *Investigating Deviance* (Los Angeles, CA: Roxbury).

Krauthammer, C. (1993) "Defining Deviancy Up", *The New Republic*, November, 22, 20–25.

Kuhn, T. (1962) *The Structure of Scientific Revolutions* (Chicago: University of Chicago Press).

Liazos, A. (1972) "The Poverty of the Sociology of Deviance: Nuts, Sluts, and Preverts", *Social Problems*, 20, 103–120.

Matthews, R. and W. Wacker (2002) *The Deviant's Advantage: How Fringe Ideas Create Mass Markets* (New York: Random House).

Merton, R. (1938) "Social Structure and Anomie", *American Sociological Review*, 3, 672–682.

Moynihan, D. P. (1993) "Defining Deviance Down", *The American Scholar*, 64, 25–33.

Musto, D. (1999) *The American Disease* (New York: Oxford University Press).

Newman, K. (1999) *No Shame in My Game* (New York: Knopf).

Pager, D. (2002) "The Mark of a Criminal Record" (PhD dissertation, Department of Sociology, University of Wisconsin, Madison).

Pontell, H. and S. M. Rosoff (2011) *Social Deviance* (New York: McGraw Hill).

Prus, R. and S. Grills (2003) *The Deviant Mystique: Involvements, Realities, and Regulation* (Westport, CT: Praeger).

Quinney, R. (1975) *The Social Reality of Crime* (Boston: Little, Brown).

Reinarman, C. and H. G. Levine (eds.) (1997) *Crack in America* (Berkeley: University of California Press).

Sanders, C. (1988) *Marks of Mischief* (Philadelphia: Temple University Press).

Schoenberger, N., A. Heckert and D. Heckert (2012) "Techniques of Neutralization Theory and Positive Deviance", *Deviant Behavior*, 33, 774–791.

Snow, D. and L. Anderson (1993) *Down on Their Luck* (Berkeley: University of California Press).

Sumner, C. (1994) *The Sociology of Deviance: An Obituary* (Buckingham, UK: Open University Press).

Sykes, G. M. and D. Matza (1957) "Techniques of Neutralization", *American Sociological Review*, 22, 664–670.

Terrell, N. E. and R. F. Meier (2001) *Readings in Deviant Behavior* (Belmont, CA: Cengage).

Tittle, C. R. and R. Paternoster (2000) *Social Deviance and Crime* (Los Angeles: Roxbury).

Tuggle, J. L. and M. D. Holmes (1997) "Blowing Smoke: Status Politics and the Shasta County Smoking Ban", *Deviant Behavior*, 18, 77–94.

Vandenburgh, H. (2004) *Deviance: The Essentials* (Upper Saddle River, NJ: Pearson).

Venkatesh, S. (2006) *Off the Books: The Underground Economy of the Urban Poor* (Cambridge, MA: Harvard University Press).

—— (2008) *Gang Leader for a Day* (New York: Penguin Press).

Weitzer, R. (2002) *Deviance and Social Control* (New York: McGraw Hill).

3
The Deviance Bubble

Joel Best

Debating the death of deviance is not especially useful. The concept's defenders argue that deviance can't be dead. After all, undergraduates continue to fill classrooms for courses in deviance, textbooks for those courses continue to sell and journalists use the term. Like status symbol or charisma, deviance is a sociological concept that has found its way into the popular vocabulary. Therefore, the argument goes, deviance can't be dead.

Okay, rumors of deviance's death may have been greatly exaggerated. But, if we ask whether deviance remains a *useful sociological concept*, an honest answer has to be "No", or at least "Not especially". The concept of deviance may not be dead, but neither is it especially healthy.

The rise of deviance as a concept

The history of the concept of deviance is a tale of a conceptual bubble, akin to a financial bubble.[1] Not so long ago, some people liked to imagine that financial bubbles were a thing of the past. But during the first decade of the new millennium, Americans – and the larger world – experienced two impressive collapses involving first the dot-com bubble and then the housing bubble, which served as reminders of bubble dynamics. A bubble – an episode of what John Kenneth Galbraith called "financial euphoria" – occurs when people begin to believe that the price of something – tulip bulbs, Internet stocks, home prices, whatever – will continue to rise, so that it makes sense to buy in anticipation

---

[1] On financial bubbles, see Galbraith (1990).

of being able sell in the future, when the price will surely be higher. Eventually, demands slow because there aren't enough buyers willing to pay the ever higher prices, the price stalls, and then begins to plunge as people rush to unload what they own before the price falls even lower. The bubble swells so long as people continue to bid up the price, only to pop when prices collapse.

The history of the concept of deviance within sociology resembles a bubble.[2] The term first appeared in the American sociological literature after World War II. This was a period of theoretical optimism in sociology; Talcott Parsons (1948), one of the first sociologists to use the term, was constructing his grand theoretical edifices. The concept of deviance promised to build upon the existing literature, to provide an overarching concept that could unify what had been separate literatures, particularly studies of crime, mental illness, suicide, drug addiction and homosexuality. The basic insight behind the concept as it was articulated in the 1950s was that these apparently very different phenomena in fact shared an underlying similarity: they all involved people violating norms. Deviance, in this early view, was simply norm violation. The literature on deviance took off during this period; the bubble was beginning to swell.

It expanded further and faster during the 1960s. This was the most creative decade in the sociology of deviance, a period that saw the publication of influential books, many of which became classic, canonical works in the field, including *Asylums* (Goffman, 1961); *Outsiders* (Becker, 1963); *Stigma* (Goffman, 1963); *Symbolic Crusade* (Gusfield, 1963); *The Other Side* (Becker, 1964); *Crimes without Victims* (Schur, 1965); *Wayward Puritans* (Erikson, 1966); *Being Mentally Ill* (Scheff, 1966); *Human Deviance, Social Problems, and Social Control* (Lemert, 1967); *Deviance and Identity* (Lofland, 1969) and *Becoming Deviant* (Matza, 1969). All of these volumes came to be associated with what would be called labeling theory, in that they argued that what different forms of deviance had in common was negative societal reaction, that is, labeling people as deviant. In other words, deviance was not a norm violation but, as Becker (1963, p. 9) famously said, "deviant behavior is behavior that people so label". During the 1960s, deviance was an undeniably hot topic within sociology, and labeling's insights were being adopted and developed outside the United States, particularly in Canada and Great Britain. The bubble swelled.

---

[2] For a more detailed summary of the history of deviance as a sociological concept, see Best (2004).

Deviance under attack

But only a few years later, the bubble popped when the concept of deviance took turn for the worse. There were two major reasons. The first concerned new – or at least newly fashionable – theoretical currents in sociology, which led to sociologists of deviance finding themselves being criticized by proponents of these new perspectives. A first critique came from conflict theorists (not a new perspective, but one that gained new life thanks to sociologists responding to the upheavals of the 1960s and early 1970s). The conflict theorists blasted the sociology of deviance for failing to address issues of power and domination. In their view, the entire social control apparatus – laws, legislatures, the criminal justice system and so on – existed largely to legitimize and maintain elites' power and privilege. By focusing their attention on interactions between cops and crooks, sociologists of deviance were themselves complicit in shifting attention away from the important economic and political inequities that, the conflict theorists argued, should be sociologists' subject.

A second critique was more novel. It came from sociologists aligned with the emerging women's movement who sought to highlight the importance of what were initially called sex roles (the terms feminism and gender were not yet well established). They criticized the sociology of deviance both for downplaying the victimization of women and for failing to challenge the ways sexism shaped how females came to be labeled deviant. In this view, sociologists of deviance bought into the sexist assumptions both mainstream sociology and the larger culture. Third, members of the rapidly growing movements for gay and lesbian rights and for disability rights challenged the classification of homosexuals and the disabled as deviants. Rather, they argued, these should be seen as political minorities and not grouped with criminals and the mentally ill.

All of these critiques – from conflict theorists, feminists and social activists – offered moral challenges, in that they argued that sociologists of deviance ignored the moral implications of their concept, that when sociologists talked about deviance, they were buying into the dominant culture's assumptions about right and wrong, normal and abnormal. These moral critiques particularly unsettled the labeling theorists, who had thought of themselves as being on the side of deviants, rather than allied with their oppressors (Becker, 1967).

In addition, there was a fourth line of criticism from mainstream sociologists, who argued that the labeling theorists' claims ignored a large empirical literature that demonstrated that societal reaction explained only a small portion of what was called deviance, that phenomena such as mental illness and addiction were more than simply artifacts of a labeling process (Gove, 1975).

By the late 1970s, the sociology of deviance had stalled as an intellectual enterprise. Scholars became wary of the concept. Invoking the term deviance had become a sort of red flag that might invite critical attention from a variety of theoretical camps. Why buy trouble? Why use the concept of deviance if it wasn't absolutely necessary?

In addition to becoming the theoretically controversial, there was a second problem: it became increasingly clear that the proponents of deviance could not define the concept's domain. The notion of deviance experienced what we might call *definitional creep*. Definitional creep becomes a possibility whenever concepts lack precise definitions. Certainly it has bedeviled sociological theorizing about deviance.

The initial popularity of the notion of deviance involved the appreciation that crime and mental illness were sociologically similar. In postwar America, this must have seemed like a startling insight, because on the surface the two seemed very different: crime was handled by the criminal justice system – laws, cops, judges, jails and so on; while mental illness was considered a medical problem – the stuff of symptoms, diagnoses, psychiatrists and mental hospitals. Criminals were held responsible for their actions, the mentally ill were not. And yet, the early sociologists of deviance argued that there were parallels: both crime and deviance involved breaking rules; both sorts of rule violators were subject to social control agents' sanctions; in both cases, offenders could find themselves locked up in total institutions; and so on.

In other words, the concept of deviance depended upon an analogy–something was deviant if it was like other forms of deviance. This turned out to be a very easy argument to make. What could be considered deviant? In *Outsiders* – probably the single most influential book of deviance – Becker argued that jazz musicians were deviant, not just because they smoked dope, but simply because they were jazz musicians. In *Stigma*, Goffman included all manner of disabilities. In no time, the concept's fuzzy boundaries were stretched to include people who were fat, people who were short, people who held unusual political or religious beliefs, people who had red hair, members of ethnic minorities, the Holocaust, positive deviants (i.e., people who displayed more virtues than other folks) and so on. This expansion of a term's definition, the application of the term to more and more kinds of cases, constitutes definitional creep.

Moreover, it was no longer clear just what all these phenomena- deviance had in common. Was there a norm against being a jazz musician or having red hair? Was there a societal reaction targeted at people who were short? Obviously, some people might consider jazz musicians less respectable than members of symphonies, and redheaded children are probably more likely to get teased on the playground than blondes. But does it make sense to argue that societal reaction encompasses everything from being imprisoned or committed to a mental hospital, to playground taunts? This sort of definitional creep threatens to equate deviance with difference, so that anything that inspires even the slightest reservation – any reaction other than wholesale approval – can be considered deviance. Imagine a party where everyone present agrees that one woman is the most attractive. Are all of the other women – all judged as somehow having fallen short – deviant? And wait, wouldn't some sociologists argue that the party's beauty is herself a "positive deviant". (Lest I be accused of sexism, let me hasten to note that, by the same logic, all of the men can be judged deviant as well.) The problem with definitional creep is it's never clear where one draws the line: it is easy to say, "Well, X should also be considered deviant", but much harder to declare, "Y is certainly not deviant".

Proponents of expanding a concept's domain may assume that a concept becomes stronger, more useful when it is applied widely. But this is exactly wrong. We can imagine that, as the concept's definition expands, it covers a broader proportion of the population. Perhaps when sociologists first started talking about deviance, they imagined that, say, 5 or 10 percent of the population was deviant. But as the concept's definition grows broader, the percentage of deviants must increase to – what? 20 percent? 50 percent? 80 percent? More? One sometimes hears sociologists casually say, "Oh, well, everyone is deviant." We can see extreme examples of such definitional creep in claims that 96 percent of families are dysfunctional, or that 96 percent of people are co-dependent (Best, 1999). If essentially all families are dysfunctional, then *dysfunctional family* becomes just another synonym for *family*. Similarly, if everyone is deviant, than *deviant* is just another word for human.

Imagine if other scientists did this. Imagine chemists allowing the definition of oxygen to creep, so that instead of restricting the term to atoms with eight protons, they started arguing that atoms with more or fewer protons also ought to be considered forms of oxygen. The concept of oxygen would lose its analytic value.

But scientists don't do this. They police the boundaries of their concepts. Consider Pluto's recent demotion from astronomers' list of planets;

Pluto is now a *dwarf planet* (Tyson, 2009). Technological improvements meant that astronomers were discovering other icy lumps orbiting on the outskirts of the solar system. They faced a choice. If Pluto – an icy lump – continued to be classified as a planet, than surely these other lumps qualified for the same designation, which could expand the list of planets to include many relatively small, quite distant, and rather uninteresting lumps of frozen matter. Alternatively, they could – and did – choose to reclassify Pluto (much as 19th-century astronomers first identified Ceres as a planet, but then demoted it to an asteroid).

Tracking deviance's trajectory

The point is that science depends upon being able to control the definitions of its concepts. We can see this very clearly when we try to track the use of the word *deviance* in the sociological literature. JSTOR is a full-text database for scholarly literature. It is possible to search JSTOR and locate every article in a set of journals that includes the word *deviance*.[3] Figure 3.1 tracks the use of the term deviance in five leading journals: *American Sociological Review*, *American Journal of Sociology*, *Social Forces* (long regarded as the field's third major general journal, although its standing has slipped somewhat in recent decades), *Annual Review of Sociology* (a venue for review articles, which began publishing in 1975, and which is now one of the discipline's three most-cited journals) and *Social Problems* (a leading specialized journal that has a long history of publishing key pieces on deviance – it began publication in 1953). I chose these journals because they are the center ring in American sociology's circus. They are widely read and widely cited; they are among the most prestigious venues for publishing sociologists' work related to deviance.

Figure 3.1 measures the average number of articles mentioning deviance in these five journals per journal per year for seven decades, beginning in the 1940s. The overall pattern is clear: usage of the term increased in the 1950s and 1960s, peaked in the 1970s, then began to decline in the 1980s. Deviance is gradually fading as a concept that is actually used by sociologists when they publish in the discipline's leading journals. This pattern is hardly unique; sociology's history is filled with concepts that once seemed promising, but wound up being abandoned (Best and Schweingruber, 2003). For instance, deviance's early-20th-century

---

[3] This is a very generous definition: it counts articles that include a single mention of deviance (even in the title of one of the cited sources).

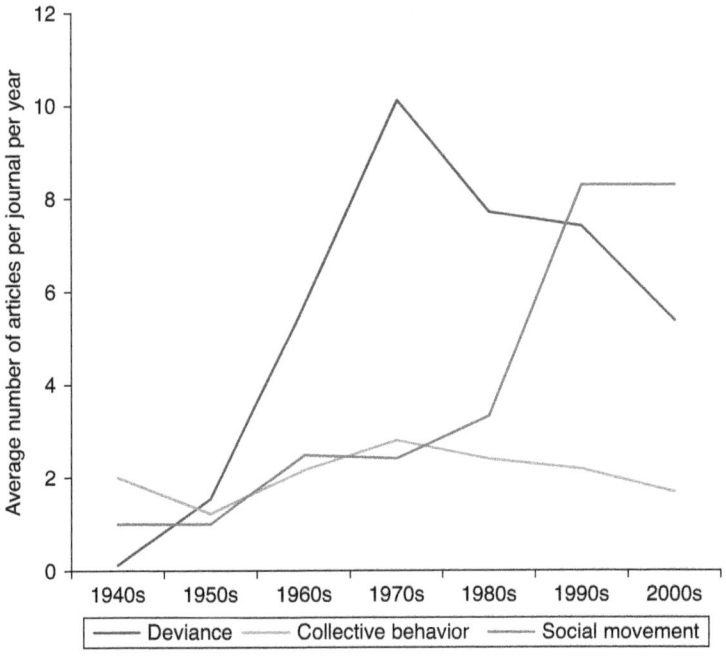

Figure 3.1 Average number of articles in five leading sociology journals mentioning deviance, collective behavior and social movements, by decade, 1940–2009

Source: JSTOR search for articles in *American Journal of Sociology, American Sociological Review, Annual Review of Sociology* (1975–2007), *Social Forces* and *Social Problems* (1953–2009).

conceptual predecessor, *social pathology*, fell out of favor long ago (Best, 2006b).

Just for the sake of comparison, Figure 3.1 also displays the usage of two other terms – collective behavior and social movement – in the sociological literature. Mentions of collective behavior have remained quite steady since the 1940s; throughout the period, the major journals averaged about two articles that referred to collective behavior per year. In contrast, references to social movements were rare in the 1940s and 1950s, but began to increase as new theoretical perspectives, such as resource mobilization and framing, revitalized the sociology of social movements. We can imagine the trajectories of other terms: interest in small groups (which received considerable attention in the 1950s and 1960s) must have fallen, even as references to gender would have increased dramatically. In other words, the trajectory of references to deviance tells us that the concept rose in popularity and has been falling out of favor in recent decades: we can't simply dismiss it by saying that usage of all concepts follows the same pattern.

Sociology's terminology – the vocabulary that sociologists use – is constantly changing. New concepts are advanced; some never catch on, while others spread because analysts find them useful. But, as new concepts come into vogue, established ideas may fall out of favor. A term like social pathology – once widely used – may come to seem dated, even archaic. Institutions vary in their susceptibility to fashion, but scholarly disciplines like sociology, which strive to constantly expand a body of knowledge, favor novelty (Best, 2006a; Blumer, 1969). Tracing the shifting popularity of particular terms in the pages of the discipline's major journals, such as *ASR* and *AJS*, let's track the influence of particular terms. And, by that measure, deviance seems to be a concept that is falling out of use.

But, deviance's advocates respond, who cares what *ASR* and *AJS* publish? They are mainstream, quantitative sociology's bastion, unreceptive to hipper, more qualitative work. We ought to look at journals that should be more receptive to studies of deviance. There are a couple problems with this argument.

First, critics worry that sociology lacks a core, that is, that sociologists don't share a set of fundamental ideas in the way that, say, economists or chemists do. Certainly sociology seems to be more fragmented: there are ever more specialized professional organizations, more specialized journals, more awards and prizes for accomplishments within particular specializations, and so on (Best, 2003). The causes of these developments aren't mysterious. As the academic marketplace has become more professionalized, expectations for faculty scholarship have risen; tenure and promotion depend on publication more than in the past, creating a demand for venues – particularly journals where all those junior scholars can place their work. As the sociological profession expands, and as the volume of published research grows, individuals cannot hope to keep up with everything, so they focus their attention on their specialties, so that most work finds only a small, fairly homogeneous (in the sense that they are likely to share the authors' interests and orientations) set of readers. Specialties need to legitimize their place within the larger profession, and thus the steady growth in organizations, journals and prizes that support particular specialized bodies of work.

One consequence of these developments is that virtually every sociological specialty can show some evidence of growth. There are more people struggling to publish more work in more venues. Publication by graduate students – relatively rare a few decades ago – has become common. If we count all venues, there are probably more articles published on nearly every subject, simply because the total amount being published is constantly increasing. At the same time, because the amount of work being published far outstrips our ability to keep up, we can suspect that much of what gets published goes largely unread. While we can't keep track of the numbers of eyeballs that focus on a particular article, studies of citations offer a crude index of readership: the number of citations tells us whether other scholars found a work worthy of being mentioned. And which journals have the greatest number of citations? Year after year, *ASR*, *AJS*, and the *Annual Review of Sociology* lead the pack; during the most recent year for which rankings were available (2011) when I wrote this, *Social Forces* and *Social Problems* were also in the top 12 (of 138 sociology journals ranked). In other words, these are the journals to which sociologists are most likely to refer in their own work. So, Figure 3.1 offers an apples-to-apples comparison; it asks how the attention paid to deviance in sociology's major journals has shifted over the decades. By this measure, we can conclude that deviance is slipping. To the degree that those journals are venues for the discipline's core contributions, it seems that the concept of deviance is deemed less useful than in the past.

Second, regardless of what the citation counts show, it is obvious that the study of deviance has been in the doldrums for decades. The theory of deviance has hardly evolved since the 1960s. Deviance-as-norm-violation was an innovative idea in the early 1950s. Similarly, deviance-as-societal reaction was a new paradigm when it emerged ten years later. It is easy to list the important books on deviance published during the 1960s – but this is the 50th anniversary of the publication of *Outsiders*. So let me invite you, my reader, to take out a blank sheet of paper and list the most important books on deviance published since 1970. Or make a list of the important theoretical models that emerged during that period. Or how about a list of the key concepts that emerged during those years? My point is not that there won't be anything on your lists, but I rather suspect your lists will be fairly short.

My list of books would begin with Jack Katz's *Seductions of Crime* (1988). It picked up on an insight – also developed in Patricia Adler's *Wheeling and Dealing* (1985) – that deviance can be pleasurable and exciting. Now this was not an unheard of notion – it had certainly been mentioned by earlier scholars (one thinks of Lofland's [1969] concept of the *adventurous deviant act*), but Katz explored the idea more thoroughly than his predecessors. When I finished his book, I thought to myself that I now understood deviance better than I had when I'd started reading it. That's not the only time I've had that reaction since 1970, but neither have I had it all that frequently, and that strikes me as a sign that the sociology of deviance isn't all that robust.

It is worth noting that although Katz does mention deviance at several points in his book, his title frames his work as a study of crime. The same device is used in Gottfredson and Hirschi's *A General Theory of Crime* (1990, p. xiv), even though they make it clear that "crime is only part of a much larger set of deviant acts, acts that include accidents, victimizations, truancies from home, school, and work, substance abuse, family problems, and disease". By the time these books appeared, it probably had become easier to speak of crime, rather than invoke the now confusing term of deviance.

Criminology is just one of the intellectual destinations that have attracted people who once might have thought of themselves as sociologists of deviance. Peter Conrad's early work on medicalization framed the process in terms of deviance (e.g., Conrad and Schneider, 1980), but his more recent writings (e.g., Conrad, 2007) seem located more clearly within medical sociology.

Perhaps the principal route away from the sociology of deviance was pioneered by such prominent labeling theorists as John I. Kitsuse and Joseph R. Gusfield, who laid much of the foundation for constructionist studies of social problems (Spector and Kitsuse, 1977; Gusfield, 1981).[4] *Social problems* was a familiar term in the sociological lexicon; it was the title of an important journal and a common lower-division course offering. However, it was not a coherent intellectual field, as Spector and Kitsuse (1977, p. 1) made clear in the opening sentence of *Constructing Social Problems*: "There is no adequate definition of social problems within sociology, and there is not and never has been a sociology of social problems". Like Herbert Blumer and Armand Mauss – who developed their own, parallel positions during the 1970s – Spector and Kitsuse argued

---

[4] It is worth noting that few of the people who wrote the most influential books about deviance published during the 1960s remained focused on the topic: in addition to Kitsuse and Gusfield promoting a constructionist approach to social problems, Goffman (whose interest in deviance always seemed peripheral) returned to the study of face-to-face interaction, Becker began concentrating on the sociology of art, Lofland turned to the study of social movements, Erikson focused on disasters and so on. These were scholars who were well-placed to remain advocates of the importance of deviance, but they chose not to adopt that role.

that social problems ought to be viewed not as objective conditions within society but as subjective constructions.

This constructionist approach had much in common with the labeling perspective toward deviance. Many of the earliest constructionist case studies focused topics that might have been considered forms of deviance, including rape (Rose, 1977), child abuse (Pfohl, 1977) and drunk driving (Gusfield, 1981). In many ways, these analyses paralleled case studies of the creation – also termed the invention, manufacture and so on – of categories of deviance; the classic example was Becker's (1963) discussion of the origins of a federal law against marijuana. Similarly, as the constructionist literature grew, there were ethnographic studies of *social problems work* (Miller and Holstein, 1997) that resembled microsociological research on labeling processes. In other words, it was possible for sociologists to conduct similar kinds of analyses; sometimes they chose to make explicit reference to deviance, sometimes not.

To be sure, constructionism is a limited perspective. Most of the research dealing with the phenomena that are considered social problems does not adopt a constructionist framework. A sociologist interested in, say, family violence might ask all sorts of questions: How common is family violence? How do violent incidents develop? What are the consequences of family violence? and so on. None of these – quite legitimate – research questions calls for a constructionist approach. And note that none of them invokes the concept of a social problem. A sociologist of social problems is likely to focus on how and why family violence came to attention as a social problem. Perhaps labeling theory – which of course closely parallels the constructionist approach to social problems – got in trouble precisely because its advocates thought of it as *the* way to understand deviance, instead of appreciating it as *one* framework useful for understanding some aspects of deviance.

The constructionist approach has inspired an extensive literature that has addressed a range of questions about the social problems process: What sort of rhetoric is needed to make effective claims that can successfully draw attention to a social problem? Who are the actors likely to play key roles in this process? How do constructions of social problems change, as they pass through the hands of the press, the public, policymakers, and social problems workers? And so on (Best, 2013). Because "social problems" is a broad label that covers a diverse range of phenomena – everything from suicide to climate change – the answers to these questions often vary from case to case. And, for sociologists of social problems, deviance simply refers to some of the phenomena that are constructed as problematic.

The future of deviance

Financial bubbles inevitably burst. Is this true for conceptual bubbles as well? The defenders of deviance argue that the concept has a secure place in the sociological lexicon; in effect, they argue that deviance, like a giant financial institution, is too big to fail.

Obviously, courses on deviance continue to have a strong place in sociology's undergraduate curriculum, and there is no reason to imagine that future cohorts of students won't be attracted to a course about sex, dope and cheap thrills. Similarly, researchers will continue to be interested in studying crime, mental illness and the like. In other words, interest in the topics that sociologists categorize as deviance is not likely to vanish.

Still, that doesn't mean that the term *deviance* is here to stay. Sociologists used to teach about – and study – sex and violence, but they used to classify those topics as forms of social pathology (the title, remember, of Edwin Lemert's pathbreaking text). No sociologist uses that term today, and there's no guarantee that deviance won't go the way of its predecessor.

And there are troubling signs. Sociologists of deviance haven't just wanted to have things both ways, they've wanted to have them every which way. They have refused to agree on a coherent definition for the concept, and they have participated in egregious definitional creep. The term is criticized by members of several theoretical camps and, at least in sociology's leading journals, it is being used less often. At the same time, sociologists of deviance have not been especially active in advancing studies within their specialty; following the excitement generated by the notion of deviance of the 1960s, there seem to have been fewer important contributions. Keeping the sociology of deviance thriving will require doing something other than just more of the same.

References

Adler, P. A. (1985) *Wheeling and Dealing: Ethnography of an Upper-Level Drug Dealing and Smuggling Community* (New York: Columbia University Press).
Becker, H. S. (1963) *Outsiders: Studies in the Sociology of Deviance* (New York: Free Press).

—— (ed.) (1964) *The Other Side: Perspectives on Deviance* (New York: Free Press).

—— (1967) "Whose Side Are We On?", *Social Problems*, 14, 239–247.

Best, J. (1999) *Random Violence: How We Talk about New Crimes and New Victims* (Berkeley, CA: University of California Press).

—— (2003) "Killing the Messenger: The Social Problems of Sociology", *Social Problems*, 50, 1–13.

—— (2004) *Deviance: Career of a Concept* (Belmont, CA: Wadworth).

—— (2006a) *Flavor of the Month: Why Smart People Fall for Fads* (Berkeley, CA: University of California Press).

—— (2006b) "Whatever Happened to Social Pathology? Conceptual Fashions and the Sociology of Deviance", *Sociological Spectrum*, 26, 533–546.

—— (2013) *Social Problems*, 2nd edn. (New York: W. W. Norton).

Best, J. and D. Schweingruber (2003) "First Words: Do Sociologists Actually Use the Terms in Introductory Textbooks' Glossaries?", *American Sociologist*, 34 (Fall), 97–106.

Blumer, H. (1969) "Fashion: From Class Differentiation to Collective Selection", *Sociological Quarterly*, 10, 275–291.

Conrad, P. (2007) *The Medicalization of Society: On the Transformation of Human Conditions into Treatable Disorders* (Baltimore: Johns Hopkins University Press).

Conrad, P. and J. W. Schneider (1980) *Deviance and Medicalization* (St. Louis: Mosby).

Erikson, K. T. (1966) *Wayward Puritans: A Study in the Sociology of Deviance* (New York: John Wiley & Sons).

Galbraith, J. K. (1990) *A Short History of Financial Euphoria* (New York: Penguin).

Goffman, E. (1961) *Asylums: Essays on the Social Situation of Mental Patients and Other Inmates* (Garden City, NY: Anchor).

—— (1963) *Stigma: Notes on the Management of Spoiled Identity* (Englewood Cliffs, NJ: Prentice Hall).

Gottfredson, M. R. and T. Hirschi (1990) *A General Theory of Crime* (Stanford, CA: Standford University Press).

Gove, W. R. (ed.) (1975) *The Labelling of Deviance: Evaluating a Perspective* (New York: John Wiley & Sons).

Gusfield, J. R. (1963) *Symbolic Crusade: Status Politics and the American Temperance Movement* (Urban: University of Illinois Press).

—— (1981) *The Culture of Public Problems: Drinking-Driving and the Symbolic Order* (Chicago: University of Chicago Press).

Katz, J. (1988) *Seductions of Crime: Moral and Sensual Attractions in Doing Evil* (New York: Basic Books).

Lemert, E. M. (1951) *Social Pathology: A Systematic Approach to the Theory of Sociopathic Behavior* (New York: McGraw-Hill).

—— (1967) *Human Deviance, Social Problems, and Social Control* (Englewood Cliffs, NJ: Prentice Hall).

Lofland, J. (1969) *Deviance and Identity* (Englewood Cliffs, NJ: Prentice Hall).

Matza, D. (1969) *Becoming Deviant* (Englewood Cliffs, NJ: Prentice Hall).

Miller, G. and J. A. Holstein (eds.) (1997) *Social Problems in Everyday Life: Studies of Social Problems Work* (Greenwich, CT: JAI).

Parsons, T. (1948) "The Position of Sociological Theory", *American Sociological Review*, 13, 156–171.

Pfohl, S. J. (1977) "The 'Discovery' of Child Abuse", *Social Problems*, 24, 310–323.

Rose, V. McNickle (1977) "Rape as a Social Problem", *Social Problems*, 25, 75–89.

Scheff, T. J. (1966) *Being Mentally Ill: A Sociological Theory* (Chicago: Aldine).

Schur, E. M. (1956) *Crimes without Victims: Deviant Behavior and Public Policy* (Englewood Cliffs, NJ: Prentice Hall).

Spector, M. and J. I. Kitsuse (1977) *Constructing Social Problems* (Menlo Park, CA: Cummings).

Tyson, N. deGrasse (2009) *The Pluto Files: The Rise and Fall of America's Favorite Planet* (New York: W. W. Norton).

4

Expanding Deviance toward Difference
A Linguistic Approach
Michael J. Coyle

Language as tool, language as architecture

Our everyday lived experience of language is that it is a tool for communication. For us, language is like the Mason's stone, the painter's brush, and the programmer's code: we viscerally have language as that which helps us get things done. In the humdrum of our daily life we use words in a myriad ways to communicate diverse things in countless circumstances. Language is lived as that which we command to do most of what we do: we experience language as the tool to ask for cereal instead of toast, to inquire for more detail on the task assigned at work, and to facilitate debate over dinner with our friends. Similarly, as students of the human world we are ever in search of the perfect word (the perfect meaning) to communicate our interpretation. In all these ways we experience and think of *language as a tool for describing human action*.

Given this primary, ongoing, and lifelong experience of language as a tool of communication, it is understandable that throughout each day we mostly lose touch with other sides of language. Examined more closely, language is a ceaseless activity of deep complexity (Foucault, 1973) that is much more than a user-directed instrument.

Indeed, this copious human action we call language can be had as more than a tool for building descriptions and arguments; it can be had as the habits that can and frequently does determine the very architecture of our descriptions and arguments. For example, the language of genocide, that is, "uncivilized barbarians" (Native Americans) and "vermin," "parasites," and "plague" (European Jews), may have become descriptions of what was taught such peoples are, but built with the habitual use of these words is the argument that we need to defend ourselves by ridding ourselves of such people (Bosmajian, 1983; 1992).

Although nowhere in these words is protection and extermination directly requested, it is everywhere suggested and implied. Similarly, in the language of sexism, of war, and of punishment, there are not only descriptions of persons, but also creations of persons which invite unambiguous interpretations of them and (sometimes require) specific actions toward them. Certainly, they make otherwise unsavory suggestions palatable: unequal treatment, killing, and torture. Reasonably, we could expect to encounter some of this complexity in the language of deviance, that is, that which occurs at first examination as simply descriptive might on further examination be found to entail something more.

Coming at language from this other end, we can see that what we call our world is made up not only of a series of words we choose each time to describe it, but also of ready words, nay entire ready architectures of words (discourses), that are habitually performed, and by their use tell that the world is one thing and not another, or put more simply, not only describe the world, but also generate it. As Sapir (1956, p. 75) phrased it, "The fact of the matter is that the 'real world' is to a large extent unconsciously built up on the language habits of the group...We see and hear and otherwise experience very largely as we do because the language habits of our community predispose certain choices of interpretation." Words, then, fabricate; not because they are false, but because their habitual everyday use is a mostly unregistered act of creation (and ceaseless re-creation). In such a fashion, words make the fabric of our lives, and they make not only the material of this fabric, but also its design. To study human action from such a perspective is to experience and think of *language as generating human action*.

Viewing the ability of our language choices to describe and define our interpretations brings to the fore the importance of studying language. In this essay I examine the language of criminalized deviance with these *two ways of looking at language: as descriptive tool and as generative action*. I do this because if we are to ask whether the language of deviance has usefulness as a concept to interpret so-called criminal behavior, then we must first inquire about the content and use of such language and then we can better assess whether it matters, if it is dead, and more. I will show that by using the deviance concept scholars can study criminalized language and develop insights that elucidate the social construction of justice performances. I will also demonstrate that given the ubiquity of harms ("crimes") in human relationships, to speak of harm-making as deviant is nonsensical and nullifies the very concept of deviance, and points to the need for a concept to distinguish how some criminalized behavior is treated differently than other criminalized behavior. Finally, I will demonstrate that we need to re-conceptualize the social response to transgression ("crime") as the management of difference (and not deviance), and study how some difference is responded to with the "criminal justice system" (is not accepted) and some by reconstructing it into something else or ignoring it (is accepted). In sum, in this chapter I argue that though the *deviance concept* has helped us develop insights that elucidate the social construction of criminalized behavior, we need the *difference concept* to study how some "criminal behavior" is responded to with the "criminal justice system" and some "criminal behavior" is responded to by reconstructing it into something else or ignoring it.

The importance and sociological usefulness of the deviance concept

Concepts such as deviance are not exactly fantasies, but they are also not brick and mortar. They are strategies that help us get somewhere; they help us accomplish goals. Concepts are all the stronger when we recognize that they arise from our assumptions about the world and our values about it. It is in this sense that the study of language (concepts) is helpful as we can ask who uses what language for what purposes and what a particular concept (language) means for how we interpret social life. Seen this way, concepts are useful or not toward particular ends, and are of questionable value (even dangerous) if the question of what they are being used for is not spelled out. Thus, to inquire about the importance and usefulness of criminalized deviance language means we must (1) distinguish with what goal we ask about its importance and usefulness, and (2) study how this language is used in everyday life. The first is simply this: how does criminalized deviance language help us accomplish our collectively espoused value of equal justice for all[1]? The second will occupy most of this section.

For the sociologist, deviant behavior, as the phrase suggests, refers to behavior that is condemned by society, that is, that which is defined as abnormal, unexpected, unusual, nonstandard, or out of the ordinary.

---

[1] By "equal justice for all" I mean the popular American (constitutionally protected) understanding of equality of all citizens under the various systems of social control (law, policing, imprisonment, etc.). For example, the US Department of Justice webpage includes a description that it is an office charged "to ensure fair and impartial administration of justice for all Americans" (The United, 2012).

While this deviance can include behavior that is both criminalized (behavior that violates formally enacted social rules, e.g., committing "crimes") and non-criminalized (behavior that violates social norms, e.g., rejecting folk customs), as already discussed, in this essay I limit myself to behavior that is criminalized.

The contributions of pragmatists, symbolic interactionists, social constructionists, and labeling theorists toward the sociology of deviance are as unmistakable as their final vision of human beings as constructs of everyday interactions. Thomas's (1923) early-20th-century work sets the foundation with his emphasis on the "definition of the situation," a straightforward distinction arguing that people enter social situations which are already defined. In other words, human beings are born into communities that have already defined the vast majority of situations which any individual will encounter. For example, I was born into a community (United States) where the act of killing a fellow community member was already defined as "murder" and carries significant criminal sanction. Mead (1934) further demonstrated the innate sociality of human action by putting forward the idea that every self not only encounters such ready-made situations, but is indeed constructed by them, that is, that everyone of us is a product of all the interactions we have had and are having with others.

Durkheim (1951) adds the critical distinction that naming (labeling) behavior a "crime," such as killing someone, is more accurately seen as an expression of society's desire to control that behavior than it is a defiance of penal regulations by the person who did the killing. In drawing this distinction he launches a way of thinking that will become known as labeling theory. Howard Becker most clearly distinguishes this power of naming things in *Outsiders* (1963), a study of marijuana users. In this work, which is as much a magnum opus for social construction and symbolic interaction as it is for labeling theory, Becker concludes that marijuana smoking is not seen by users or others as deviance, until social groups make it so by creating it as an infraction (a "crime").

What emerges from this foundational scholarship is that "deviance" does not refer to the quality of a person's behavior, but to the actions of those naming the person's behavior; that "the deviant" is nothing other than the person to whom that behavior has been attached; and that "deviant behavior" is only the behavior that has been labeled as such (Becker, 1963). Thus, from the interactionist/constructionist/labeling perspective, the study of criminalized deviance language promises insight into who is labeling criminality, who is being labeled a "criminal," and what behavior is being labeled criminal. Importantly, using this paradigm scholars can study the language of criminalized deviance and develop insights that elucidate the social construction of justice performances, that is, the routines of the so-called criminal justice system, the development of justice discourse and justice policy, and consequently, justice outcomes (Coyle, 2013).

The importance and usefulness of analyzing criminalized deviance language is easily showcased with examples of studies that examine the everyday language of justice performances. In Mason's edited work *Captured by the Media: Prison Discourse in Popular Culture* (2006), authors highlight how media engage in a process that both reflects and creates a specific discourse about prisons and punishment. The authors demonstrate that the collective performance of media culture constructs punitive public attitudes which, in turn, encourage punitive constructions of "offenders," punitive public policy, and ultimately the greater use of increasingly punitive prisons. Sloop's *The Cultural Prison: Discourse, Prisoners, and Punishment* (1996) pursues similar themes of cultural discourse on prisons and punishment by carefully tracing media discourse from the perspective of rhetorical studies. In a 50-year study of US media coverage, he theorizes four distinct periods of imagining people in prison as either redeemable or "criminal": in the 1950s the person in prison is characterized as an essentially "good" white male facing challenging life circumstances; in the 1960s as an angry black male; in the 1970s this black male in prison is "unmasked" as trapped between his violent nature and an unfairly racially charged society; and in the 1980s he is seen as an incorrigible "bad" person whose behavior justifies a "tough on crime" attitude. These authors show that the study of criminalized deviance language gives insight, for example, into who is labeling deviant behavior (moral entrepreneurs, the media), or who is being labeled a deviant (a group of persons named "offenders," a white male lacking opportunity, and a black male).

Another example demonstrating the importance and usefulness of investigating criminalized deviance language is a series of studies examining deviance language in the legal process. In "Is it Sex or Assault? Erotic versus Violent Language in Sexual Assault Trial Judgments" Bavelas and Coates (2001) scrutinize the language used to describe sexual offenses in British Columbia trial judgments. They find that descriptions are more frequently likely to employ sexual (erotic or affectionate) language than to employ language which demonstrates violence or force. The authors argue that such sexualized descriptions hide both the violence of sexual assault and the experience of the, usually female, victims. In "'Baby' or 'Fetus'?: Language and the Construction of Reality in a Manslaughter

Trial," Danet (1980) highlights how words do not describe so much as they construct facts and intentions in the trial of a doctor who had performed a late term abortion. She details how opposing lawyers create opposite realities through word choice. Depending on the intent to prosecute or defend, the lawyers used either "baby," "child," "the deceased," and "person," or "fetus," "embryo," and "products of conception" language. Finally, in *Just Words: Law, Language, and Power*, Conley and O'Barr (2005) examine how power and ideology pervade the legal process. They show that the work of law is done through careful and intelligent manipulation of language to the distinct advantage of some and to the loss of others. In one example, the authors detail the use of language in court by a lawyer constructing a rape "victim" as being "interested" in her attacker, and in another how language work resulted in the advantageous positioning for one party in a divorce mediation. These studies of language in the legal process demonstrate the work to make a label – and the work to avoid a label. Here, "deviance" does not refer to the quality of a person's behavior, but to the actions of those naming the person's behavior. Similarly, "the deviant" is the person to whom that behavior has been successfully attached, and "deviant behavior" is only the behavior that has been labeled as such.

A final example is taken from my own work – a series of language studies driven by various goals – that I term *Language of Justice* research (see Coyle, 2002; 2010a; 2010b; 2013). I argue that everyday justice discourse takes place within a body of interpretations, metaphors, rhetorical frames, and ultimately ideology, which is rarely acknowledged and is instead accepted as self-evident. In my research, I conduct language studies, which are individual investigations into a word or a phrase commonly used in "criminal justice" discourse. I do these language studies to interfere with and disrupt everyday justice discourse in order to get to the language habits that we have forgotten are generating (and not just describing) our "criminal justice system." In this research, I discover that the language of social control, and "criminal justice" in general, is designed to encounter people of color, as well as those of lower socio-economic status and of certain gender (Coyle, 2010b; 2013).

In another project, a colleague and I demonstrated that the currently occurring discursive shift from "tough on crime" to "smart on crime" does not reflect a change in "criminal justice" ideology that somehow recognizes the racist consequence of the "tough on crime" movement (Altheide and Coyle, 2006). Instead, the shift to "smart on crime" denotes a rhetorical device that is designed to mask the political and economical infeasibility of sustaining the funding of what has become the gargantuan "criminal justice system" (see Kappeler and Kraska, 1999 for a similar analysis of the shift from law enforcement and "crime control" to community policing).

This brief literature review and series of examples demonstrate the interactionist-constructionist understanding that "deviance" does not refer to the quality of a person's behavior, but to the actions of those naming the person's behavior; that "the deviant" is nothing other than the person to whom that behavior has been attached; and that "deviant behavior" is only the behavior that has been labeled as such. The examples of studies that examine the everyday language of justice performances demonstrate the power of studying language to elucidate the social construction of these performances. Finally, the research examined in this section also demonstrates the power and importance of asking the key question of how our "deviance-making" and "justice-making" work correspond with our supposedly commonly accepted values, such as "equal justice for all" (i.e., who is served with such language and who loses). In sum, using the deviance concept scholars can study criminalized language and develop insights that elucidate the social construction of justice performances, that is, the various performances of the so-called criminal justice system, the construction of public justice discourse and justice policy, and consequently justice outcomes.

The boundaries of the deviance concept

As just demonstrated with the example of criminalized language, deviance theory examines abnormal, unexpected, unusual, nonstandard, or out of the ordinary behavior, and provides insight into who labels, who is being labeled, and what behavior is being labeled. As a consequence, deviance sociologists are often examining marginalized behavior (uncommon sexual expressions), marginalized actors (the "criminal"), and marginalized situations (mental illness). Appropriately, students of deviance are thus ever in search of the unusual or non-standard other who is being dominated.

With its emphasis on marginalized minorities, the concept of deviance has had a very specific impact on the study of criminalized behavior. As I showed in the examples of the previous section, this emphasis has fruitfully been employed to deconstruct and analyze some disturbing trends in modern "criminal justice" performances, for example, how the work of law is done through careful and intelligent manipulation of language to the distinct advantage of a privileged few, how "criminal justice" practices in general are designed to encounter people of color (especially black males), and how in courtrooms language is used to transform the violence and force of sexual assault on women into an erotic and affectionate encounter. *However, the emphasis has also come at a cost because the full study of criminalized behavior shows that it is more a deeply shared human expression than it is an aberration.*

To demonstrate this argument I will deconstruct the presentation of the ultimate American liberal "criminal justice" worker who in his 32-year career – more than anyone else in his profession – recognized the very insights about the construction of criminalized behavior that deviance theory so effectively demonstrates. Michael Hennessey, sheriff of the county and city of San Francisco, retired in 2012 as the longest-serving elected official in the history of San Francisco.[2] In a city known for leading the nation in liberal politics, Hennessey distinguished himself as a reformist advocating for education in the jails and the legalization of marijuana in the streets. He took these views long before they were popular – even with progressives – and has been a leading liberal voice throughout his career. However, his constructions also typify the far more common misunderstanding of criminalized behavior.

An analysis of a Hennessey interview (Kransky, 2011), conducted on the occasion of his retirement, reveals all this and more. The very first topic of the interview is the county's jail population. When Kransky asks directly about "what kind of people go to jail," and suggests that it is "the rabble," or "drunks and homeless," "petty criminals," and "petty thieves," Hennessey is quick to agree. Hennessey also adds that "40 percent of people in jails are there for drugs," "25 percent are in for a violent crime," and "a smaller percentage for public nuisance." He then invokes the influence of his friend, the late sociologist and convict criminologist John Irwin, who argued that "county jails keep the undesirables out of the view of the public eye." While he finds this claim to be "to some degree true," he emphasizes that jails are "also a place where people who are charged with very serious violent crimes await disposition of their case" as "society fears violent criminals more, and rightly so." As the interview continues he applauds religion in the jail as it can "get people the values they need to avoid future criminal activity." As I will show, all of this is important.

When the conversation turns to race, the discussion about who is in prison takes a new turn. Hennessey is asked to comment on the fact that while African Americans constitute only 5 percent of the general

---

[2] This discussion was first developed in Coyle (2013).

population, they constitute 55 percent of the jail population. He declares that the imbalance "is one of the most troubling issues that I have had to deal with and had to look at during my entire 32 years as sheriff" and plainly names it "just scandalous" and "a real tragedy." His explanation is that "it comes down to a lot of social factors such as unemployment and unemployment leading to people going to the underground economy to make a living selling drugs" and "many African American families having had generations of people incarcerated and therefore it sort of seems inevitable." He concludes, "It is something that I've brought to the public's attention many times but [it] does not seem to be abating."

When the interview turns to "jail rehabilitation" and "programs," Hennessey declares that "people can change their worldview" and that "people can change," "rehabilitate themselves," and "become productive members of society." As Kransky congratulates him for all his efforts in this area, Hennessey says, "I do think San Francisco is a compassionate city, and will continue to support programs that help ex-offenders get back on their feet." Hennessey also calls for "giving people in custody education," for "getting the riskier population...counselors and therapists," for helping "these men to first recreate their own life and what has caused them to commit violence." Finally, although Hennessey may see problems in his jails, on the whole he likes them. As he says, "People can also learn while they are in jail and essentially take advantage of the time they have to change their lives for the better."

Hennessey's speech about "what kind of people go to jail" is so familiar that most would be hard pressed to recognize its profound inaccuracies. He identifies the people who go to jail as "criminals," drug addicts, and those committing very serious violent "crimes." Yet research tells us otherwise. The first problem is that the complete population of "criminals," drug addicts, and those committing very serious violent "crimes" would include the vast majority of Americans. Research shows that most people habitually violate the law (committing a variety of both nonviolent and violent "crimes" in their lifespan; see Gabor, 1994), that a large proportion of people experiment with or regularly use illegal drugs [more than one-third of all Americans have tried an illicit drug and 22.6 million (one in 13 Americans) are currently illicit drug users; see America's Drug, 1997 and Results From, 2011], and that high numbers of people commit very serious violent "crimes" (e.g., one in four college women in the United States is sexually assaulted and one in six women in the United States will be sexually assaulted in their lifetime – all these usually by someone they know personally; see Fisher et al., 2000 and Tjaden and Thoennes, 1998).

A second problem with Hennessey's construction of "what kind of people go to jail," and with the accompanying constructions of "crime," "criminals," and "criminal justice," is that he never acknowledges that the majority of social harms (economic damage, violent acts, and death) derive from the widely ignored white collar "crimes," environmental "crimes," and corporate or state "crimes." By consequence, he fails to recognize that instead of being in his jails, these persons are rarely counted, massively under-policed, and even less frequently arrested, prosecuted, or incarcerated. Research shows that the annual cost of white collar "crime" alone is more than 80 times that of the total amount stolen in all thefts (Reiman and Leighton, 2010). Similarly, the annual cost of antitrust and trade violations has been reported as more than 60 times that of the total amounts in all thefts (Cullen et al., 1987). Although the sum of a year's worth of robberies, burglaries, larcenies, and motor vehicle thefts will represent only a fraction of the cost of a single corporate "crime" (e.g., Enron), most harms committed by corporations will go as unnoticed and unstudied as they are unprosecuted (in its first and last study of the kind, the Justice Department found that approximately two-thirds of large corporations violated the law; see Clinard and Yeager, 1987). Finally, while the FBI reports the annual US murder rate is about 16,000 people, more than 70,000 die in the same time period from product-related accidents (Friedrichs, 1996), and these numbers do not include the thousands of annual deaths connected to corporate pollution, such as the more than 11,000 who die annually from industrial pollution alone (Steingraber, 1997).

Hennessey's constructions – and for that matter almost all constructions of the "criminal justice system" – not only fail to recognize the mythology of "the criminal" deviant, but in fact perpetuate it. Hennessey does this most clearly when he speaks about the need for religion in jail to "get people the values they need to avoid future criminal activity," for "getting the riskier population...counselors and therapists," for helping "these men to recreate their own life and what has caused them to commit violence"; or the need for "rehabilitation," "giving people in custody education," and "programs" where "people can change," where "people can change their worldview," "rehabilitate themselves," and "become productive members of society." Yet the meaninglessness of his construction in the face of the ubiquity of serious and non-serious "crimes," and the targeting of only some for participation in the "criminal justice system" appear to escape him.

When asked about race and incarceration rates in his jails, Hennessey finds the reality that African Americans constitute only 5 percent of the general population, yet constitute 55 percent of the jail population "just scandalous" and "a real tragedy." His explanation blames the "victims" (they are "unemployed," "sell drugs," and "come from families with incarceration history"). Blind to the selection process, he concludes that inequity is inevitable, and comforts himself by assuring us that he has done his job by "bringing it to the public's attention many times."

The words that the hyper-liberal – for the United States – Hennessey uses to talk about the people living in his jails and the images that they evoke are all *cliché*. The discourse of his less liberal colleagues is only more entrenched in this mythology of "the criminal." As social construction-ists argue, these justice interpretations are maintained as "real" because we continue to use them and assume that they are valid and "objec-tively" true (Berger and Luckmann, 1966). In Thomas's (1923) terms, our society has been remarkably consistent in "defining the situation" of "what kind of people go to jail"; so successful in fact that moral entre-preneurs anywhere on the political spectrum employ the same "crime" and "criminal" language.

In more ways than one, as it turns out, the only accurate way to speak about "what kind of people go to jail" is to ask "what kind of people are selected for jail?" This conclusion comfortably fits the interactionist/ constructionist/labeling understanding that "deviance" does not refer to the quality of a person's behavior, but to the actions of those naming the person's behavior, that "the deviant" is nothing other than the person to whom that behavior has been attached, and that "deviant behavior" is only the behavior that has been labeled as such. *But there is something that is wanting in the face of this ubiquity of "deviance," "deviants," and "deviant behavior" in our social life: a way to think about whose "deviancy" is socially tended to and whose is not.*

Put another way, given the ubiquity of harms ("crimes") in human relationships, to speak of harm-making as deviant is nonsensical and nullifies the very concept of deviance that got us this far. Sociologically speaking, we now need a concept to distinguish how some criminalized behavior is treated differently than other criminalized behavior. I think negotiating all this with the concept "difference," as I already did in the previous sentence, is the way forward.

That the sociological usefulness of the deviance concept has bounda-ries in the study of criminalized human behavior does not mean that the concept is dead or any less helpful than we thought before. As discussed earlier, concepts are strategies that help us get somewhere and help us accomplish goals. In the study of criminalized behavior, using the concept of deviance has allowed us to develop insights and critiques that elucidate much of the social construction of justice performances, including having brought us to the point of recognizing that the social control work of the "criminal justice system," far from referencing an unusual and non-standard other, can only reference attempts of dominance by some over others. I am simply recognizing here that criminalized deviance language, like the language of genocide discussed earlier, is a language whose habitual use does more than simply describe: it constructs and continuously regenerates not only the very architecture of our descriptions and our arguments about persons, but followed also creates unambiguous interpretations of them and invites (and often requires) specific actions toward them. Certainly, as we saw in the Hennessey case, such language makes otherwise unsavory dominance palatable: inequity, racism, sexism, classism, and the unimaginable horror we call the "criminal justice system."

Shifting concepts: from deviance to difference

The deviance concept is critical for understanding the mythology of "crime," "criminal," and "criminal justice" situations – an altogether sacred discourse that is rarely challenged. The deviance concept also helps us distinguish the human work to sustain social norms and minimize transgressions. But where the deviance concept has not helped us get to and the goal it has not helped us achieve is the analysis of how some criminalized behavior is treated differently than other criminalized behavior. Put differently, the deviance concept has not helped us think about whose criminalized behavior is socially tended to and whose is not.

In the end, within the study of criminalized behavior, the deviance concept has brought us to the distinction that because transgression ("crime") is a ubiquitous social performance, we are all, at least in part, deviants.[3] If we remain with Durkheim's (1951) distinction that naming

---

[3] As Gottfredson and Hirschi (1986) first demonstrated, the concept of "career criminals" (also known as "chronic offenders," "habitual offenders," and the like) that claims there exists a group of "offenders" whose "criminality" spans the length of a career cannot in any way be demonstrated. In fact, the opposite case (that after 13 years of age "offending" rates drop precipitously and continuously) is probably the most clearly demonstrated fact in the disciplines of criminology and criminal justice. Yet, to this day, the most frequent justification for incarceration schemes is the argument for imprisoning "career criminals," and addressing this fictional population remains a staple of criminal justice research, federal funding of such research, and criminal justice policy.

(labeling) transgressive behavior a "crime" is a healthy expression of society's desire to control that behavior, that is, that we are socially organized to reject norm violations, then *we need to re-conceptualize the social response to transgression ("crime") as the management of difference (and not deviance), and study how some difference is responded to with the "criminal justice system" (is not accepted) and some difference is responded to by reconstructing it into something else or ignoring it (is accepted).*

While I have not encountered research that examines the social negotiation of transgression ("crime") with the difference concept, there are studies that, when examined in this light, clearly illustrate its promise. One example is Evans's (2002) study of the hurdles indigenous peoples face in Australian courts. As he says of them, "In the case that the social and economic problems can be overcome, they face problems related to the intellectual structures of the court and the language and philosophical beliefs that the court systems are based on" (p. 127). Evans is pointing to how the dominance of Australian (Euro-centric) justice discourse in the courts makes it difficult, if not impossible, for a non-European people to get anything resembling meaningful legal justice. In the United States, the debate about the constitutionality of peyote use between federal courts and some Native American communities is a parallel issue (Pohlman, 2004). Evident here is that the dominant justice discourse, whether in Australia or the United States, is *different* than that of the indigenous peoples, and this prevents them from receiving a fair hearing as the social and "criminal justice system" they encounter is constructed on the ontology and epistemology of the first; their justice discourse *differs*, and because it is subordinate it is suppressed.

Haviland's "Ideologies of Language: Some Reflections on Language and US Law" (2003) shows how language ideologies influence legal outcomes. In this study he exposes how in the US actors using a language *different* than English are interpreted as inherently offensive and dangerous. Bower's (1989) analysis of legislative language sheds light on how certain legal processes, such as political trials, fundamentally occur within an established body of written law that fails to consider how our justice discourse ignores the reality of dominant discourse that *differs* from that of silenced others.

Arrigo (2001) examines the impact of *differing* discourse on the lives of persons characterized as Mentally Ill Offenders (MIOs). Through ethnography of the lives of three MIOs, Arrigo powerfully demonstrates the impact of medico-legal discourse by showing their entrapment in either "mad" or "bad" identity categories and their subsequent transcarceration (being shuffled between the mental health and "criminal justice" systems). In sum, Arrigo argues that powerful agents (medico-legal professionals) choose language (labels such as "dangerous" or "insane") that construct *different* discourses (medical, legal) with immense power to define MIOs.

With these examples I aim to demonstrate that difference is a socio-logical concept which grows out of the deviance concept and that it is an analytic tool for the study and encouragement of justice. While it was the concept of deviance that brought us to the distinction that we are all maintainers and transgressors of the social order, the concept of difference will take us to the next step of negotiating with what variance we want to live and with what variance we do not want to live. Put differently, having traveled long and well with deviance, we arrive at difference which invites sociologists to analyze human relationships from a perspective that moves beyond normal and deviant, and toward an equality based on similar participation in difference. It also opens new conceptual roadmaps to think about nonviolent, non-punitive, and abolitionist social control efforts.

The importance and sociological usefulness of the difference concept

In this essay I am arguing for a paradigm shift in our study of crimi-nalized deviance. I advocate using the difference concept to grow our understanding and analysis of how some "criminal behavior" is treated differently than other "criminal behavior" and what this difference demonstrates.

There are other reasons to be excited about using the difference concept. For one, it invites a rethinking of labeling, or the theory of under-standing criminalized deviance as that which is painted as abnormal. It could finally force our attention on the fact that this "abnormality" is commonly not very deviant, but rather a norm, that is, that which we have judged non-normative is hardly so. In the criminological sense, deviance is a category that belongs to us all, for as far this deviancy goes, we are all deviant, which is to say we are all normal. The difference concept can help us negotiate an equitable balance of deviancy at the dinner table.

Another is that since, as Matza (1969) pointed out, applying stigma-tizing deviant labels only promotes such behavior in a self-fulfilling fashion, employing a discourse of difference will avoid this problem by encouraging recognition that we are all faced with living amid difference.

As Tannenbaum (1938, p. 20), the grandfather of labeling theory put it, "The way out is through a refusal to dramatize the evil."

Difference also invites us to significantly reconsider Becker's *Outsiders* (1963), as it is not only that social groups create deviance by making the rules whose infraction then constitutes deviance, but it is also that social groups respond to only some of the deviance that actually all are involved in. In other words, while all are outsiders, only some are singled out to be named as such.

Most importantly, using difference to conceptualize justice in human relationships shifts sociological analysis from distinctions of abnormal, unexpected, unusual, nonstandard, and out of the ordinary criminal behavior (mostly a myth), to an analysis of justice as fair and similar participation of dissimilar (diverse) persons living in different languages as well as different discourses. This is the unavoidable semiotic conclusion that all language work is actually ideology work (Voloshinov, 1973) and the insight that while every conception of justice rests on a conception of rationality, there is no rationality that is not a rationality of some discourse (MacIntyre, 1998).

Ahead await more potential disagreements than anytime has afforded us before. Given our environment – where with time communication only increases in quantity and speed – our differences are closer to each other and more in competition than ever before. Thinking in terms of difference not only accurately articulates our growing experience of each other, it might also be a required conceptual tool for our very survival.

References

Altheide, David and Michael J. Coyle (2006) "Smart on Crime: The New Language for Prisoner Release", *Crime, Media, Culture*, 2(4), 286–303.

America's Drug Abuse Profile (1997) National Criminal Justice Reference Service. Retrieved 30 June, 2012 (https://www.ncjrs.gov/htm/chapter2.htm).

Arrigo, Bruce (2001) "Transcarceration: A Constitutive Ethnography of Mentally Ill 'Offenders'". *The Prison Journal*, 81(2), 162–186.

Bavelas, J. and L. Coates (2001) "Is it Sex or Assault? Erotic versus Violent Language in Sexual Assault Trial Judgments", *Journal of Social Distress*, 10(4), 29–40.

Becker, Howard (1963) *Outsiders* (New York: Free Press).

Berger, Peter and Thomas Luckmann (1966) *The Social Construction of Reality: A Treatise in the Sociology of Knowledge* (New York: Anchor Books).

Bosmajian, Haig (1983) *The Language of Oppression* (Lanham, MD: University Press of America).

—— (1992) *Metaphor and Reason in Judicial Opinions* (Carbondale, IL: Southern Illinois University Press).

Bowers, F. (1989) *Linguistic Aspects of Legislative Expression* (Vancouver, Canada: University of British Columbia Press).

Clinard, M.B. and P.C. Yeager (1987) "Illegal Corporate Behavior, 1975–1976", ICPSR07855-v3. Ann Arbor, MI: Inter-university Consortium for Political and Social Research.

Conley, J.M. and W.M. O'Barr (2005) *Just Words: Law, Language, and Power* (Chicago, IL: University of Chicago Press).

Coyle, Michael J. (2002) "Language, Culture and the Interpretation of 'Victim': An Analysis of 'Innocent Victim' in Media", Presented at the annual meeting of the American Society of Criminology, Chicago, IL.

—— (2010a) "Language, Metaphysics and Deviancy: Delineating the 'Evil' Criminal Other", in M. Herzog-Evans and I. Dréan-Rivette (eds.), *Transnational Criminology* (Nijmegen, The Netherlands: Wolf Legal Publishers).

——(2010b) "Notes on the Study of Language: Toward a Critical Race Criminology", *Western Criminology Review*, 11(1), 11–19.

—— (2013) *Talking Criminal Justice: Language and the Just Society* (London, England: Routledge).

Cullen, F.T., W.J. Maakestad, and G. Cavender (1987) *Corporate Crime under Attack: The Ford Pinto Case and Beyond* (Cincinnati, OH: Anderson Publishing Company).

Danet, B. (1980) "'Baby' or 'Fetus'?: Language and the Construction of Reality in a Manslaughter Trial", *Semiotica*, 32(3), 187–219.

Durkheim, Emile (1951) *Suicide: A Study in Sociology* (Glencoe, IL: Free Press).

Evans, J. (2002) "Indigenous Australians: Language and the Law", *International Journal for the Semiotics of Law*, 15(1), 127–141.

Fisher, B.S., F.T. Cullen, and M.G. Turner (2000) *The Sexual Victimization of College Women* (Washington, DC: National Institute of Justice and Bureau of Justice Statistics).

Foucault, Michel (1973) *The Order of Things: An Archaeology of the Human Sciences* (New York: Vintage).

Friedrichs, D.O. (2003) *Trusted Criminals: White Collar Crime in Contemporary Society* (Belmont, CA: Wadsworth Publishing).

Gabor, T. (1994) *Everybody Does It! Crime by the Public* (Toronto, Canada: University of Toronto Press).

Gottfredson, Michael and Travis Hirschi (1986) "The True Value of Lambda Would Appear to be Zero: An Essay on Career Criminals, Criminal Careers, Selective Incapacitation, Cohort Studies and Related Topics", *Criminology*, 24(2), 213–234.

Haviland, J.B. (2003) "Ideologies of Language: Some Reflections on Language and US Law", *American Anthropologist*, 105(4), 764–774.

Kappeler, Victor E. and Peter B. Kraska (1999) "Policing Modernity: Scientific and Community-Based Violence on Symbolic Playing Fields", in Stuart Henry and Dragan Milovanovic (eds.), *Constitutive Criminology at Work: Applications to Crime and Justice* (Albany, NY: SUNY Press).

Kransky, M. (2011) "Exit Interview with Sheriff Michael Hennessey", *Forum*, KQED. Retrieved 27 June, 2012 (www.kqed.org/a/forum/R201112151000).

MacIntyre, Alasdair (1998) *Whose Justice? Which Rationality?* (Notre Dame, IN: University of Notre Dame Press).

Mason, P. (2006) *Captured by the Media: Prison Discourse in Popular Culture* (Portland, OR: Willan).

Matza, David (1969) *On Becoming Deviant* (Englewood Cliffs, NJ: Prentice Hall).

Mead, George H. (1934) *Mind, Self and Society: From the Standpoint of a Social Behaviorist* (Chicago, IL: The University of Chicago Press).

Pohlman, H.L. (2004) *Constitutional Debate in Action: Civil Rights and Liberties* (Lanham, MD: Rowman & Littlefield Publishers).

Reiman, J. and P. Leighton (2010) *The Rich Get Richer and the Poor Get Prison: Ideology, Class and Criminal Justice*, 9th edn. (Cambridge, UK: Pearson).

Results from the 2010 National Survey on Drug Use and Health (2011) Summary of National Findings. Rockville, MD: Substance Abuse and Mental Health Services Administration.

Sapir, Edward (1956), as cited in Whorf, Benjamin Lee (1956) *Language, Thought, and Reality* (Cambridge, MA: The Technology Press of MIT).

Sloop, J. (1996) *The Cultural Prison: Discourse, Prisoners, and Punishment* (Tuscaloosa, AL: The University of Alabama Press).

Steingraber, S. (1997) *Living Downstream: An Ecologist Looks at Cancer and the Environment* (New York: Addison-Wesley).

Tannenbaum, Frank (1938) *Crime and Community* (New York: Columbia University Press).

Thomas, William I. (1923) *The Unadjusted Girl: With Cases and Standpoint for Behavior Analysis* (Boston, MA: Little, Brown and Company).

Tjaden, P. and N. Thoennes (1998) *Prevalence, Incidence and Consequences of Violence Against Women Survey* (Washington, DC: National Institute of Justice and Centers for Disease Control & Prevention).

The United States Department of Justice (2012) "Mission Statement", Retrieved 19 June, 2012 (www.justice.gov/about/about.html).

Voloshinov, V. (1973) *Marxism and the Philosophy of Language*. Translated by M. Ladislav and I.R. Titunik (New York: Seminar Press).

5
The "Death of Deviance" and Stagnation of 20th-Century Criminology

Mark Horsley

Introduction

The publication of Colin Sumner's *The Sociology of Deviance: An Obituary* (1994) marked a critical transformation in the theorization of crime and criminality. In a work that offered a narrative history of criminological theory from Durkheim's *Sociological Method* (1982 [1895]) to Taylor et al.'s *The New Criminology* (2003 [1973]), Sumner explored the rise and fall of early sociological explanations for criminality, the emergence of a new perspective and a radical transformation of the discipline during the middle decades of the 20th century. The original "sociology of deviance" – the book's initial object of study – emerged during the 1920s as an early attempt to offer a sociological theory of criminal causation. Its reliance on a normative perspective, however, left little room for the putative plurality of social norms in light of the counter-cultural ideals of the 1960s. In these circumstances Sumner goes on to identify an increasingly forceful pluralist critique that placed greater emphasis on the potential illegitimacy of normative prohibitions, the censorious nature of centralized power and hysterical social reactions to the perceived deviance of subordinate groups.

In Sumner's estimation this social reaction perspective became increasingly symptomatic of criminological theory during the latter decades of the 20th century to the extent that the discipline looked to be undergoing a marked paradigm shift leaving behind many of its founding concepts for a more "mature", "enlightened" interpretation of its subject matter. While noting that the old "sociology of deviance" seemed to be running out of steam, variously describing it as "outmoded", "stagnant" or "stalled" and even likening it to the terrain of a battlefield – empty, scarred, deathly silent – the emerging social reaction perspective attracted far more affirmative discussion. In Sumner's (2012, p. 165) analysis, "The concept of social censure has considerably more descriptive and explanatory power, is research generative and can be deployed irrespective of politics". In this way, Sumner's narrative, while not uncritical of the developing perspective, effectively captured the criminological zeitgeist providing a key statement of how the discipline saw itself during the decades running up to the new millennium, finding a deeply appreciative audience and a ready-made home amid the wider criminological literature (for typical assessments, see O'Connell, 1995; Venkatesh, 1995; Roberts, 1996).

In this way an emerging "sociology of censure" arguably altered the discipline's surface texture, repurposed criminological theory and even realigned the ultimate aims of criminological analysis to focus more on media discourse, political portrayal and the effects of representation. In this chapter we look back on the resultant intellectual transformation from a 21st-century perspective in order to critically explore its long-term impact. We divide this discussion into three component parts. The first part puts a little more flesh on Sumner's observed transformation in order to fully appreciate the ideas and concepts that define both the "sociology of deviance" and the subsequent "sociology of censure". We then look again at social censure's explanatory capacity based on a growing critique of its political, philosophical and ideological roots (see, for instance, Hall et al., 2008; Hall, 2012). The final part considers the possibility that criminology is currently returning to some of the ideas that once characterized "sociology of deviance" with particular reference to growing interest in the socio-cultural forces behind criminality.

From "deviance" to "censure"

The "sociology of deviance" grew out of Durkheimian social theory and its attempts to establish a "realist" social science that would locate social interaction within a broader cultural, political and economic context. Its purpose was to move beyond the "methodological individualism" that marked 19th-century positivism's theorization of crime and deviance to offer a holistic analysis of relationships between social context and individual action based on empirical observation of the social world. Where most pre-existing theoretical frameworks held "social facts" such as crime to be artifacts of individual pathology, Durkheimian sociology began to recognize the ineffable contingency of social action. In other words,

Durkheim began to offer explanations for social phenomena grounded in practical and philosophical context, promoting a "phenomenological perspective ... which challenged the crude [individualist] empiricism of the positivist vision, and offered new images of the thoroughly social character of vision ... [making] it altogether more difficult to separate the phenomenon allegedly observed from the emotional, political, linguistic and cultural conditions of the observation" (Sumner, 1994, p. 10).

While there is much more to be said about the complexities of Durkheimian sociology, the assertion that social interaction is driven by much more than the internal nature of the individual was quite a radical idea for the early part of the 20th century. It held that the social world was a product of socio-ethical ideals, practical circumstances and the interplay between people, organizations and collective moral sentiments rather than the clash of isolated individuals, some of whom with singular pathological defects. This basic idea appeared in a few different guises throughout Durkheim's work but perhaps most instructively in his assertion that increasingly complex modern societies were losing many of their old moral certainties amid the creeping decline of organized religion and the rise of an industrial economy that severed individual attachments to instructive moral sentiments. Where Western society perhaps seemed to have come from a single moral order, Durkheim (2002 [1897]) noted that the growing complexity of social relations seemed to isolate individuals from the normative values that structured interaction heralding a condition of normlessness that turned pre-existing social dispositions toward self-preservation – greed, interpersonal competition and material acquisition – resulting in growing deviation from established norms amongst those worst affected by the rapid pace of social change in industrializing societies.

The Chicago School of Sociology started out with the assertion that crime and deviance needed to be treated as concrete aspects of social reality rooted in contingent circumstance rather than the base nature of the individual. With this in mind they set out to explore the significant context of deviance and quickly noticed that all manner of social problems, including criminality, seemed to map disproportionately onto run-down inner city areas primarily inhabited by disadvantaged groups. It started to look as if there is a connection between the two, as if "disorganized" circumstances lead into increased deviance from pre-existing social norms, including acquisitive and violent criminality. In this way, much of the Chicago School's theoretical approach, heavily influenced by Durkheim, shows more than a passing concern for the possibility that deleterious social circumstances, as a result of their effect on moral life, effectively pushed those in dire straits to otherwise alien forms of social action. Within this theoretical framework we find the foundations of social disorganization theory (Shaw and McKay, 1972 [1942]), Sutherland's (1992 [1924]) differential association and Mertonian (1938) strain all of which came out of a tacitly Durkheimian concern for collective morality, the cultural pressures of industrial/consumer society and their deviant implications. In the latter case, for example, Robert Merton specifically argued that people confronted by the inability to live up to social goals within a materialistic culture potentially adapt to the resultant sense of inadequacy by dropping any remaining allegiance to prohibitive moral norms in favor of more forceful competition for wealth and status.

In other words, the "sociology of deviance" was primarily interested in criminal motivation, in the forces that drive people into the acquisitive, combative and often violent behaviors that generally constitute criminality. It may well be the case that none of the Chicago School's ideas, nor, for that matter, any of the theories that followed in their wake, provide an entirely persuasive account of motivating cultural forces but as foundations on which to build they collectively represent an interesting and engaging attempt to explore a vital aspect of criminology. The sociology of deviance was a distinct and purposeful attempt to grapple with the fundamental problem of criminal causation, or, as recently phrased, to explain, "why individuals or corporate bodies are willing to risk the infliction of harm on others in order to further their own instrumental or expressive interests" (Hall, 2012, p. 1).

Most importantly, however, Sumner (1994) notes that the "sociology of deviance" was bound up with the radical change of direction in Western politics that gave rise to European social democracy and the American "New Deal". The privations of the Great Depression, not to mention two world wars, soured Western cultural relationships with 19th-century *laissez faire,* leading British and American populations to demand major improvements in their social circumstances through new institutions and egalitarian policy change (see Galbraith, 1994; Freiden, 2006).

The sociology of deviance became entwined with the resulting political project as the empirical elaboration of the social world allowed for clearer identification of problems and more purposeful formulation of corrective policy. Its understanding of social ills and their apparent relationship with industrialism's rapid pace of social change naturally flowed into welfare programs, job creation schemes and new social institutions that dramatically improved everyday life (see Hutton, 1996,

2003) while working against the forces that notionally pushed people into criminality. In the hands of administrators and political pragmatists, however, the sociology of deviance, even within its apparently Durkheimian perspective, quickly returned to much older concepts of individual pathology and personal failing. The conceptual advances of the early 20th century reverted to "casual condescension and mindless jargon justifying full intervention in the lives of the powerless and poor...theoretical advances became mere subliminal references and the old concepts and prejudices openly structured the surface text" (Sumner, 1994, pp. 130–131). The sociology of deviance, it seemed, simply provided a veneer of intellectual respectability for those with a political interest in castigating the disadvantaged and justifying authoritarian intervention in their lives.

Where the sociology of deviance concerned itself with social ills and their causative impact on criminality, the decline of those problems coupled with a seemingly inexorable rise in recorded crime in step with an increasingly authoritarian response all but forced a change of perspective. If criminality was not simply the product of social ills – an observation amply demonstrated by rising crime amid vaguely egalitarian social policy and massive improvements in social conditions on both sides of the Atlantic (Reiner, 2007) – its causation, it seemed, must lie elsewhere, perhaps even in the social democratic intrusion of the state into everyday life. With this possibility ringing in their ears, the 1960s generation of social theorists internalized the growing philosophical rejection of centralized power at the heart of contemporary politics (Frank, 1999) molding it into the criminological observation that the state's efforts to maintain social control exacerbated the "crime problem" through constant expansion of the criminal law and the effects of getting wound up with justice systems. In line with a broad labeling perspective adapted from the sociological work of Erving Goffman (1963) and Edwin Lemert (1972), criminology started to concentrate more on how the power to create laws and apply their associated censures effectively generates "crime" and "deviance" where earlier there may have been only neutral social action. In Becker's (1963) often repeated terms,

> social groups create deviance by making the rules whose infraction constitutes deviance, and by applying those rules to particular people and labelling them outsiders. From this point of view deviance is not a quality of the act...but rather a consequence of the application by others of rules and sanctions to an "offender". (p. 9)

In other words, the discipline turned its attention to the "deviance of the lawmakers", the "censorious" advancement of social control over individual freedom, the power of definition vested in political institutions and the role of public discourse in criminal justice. What we have in the work of early labeling theorists is the beginning of a paradigm shift in criminological theory, a set of ideas that have come to dominate the discipline over the next few decades at least partially eclipsing the concept of crime as normative transgression leading to the assertion that this latter disposition was all but dead, the core assertion of Sumner's (1994) obituary.

After the "death of deviance"

The "sociology of censure" entered criminology during the 1960s with symbolic interactionism's adaptation of American phenomenology and the assertion that the societal reaction to perceived deviance was perhaps the most important factor driving the escalation of recorded crime rates on both sides of the Atlantic. In this original form what became labeling theory argued that minor lifestyle differences become the first movements of sustained deviance by provoking wider society into an excessive crackdown on youthful hijinks. The application of a deviant "label" then forces affected individuals to construct social identity amid ongoing records of past misdeeds that color their social relationships, erode legitimate opportunities and, as a result, ensure their allegiance to deviant lifestyles. In other words, the label effectively "spoils" (Goffman, 1963) individual identity creating a self-fulfilling prophecy in which society's attempts to buttress social norms exacerbate deviancy, increase the profile of social problems and generate public demand for a punitive response.

If we jump forward into the 1960s, we find these ideas rapidly assuming the mantle of dominant paradigm. In his well-known study of London drug culture, for example, Jock Young (1971) argued that society's punitive reaction tied his research subjects into their drug-taking identity, amplifying initially insignificant levels of deviance by raising the public profile of their offenses. Much the same narrative is to be found in Cohen's (2002 [1972]) work on British "subcultures" in which he argued that efforts to maintain social norms and regulate interpersonal conduct reinforce potentially criminal deviancy by further alienating offenders from mainstream social norms, driving their deviancy to new heights and generating demand for an even more punitive response. These ideas, however, came to a head with critical criminology and its attempts to locate both crime and criminal justice discourse within inalienable class conflict. In Hall's (2012) terms,

> Generally, there are three major themes to critical criminology: 1) criminologists should focus on why some people and not others are labelled as criminals rather than ... the characteristics that distinguish criminals from non-criminals; 2) moral panics about street crime are engineered to justify harsh and authoritarian laws; 3) the criminal justice system is a tool used for the maintenance of the status quo and serves the interests only of the powerful members of society. (p. 109)

Taylor et al. (2003 [1973]), for instance, asserted that criminal justice places undue emphasis on the "crimes of the powerless" whilst the far more troublesome transgressions of the relatively powerful classes often pass without comment because justice itself is an artifact of class power. What's more, they argued, the fundamental conflicts at the heart of Marxist philosophy meant that all manner of "deviants", through their rejection of biased social norms, constituted a proto-revolutionary vanguard whose "creative resistance" to mainstream society engendered wholly disproportionate criminalization and reactionary social control. With this in mind the business of criminological theory was to redress the balance; to portray "criminals" as potential folk heroes rather than the "folk devils" they were made out to be by authoritarian powers. What mainstream society successfully portrayed as disintegrative, harmful forms of social interaction inimical to social order were, for the new criminologists, actually reassertions of human freedom amid the over-bearing oppression of social democratic – in America read "New Deal" – bureaucracy. In their terms, "for us ... *deviance* is normal – in the sense that men are now consciously involved (in the prisons that are contemporary society and in the real prisons) in asserting their human diversity ... The task is to create a society in which the facts of human diversity, whether personal, organic or social, are not subject to the power to criminalise" (p. 282).

In this way criminological theory benefited from a notable paradigm shift in which social reaction theory, labeling, criminalization and moral panics repurposed the discipline, turning it away from underlying socio-cultural motivations toward the castigation of "authoritarian" state power, social control, media discourse and inequalities of representation. Furthermore, these ideas remain a substantial force in 21st-century criminology. Cohen's (2002 [1972]) take on moral panics, for example, seems to have found its way into the common lexicon as an abstract but apparently naturalistic description of social life that is constantly recycled with every new turn in criminal justice discourse. Whether it's child abduction and pedophilia (Cavanagh, 2007; Marsh and Melville, 2011), white-collar crime (Levi, 2009) or 9/11 and the threat of terrorism (Rothe and Muzzatti, 2004) someone takes the opportunity of a publication in which, no matter what the subject, it's all just an issue of over-representation.

The same emphasis on social reaction also finds its way into "cultural criminology", perhaps the most significant development of the 1990s, which "references the increasing analytical attention that many criminologists now give to popular culture constructions, and especially mass media constructions, of crime and crime control" (Ferrell, 1999, p. 395). In fact, cultural criminology continually draws on the labeling and critical criminology tradition to construct a narrative of political opposition around low-level criminality and frequently claims to have uncovered forms of "creative resistance" to authoritarian governance (see, for instance, Presdee, 2000). Many of cultural criminology's research conclusions follow a pattern that has not changed all that much in the past 40 years running from the observation of low-level deviance through public reaction to amplification. Ferrell et al.'s (2008) recent invitation to broader "cultural" analysis of criminal justice discourse, for instance, summarizes some of their recent work on "crime and resistance":

> When gentrification and "urban redevelopment" drive late capitalist urban economies, when urban public spaces are increasingly converted to privatized consumption zones, graffiti comes under particular attack by legal and economic authorities as an aesthetic threat to cities' economic vitality. In such a context legal authorities aggressively criminalize graffiti, corporate media campaigns construct graffiti writers as violent vandals – and graffiti writers themselves become more organized and politicized in response. (p. 17)

In this vein, the social reaction perspective has contributed much to the continued development of criminological theory, which has singularly benefited from a variety of new ideas, each of which was associated with a critical perspective on the effects of official discourse. We might point, for example, to the role of politicians and corporate media in stoking up public fears, the reasons why some harmful acts and not others attract criminal prohibition and the political function of a "culture of fear" in legitimizing the sort of authoritarian governance that threatens to erode civil liberties.

If we return our analysis to the philosophical context, however, we might suggest that the "sociology of censure" was also rooted in political philosophy. Where it is only slightly simplistic to say that post-war society invested in bureaucratic regulation for the betterment of social conditions, the dominant political ideals of the 1960s and 1970s identified the same regulation as the root of socio-economic stagnation along with a consequent need to reassert "every person's claim to maximized private freedom ... the unrestrained liberty to express autonomous desires and have them respected and institutionalised by society at large" (Judt, 2010, p. 87). It rejected "any form of *determination* liable to restrict the self-definition and self-fulfilment of *individuals* [original emphasis]" (Boltanski and Chiapello, 2005, p. 433) and associated the expansion of social regulation with anything perceived to be wrong with that system of governance.

In other words, mainstream political philosophy came to argue for the sanctity of the individual, the moral correctness of radical self-determination and, conversely, the illegitimacy of social expectation, restrictive norms and other constraints on "freedom of choice". The idea that "the state" excessively constrained individual freedom came to typify cultural discourse during the latter decades of the 20th century as various groups claimed that one or another social norm prevented them from fully expressing their individuality, "letting it all hang out" and generally "being themselves". The new political and cultural paradigm preached the separation of the individual from collective authority, the ethical sanctity of self-determination and the necessity of "tolerance", all of which quickly ascended to the status of dominant ideology (see Frank, 1999; Hedges, 2011) becoming incredibly forceful in both the cultural and economic fields of social activity. Where some adopted the idea of individual liberty to call for increased cultural freedom, emancipation from the monotony of work and greater flexibility in social life, others claimed the same rejection of centralized power for their attempts to roll back economic oversight, liberate the finance industry and bring the state into line with the demands of continued capital accumulation (Galbraith, 2008).

When these ideas filtered into criminological theory, they turned the discipline toward a detailed study of the application of stigma and the possibility that "deviant" labels effectively push people into criminality as they try to maintain social identity within reduced life chances. The social reaction perspective thus came with its own take on criminal causation, its own way of explaining why and how people get involved in socially destructive criminality. In this schema, however, criminal causation rests not on odious circumstances – poverty, deprivation, exclusion – and deteriorating social ethics but on the idea that deviance signals active construction of social meaning on the part of labeled individuals and provides criminology with a significant illustration of "innate human freedom". In other words, it suggests that criminality allows labeled individuals to negotiate and construct meaning within a society that holds them in contempt, coming up with all manner of justifications, explanations, excuses and dismissals (Albas and Albas, 2003) that allow them to freely integrate deviance into their understanding of selfhood and claim a sense of identity from a society that excludes them from legitimate pursuits. The social reaction schema, drawing on symbolic interactionism and C. Wright Mills's (1940) "vocabularies of motive", effectively argues that crime and deviance are artifacts of self-determination, expressions of inalienable freedom, amid the conservative moralization common to over-bearing states and corporate media outlets. The key intimation of course being that the labeled individuals would have no need and possibly no reason to construct social meaning by amplifying their deviance if society could simply refrain from putting them in that position.

The idea that crime and deviance are products of stigmatized individuals' attempts to negotiate, acquire and preserve social meaning on an ad-hoc basis, however, brings us to one of the greatest problems with the social reaction paradigm and late-20th-century criminological theory. When it comes to actually explain why people get involved in criminality, social reaction relies on a concept of motive that excludes ideology and social ethics in favor of a distinctly individualist, almost rationalist interpretation of criminal causation. The idea that motive comes down to explanations and excuses offered by self-positing subjects in light of socially assigned stigma concentrates on surface detail at the expense of underlying causes – any form of social action, we might suggest, involves an immediate choice of whether to partake or refrain and that choice necessarily occurs within a single mentality but social reaction mistakes the internality of said choice for motivation. In other words, it trades on the everyday meaning of "motivation" as a proximate, conscious and inherently individual reason that colors social action in the moment so as not to engage with the more sociological possibility of subconscious ideological precepts that inform momentary decision making at a much deeper level, influencing the ideas and preconceptions that affect the way such choices are made. In this vein, Hadfield (1955, quoted in Campbell, 1996, pp. 102–103) suggested that "motivation" can be interpreted in one of two ways: "when…we say that the 'motive for the crime was theft', we mean that this was the 'end in view' which moved the prisoner to commit the crime ... it would be equally true to say that the motive for the crime was avarice ... in which case we use 'motive' to mean the instinctive motive or *force* which impelled him to perform the theft [original emphasis]". What's missing from the social reaction perspective is any deeper understanding of social ethics, the ideas, concepts and common philosophical dispositions which, in keeping with Hadfield's example, might build "avarice" into broader socio-cultural ideals turning it into an operant force capable of impelling social action. In taking the immediate offending choice for an illustration of agency and free will, social reaction theory sidesteps the vital ideological context that might bring criminology to an analysis of the ideas, common understandings and philosophical precepts that made crime seem worthwhile.

In this light, Hall (2012, p. 109) suggests that social reaction theory has "nothing to do with the social scientific and philosophical investigation into why individuals are willing to do harm to others in the interests of the self" leading to the increasingly forceful assertion that criminology's portrayal of the deviant/criminal as wronged victim of over-bearing power may well be insufficient. Many of our key theorists are beginning to recognize that the discipline's allegiance to individualist notions of liberty and agency have left it unable to offer a perspective on the second meaning of motivation, on differential social ethics and how certain dispositions might drive the infliction of harm. If we return to Steve Hall, for example, we might even suggest that "decades of liberal dominance, controlling research programmes and selecting and deselecting theoretical frameworks, has denied us any insight into the vital ontological category of the subject of ideology" (p. 94). The discipline's predilection for portraying the "deviant" as a free-thinking individual rather than a subject of ideology has arguably prevented the emergence of a properly critical perspective on criminal motivation including its relationship with what Weber might have called the underlying "spirit" of late capitalism (see Boltanski and Chiapello, 2005; Campbell, 2006)

The major problem for contemporary criminological theory is that our decades-long dalliance with social reaction seems to have produced little of any value when it comes to actually explaining the socio-ethical basis for criminality and the cultural ideals that apparently justify the infliction of harm in the service of instrumental or expressive interests. Its underlying liberal narrative has left us struggling to explain persistent forms of criminality appearing throughout the social structures of late modern capitalism by placing undue emphasis on self-determination and the ethical autonomy of the individual at the expense of the relationship between individuality and ideology. In Hall et al.'s (2008) estimation, the

> early criminological work correlating crime rates with poverty, inequality and unemployment was largely ignored and dismissed as "reductionist" by both the Left and Right...The left were keen to downplay working-class deviancy and focus on the crimes of the powerful, and the right were keen to ignore consumerist values, political economy and the social conditions of existence to press their traditional case for personal responsibility. (p. 5)

In this context, however, the past few years have seen a marked return to theorizing criminal motivation and a greater willingness to look beyond public discourse in favor of political economy and socio-cultural explanations for criminality. The final section of this chapter turns our attention to these latest movements in our discipline's immediate intellectual lineage as it attempts to counter the over-bearing influence of social reaction theory and develop a more holistic, explanatory perspective on crime and deviance.

The "return to motivation"

When it comes to social reaction theory's dominance of criminology, there have undoubtedly been a number of notable countertrends including left realism's ongoing attempts to move beyond debating the power to define crime and deviance to look at real-world impact (see Currie, 2010) as well as a small but steady undercurrent of political-economic theorization (see, for instance, James, 1995; Taylor, 1999). Nevertheless, such contributions are far outweighed by the sheer volume of social reaction theory. Hall and Winlow (2007, p. 83), for example, observe that critical exploration of relationships between criminality and socio-cultural ideals have been confined to "a dismissive aside in undergraduate texts or a sporadic volley launched from a disgruntled Mertonian or a lonely neo-Marxist". Meanwhile the largest part of the discipline "followed the prevailing trend in radical liberal philosophy and decided it was no longer hip to posit the capitalist economy and its relations of production as the bedrock of social life", rejecting the analysis of driving forces in favor of public representation, criminal agency and the idea of proto-political deviation.

What's missing from the resultant social reaction narrative is an account of criminal motivation beyond a vague, nameless and supposedly proto-political dissatisfaction with existing social norms that contributes little to any analysis of the "spirit" of criminality. It proffers a critical perspective on inherently unjust social relations and their tendency to exclude, impoverish, label and confine but apparently chooses not to engage with the underlying forces of liberal capitalism's accumulation imperative and the increasingly forceful suggestion that it has created a swath of "high-crime societies" (Garland, 2000; Hall and McLean, 2009; Reiner, 2006; 2012) by promoting the socio-ethical pre-requisites of increased criminality. The discipline's over-arching subscription to late-19th-century liberalism foregrounded the assertion that crime and deviance were often problems of social reaction to the extent that these ideas took up the lion's share of research funding, caught the attention of new students and future researchers and filtered into teaching programs as "contemporary" criminological theory eventually acquiring the status of dominant analytical paradigm. In the process, however, it also blocked the analysis of the ideological forces – beliefs, ideals, common understandings, philosophies of social life and, above all, social morality – that arguably drive people into criminality by providing the social-psychological impetus for violent and acquisitive interactions.

The past few years have seen a marked return to theorizing crime's driving forces with a number of prominent figures adopting a more explanatory, motivation-centered approach that arguably points the way beyond social reaction and underlying adherence to late-20th-century individualist liberalism. It is an exercise in complimenting criminology's thoroughgoing engagement with inequalities of representation by building in a greater awareness of the ideological forces that drive violent and acquisitive behaviors in the service of instrumental goals and self-determinative subjectivity. In this vein, Colin Sumner (2012, p. 174), while offering a critique of ongoing attempts to resurrect the sociology of deviance in the service of a "right-wing ideology", acknowledges that "there is a need for a critical re-moralization of society" and a much deeper understanding of the "influence of the amoral culture of the rich and powerful". What's being suggested is not so much the abandonment of censure – a paradigm that has undoubtedly hatched a number of useful ideas even where it may have blocked others – as a critical re-balancing of criminology to bring the analysis of crime's ideological foundations back into our collective research agenda, to once again make it a full and vibrant part of the discipline instead of a minority offshoot. It is an attempt to move beyond endlessly debating inequalities of representation by accepting the proliferation of harmful criminality over the past half decade (see Reiner, 2007) and turning our attention to the possibility that "something somewhere is going badly wrong [which] can no longer be passed off as the mere product of a conspiratorial attempt to generate fear among the population with the aim of legitimising current modes of authoritarian control" (Hall et al., 2008, p. 2).

The resultant "return to motivation" (p. 2) presents us with a partial change of trajectory that argues for deeper critical analysis of prevailing social ideals in light of the unchecked growth of recorded crime and the consequent proliferation of flailing, vaguely authoritarian attempts at control (Garland, 2001). It often begins with some acknowledgment of the dominance of neoliberal political economy since the early 1980s (Harvey, 2005; Saad-Filho and Johnson, 2005) and, more specifically, the impact of its highly Randian social ethics on cultural interaction. In short, "neoliberalism" brought with it a set of social ideals that promoted a deeply attractive picture of virtuous lives free from the demands of community and social integration with a primary responsibility to self. In Gray's (2007, p. 109) terms, it came with a new "individualist ethos of personal responsibility" in which relying on pre-existing social structures – family, occupation, class and so on – to provide a sense of purpose, fulfilment, security and respect was little more than a sign of advanced moral degeneracy wholly inferior to going our own way and negotiating the marketplace in such a way as to become self-made men and women. If we briefly dip into Randian philosophy, for instance, we find the repeated assertion "of man as a heroic being, with his own happiness as the moral purpose of his life, with productive achievement as his noblest activity" (Rand, 1992, p. 1170) – a concept of human value measured by the acquisition and display of wealth and power, by the ability to have the world conform to an individualist exercise of will. For those who fail in this primary ethical duty it offers only the ignominy of defeat and the black mark of relative incapacity rooted in the deeper moral failing of not having worked as hard as those who rose above the herd by their own grit and determination.

This vaguely Randian schema (see Rand, 1961, for more philosophical discussion) altered the signifiers of "value" – that which defines the relative worth of individual life – by which we acquire and preserve a sense of purpose and respect explicitly rooting them in the acquisition and display of material commodities and enjoyable experiences. The "consumer society" (Bauman, 2007) has tied our sense of purpose, achievement and "social identity" to the acquisition and disposal of pecuniary resources in such a way that we primarily construct meaning as desiring subjects within a system that exists to "enchant…with dreams (of freedom, of how your success depends on yourself, of the run of luck which is just around the corner, of unconstrained pleasures)" (Žižek, 2009, p. 26). What this means, in practice, is that our place within society and our access to positive mental states – happiness, fulfilment and so on (Belliotti, 2003; Schumaker, 2006) – exist only to the extent that we engage with the endlessly saccharine allure of consumer solipsism as a primary means of self-determination within a socio-cultural firmament that lauds the self-made, self-reliant individual while denigrating anyone who finds themselves at the bottom of the pile. It is a picture of social interaction in which consumptive solipsism is seen as a morally praiseworthy mode of being-in-the-world while anything outside those confines indicates a moral failing, a despicable incapacity that displays nothing less than incoherence, inferiority and outright inhumanity.

The result is to tie our sense of selfhood into a Sisyphean labor that requires the constant acquisition of pecuniary wealth and its rotating disposal amongst a sea of proffered experiences, and commodities each of which provides a momentary symbolic contribution to the maintenance of selfhood constituted amid the ever-present threat of socio-cultural insignificance. If we do not work hard enough, if we do not participate to our fullest in the virtuous round of acquisition and disposal, then ours is an ignominious place at the bottom of the pile cut off from everything that communicates the Randian value of self-identity. The assertion that this self-determinative ideal has become one of late modernity's primary ethical forces has been a substantial part of the sociological literature for decades (see, for instance, Bauman, 2000a; 2000b; Beck and Beck-Gernsheim, 2002) along with its attendant inversion: failure to self-determine or otherwise live up to the "ultimate sustaining fantasy" of autonomous selfhood is to acquire the black mark of the postmodern *untermensch* excluded from the virtuous construction of social identity through value-laden acquisition of symbolic objects. In this way a "liberal" society nominally based on the inalienable freedom of the individual communicates both success and failure conditions, the former desirable and "virtuous", the latter presenting us with an ever-present threat to the future maintenance of social identity, turning it into a labor of constant anxiety at the fragility of carefully constructed lifestyle projects (Becker, 1985).

Where social reaction theory largely proceeded from the assertion that crime and deviance were constituted in opposition to these over-arching cultural forces, the "return to motivation" takes a slightly different approach. It comes at the problem of crime in light of late-20th-century liberalism's ascent to the status of dominant ideology

(Hedges, 2011) noting the integral position of success/failure conditions when it comes to impelling social action. In the past few decades criminology's major theoretical assertion with regard to motivation has been the idea that low-level deviance is the product of individuals expressing their free-will and drive to self-determination amid a social system that sought to constrain them through its ability to label and punish. It is an assertion born, more often than not, of Foucault's (1991) contention that disciplinary technologies and discourses bear down on helpless individuals, erode their innate freedom and ultimately create "normalized" subjects wholly integrated into the needs of a power-elite. The "return to motivation", on the other hand, starts with the observation that individualist liberalism has become something of a key determining ideology and, in the process, "taught a concept of humanity according to which "what is most 'human' about people is...their need to incorporate 'more and more' – goods, money, experience, everything" (Frank, 1999, p. 20) to the extent that criminology needs to develop new ideas to explain how these emergent cultural ethics effect social interaction.

Instead of arguing that criminality represents a vanguard rejection of restrictive social norms, the "return to motivation" takes account of consumer capitalism's ascent to the status of dominant ideology in order to consider the possibility that current social problems, including criminality, perhaps result more from a broad cultural allegiance to the ideals of late-20th-century capitalism. It proceeds from the observation that we are less constrained than constantly and unendingly enjoined to express ourselves through consumer markets (Žižek, 1997, 2006, 2009) even as our increasingly unequal societies effectively exclude large sections of the population from legitimate means of identity construction (see Lansley, 2006). What's more, the resultant failure to live up to our primary ethical duty – the self-determinative construction of consumer identity – contributes one of the primary motivating forces of life under late capitalism experienced as a radical and potentially transformative sense of anxiety, incompleteness and impending loss that looms over subjective experience inspiring us to greater heights in an effort to live up to dominant notions of virtuous action and value-laden selfhood.

In other words, Western culture's socio-ethical emphasis on consumer subjectivity seems to have recalibrated or restructured dominant ethical norms in relation to instrumental and expressive interests that have perhaps changed "what is regarded as acceptable and unacceptable, proper and improper, legitimate and illegitimate, or praiseworthy and blameworthy behaviour in the light of the moral principles (e.g., justice...fairness, decency...authenticity, reliability)...changing the criteria by which people evaluate their own and each other's actions" (Weigratz, 2010, p. 124). What is being suggested, in other words, is that the socio-ethical ideals associated with the liberalization of Western society placed a set of pressures on individuals, which have reconstituted social morality providing the impetus for self-serving criminality.

It is immediately apparent that there are more than a few shades of the old sociology of deviance in this idea and many of the early proponents of this return to motivation tend to reference Chicago School scholars with notable frequency, if only because they provide a disciplinary touchstone for what is essentially an argument in favor of political-economic causation. The influence of Mertonian Strain theory (see also Messner and Rosenfeld, 2006), for instance, is quite obvious in Robert Reiner's (2007) recent output as well as some of the more responsive cultural criminologists such as Keith Hayward and Yar (2006) and Jeff Ferrell (2012, pp. 245 and 248) whose recent exploration of the "criminology of drift" highlights "the degree to which, amidst the dynamics that define late capitalist economies, both failure and success engender dislocation...[as] mortgage fraud and insider trading costs millions their homes and their livelihoods...others lose home, neighbourhood or career to the economic bulldozer of 'consumption driven urban development'".

While such assertions may provide the opening refrain for a new approach to the sociological theorization of criminality with its roots in the early part of the 20th century rather than mid-century symbolic interactionism, it is fair to say that the "return to motivation" aspires to rather more than simply recapitulating the sociology of deviance for a late-modern audience. Its ultimate purpose is to offer a "deeper exploration of...direct yet complex relationships between our core values and practices, our current conditions of existence and the individual's motivation to commit crime" (Hall et al., 2008, p. 5). With this goal in mind, a number of British criminologists, often influenced by Steve Hall (2012, p. 245) and his thoroughgoing engagement with contemporary social philosophy, have begun developing new explanations for "why liberal-capitalist life constitutes and reproduces throughout the social structure conspicuous and influential subjectivities that reject solidarity for a form of competitive individualism, one which is willing to risk harm to others as it furthers its own interests". In a wide-ranging and highly complex body of work Hall (see also Hall and Winlow, 2005a, 2005b; Winlow and Hall, 2006, 2012) argues for a renewed analysis of criminality as an integral feature of a dialectical process in which the people of Western societies are perpetually enjoined to equate positive mental states with discerning consumption while subject to psychosocial dynamics of relative incapacity resulting from the political-economic reality of neoliberal society. The dynamic tension between these forces inspires "an economically energizing form of competitive individualism fuelled by a struggle for social distinction" which in turn fuels "destructive, competitive drives and desires and the concomitant expansion and sophistication of external and internal control measures in a relation of mutual amplification" (Hall, 2012, pp. 254–255).

In other words, socially destructive criminality can be seen as a by-product of the self-same forces that drive liberal capitalism and its consumer-finance economy with just as much influence in criminal causation as everyday, law-abiding consumption, borrowing and many other prominent forms of social interaction. The major problem with the social reaction narrative was its excessively simplistic, non-dialectical theory of criminality, which uncritically posited a causal relationship between punitive statist attempts at social control and individual deviance. Where the dominant criminological paradigm of the late-20th century saw crime as the product of proto-political sentiments inspired by oppressive social norms, that of the early 21st century proffers a far more satisfying explanation rooted in the internalization of liberal ideals at the confluence of dynamic cultural pressures culminating in "hyperconformist" attempts to rise above the herd and acquire the value-laden symbolism of "consumer society" by means fair or foul.

Conclusion

The core thesis of Sumner's obituary for the sociology of deviance made two key assertions about the philosophical and theoretical development of criminology during the latter decades of the 20th century, the first of which can be seen as a historical observation while the second provides a consequent assessment of potential contribution to sociological understandings of crime and deviance. In the former case, it is probably fairly safe to say that Sumner's analysis was right on the money. There is a great deal of evidence to suggest that criminology did undergo something of a paradigm shift after 1970 in which the discipline as a whole substantially de-emphasized a normative, realist take on crime and deviance in favor of far more postmodern, relativist emphasis on discourse, representation and imbalanced powers of definition. This new paradigm began with symbolic interactionism and the labeling perspective as they came out of American phenomenology but eventually played a defining role in much of criminology's recent theoretical output including radical and critical criminology, the moral panics tradition and our discipline's version of the "cultural turn". What we collectively term "social reaction theory" or the "sociology of censure" proffered a detailed analysis of the impact of criminal labels and statist censure.

Where we might depart from Sumner's analysis, however, is in his second assertion and the benefit of an extra 20 years' hindsight into the overall distribution of criminological research. If we look back at the contemporary literature, despite a few notable and prominent countertrends, we can identify a discipline that seems to have collectively identified social reaction as a positive source of future development with which to extricate the sociological study of crime and deviance from a problematic relationship with bureaucratic pragmatism. The result, however, seems to have been a criminological paradigm that bought into the anti-bureaucratic and anti-authoritarian spirit of the late 20th century with its over-riding emphasis on liberating individual will from social expectation and collective responsibility. In the process, the lion's share of criminological theory apparently subscribed to an increasingly dominant, all but unchallenged ideology that recalibrated social, political and economic fortunes across the Western world as it communicated and valorized a set of ideals that placed greater emphasis on the individual's responsibility for the "virtue" and "value" of their lifestyle measured by the symbolic content of material commodities and the enjoyment we gain from their disposal.

When the discipline subscribed to this paradigm shift, however, it created a block between criminological theorization and the socio-ethical dominance on Randian liberalism leading us to ignore increasingly forceful ideals because we were too busy imagining the liberation of the individual from censorious corporate media and reactionary authoritarian state. The consequence of this realignment is a discipline that certainly offers a fairly thoroughgoing appraisal of media effects and political discourse at the expense of any substantial appreciation of how ethical concepts influence social interaction and manifest in lived experience to the extent that they might create the scope for transformations in human behavior. While censure might have provided a number of very useful ideas and interpretations, it is distinctly lacking in the crucial respect of criminal motivation to the extent that the discipline's amassed output no longer comes close to answering some of the most fundamental questions of criminological enquiry. The dominance of censure, it seems, has led criminological theory into a stagnatory phase that is only now being rectified by growing research interest in the ethical concepts underlying an observed profusion of self-serving, acquisitive and violent interactions.

References

Albas, C. and D. Albas (2003) "Motives", in L. Reynolds and N. Herman-Kinney (eds.) *Handbook of Symbolic Interactionism* (Walnut Creek, CA: Altamira Press).

Bauman, Z. (2000a) *The Individualized Society* (Cambridge: Polity Press).

—— (2000b) *Liquid Modernity* (Cambridge: Polity Press).

—— (2007) *Consuming Life* (Cambridge: Polity Press).

Beck, U. and E. Beck-Gernsheim (2002) *Individualisation: Institutionalised Individualism and Its Social and Political Consequences* (London: Sage).

Becker, E. (1985) *Escape from Evil* (London: Free Press).

Becker, H. (1963) *Outsiders: Studies in the Sociology of Deviance* (New York: Free Press).

Belliotti, R. A. (2003) *Happiness Is Overrated* (London: Rowman & Littlefield).

Boltanski, L. and È. Chiapello (2005) *The New Spirit of Capitalism* (London: Verso).

Campbell, C. (1996) "On the Concept of Motive in Sociology", *Sociology*, 30 (1), 101–114.

—— (2006) "Do Today's Sociologists Really Appreciate Weber's Essay 'The Protestant Ethic and the Spirit of Capitalism'?", *The Sociological Review*, 54 (2), 207–223.

Cavanagh, A. (2007) "Taxonomies of Anxiety: Risks, Panics, Paedophilia and the Internet", *Electronic Journal of Sociology*, http://www.sociology.org/content/2007/__cavanagh_taxonomies.pdf, date accessed May 22, 2013.

Cohen, S. (2002 [1972]) *Folk Devils and Moral Panics*, 3rd edn. (London: Routledge).

Currie, E. (2010) "Plain Left Realism: An Appreciation and Some Thoughts for the Future", *Crime, Law and Social Change*, 54, 111–124.

Durkheim, E. (1982 [1895]) "The Rule of the Sociological Method", in S. Lukes (ed.) *The Rules of the Sociological Method and Selected Writings on Sociology and Its Method* (London: Free Press).

—— (2002 [1897]) *Suicide: A Study in Sociology*, 2nd edn. (London: Routledge).

Ferrell, J. (1999) "Cultural Criminology", *Annual Review of Sociology*, 25, 395–418.

—— (2012) "Outline of a Criminology of Drift", in S. Hall and S. Winlow (eds.) *New Directions in Criminological Theory* (London: Routledge).

Ferrell, J., K. Hayward and J. Young (2008) *Cultural Criminology: An Invitation* (London: Sage).

Foucault, M. (1991) *Discipline and Punish: The Birth of the Prison* (London: Penguin).

Frank, T. (1999) *The Conquest of Cool: Business Culture, Counterculture, and the Rise of Hip Consumerism* (London: University of Chicago Press).

Frieden, J. A. (2006) *Global Capitalism: Its Fall and Rise in the Twentieth Century* (London: W. W. Norton).

Galbraith, J. K. (1994) *The World Economy Since the Wars: A Personal View* (London: Sinclair-Stephenson).

—— (2008) *The Predator State: How Conservatives Abandoned the Free Market and Why Liberals Should Too* (New York: Free Press).

Garland, D. (2000) "The Culture of High Crime Societies", *British Journal of Criminology*, 40 (3), 347–375.

—— (2001) *The Culture of Control: Crime and Social Order in Contemporary Society* (Oxford: Oxford University Press).

Goffman, E. (1963) *Stigma: Notes on the Management of Spoiled Identity* (Englewood Cliffs, NJ: Prentice Hall).

Gray, J. (2007) *Black Mass: Apocalyptic Religion and the Death of Utopia* (London: Penguin).

Hall, S. (2012) *Theorizing Crime and Deviance: A New Perspective* (London: Sage).

Hall, S. and C. Mclean (2009) "A Tale of Two Capitalism's: Preliminary Spatial and Historical Comparisons of Homicide Rates in Western Europe and the USA", *Theoretical Criminology*, 13 (3), 313–339.

Hall, S. and S. Winlow (2005a) "Anti-nirvana: Crime, Culture and Instrumentalism in the Age of Insecurity", *Crime, Media, Culture*, 1 (1), 31–48.

—— (2005b) "Night-Time Leisure and Violence in the Breakdown of the Pseudo-Pacification Process", *Probation Journal*, 52 (4), 376–389.

—— (2007) "Cultural Criminology and Primitive Accumulation: A Formal Introduction for Two Strangers Who Should Really Become More Intimate", *Crime, Media, Culture*, 3 (1), 82–90.

Hall, S., S. Winlow and C. Ancrum (2008) *Criminal Identities and Consumer Culture: Crime, Exclusion and the New Culture of Narcissism* (Cullompton: Willan).

Harvey, D (2005) *A Brief History of Neoliberalism* (Oxford: Oxford University Press)

Hayward, K. and M. Yar (2006) "The 'Chav' Phenomenon: Consumption, Media and the Construction of the New Underclass", *Crime Media Culture*, 2 (1), 9–28.

Hedges, C. (2011) *Death of the Liberal Class* (New York: Nation Books).

Hutton, W. (1996) *The State We're In*, rev. edn. (London: Vintage).

—— (2003) *The World We're In*, rev. edn. (London: Abacus).

James, O. (1995) *Juvenile Violence in a Winner–Loser Culture* (London: Free Association).

Judt, T. (2010) *Ill Fares the Land: A Treatise on Our Present Discontents* (London: Allen Lane).

Lansley, S. (2006) *Rich Britain: The Rise and Rise of the New Super-Wealthy* (London: Politico).

Lemert, E. (1972) *Human Deviance, Social Problems and Social Control*, 2nd edn. (Englewood Cliffs, NJ: Prentice Hall).

Levi, M. (2009) "Suite Revenge?: The Shaping of Folk Devils and Moral Panics about White-Collar Crimes", *British Journal of Criminology*, 49 (1), 48–67.

Marsh, I. and G. Melville (2011) "Moral Panics and the British Media – A Look at Some Contemporary 'Folk Devils'", *Internet Journal of Criminology*, http://www.internetjournalofcriminology.com/Marsh_Melville_Moral_Panics_and_the_British_Media_March_2011.pdf, date accessed May 22, 2013.

Merton, R. (1938) "Social Structure and Anomie", *American Sociological Review*, 3, 672–682.

Messner, S. and R. Rosenfeld (2006) *Crime and the American Dream*, 4th edn. (Belmont, CA: Wadsworth).

Mills, C. W. (1940) "Situated Actions and Vocabularies of Motive", *American Sociological Review*, 5, 904–913.

O'Connell, M. (1995) "Review of Sumner's Sociology of Deviance: An Obituary", *Discourse and Society*, 6 (4), 549–550.

Presdee, M. (2000) *Cultural Criminology and the Carnival of Crime* (London: Routledge).

Rand, A. (1961) "The Objectivist Ethics", in Ayn Rand (ed.) *The Virtue of Selfishness: A New Concept of Egoism* (London: Penguin).

—— (1992) *Atlas Shrugged*, 35th anni. edn. (New York: Dutton).

Reiner, R. (2006) "Neo-liberalism, Crime and Criminal Justice", *Renewal*, 14 (3), 10–22.

—— (2007) *Law and Order: An Honest Citizen's Guide to Crime and Control* (Cambridge: Polity Press).

—— (2012) "Political Economy and Criminology: The Return of the Repressed", in S. Hall and S. Winlow (eds.) *New Directions in Criminological Theory* (London: Routledge), pp. 30–51.

Roberts, P. (1996) "From Deviance to Censure: A New Criminology for the Nineties", *Modern Law Review*, 59, 125–144.

Rothe, D. and S. Muzzatti (2004) "Enemies Everywhere: Terrorism, Moral Panic and US Civil Society", *Critical Criminology*, 12, 327–350.

Saad-Filho, A. and D. Johnson (eds.) (2005) *Neoliberalism: A Critical Reader* (London: Pluto Press).

Schumaker, J. F. (2006) *In Search of Happiness: Understanding an Endangered State of Mind* (London: Praegar).

Shaw, C. and H. McKay (1972 [1942]) *Juvenile Delinquency in Urban Areas* (Chicago, MA: Chicago University Press).

Sumner, C. (1994) *The Sociology of Deviance: An Obituary* (Buckingham: Open University Press).

—— (2012) "Censure, Culture and Political Economy: Beyond the Death of Deviance Debate", in S. Hall and S. Winlow (eds.) *New Directions in Criminological Theory* (London: Routledge).

Sutherland, E. (1992 [1924]) *Principles of Criminology* (Plymouth: Altamira Press).

Taylor, I. (1999) *Crime in Context: A Critical Criminology of Market Societies* (Cambridge: Polity Press).

Taylor, I., P. Walton and J. Young (2003 [1973]) *The New Criminology: For a Social Theory of Deviance* (London: Routledge).

Venkatesh, S. (1995) "The Sociology of Deviance: An Obituary by Colin Sumner", *American Journal of Sociology*, 100 (6), 1632–1634.

Weigratz, J. (2010) "Fake Capitalism? The Dynamics of Neoliberal Moral Restructuring and Pseudo-Development: The Case of Uganda", *Review of African Political Economy*, 37, 123–137.

Winlow, S. and S. Hall (2006) *Violent Night: Urban Leisure and Contemporary Culture* (London: Berg).

—— (2012) "What Is an Ethics Committee: Academic Governance in an Era of Belief and Incredulity", *British Journal of Criminology*, 52, 400–416.

Young, J. (1971) *The Drugtakers: The Social Meanings of Drug Use* (London: Paladin).

Žižek, S. (1997) *The Plague of Fantasies* (London: Verso).

—— (2006) *The Parallax View* (London: MIT Press).

—— (2009) *First as Tragedy, Then as Farce* (London: Verso).

6

Subcultures and Deviance

J. Patrick Williams

Introduction

In this chapter, I outline a genealogy of the concept of *subculture*. My interest is in the degree of assumed connections between subculture and deviance, as well as with other related social scientific concepts such as marginalization, resistance and lifestyle. What I argue in short is that there has been a diverse set of uses for the term subculture that do not necessarily fit well with one another. Early work by Chicago School sociologists predates the term's entry into sociology's standard vocabulary but was nevertheless crucial in developing a cultural understanding of group meanings. Later, Birmingham School cultural studies cemented a Marxist, structuralist view of subcultures that has had perhaps the most influence on scholars researching subcultural studies. At the millennium, a concerted effort was made among some cultural scholars to move on to the study of the so-called post-subcultures. This effort had mixed success, with subculture remaining an oft-used term and with some scholars explicitly maintaining the validity of the subculture concept (see, e.g., Muggleton and Weinzierl, 2003).

In all this, subculture's relation to deviance has been mixed. While deviance was an implicit part of early American subcultural studies, the term has been missing in the British tradition, where continental theories of first class and then postmodernism have taken precedence. Of course, long before any of these academic strands emerged in the social sciences, people were writing about group cultures in terms of deviance and delinquency. Therefore, I begin the genealogy in the mid-16th century to suggest a literary (rather than social science) origin myth for subcultures.

I rely on an interpretive perspective that frames neither subculture nor deviance in terms of "things", but rather in terms of processes of meaning-making. As the other chapters in this volume similarly make clear, an interpretive approach recognizes that deviance may be seen as a product of collective meaning-making whereby people construct the boundaries of acceptability and then enforce those boundaries in various ways. As such, deviance is a more complicated term than it first appears because defining a case requires understanding the meanings that people attach to the event, action or attribute being judged. Nevertheless, most people assume to know exactly what or who is deviant in a given time or place and have few qualms judging those who transgress moral boundaries.

Culture, on the other hand, is a term that many people have trouble defining. Raymond Williams (1983, p. 87) went so far as to claim that culture "is one of the two or three most complicated words in the English language". One of the reasons for this complexity is its use "in several distinct intellectual disciplines and in several distinct and incompatible systems of thought" (ibid.), as I mentioned earlier. The subculture concept has been well-used to build a sociological understanding of deviance and delinquency. But it has also been employed by other scholars for other things, which has led to quite distinct traditions and uses of the term. My task then, as I see it, is to describe some of these different traditions of subculture scholarship and then offer some tentative answers to the question of whether subculture and deviance can or will remain useful to one another in social theory.

Subculture's literary beginnings

Deviant subcultures were visible beginning in the mid-16th century via a new genre called rogue literature. This is not the standard origin myth for subcultures but is nevertheless significant, not least because it pushes the roots of subcultures back a few hundred years. Most research on subcultures frames 20th-century consumer society as the social milieu from which subcultures emerged. Yet as literary scholars and historians have demonstrated, early modern societies such as England manifested a clearly stratified social hierarchy with coinciding class-based culture. Thus another reason the idea of a roguish beginning to subcultures is important has to do with the specificities of cultural difference. The rogue literature "manufactured an imaginary criminal underworld for London's growing metropolis, displacing dominant notions of social hierarchy and order onto the growing populations of homeless" (Dionne and Mentz, 2004, p. 7). The rogue, a common and well-understood identity by today's standards, was created at that time as a foil for the upstanding citizens of both rural and urban England. From Gilbert Walker's *A Manifest Detection of Dice-Play* (1552) to John Awdeley's *The Fraternity of Vagabonds* (1561) to Robert Greene's pamphlet series (1591a, 1591b, 1592a, 1592b) on cozening and coney-catching[1] and beyond, rogues were manifested in a way similar to Simmel's (1921) "stranger" – members of society who were understood foremost in terms of their difference from normal society. However, whereas Simmel's stranger remained a dark silhouette against a bright background, the image of the rogue as a cultural icon was characterized in great detail.

The rogue comprised a number of different social lifestyles and roles, including card sharps, pimps and prostitutes, cutpurses and other thieves and cheats. Stories ranged from cautionary tales of well-intentioned farmers visiting the city who were enticed by pretty girls into situations where modesty was compromised and only money paid to the girls' "brothers" and "uncles" could save his honor, to drunken gentlemen placing too much trust in strangers in the tavern, only to be robbed or murdered in dark alleys on their way home. Such diverse roles coalesced around their collective and cultural differences from those invited to read the pamphlets: "gentlemen, citizens, apprentices, country farmers and yeomen, that may hap to fall into the company of such coosening companions" (Greene, 1591a, p. 1). The tales were a mixture of fantastic crime novel and citizen education campaigns, using the rogue to simultaneously entertain and educate England's growing, literate, respectable classes about the devious methods through which the poor allegedly made their living. Through a steady supply of such stories across the second half of the 16th century, the rogue literature was the first to construct a relatively coherent vision of the cultural worlds of England's landless poor. This coherence of various character types as rogues was predicated on a narrow emphasis on deviant behavior and criminality. As Gelder (2007) notes, the historical record is replete with stories of criminals, slackers and others whose behaviors (or lack thereof) set them apart from respectable society, but it was

---

[1] "Cozening" referred to the act of swindling someone in a deal, while "coney-catching" alluded to the process of professional criminals, often working in small groups, baiting an unsuspecting person – a "coney", or tame rabbit – into some sort of trap where he or she could be robbed or extorted.

Elizabethan English literature that discursively constructed such characters in cultural terms, including their landlessness in a society where one's connection to land was a primary identifier; the development of argots and secret languages to hide the meaning of their talk from outsiders and the fraternities and communities they seemed inclined to subscribe to (ibid.).

In the 19th century, chronicling the cultural distinctiveness of England's urban poor was still seen as prototypical of subcultural scholarship. Several scholars have pointed to Henry Mayhew as the man responsible for bringing "a particular kind of social perspective, a 'sociological gaze', which [began] to emerge in the 1830s and 1840s" (Tolson, 1990, p. 114) to bear on the lived culture of London's working-class poor (see also Hebdige, 1988, pp. 19–22; Thompson and Yeo, 1973). Mayhew was a newspaper journalist who published a series of character profiles on representatives of various working-class cultures in the London paper *Morning Chronicle*, in 1849–1850 (subsequently published in 1851–1852 as *London Labour and the London Poor*). Like the rogue pamphlets, Mayhew's work was literary in scope – he earned his living by telling stories of interest to the literate classes. Yet unlike the rogue literature, which some have argued was based more on fiction than fact (see Dionne, 2004; Woodbridge, 2001), Mayhew engaged in what today would be called field work, moving through the streets of London observing the behaviors of those his society saw as deviant and collecting their stories through interview-like conversations with them. His work again brought to life groups of citizens who were more or less treated as subhuman by England's landed classes in everyday life. Andrew Tolson (1990, p. 114) argued that Mayhew's work, while liberal and reformist in nature, opened up "a range of approaches to the classification, supervision and policing of [these] urban populations."

Urban gangs and deviance

The range of approaches, methodologically and theoretically speaking, through which academics and social reformers might come to understand the inequalities and cultural diversity of urban environments became a shared focus among sociologists at the University of Chicago, who systematically studied the social dimensions of urban life in the early 20th century. Sociology at the University of Chicago meant the sociological study of Chicago itself. The city had emerged over the previous half-century from a small town of approximately 10,000 inhabitants in

1860 to more than 2,000,000 in 1910 and thus offered a useful setting for the development of empirically based urban research. A key player in the so-called Chicago School of sociology was Robert Park (1925, p. 26), who wrote that the rapid improvements in modes of transportation and communication had changed the social organization of modern cites such "that all sorts of people meet and mingle together who never fully comprehend one another". For Park, such a lack of comprehension was dysfunctional, leading to a breakdown in social cohesion and hence to the coherence of smaller group culture rather than a homogenous urban culture.

Park, who had worked for years as a journalist, encouraged his students to leave the classroom and explore the city in order to "seek rich personal experience with the topics of their interest; to get inside the subject and even live it as far as possible" (Faris, 1967, p. 30). The development of urban ethnographic research became a key dimension of Chicago sociology and led to graduate students such as Paul G. Cressey, Frederic Thrasher and later William Foote Whyte and Howard Becker (among others) undertaking detailed empirical studies of urban subcultures. The hallmark of their subcultural work was an emphasis on deviant collective behavior. Numerous studies had found that most patterns of criminal behavior were acquired during the "youthful days" of criminals' lives, and research into the origins of juvenile delinquency and deviance appeared to be of strategic importance for explaining social dysfunctions. Therefore, significant effort was put into the empirical study of deviance, not least because sociologists were convinced that the roots of deviant behavior were to be found in social phenomena rather than in biological or psychological profiles of delinquents, which was the common practice among physicians, psychologists and correctional officers. Frederic Thrasher's (1927) study of 1,313 youth gangs in Chicago is one example of earlier sociological work on deviant subcultures and his goal was to map out the social processes that underlay gang behaviors. He noted that gangs originally formed through casual interaction but were subsequently integrated through conflict, presumably with people in other areas of the city. Thrasher characterized gangs in terms of routinized behaviors including "meeting face to face, milling, moving through space as a unit, conflict, and planning", the results of which were "the development of tradition ... esprit de corps, solidarity, morale ... and attachment to a local territory" (Thrasher, cited in Faris, 1967, p. 73). Thrasher's findings were explicit: gangs were not formed by psychological abnormality, but rather by sociability and a shared sense of adventure and excitement. These ideas were elaborated in case studies of delinquents as well. In *The Jack-Roller*, for example, Clifford Shaw (1930) noted that

> the human being as a member of a social group is a specimen of it, not primarily, if at all, because of his physique and temperament but by reason of his participation in its purposes and activities. Through communication and interaction the person acquires the language, tradition, standards, and practices of his group. Therefore, the relation of the person to his group is organic and hence representative upon a cultural rather than upon a biological level. (p. 186)

Shaw used a narrative case study approach, but many performed ethnographic research into deviant lifestyles among the marginalized urban poor. Paul Cressey's (1932) *The Taxi-Dance Hall* studied the social worlds of private clubs, popular in many large American cities of the day, where women were employed to dance with men. A young woman who worked as a "taxi-dancer" was so named because, "like a taxi-driver with his cab, she is for public hire and is paid in proportion to the time spent and the services rendered" (p. 3). One of Cressey's concerns was how young women regressed through a taxi-dancing career, from dancing to some eventual form of prostitution before returning to "normal" society. Dancers tended to come from eastern European immigrant families, who clustered together in Chicago's ethnic neighborhoods and whose career choices were relatively limited to things like rolling cigars or providing menial office labor. Taxi-dancing offered a temporary respite to young immigrant women's dissatisfactions with their lives in home and neighborhood. Rather than surrender to immediate prospects of dead-end jobs or marriage, these women chose an alternative means of securing satisfaction in their everyday lives that was grounded in the desire for the excitement of the dance hall and the increased prestige that accompanied a job earning much more money than their mainstream peers.

These early studies tended to ignore the socially constructed nature of deviance, or at least they lacked an explicit emphasis on problematizing the relationship between such groups and normal society. Instead, the emphasis was on the function or dysfunction of culture and social action for solving the problems of modern life. One of the major functionalist theories of culture to emerge during this time was strain theory, which postulated that a society's structure provided both cultural goals – aspirations that society's members share – and institutionalized means of achieving those goals and that a society in perfect equilibrium would provide everyone with goals as well as the means to achieve them

(Merton, 1938). The problem was that modern societies were not in equilibrium and their social structures provided unequal access to the institutionalized means of achieving cultural goals. Disjuncture between cultural goals and the ability to achieve those goals arose for some groups, which would seek alternative means to achieve those goals. For example, working-class youths who were socialized via mainstream culture to recognize the value and prestige associated with driving a new car, and yet could not foresee themselves having legitimate opportunities to own one by conforming to traditional roles (i.e., get a good job, work hard) were likely to engage in delinquent behaviors that would enable them to satisfy the cultural goal, such as auto theft. In short, the psychological strain some people feel at being unable to achieve mainstream cultural goals forced them to engage in delinquent behavior.

Merton's theory of culture and deviance became crucial to many sociological studies during the 1940s. But while Merton believed that marginalized groups would seek ways of overcoming strain in order to fit into the larger society, his student Albert Cohen argued instead for a more subcultural understanding of deviant behavior. In particular, Cohen emphasized a link between strain and a person's frame of reference. According to Cohen (1955, p. 59), a subculture's emergence required "the existence, in effective interaction with one another, of a number of actors with similar problems of adjustment". From this perspective, the frustration some people experienced when they felt pressure to conform to dominant culture led to a reaction formation whereby they inverted sets of values and norms to legitimize alternative lines of action. Rather than struggle to meet society's cultural goals, subcultures emerged that legitimated not achieving them. As Gibbons (1970) noted, this line of work on delinquent subcultures

> indicated that most lawbreakers...were members of gangs and peer association in which delinquent conduct was defined positively, young boys were inducted into lawbreaking by older youths, and juveniles were taught the skills of delinquency in much the same way that youths in socially-favored circumstances learn to become boy scouts or "good boys" of some other brand. (p. 113)

Cohen's study renewed the vigor with which sociologists and criminologists investigated the relationship between subculture and delinquency. However, much of that work tacitly operated from the point of view that delinquency was an objectively real category. The reification of deviance and delinquency has continued with mainstream criminology and criminal justice studies, though more explicitly constructionist and critical traditions such as cultural criminology (Ferrell, 1999) have emerged to ensure the continuing debate about the role of culture in deviance studies.

Post-war consumerism and resistance

While the American tradition of subculture studies has typically been pegged to criminology, things were different elsewhere. The field of cultural studies emerged in the 1960s and 1970s in Britain, in large part thanks to the Center for Contemporary Cultural Studies (CCCS) at the University of Birmingham. There, scholars from the social sciences and humanities had joined together to study various aspects of culture and society. Their first collective work, *Resistance through Rituals* (Hall and Jefferson, 1976), represented a heavily Marxist and structuralist "reading" of working-class youth culture that differed drastically from the American ethnographic tradition. The most significant differences were the rejection of the concept of deviance and the methods of field research in favor of the concept of resistance and the methods of semiology.

The CCCS took its interest in resistance from Gramsci (1971), who is best known for his reworking of Marx's theory of conflict through the concept of cultural hegemony. At its simplest, hegemony is the idea that the ruling class in any society seeks to maintain its power by gaining the consent of subjugated classes through cultural means. The quest for control, however, is never complete and those subjugated are always finding ways to resist the machinations of the more powerful. Althusser (1970) drew from, but extended, Gramsci's theory of hegemony, arguing for a more ideological conceptualization that explained how hegemony worked its way into people's very conceptions of self, rather than limiting the theory to the realm of politics. He argued that it was hardly possible for people *not* to be socialized to accept power as a natural, common-sense structure that shaped their everyday lives because the most basic institutions in society – family, religion, education, work – functioned as sites of power and control. These institutions he called *ideological state apparatuses* and they offered insight into the *structures* responsible for socializing individuals.

Following Althusser, CCCS scholars sought to explain the emergence of youth subcultures in *post-war Britain* (not all subcultures across time and space). Accordingly, they believed that British subcultures represented working-class youths' struggles for identity and collective consciousness in the face of conflicting cultural messages: one from their parents' working-class culture and another propagated by bourgeoisie culture. While Britain is known historically for caring a lot about class affiliation, the post-war national economy shifted in a way that simultaneously worked to destroy traditional working-class cultural forms and open up new opportunities for class mobility (Cohen, 1997 [1972]). The expansion of working-class jobs to rebuild the country, the restructuring of the urban landscape to deal with population growth and the ability of new media technologies such as television and vinyl records to disseminate popular youth culture all came together to create a conjuncture within which, according to the CCCS, consumption-based youth subcultures emerged.

Subcultures were not understood in terms of *psychological* strain or deviance, but rather as forms of collective, class-based resistance to cultural hegemony. Young people were torn between the threat of the destruction of their working-class heritage, on the one hand, and the allure of a middle-class consumer lifestyle, on the other, and reacted to this *ideological* strain by producing new styles that represented their liminal cultural positions. The teddy boy's Edwardian suit, the skinhead's shaved head and boots, the mod's pills and scooters – each became a homological icon of the tension between consumption and the ability of marginal groups to resist mainstream culture by rewriting the meaning of cultural symbols. Their resistance was conceptualized as economically impotent because it failed to improve their marginal positions in society. Symbolically though their resistance impacted dominant cultural institutions, which had to work actively to dismiss, marginalize or appropriate the resistant meanings (Clarke, 1976).

The emphasis on consumption and resistance represented a major methodological difference between the American and British traditions of subcultural studies. Instead of an ethnographic approach, CCCS studies were primarily grounded in semiotic analyses. The semiotician's job was to unpack the taken-for-granted meanings that were attributed to subcultural objects and practices. This unpacking required the semiotician to interrogate how taken-for-granted meanings were created, distributed and consumed. What CCCS scholars seemed to find, everywhere they looked, was that subcultures appropriated and inverted cultural meanings, often through the consumption of clothing, music and other leisure commodities. From this perspective, all meaning was ideology-laden and subcultural youths themselves did not always understand what their objects and practices "really" meant. Only the trained semiotician could see the ideological dimension of subcultural style.

Thus, in reading CCCS scholarship from the 1970s, one finds very little in the way of insight into the meaning-making processes of subcultural-ists themselves. Research, which was more of a humanities-style under-taking than social-scientific, was driven by a preoccupation with theories of class and by a seemingly willful ignorance of how youths made sense of their own experiences (see, e.g., Hebdige, 1979). Ironically, it has nevertheless come into its own hegemonic position within subculture studies, with new (especially British) generations of scholars constantly invoking the CCCS's origin myth.

Post-subcultural lifestyles

To paraphrase Gramsci, hegemony highlights that power is never a done deal. And though the cultural studies tradition has flourished since the 1970s, the CCCS's over-emphasis on the white male working-class subcultural hero and the methods used to theorize his identity and value have come under sustained criticism (e.g., McRobbie, 1980; Muggleton, 2000; Widdicombe and Wooffitt, 1995; Williams, 2011). That critique was embodied in the early 1990s by club-cultures research, the goal of which was "to continue the ... traditions of 1960s and 1970s CCCS, but in the very different theoretical and political environment of the 1990s" (Redhead, 1997a, p. 2).

Club-cultures research emerged in part because of the belief among some cultural scholars that acid house and rave music forms, which gained so much popularity among youths in the 1990s, facilitated the rebuilding of subcultural sensibilities within a distinctly more troubling political-economic era. Ravers and other types of club-music fans flocked to the safety of the club and the all-night party, much as Hedbige's (1976) mod had a generation before. However, this new generation of youths was much less coherent in its alleged affiliations with class and style. In Redhead's view (1997b), the 1990s were better characterized through the lens of postmodernism – through pastiche, playfulness and irony. Many other scholars were quick to agree that the coherence, seriousness and ultimate impotence of the CCCS's subcultures were not adequate to describe the diverse array of alternative youth cultures of the 1990s. Redhead's (1993) prior work in dance culture had gone a long way in establishing not only the significance of music in what was called a post-CCCS perspective, but also in breaking down the assumed relationship between music preference, style and subcultural affiliation. Subcultural style was no longer understood as a representation of ideo-logical strain among working-class youths. The styles of punk, mod, skinhead and hippy, all of which could be found mixed together in rave clubs and parties, signaled "entirely new ways of understanding how young people perceive the relationship between music taste and visual style ... revealing the infinitely malleable and interchangeable nature of the latter as these are appropriated and realized by individuals as aspects of consumer choice" (Bennett, 1999, p. 613). Club cultures represented a new era of youth hedonism, academically framed in a way that celebrated agency and affirmation rather than impotence.

The shift from subcultures to club cultures signified an emerging alignment of youth studies with a post-CCCS sensibility that did not assume to speak on behalf of absent subcultural members, that treated subcultures as something more than a series of successive moments of "spectacular" resistance and that looked beyond an over-simplified us-versus-them portrayal of subcultures as "externally differentiated, yet internally homogenous collectivities, existing in clear opposition to each other and to conventional [culture]" (Muggleton, 1997, p. 192). Sarah Thornton's book *Club Cultures* (1996) is a key study of the 1990s because it brought back key texts from the American tradition of deviance scholarship such as Becker's *Outsiders* (1963) and merged them with a more British version of subculture. Her study was the result of years of participation in and observation of clubbing activities, beginning as avid insider and ending as a more mature but knowledgeable outsider, and she was concerned with understanding youth culture from an insider's perspective. Thus rather than characterize clubbers in terms of deviance, Thornton highlighted more emotional concerns such as the quests for authenticity and status. Such a perspective allowed the researcher to explore the functional, participatory and lived aspects of young people's material and non-material cultures in ways that outsiders would find more difficult. There was a conscious movement beyond simplified divisions between middle-class and working-class, high-brow and low-brow cultures, as well as reconsiderations of the role of media *vis-à-vis* as tools of the powerful for controlling problem youths.

Since the late 1990s, a number of British scholars have staked claims to one or another concept that attempts to better characterize youth cultural formations, just as American sociologists had done in previous decades. David Muggleton (1997) offered a vision of the "post-subculturalist" in his contribution to Redhead's (1997a) reader. Drawing heavily from postmodern theory, Muggleton's post-subculturalist wore style for its look alone rather than for any underlying meaning and reveled in the availability of cultural choices afforded by the decades of cross-fertilization and collapsing boundaries among youth subcultures after punk. Muggleton's work was followed by that of Andy Bennett, who introduced the concept of "neo-tribe" into youth subculture studies. Relegating subculture to "little more than a convenient 'catch-all' term for any aspect of social life in which young people, style and music intersect", Bennett (1999, pp. 599, 600) argued that youth "groupings which have traditionally been theorized as coherent subcultures are better understood as a series of temporal gathering characterized by fluid boundaries and floating memberships". Like post-subculture, neo-tribe emphasized a general decline in the willingness of many young people to commit to a subcultural identity, preferring instead a more playful approach to youth cultural lifestyles. These ideas collectively moved beyond bifurcated conceptions of youth culture as either mainstream of heroically resistant and embodied a desire to theorize youths' cultural proclivities in less monolithic terms. To do this, its authors sought to reduce subculture to an outdated macro-oriented concept, too rooted in theories of class or deviance to fit alongside millennial conceptions of youth.

The deaths of deviance and subculture?

In the 21st century, cultural scholars have continued to weigh in on the relevance of "subculture" as a sociological concept. This has sometimes taken the form of re-summarizing criticisms of the concept as it was used by the CCCS (e.g., Bennett and Kahn-Harris, 2004; Muggleton and Weinzierl, 2003) and other times by defending its continued relevance to social life while striving to refine its analytic utility (e.g., Blackman, 2005; Gelder, 2007; Williams, 2011). Beyond this, there are several academic fields within which subculture continues to be used analytically. In criminology, subculture is used often to refer to the transgressive values, styles and behaviors of delinquents, usually with an emphasis on class, race or gender (e.g., Hamm, 2004; Holt, 2007; Martin, 2009). Such work comes out of the American tradition of deviance and delinquency studies noted earlier. In cultural sociology, scholars such as Gary Fine have used subculture as an explanatory concept in the study of small groups (e.g., Fine, 1983, 2012; Fine and Kleinman, 1979). This work shares with criminology theoretical roots in early Chicago School studies of delinquent groups. However, in cultural sociology the subculture concept has broader analytical function by virtue of an emphasis on the universal creation of culture among interacting groups rather than a focus on non-normative values, beliefs or behaviors. Indeed, research on local activities and groupings that involve music, and that would have previously invoked the concept of subculture, has gravitated toward the more useful concept of *scene* (Bennett and Kahn-Harris, 2004; Kotarba et al., 2009), thus addressing Bennett's (1999) concern for "fluid boundaries and floating memberships". There has also been continued use of subculture within the sociology of sports, particularly in terms of how sports may invoke subculturally relevant processes such as identity, consumption and resistance (e.g., Atkinson and Young, 2008; Donnelly and Young, 1988; Wheaton, 2000).

With the exception perhaps of the field of criminology, little of this literature uses the term "deviance" explicitly. I suggest three reasons for this. First, the social constructionist paradigm that arose in the second half of the 20th century called into question earlier studies that took deviance for granted as a universal function in society. Deviance is now recognized by most social science scholars as a process or condition organized in the service of power. As such, there are few assumptions among researchers about the relative good or bad of the cultures being studied and therefore it is rarely assumed that certain cultures are or are not deviant. Even criminology has been impacted by the linguistic and cultural turns and is today a field where deviance is a contested terrain.

Second, the theoretical significance of the CCCS on subculture studies cannot be underestimated. A look at the social science literature on subcultures today reveals how many scholars derive their own conceptual frames from CCCS scholarship. And because the CCCS explicitly rejected a deviance approach to the study of working-class youth culture, many studies no longer rely on that older literature for insight. This has its own set of benefits and problems. On the problems side, the CCCS version of subculture is hegemonic in that few scholars seem willing to leave it alone. Flippant references to *Resistance through Rituals* (Hall and Jefferson, 1976) and *Subculture: The Meaning of Style* (Hebdige, 1979) are often used to justify the use of "subculture" without sufficient understanding of the theoretical and methodological baggage involved. On the benefits side, there has been much more research that takes an insider's view of subcultural participation seriously, with the result that things once considered deviant are now being theorized as resistant or even heroic instead.

Third, much of the contemporary literature has shifted focus either toward the subcultures of marginalized or non-normative groups. The research on marginal cultures tends to rely on political-economic discourses where deviance is a tangential concept. And for those studies that frame subcultures in terms of non-normativity, concepts like resistance are preferred since the emphasis is more likely to be on insiders, who rarely use a term like "deviant" except as a badge of honor.

This shift toward insider research is perhaps the single most significant development in the field of subculture studies in the 21st century. As more individuals – who themselves participated in youth subcultures and were likely labeled as deviant by their parents, peers and other subscribers to mainstream culture – engage in the academic study of subculture, the story of the significance of subculture as a meaningful dimension of everyday life is retold time and again. This is consequential for subcultural theory, as W. I. Thomas (1928, p. 572) noted more than 80 years ago when he wrote that "if [people] define situations as real they are real in their consequences". To the extent that being "subcultural" is positively meaningful to people, while being "deviant" is not, deviance and subculture will continue to drift apart.

References

Althusser, L. (1970) "Ideology and Ideological State Apparatuses", in L. Althusser *Lenin and Philosophy and Other Essays* (New York: Monthly Review Press).

Atkinson, M. and K. Young (2008) *Tribal Play: Subcultural Journeys through Sport* (Bingley, UK: JAI Press).

Awdeley, J. (1561) "The Fraternity of Vagabonds", in A. V. Judges (1965 [1930]) (ed.) *The Elizabethan Underworld* (London: Routledge & Kegan Paul).

Becker, H. (1963) *Outsiders: Studies in the Sociology of Deviance* (New York: Free Press).

Bennett, A. (1999) "Subcultures or Neo-tribes? Rethinking the Relationship between Youth, Style, and Musical Taste", *Sociology*, 33 (3), 599–617.

Bennett, A. and K. Kahn-Harris (eds.) (2004) *After Subculture: Critical Studies in Contemporary Youth Culture* (New York: Palgrave).

Blackman, S. (2005) "Youth Subcultural Theory: A Critical Engagement with the Concept, Its Origins and Politics, from the Chicago School to Postmodernism", *Journal of Youth Studies*, 8 (1), 1–20.

Clarke, J. (1976) "Style", in S. Hall and T. Jefferson (eds.) *Resistance through Rituals* (London: Routledge).

Cohen, A. (1955) *Delinquent Boys: The Culture of the Gang* (New York: Free Press).

Cohen, P. (1997 [1972]) "Subcultural Conflict and Working Class Community", in P. Cohan *Rethinking the Youth Question: Education, Labor and Cultural Studies* (Basingstoke: Macmillan).

Cressey, P. G. (1932) *The Taxi-Dance Hall* (New York: Greenwood Press).

Dionne, C. (2004) "Fashioning Outlaws: The Early Modern Rogue and Urban Culture", in C. Dionne and S. Mentz (eds.) *Rogues and Early Modern English Culture* (Ann Arbor: University of Michigan Press).

Dionne, C. and S. Mentz (2004) *Rogues and Early Modern English Culture* (Ann Arbor: University of Michigan Press).

Donnelly, P. and K. Young (1988) "The Construction and Confirmation of Identity in Sport Subcultures", *Sociology of Sport Journal*, 5 (3), 223–240.

Faris, R. E. L. (1967) *Chicago Sociology 1920–1932* (San Francisco: Chandler).

Ferrell, J. (1999) "Cultural Criminology", *Annual Review of Sociology*, 25, 395–418.

Fine, G. A. (1983) *Shared Fantasy: Role-Playing Games as Social Worlds* (Chicago: University of Chicago Press).

—— (2012) *Tiny Publics: A Theory of Group Action and Culture* (New York: Russell Sage Foundation).

Fine, G. A. and S. Kleinman (1979) "Rethinking Subculture: An Interactionist Analysis", *American Journal of Sociology*, 85 (1), 1–20.

Gelder, K. (2005) "Introduction: The Field of Subcultural Studies", *The Subcultures Reader*, 2nd edn. (London: Routledge).

—— (2007) *Subculture: Cultural Histories and Social Practice* (London: Routledge).

Gibbons, D. C. (1970) *Delinquent Behavior* (Englewood Cliffs, NJ: Prentice Hall).

Gramsci, A. (1971) "Selections from the Prison Notebooks of Antonio Gramsci", in G. Smith and Q. Hoare (eds. and trans.) (London: Lawrence and Wishart).

Greene, R. (1591a) "A Notable Discovery of Coosnage", in A. V. Judges (1965 [1930]) (ed.) *The Elizabethan Underworld* (London: Routledge & Kegan Paul).

—— (1591b) "The Second Part of Conycatching", in A. V. Judges (1965 [1930]) (ed.) *The Elizabethan Underworld* (London: Routledge & Kegan Paul).

—— (1592a) *A Disputation between a Hee Conny-Catcher and a Shee Conny-Catcher.*

——. (1592b) "The Third and Last Part of Conycatching", in A. V. Judges (1965 [1930]) (ed.) *The Elizabethan Underworld* (London: Routledge & Kegan Paul).

Hall, S. and T. Jefferson (eds.) (1976) *Resistance through Rituals* (London: Routledge).

Hamm, M. S. (2004) "Apocalyptic Violence: The Seduction of Terrorist Subcultures", *Theoretical Criminology*, 8 (3), 323–339.

Hebdige, D. (1976) "The Meaning of Mod", in Stuart Hall and Tony Jefferson (eds.) *Resistance through Rituals* (London: Routledge).

—— (1979) *Subcultures: The Meaning of Style* (London: Methuen).

—— (1988) *Hiding in the Light: On Images and Things* (London: Routledge).

Holt, T. J. (2007) "Subcultural Evolution? Examining the Influence of On- and Off-line Experiences on Deviant Subcultures", *Deviant Behavior*, 28 (2), 171–198.

Judges, A. V. (1965 [1930]) *The Elizabethan Underworld* (London: Routledge & Kegan Paul).

Kotarba, J. A., J. L. Fackler and K. M. Nowotny (2009) "An Ethnography of Emerging Latino Music Scenes", *Symbolic Interaction*, 32 (4), 310–333.

Martin, G. (2009) "Subculture Subculture, Style, Chavs and Consumer Capitalism: Towards a Critical Cultural Criminology of Youth", *Crime, Media, Culture*, 5 (2), 123–145.

McRobbie, A. (1980) "Settling Accounts with Subcultures: A Feminist Critique", *Screen Education*, 34, 37–49.

Merton, R. (1938) "Social Structure and Anomie", *American Sociological Review*, 3 (5), 672–682.

Muggleton, D. (1997) "The Post-subculturalist", in S. Redhead (ed.) *The Clubcultures Reader: Readings in Popular Cultural Studies* (Oxford: Blackwell).

—— (2000) *Inside Subculture: The Postmodern Meaning of Style* (Oxford: Berg).

Muggleton, D. and R. Weinzierl (eds.) (2003) *The Post-subcultures Reader* (Oxford: Berg).

Park, R. E. (1925) "The City: Suggestions for the Investigation of Human Behavior in the Urban Environment", in R. E. Park, E. W. Burgess and R. D. McKenzie (eds.) *The City* (Chicago: University of Chicago Press).

Redhead, S. (1993) "The End of the End-of-the-Century Party", in S. Redhead (ed.) *Rave Off: Politics and Deviance in Contemporary Youth Culture* (Aldershot: Avebury).

—— (1997a) *The Clubcultures Reader: Readings in Popular Cultural Studies* (Oxford: Blackwell).

—— (1997b) *Subcultures to Clubcultures: An Introduction to Popular Cultural Studies* (Oxford: Blackwell).

Salgado, G. (1977) *The Elizabethan Underworld* (London: J.M. Dent & Sons).

Shaw, C. R. (1930) *The Jack-Roller: A Delinquent Boy's Own Story* (Chicago: University of Chicago Press).

Simmel, G. (1921) "The Sociological Significance of the 'Stranger'", in R. E. Park and E. W. Burgess (eds.) *Introduction to the Science of Sociology* (Chicago: University of Chicago Press).

Thomas, W. I. and D. Thomas (1928) *The Child in America* (New York: Knopf).

Thompson, E. P. and Eileen Yeo (1973) *The Unknown Mayhew* (Harmondsworth: Penguin Books).

Thornton, S. (1996) *Club Cultures: Music, Media and Subcultural Capital* (Middletown, CT: Wesleyan).

Thrasher, F. (1927) *The Gang: A Study of 1,313 Gangs in Chicago* (Chicago: University of Chicago Press).

Tolson, A. (1990) "Social Surveillance and Subjectification: The Emergence of 'Subculture' in the Work of Henry Mayhew", *Cultural Studies*, 4 (2), 113–127.

Walker, G. (1552) "A Manifest Detection of Dice-Play", in A. V. Judges (1965 [1930]) (ed.) *The Elizabethan Underworld* (London: Routledge & Kegan Paul).

Wheaton, B. (2000) "'Just Do It': Consumption, Commitment, and Identity in the Windsurfing Subculture", *Sociology of Sport Journal*, 17, 254–274.

Widdicombe, S. and R. Wooffitt (1995) *The Language of Youth Subcultures* (New York: Harvester-Wheatsheaf).

Williams, J. P. (2011) *Subcultural Theory: Traditions and Concepts* (Cambridge, UK: Polity Press).

Williams, R. (1983) *Keywords: A Vocabulary of Culture and Society*, rev. edn. (New York: Oxford University Press).

Woodbridge, L. (2001) *Vagrancy, Homelessness, and English Renaissance Literature* (Urbana: University of Illinois Press)

Part II
Productive Deviance

7
Debating the Death of Deviance
Transgressing Extremes in Conspiracy Narratives
Daniel Dotter

Introduction

In recent years the sociology of deviance has been marked by an ongoing, lively and emergent intellectual debate. The parameters of the competing arguments are both conceptual (Best, 2004a, 2004b, 2006; Goode, 2006) and ideological (Hendershott, 2002; Sumner, 1994), reflecting shifting contemporary theoretical concerns (Adler and Adler, 2006; Dotter, 2002). Questions regarding the intellectual coherence of the field (Goode, 2004a), its present-day relevance (Goode, 2004b) and even of its "death" (Goode, 2002, 2003, 2004a; Sumner, 1994) have been taken up by scholars, creating a terrain no less fertile than that represented by the growth of interactionist theories in the 1960s and 1970s (Becker, 1973 [1963], 1964, 1967).

This chapter has three purposes. First, I outline the contemporary theoretical controversy in the sociology of deviance: the claim of its morbidity. Central here is the work of Joel Best (2004a, 2004b), as well as that of Erich Goode (2002, 2003, 2004a, 2004b) – the latter, particularly as a response to Colin Sumner's (1994) "obituary" announcement.

Second, I frame this debate within the context of cultural criminology and what has been called the "carnival" of crime (Presdee, 2001; Dotter, 2011): images of deviance and their cultural significance are constantly shifting position, especially in narratives of popular culture. The carnival as a scenario of stigmatization is framed by the overlapping processes of transgression and extremity: Deviance is less and less a matter of disvalued behavior or status and increasingly generated within cultural storylines as the construction of extreme knowledge.

Deviance-labeling is situated in a process of meaning generation (Dotter, 1997, 2004, 2011), mediated in cultural scenarios of textual meaning. In the scenario (Dotter, 2004), deviance is layered in a complex narrative which shifts the emphasis from traditional legal categories to broader socio-cultural "stigma contests" (Schur, 1980). In this context, cultural politics (Jordan and Weedon, 1995) are animated by transgression or the crossing of boundaries (Foucault, 1977; Jenks, 2003), and meaning generation is increasingly a battle to cast knowledge and its proponents as extreme and therefore having no legitimate claim to acceptance.

Third, the concept of extreme deviance (Goode and Vail, 2008) extends the reach of carnival and is a valuable description of this changing context of deviance and cultural meaning production. As mediated, increasingly virtual boundaries dissolve and transmute, narratives of "extreme" experience are afforded space in mainstream culture. An example I preliminarily offer as prototypical scenarios of extreme deviance is UFO conspiracy narratives. The concept of conspiracy panics (Bratich, 2008) illuminates a doubling process in media culture: As meaning generation, UFO conspiracy stories – "exopolitics" (Salla, 2004) – overlap with paranormal knowledge (Goode, 2000; Dean, 1998) and are nearly universally stigmatized as irrational, fear-mongering "theories."

The deviance debate: the shifting context of meaning

Initial considerations

Theoretical development in the sociology of deviance has followed two intersecting paths. First, from the inception of the specialty, deviance theorizing has closely mirrored trends found in sociology generally (Davis, 1975; Best, 2004a; Rubington and Weinberg, 2010). Durkheim's (1951 [1897]) classic study, *Suicide*, is simultaneously sociological and deviance theorizing (Douglas, 1967). Micro- and macro-sociological perspectives were adapted to study normative violation, whether such violation was described as social pathology, social disorganization, social problems or deviance (Mills, 1943).

Best (2006, p. 535) neatly summarizes the conceptual dilemma originally faced by social pathology and, over time, confronted by each of the other terms as well: "The real problem that bedeviled social pathology – and that has plagued its conceptual cousins, including social problems, social disorganization (and as we shall see) deviance – is that its proponents could not agree on a workable way to define the concept." From the beginning, then, deviance – and related concepts – evidenced "definitional creep" (Best, 2004a, pp. 33–34): anything and anybody could be considered as possibly deviant under specific circumstances.

Second, included in the study of deviance was the overlapping subject area of criminality (Hester and Eglin, 1992). In the early 20th century conceptual problems of "deviation" were part of the larger dialogue on the problems of social order. The early Chicago School formation and development reflected this bifurcated, uneven theoretical development (Faris, 1970; Rock, 1979). Within it were perspectives on systemic social disorganization (arguably a more reasoned social pathology narrative), deviance (an early interactionist focus on meaning generation) and eventually the seeds of criminology as a distinct subfield, embedded in Sutherland's (1983 [1949]) analysis of white collar crime and differential association (Sutherland et al., 1992) as value conflict. In the 1960s labeling – including what Howard S. Becker (1973 [1963]) specifically conceptualized as an "interactionist" viewpoint – and the "new" Marxist criminology (Taylor et al., 1973) continued the bifurcated emphasis on deviance and crime. Perspectives on deviance stressed a broader concern with the multiple contexts of stigmatization (Goffman, 1986 [1963]) and normative violation as disvaluement (Sagarin, 1975; Schur, 1971); those on criminology focused on the singular importance of the criminal label, as a method of differentiating crime types (Clinard et al., 1994) or as the genesis of a self-fulfilling prophecy in a criminal career (Davis, 1975).

Joel Best: "labeling under attack"

Best (2004a, p. 71) maintains that by 1975 "as deviance began to lose its importance as a center of intellectual action, criminology underwent a substantial revival". He sees this emergence and spread of criminology as a field, heretofore a less prestigious area, as evidence of a wider trend of "labeling under attack". From all sides – conflict theory, feminism, identity politics, even mainstream sociology – labeling was constantly challenged (not infrequently, assailed) for its definitional inadequacies and imprecise conceptualization (pp. 33–51). In short, the halcyon days of the 1960s were over for interactionist theories and the field of deviance generally. Certainly neither disappeared from intellectual discourse, but both gave ground in the face of the rise of criminology and, eventually, that of criminal justice as well (Best, 2006, pp. 537–539; Dotter, 2004, p. 278).

Best (2004a, pp. 54–60) recognizes that labeling left an intellectual legacy following the 1970s, including a renewed interest in the construction of social problems (Spector and Kitsuse, 1987 [1977]; Holstein and Miller, 1993); studies of medicalization – that is, the recasting of deviance and social problems as medical issues (Conrad and Schneider, 1980); and research into social movements. Also, within the field of deviance he summarizes the renewed research interest in qualitative/ethnographic studies. While apparently not insignificant, these developments did not arrest the relative decline of deviance or labeling perspectives. Best (2004a) writes:

> This sympathy for the labeling approach allowed people to develop ideas in various directions. Some largely dropped the language of deviance in favor of talking about social problems or social movements. Others asked a variety of different research questions that emerged to guide studies of various topics related to deviance (e.g., about deviant transactions, emotion, or gender), but none of these questions captured the imagination of the field in the way that the labeling perspective had in the 1960s. In the aftermath of the attacks on labeling theory, there were no dramatic theoretical developments. No new paradigm emerged to transform the field. (p. 68)

To this point Best's analysis of the historical trajectory of deviance as a concept and a field is concise and well-argued; it is also incomplete.

Two other strands of the deviance debate bring the narrative into the present. One strand is the "death" of the sociology of deviance, with the obituary written by Colin Sumner (1994); the other is a reaffirmation of constructionist/interactionist perspectives (Schur, 1980; Douglas, 1984; Goode, 2002, 2003, 2004a, 2004b; Dotter, 2004). The former is pessimistic to the extreme, while the latter attempts to go beyond Best in shaping a contemporary interactionist narrative.

Colin Sumner: the "death" of the sociology of deviance

In sounding the death knell of the sociology of deviance, Sumner (1994, p. x) interjected more than a bit of drama into the debate: "We have changed the world that gave rise to the sociology of deviance and those changes have altered the way we look at that old world. The sociology of deviance no longer expresses our vision in the very new world of the 1990s. In that sense it is dead. Its voice cannot speak." He adds even more feeling to his narrative: "The terrain now resembles the Somme in 1918, It is barren, fruitless, full of empty trenches and craters, littered with unexploded mines and eerily silent. No one fights for hegemony over a dangerous graveyard" (p. ix).

Unfortunately, Sumner's death metaphor does little more than dramatize the terms of the debate; it does not illuminate what has changed so radically about the sociology of deviance to merit such a claim. With less flourish he argues that "the behavioral concept of social deviance had run its course by 1975"; that "there was no logical reason why the deviance should be said to inhere in the behavior and not the relation between the behavior and the norm"; and, finally, that "the relations between deviance, crime, and difference were totally incoherent" (p. 309). His lurid descriptions and his more reasonable claim of conceptual difficulties bookend his history of the field, which, like that of Best, is hardly controversial. In the end Sumner argues that ideology led to the field's demise:

> Whether it was the ideology of the law-makers, or the morality-definers, whether it was widely shared or not, and whether it was the ideology of the deviants reflecting the contradictory social relations within which they lived, deviance was now ideological – both as a category of moral censure and as a category of behavior. (p. 308)

Erich Goode's response: the field reclaimed

In several articles Goode (2002, 2003, 2004a, 2004b) thoroughly dismantles Sumner's death claim. At the same time, he takes Best to task for underestimating the health of the field, although to be fair, Best (2004b, p. 487) himself has called the "death" of deviance a red herring. In Goode's (2004a, pp. 505–506) view, criticizing the conceptual relevance of deviance is overdone and more than a bit of a fad. He sees critics as being "mesmerized" by a word – deviance – without proper regard for its meaning.

Goode (2002) recognizes that, especially over decades, interactionist deviance theorizing has changed contexts, even waxed and waned in popularity. Still, he argues that disvaluement – of behavior, status, categories of people and so on – remains crucial to the conceptual clarity of deviance, and that stigma is afforded the widest appreciation in constructionist perspectives. Where Best, Sumner and others see continued conceptual inadequacy, Goode senses far-from-exhausted potential. The current debate is thus evidence of the vitality of deviance – the concept, the field and its constructionist narrative.

Goode (2004a) places the critical dialogue in the following wider context:

> It's true that many sociologists-from conventional positivists to postmodernists-imagine that the field of the sociology of deviance has been "discredited." But in thinking about how the social world

operates, they themselves use the concept in much the same way that sociologists of deviance use the concept. I suspect they don't like the term; it sounds...politically incorrect. In my view, the objection that feminists, po-mo types, queer theorists, identity politicos, and conflict theorists make to the field is completely bogus. They misunderstand what the field is about. They use the concept without understanding what it means. (p. 506)

Criticism – both from within and outside the field of deviance – misconstrues the constructionist emphasis on stigmatization in two possible ways: from the left as itself a negative label, even a condemnation, of behavior and people; or, alternately, from the right as a sign that all labels are almost hyper-relative (Costello, 2006; Hendershott, 2002) and any context is fruitless.

As arguably the most influential critics, even Best (more moderately) and Sumner (somewhat offhandedly) recognize the continued importance of meaning generation and disvaluement. Sumner (1994, p. 304) sees the concept of censure as the successor to that of deviance. Best (2006, pp. 543–544) is not so certain of possible paths. He muses that a new approach may be forthcoming, "taking a fresh look at the concept, perhaps framing it in slightly different terms", or that "sociologists might devise new sets of questions to ask about deviance, questions that might guide researchers".

Building bridges: interactionist theorizing and the politics of deviance

Elsewhere I describe the death of the sociology of deviance as "an obituary absent a demise" (Dotter, 2004, p. 277). Like Goode, I view the current controversy in the field as a sign of its intellectual vitality rather than its decline. As I pointed out, Best (2004a) has written of the 1970s as a time of "labeling under attack" as if the situation were fundamentally negative or fatal to the theory; I think not. By the 1980s, Jack Douglas (1984) had begun to conceptualize a number of "special interactionist theories" of deviance, all sharing a focus on meaning construction and generation. These perspectives include all variations of Chicago labeling and interactionism; interactional conflict; and sociological phenomenology. At very nearly the same time, Edwin Schur (1980) published a monograph clearly arguing for the "politicality" of deviance, thereby recasting traditional interactionist concerns with societal reaction (Dotter and Roebuck, 1988) in a wider socio-cultural context.

Schur (1980, pp. 18–21) summarizes two vitally important aspects to the politicality of deviance. First is "the amplification of deviance" by the mass media. This may include selective reporting and – intentionally or not – the reinforcement of negative stereotypes. The second aspect of the politics of deviance is the increasing role of formal organizations that process deviance, both legal and extra-legal. Schur (1980, p. 21) explains "that the state itself clearly plays a significant role, direct or indirect, in virtually all the broad deviant situations (e.g., 'the drug problem', 'the war against crime', 'treatment of the mentally ill') that preoccupy the citizenry in a modern society". David Matza (2010 [1969], pp. 143–144) had earlier hinted at Schur's argument in his analysis of labeling as signification a process dominated by governmental organizations that Matza characterizes as "Leviathan".

The interconnection of media amplification and formal organizational labeling activity is thus evident in the politicized deviance-defining process. Traditional interactionism (Becker, 1973 [1963]; Dotter and Roebuck, 1988) tended to focus on the problematic of labeling as a criminal justice outcome (i.e., who is more or less likely to be criminalized, particularly along racial and class lines). Schur (1980, p. 21) casts a wider interpretive net by maintaining that "there is considerable disagreement regarding the precise nature, extent, and overall implications of this [state] role". In coining the richly descriptive term "stigma contest", Schur illuminates the political context of deviance-labeling (p. 8). Such contests are not neutral; play out in both media narratives and governmental activities aimed at social control, in which relative rather than absolute power holds sway; and are a mixture of norms, enforcement groups and mechanisms and labels.

Interactionism and cultural studies: the scenario and meaning generation

Interactionism and cultural studies

The centrality of symbolic interactionist conceptions of deviance (Downes and Rock, 2007 [1982]) ensured that the field was somewhat sensitive to wider theoretical developments in sociology. By the 1990s symbolic interactionism was overlapping with the emerging field of cultural studies (Surber, 1998; Hall and Birchall, 2006; Denzin, 1992), and this contact influenced deviance theorizing (Dotter, 2004).

Cultural studies is an interdisciplinary project which focuses on the importance of mass communication and meaning generation in contemporary society (Carey, 2009 [1989]; Dotter, 2004, pp. 135–164). British cultural studies (Cohen, 2002 [1972]; Hall and Jefferson, 2006 [1975]; Hebdige, 2002 [1979]) from the beginning greatly overlapped with interactionist labeling, especially Becker's work on moral panics; American proponents (Best and Kellner, 2001; Denzin, 1992; Kellner, 1995) cast a wider interpretive net to include the so-called postmodern turn in social theory (Best and Kellner, 1997, 2001; Dotter, 2004, pp. 164–181), focusing on "media culture" (Kellner, 1995) and, particularly, the manner in which meaning is created and changed.

An interactionist-cultural studies articulation reinvigorates the study of deviance; stigmatization is part of the same process responsible for all cultural meaning production. This includes disvalued behavior and cultural identities (Young, 1996) as well as "stigmatized" knowledge (Barkun, 2003).

To describe this process, I offer the concept of scenario: an interactional moment of meaning creation (Dotter, 1997, 2011), the narrative presentation of an event or historical context within media culture. The term is an early designation in film history for screenplay (Katz, 1994, p. 1205), and simultaneously serves as a metaphor for the "voyeur's gaze" in contemporary society (Denzin, 1995).

The scenario, as ongoing media process, has three layers (Dotter, 2004, pp. 37–41). The first is the *deviant event*, an occurrence in space and time that most often triggers the other layers. The significance of the event, especially as it becomes public knowledge, may or may not be clearly communicated. The meaning of the event emerges in media culture over time and calls into question the relationship of laws to other types of norms. Societal reaction may take the form or criminal charges, informal sanctions, both, or neither. Criminal labeling is not an entirely independent reaction to other forms of judgment in this layer, as informal reactions may also transpire. Also, there may be multiple events, deviant and otherwise, that frame the scenario, describing real people, their putative actions, situational normative constructions and possible societal reactions.

The second layer is that of *media reconstruction*, "bounded by the expanded activities of media, law enforcement, and other audiences in offering interpretations of the deviant event" (Dotter, 2004, p. 38). As potential actors, these audiences, both formal organizations or as individuals, not infrequently begin to generate a second-layer drama via television or the Internet. The familiar interactionist concepts of moral entrepreneurs (Becker, 1973 [1963], pp. 147–163) and moral panic (Goode and Ben-Yehuda, 2009 [1994]; Thompson, 1998) most often first appear at this point, framed by typification (Best, 1989) and claims-making (Spector and Kitsuse, 1987 [1977]; Ibarra and Kitsuse, 1993; Miller, 1993) as instances of deviance as well as emerging social problems. In this layer, meaning continues to be negotiated and clarified, both factual and opinion strands.

The third layer is the *stigma movie*, representing the point (never discreetly identifiable) at which media reconstructions not only share cultural space with the deviant event, but may eventually compete with and overshadow the significance of the original. Herein, meaning generation becomes amplified in various media as the movie gradually defines and justifies its own existence – the process Jean Baudrillard (1994 [1981]) describes as implosion of reality. As a concept, the stigma movie is generally synonymous with implosion, whereby "the commodification of deviance as a cultural representation becomes its own experience" (Dotter, 2004, p. 40). The term is a metaphor for the meaning generation process; the meaning itself may be created within any type or combination of cultural texts.

In the scenario, then, meaning generation assumes significance well beyond simple criminal labeling. Although every deviant event does not transmute into a stigma movie, Schur's (1980) politicality of deviance and his concept of stigma contest are given a thoroughgoing mediated context. The intersecting layers of meaning in the scenario reconstitute moral boundaries; definitions of deviance are "ideologized" or commodified. Most important, the movie is the layer in which the stigma contest is so completely realized. It often showcases celebrity actors and is "scripted around the master statuses of age, gender, race, and class" (Dotter, 2004, p. 42).

In the stigma movie, definitions of deviance and crime continue to overlap with the related process of social problems construction as "a dialogue, a narrative stigma contest among claims-makers (i.e., moral entrepreneurs, rule creators, and enforcers, as well as other general audiences) and those symbolically stigmatized" (Dotter, 2002, p. 441). This discourse may also include claims-making by marginalized groups (Miller, 1993). Initially generated in the media reconstruction layer, meaning-as-typification remains a key dynamic of the stigma movie, that is, the media- and professionally provided situational context to the behavior, events and/or problem (Best, 1989, p. xx). Typing is a necessary if not sufficient prelude to the political genesis of a moral panic (Cohen, 2002 [1972], pp. 90–93).

In the layered, cinematic scenario, deviance and crime narratives are cited in broader mediated contexts of social control (Cohen, 2002 [1972]; Foucault, 1983). Control may be exercised through traditional criminal labeling, or it may be largely unconscious and not so apparent (i.e., ideological), whereby what is defined as deviance in media culture is pre-empted in its presentation. In short, the scenario – however messily and incompletely – links Debord's (1994 [1967]) society of the spectacle to what Patricia and Peter Adler (2006) have called the deviance society. The former exposes the emptiness of appearance, while the latter describes "a growing paradigm that uses definitions of deviance to disempower and control people who dissent from the majority opinion" (p. 135).

It is not only social categories such as age, gender, race and class that frame meaning in the scenario; as both ideology (i.e., control of meaning production) and spectacle (i.e., appearance as its own justification), media culture inundates audiences with extremes of meaning, including novel perspectives on what may pass as deviance.

The carnival of deviance: stirrings of the uncanny

As a concept articulated from film studies, the scenario locates meaning generation in media culture, in the play between the society of spectacle and that of deviance. To be more precise, the shorthand use of "society" to characterize these two situations (i.e., the centrality of appearance and ideology in meaning creation) is a textual frame; the cinematic quality of the scenario is captured in what Denzin (1995) calls "the voyeur's gaze." Definitions of deviance are negotiated as narratives, emerging from "real" events, from fictional sources or a combination of the two (Dotter, 2004, p. 44).

The scenario presents images of deviance as both documentary (i.e., factual) and dramatic (i.e., entertainment) narratives. The voyeuristic quality of both textual presentations lies in the "invitation" to audiences to vicariously enter the experiences of characters in the narrative (Culler, 2000); in "sharing" and thereby consuming the text as the stigma movie, the audience, all of us, are part of the meaning-making process. The scenario is thus a form of postmodern story-telling (i.e., description and interpretation), emerging from media culture and predicated on the transformative quality of *all* cultural meaning as narrative stories (Dotter, 2004, pp. 44–45). Definitions of deviance, crime and conformity emerge from these stories, generated in media culture.

In the scenario, labeling evolves into transgression through presentation of the stigma movie in media culture: the continuous negotiation, transformation, re-emergence and consumption of meaning (Foucault, 1977). The meaning may be simultaneously overblown and of substantial depth. A fitting descriptor for transgression is the concept of carnival:

> The symbolism of carnival is rich; in reality it was much more than a period of release, or even contained anarchism. Carnival acts through strategies that ape, parody and indeed parallel the dominant social order. There is a calculated inversion of existing social forms and cultural configurations: coronations take place (Lords of Misrule are elected), laws are passed, trials are held, punishments are executed. (Jenks, 2003, p. 162)

In the carnival, transgression activates criminal and other kinds of labels and in the process marks the cultural dynamic of self and other (Dotter, 2011). This dynamic is anchored in the labeling process – that is, signification – as Matza (2010 [1969], p. 156) brilliantly explicates:

> To make someone or something stand for yet something else is an act of genuine creation requiring an investment of meaning. Thus signifying makes its object more significant-as we might expect. The object enjoys – or suffers – enhanced meaning. To be signified a thief is to lose the blissful identity of one who among other things happens to have committed a theft. It is a movement, however gradual, toward being a thief and representing theft. The two movements are intimately related; without a population selected and cast as thieves, we might have to look everywhere to comprehend the prevalence of theft.

The labeling process, formal and informal, involves signification of the other (i.e., disvalued persons and groups). In the stigma contest (Schur, 1980) political context is amplified through media stereotyping; in the stigma movie of the scenario, the other is a transgressing narrative, "what is expelled as unacceptable or unthinkable, or reduced to inferior status", "a carrier of pollution, irrationality and danger" (Jervis, 1999, p. 1). Transgression captures movement across permeable boundaries; it places disvaluement in the cultural politics of dominant/marginalized voices and in the contested narratives of cultural knowledge.

Thus the stigma movie is a contemporary site for the appearance of "the uncanny" in media culture. Sigmund Freud (2003 [1919], p. 132) conceptualized the uncanny as referring to "everything that was intended to remain secret, hidden away, and has come into the open". The meaning strands of the uncanny include fear and anxiety, but are not limited to them; familiarity and strangeness are simultaneously present as well. Freud continues: "An uncanny effect often arises when the boundary between fantasy and reality is blurred, when we are faced with the reality of something that we have until now considered imaginary, when a symbol takes on the full function and significance of what it symbolizes, and so forth" (p. 150).

In his contemporary articulation of the concept, Nicholas Royle (2003, p. 24) describes the uncanny as a "critical spectralization of feeling and belief", joining the discourses of psychoanalysis and deconstruction. Furthermore, the uncanniness of meaning is an emergent quality of modern and postmodern media culture: "the issue of the uncertain status of originality and the haunting of what seems new in the present by the residues of the past" (Jay, 1998, p. 157). Finally, the uncanny may encompass nostalgia (Vidler, 1992, pp. 7–8); the shock of urban life experience (Benjamin, 2007 [1968]); the haunting of the divided self by ghostly doubles (Kearney, 2003); and Max Weber's "disenchantment of the world" (Collins and Jervis, 2008). To these extremes of meaning creation, we may add contemporary ever-present conspiracy narratives.

Conspiracy as stigmatized knowledge: exopolitics and UFO conspiracies

The carnival and extreme deviance

As a scenario of cultural meaning generation, the carnival is marked by extremes of stigmatized behavior, groups and knowledge; it blends multiple realities and identities into the stigma movie. In short, the carnival metaphor suggests that media culture increasingly projects life in the interplay of extreme boundaries and the cultural uncanniness of experience.

The concept of extreme deviance (Goode and Vail, 2008) is important here for two reasons. First, it expands the context of labeling beyond the traditionally recognized sites of stigmatized behavior and status to include beliefs, worldviews, cosmologies and so on. These ideas represent narratives or stories, within which deviance and stigma are situated as frequent and recurring themes. In other words, extreme deviance is socially constructed within these wider scenarios of meaning. The disvaluement is never absolute, but exists alongside definitions of conformity or expected outcomes.

Second, extreme deviance is arguably a pure form of transgression (i.e., boundary crossings in media culture): the extremity of the stigma depends on the boundary transgressed in multiple layers of mainstream, especially popular, culture. Mediated storylines of extreme deviance are often embedded within "paranormal" knowledge and beliefs: "the view that under certain circumstances what are regarded by traditional scientists as the laws of nature can be bent, broken, suspended, violated, superseded, or subsumed under entirely different principles" (Goode, 2000, p. 23). Examples of paranormal knowledge include occult beliefs and prophecies, spiritualism, UFOs and contact with alien life forms, prediction of the future, faith-healing, telekinesis and so on. These paranormal narratives overlap in popular culture through the twin themes of apocalypse and conspiracy (Dotter, 2011).

The historical linking of conspiracy and apocalypse is found in Richard Hofstadter's classic description of "the paranoid style in American politics." The concept was introduced in 1964, as both a *Harper's Magazine* article and as the extended title chapter in a book of essays (Hofstadter, 1979 [1964]); he carefully makes clear that his use of the term "paranoid" is not in the clinical sense. It is more a historical, cultural marker and less a purely psychological one.

In general, paranormal refers to descriptions and explanations "outside of" conventional scientific ones, beyond a naturalistic cause-and-effect model (Goode, 2000, p. 18). Especially in the past decade, cultural images of apocalypse have proliferated, going beyond stark religious prophecies (i.e., of revelation and/or destruction) (Weber, 1999) to include secular scenarios of global catastrophe (Boyer, 1992). Similarly, conspiracy narratives cover all sorts of stories: political machinations, extraterrestrial invasion and everything in between (Fenster, 2008 [1999]; Knight, 2002a; Birchall, 2006). Michael Barkun (2003) cogently summarizes the interplay of apocalyptic and conspiratorial themes, labeling the latter as a generic form of "stigmatized" knowledge. In the context of the scenario, conspiracy stories represent continuous transgressions or boundary crossings. As cultural knowledge, conspiracy narratives are ever-present and the subject of constant controversy, if not outright declarations of illegitimacy.

Exopolitics: transgressing cultural boundaries of UFO knowledge

In postmodern culture, transgression represents a kind of "mediated signification". The dissemination of conspiracy knowledge begins to permeate more mainstream outlets, and the audience(s) for the narrative expands and becomes increasingly diverse, if not sophisticated. Barkun (2003) marks this softening of conspiracy as extreme political belief to its contact with the fairly politically non-threatening UFO scenarios:

> As long as conspiracy theories, such as those that posit a New World Order plot, were strongly linked to antigovernment militants, anti-Semites, and neo-Nazis, the audience for conspiracism was limited. This was true even though conspiracism has also found a niche among religious fundamentalist as part of Antichrist theology. This political exile, however, now seems to be over, thanks to the incorporation of New World Order conspiracy into UFO beliefs. (p. 178)

Thus, conspiracism discursively blends with multiple forms of paranormal knowledge, including ufology. Certainly this blending is not seamless, nor is it apolitical:

> Ufology is political because it is stigmatized. To claim to have seen a UFO, to have been abducted by aliens, or even to believe those who say they have is a political act. It may not be a very big or revolutionary political act, but it contests the status quo. Immediately it installs the claimant at the margins of the social, within a network of sites and connections that don't command a great deal of mindshare, that don't get a lot of hits. (Dean, 1998, p. 6)

Increasingly, conspiracy narratives enter mainstream cultural space, and through transgression (of audiences, media and so on) the stigma attached to the knowledge is rendered less extreme. This neutralizing of extreme deviance is particularly accomplished in popular culture. The conspiracy scenario is consumed by audiences at once as information and entertainment; in the process, boundaries appear, transform, blur, disappear and reappear continuously (Gergen, 2000 [1991], p. 119). Thereby, the conspiracy story can become "paranoia within reason" (Marcus, 1999). In effect, the layering of conspiracy stories throughout media culture to a certain degree institutionalizes paranoia and secretive knowledge contexts. Extremely stigmatized narratives indeed do not disappear. Rather, their signification as deviant knowledge is highly situational and political, the meaning evolving and regressing in time and space. Jodi Dean (1998, p. 8) presses the argument further: "I am convinced that many contemporary political matters are simply undecidable. My particular interest is in those, like ufology and abduction, that not only turn on questions of evidence, but involve charges of conspiracy and are in conflict with what is claimed as 'consensus reality' or 'common sense'".

In his contemporary take on the "paranoid style", George E. Marcus (1999, pp. 2–3) sees conspiracy narratives as a predictable extension of Cold War politics and policy: "The effects of decades of paranoid policies of statecraft and governing habits of thought define a present reality for social actors in some places and situations that is far from extremist or distortingly fundamentalist, but is quite reasonable and commonsensical". Following World War II, Cold War culture presented two sustained conspiracy threads. First was the political narrative of Communism as an aggressive existential threat, constructed domestically as "enemies within". Robert Alan Goldberg (2001, pp. 22–23) traces this master conspiracy over more than half a century from the 1950s Red Scare to contemporary fear of the New World Order.

Second was the narrative of a government cover-up of extraterrestrial sightings, contact and knowledge, proceeding from the 1947 incident at Roswell, New Mexico:

> In the late evening of July 3, 1947, a severe thunder and lightning storm raked central New Mexico. During the height of the storm, local ranchers would later describe hearing a loud explosion that did not sound like the other thunderclaps. Civilians would arrive at the site first. Some would attempt to report it to the local sheriff. Others would later describe what they saw, but they would wait many years before finally admitting to their closest family members and friends facts that still defy all reasonable and conventional explanation...."These people, members of America's 'Greatest Generation', believed that they witnessed, up close and personal, the remains of an interplanetary vehicle of unknown origin – a crashed *flyingsaucer*". (Carey and Schmitt, 2009 [2007], p. 21; italics in the original)

As a paranormal conspiracy story, the Roswell event is significant: interest in it has, arguably, increased through the years. From the original event to the present, the US government has offered no less than four distinct explanations to the public, responding to various criticisms over the years and thereby admitting some degree of lying. The first two explanations were given within hours of the event: the crash of a flying saucer and – in a complete reversal – a misidentified weather balloon. The third explanation appeared in 1994 (along with acknowledgment of the earlier prevarication): "What crashed was now a high-flying contraption composed of multiple weather balloons, multiple radar targets, and a listening device belonging to a special project – Project Mogul – that fell to earth near Roswell" (pp. 29–30).

The fourth explanation came in 1997 – the 50th anniversary of the crash – and was meant to dispel eyewitness accounts of alien bodies at the scene. Rather, the objects were revealed to be full-size (six-foot-tall) mannequins in several Air Force projects involving high-altitude parachute drops, carried out in New Mexico in the 1950s as preparation for our country's manned space program. The obvious time disparity was a result of witnesses suffering "time compression" in which "recollections of past events tend to contract the time frames in which they took places as a person ages" (Carey and Schmitt, 2009 [2007], pp. 29–30).

The Roswell scenario framed the emergence of ongoing governmental UFO cover-ups in both mainstream and popular culture. As suggested earlier, it is this paranormal governmental conspiracy to deceive which has tended to neutralize the stigma of UFO apocalyptic knowledge as well as to legitimate "reasonable" suspicion of governmental accounts. In a massive two-volume history titled *UFOs and the National Security State*, Richard M. Dolan (2002 [2000], 2009) presents a hidden history of the US government's active and ongoing cover-up of both alien sightings and visitations over the past half-century. In the process he suggests how ufology as transgressed knowledge has evolved:

> Leading edge thinking on the topic was in a very different place in 1991 than it had been during the early 1970s. How researchers got from the one place to the other is a fascinating story. What had once seemed like a somewhat straightforward proposition-extraterrestrials visiting Earth in spaceships-went through many permutations. Researchers began to discuss subjects previously off-limits, such as dimensions, time travel, remote viewing, abductions, animal mutilations, black helicopters, crop circles, and the Nazi "legacy". Included in this explosion of new ideas were claims and details of the cover-up, and even discussion of whether or not there was a "human-alien deal" involving abductions and technology transfer. Much of the new thinking was based on solid foundations, such as government documents, open source research, or new developments in science. Some of it was fantastic and impossible to verify. (Dolan, 2009, p. 4)

This proliferation and dissemination of heretofore stigmatized paranormal conspiracy knowledge has helped in the creation of a "conspiracy culture" (Knight, 2000), both as explanation and entertainment. Disentangling its discursive threads and evaluating the level, quality and context of deviant signification is no easy task:

Conspiracy theories are now less a sign of mental delusion than an ironic stance toward knowledge, and the possibility of truth, operating within the rhetorical terrain of the double negative. They are now presented self-consciously as a symptom that includes its own in-built diagnosis. The rhetoric of conspiracy takes itself seriously, but at the same time casts satiric suspicion on everything, even its own pronouncements. (pp. 2–3)

Moreover, the presentation of conspiracy as popular culture extends the very idea of audience to its own extremity: "We are all conspiracy theorists now: you can hear it, read it, watch it, play it, and buy it everywhere – without necessarily having to buy into it. In short, a self-conscious and self-reflexive entertainment culture of conspiracy has become thoroughly mainstream" (Knight, 2002b, p. 6).

This movement of knowledge (i.e., transgression) from the extreme toward the mainstream is marked by the dissolution and reconstitution of boundaries and the increasingly popular dissemination of ufology as conspiracy narrative; the emergence of exopolitics (Webre, 2005) describes the effort to expose the conspiracy at the heart of UFO scenarios:

The extraterrestrial presence goes to the very core of how key actors, processes and institutions operate in international politics. An international political system based on disinformation, intimidation and manipulation has been constructed to hide the truth about the extraterrestrial presence and to maintain a nondisclosure policy that has existed for nearly 70 years. (Salla, 2004, p. vii)

Exopolitics views the ET/UFO conspiracy as the hidden, unsolved mystery of the new millennium. The shifting boundaries of such deviant knowledge is a key to the persistence of the narrative. The appearance of exopolitics has largely coincided with the explosion of stigmatized knowledge, the transgression of its boundaries and the layering of conspiracies within various scenarios. Barkun (2003) describes this cultural terrain as movement from conspiracism to millennialism; in transgression the movement involves the following:

A heterogeneous assortment of beliefs and ideas. They concern an alleged shadow government, the secret circles of religious and fraternal organizations, a hidden world beneath our feet, and the machinations of alien intelligences. The elements can be arranged in innumerable permutations. Because all that is visible is deception, one permutation may seem as likely as any other. All claim empirical truth, but none trusts conventional canons of evidence. Thus the empirical claims coexist with nonfalsifiability. (pp. 183–184)

This layering of conspiracy and millennial narratives is an inevitable product of media culture, especially the consumption of popular images as largely uncontested factual claims. This latter process, referring to the transgression of empirical truth, is marked by its fragmentation (p. 188) and disinformation. Regarding the UFO conspiracy narrative, efforts of governmental cover-up are aided by popular culture narratives.

UFO conspiracy scenarios are ultimately global, universal narratives. Their dissemination is an artifact of postmodern media culture, the context of which is constantly shifting from informational reality to entertainment and back again in multimedia stigma movies. In the process the boundaries of signification (of behavior and status) are blurred, enabling the internalization of social control as conspiracy narratives are popularly consumed. Matza (2010 [1969], pp. 150–152) foresaw this possibility in the opacity of labeling in the narrow sense; the scenario transposes the opaque to wider and deeper currents of cultural meaning construction.

Conclusion: conspiracy panic and the alien as other

In this chapter, I have attempted to chart a course for the construction of deviance within a media culture of increasing complexity. The debate over the contemporary importance of deviance as a concept (or of the relevance of the field itself) is a bridge to the interdisciplinary problems of meaning generation. The term deviance studies (Schur, 1979; Dotter, 2004) has been used in reference to this broader interpretive theoretical stance. The vitality of interactionist deviance theorizing, with a cultural studies articulation, is reaffirmed in the concept of scenario, and any declaration of the death of deviance is faddishly premature. In my example, stigmatization of behavior and status are increasingly embedded as deviant cultural knowledge in conspiracy narratives.

In a similar vein Jack Z. Bratich (2008, p. 11) attempts to update the traditional interactionist importance of moral panic (Goode and Ben-Yehuda, 2009 [1994]; Cohen, 2002 [1972]); he frames a wider context of cultural meaning construction and conspiracy narratives. In the moral panic, the threat is a specific identifiable social group; in the conspiracy panic, the threat is diffuse, even unspecified. Bratich (2008) then goes deeper into the ideological component of conspiracy "theories" in contemporary scenarios of meaning:

> We can say that the inability to define conspiracy theory is no failure or flaw. It is precisely the motor that allows the conspiracy panic to operate. By never having final criteria for what counts as a conspiracy theory, the term can be wielded in a free-floating way to apply to a variety of accounts. (p. 12)

Conceptually, conspiracy panic sets the terms under which conspiracy theories can be discussed and treated as meaningful social realities. As scenarios of meaning construction, conspiracy stories are discursive, subjugated forms of knowledge, resisting and "outside of" what Foucault (1980) calls the "regime of truth" in media culture:

> Each society has its regime of truth, its "general politics" of truth: that is, the types of discourse which it accepts and makes function as true; the mechanisms and instances which enable one to distinguish true and false statements, the means by which each is sanctioned; the techniques and procedures accorded value in the acquisition of truth; the status of those who are charged with saying what counts as true. (p. 131)

Indeed, the practically universal connotation of conspiracy-as-theory is just such a marker of subjugated, marginalized knowledge: As theory, the truth of the conspiracy cannot be proven, nor even seriously considered (Bratich, 2003). As the context of legitimate knowledge, the regime of truth constitutes a largely unexamined form of social control: this ideology-as-discourse discriminates among acceptable and unacceptable forms of cultural meaning (i.e., transgression) and establishes the intersubjective narrative of actors in the scenario (Foucault, 1983; Melley, 2000, pp. 38–39). In effect, the scenario is the relational presentation of knowledge which is stigmatized (i.e., "outside of" the regime of truth), rather than a focus on behavior or person as in traditional interactionist labeling. As Bratich (2008) argues:

> Studying conspiracy theories as subjugated knowledges would demonstrate how some accounts become dominant only through struggle. An official account comes to *be* official only through a victory over, and erasure of conflict with, conspiracy accounts. Among the competing accounts for any event, the official version is not merely

the winner in a game of truth-it determines who the players can be. (p. 7; italics in the original)

The paranormal conspiracy linking the US political culture with UFO deception may be just such a panic, a stigma movie portraying symbolic displacement: Extraterrestrial life is the "extreme" unknowable other in a narrative with shifting status boundaries. In this intersubjective turn, science fiction mirrors the everyday, and "some prominent contemporary aliens click on current insecurities about technology, otherness, and the future. The most obvious link is between the space alien and the noncitizen" (Dean, 1998, p. 155).

This link between space alien and other was most chillingly dramatized in the 1956 science fiction film "Invasion of the Body Snatchers" (Arnold, 2008, pp. 34–36; Grant, 2010). Inert extraterrestrial seed pods arrive on Earth with the potential to produce alien replicas of humans, down to the finest physical detail. When the transformation is complete, the original humans die in their sleep and the alien copies take their places.

On its release, the film was critiqued as a metaphor of McCarthyism and the 1950s Red Scare. Viewed through today's lens of cultural politics, the narrative suggests a transgression of meaning, whereby deviant behavior and status are blurred by the disappearance of normative boundaries. For this reason, all is not as normal as may appear in day-to-day life, nor can people be trusted (Arnold, 2008, p. 36). The gradual takeover of human society by alien beings who are exact physical duplicates has a basis for metaphor in the contemporary issues of illegal immigration and terrorist infiltration of the democratic polity. In the face of these two threats, other types of contested difference (e.g., age, gender and class) seem, for the moment, to be of secondary importance. Not only do normative boundaries become unstable, but the markers of self-identity are increasingly precarious in scenarios of media culture. Conspiracy narratives, in the transgressive carnival, are textual expressions of normative boundaries between self and other (Jervis, 1999).

The concept of conspiracy panics, as realized in stigma movies with extraterrestrial storylines, exposes an uncanny doubling process in contemporary culture: the free-floating anxiety of the not-to-be proven conspiracy plot is externalized into the arrival of the alien, otherworldly, other. As meaning generation scenarios, narratives of UFO "exopolitics" overlap with paranormal knowledge (Goode, 2000; Dean, 1998) and are nearly universally stigmatized as irrational, fear-mongering "theories". Such storylines have percolated for decades in the ambiguous voyeuristic imagination of media culture and the number is not likely to decrease.

References

Adler, P. A. and P. Adler (2006) "The Deviance Society", *Deviant Behavior*, 27, 129–148.

Arnold, G. B. (2008) *Conspiracy Theory in Film, Television, and Politics* (Westport: Praeger).

Barkun, M. (2003) *A Culture of Conspiracy: Apocalyptic Visions in Contemporary America* (Berkeley: University of California Press).

Baudrillard, J. (1994 [1981]) *Simulacra and Simulation* (Ann Arbor: University of Michigan Press).

Becker, H. S. (ed.) (1964) *The Other Side: Perspectives on Deviance* (New York: Free Press).

—— (1967) "Whose Side Are We On?", *Social Problems*, 14, 239–247.

—— (1973 [1963]) *Outsiders: Studies in the Sociology of Deviance*, enl. edn. (New York: Free Press).

Benjamin, W. (2007 [1968]) "On Some Motifs in Baudelaire", in W. Benjamin and H. Arendt (eds.) and Leon Wieseltier (pref.) *Illuminations: Essays and Reflections* (New York: Schocken Books).

Best, J. (ed.) (1989) *Images of Issues: Typifying Contemporary Social Problems* (Hawthorne, NY: Aldine de Gruyter).

Best, J. (2004a) *Deviance: Career of a Concept* (Belmont, CA: Wadsworth).

—— (2004b) "Deviance May Be Alive, But Is It Intellectually Lively? A Reaction to Goode", *Deviant Behavior*, 25, 483–492.

—— (2006) "Whatever Happened to Social Pathology? Conceptual Fashions and the Sociology of Deviance", *Sociological Spectrum*, 26, 533–546.

Best, S. and D. Kellner (1997) *The Postmodern Turn* (Oxford: Blackwell).

Birchall, C. (2006) *Knowledge Goes Pop: From Conspiracy Theory to Gossip* (Oxford: Berg).

Boyer, P. (1992) *And Time Shall Be No More: Prophecy Belief in Modern American Culture* (Cambridge, MA: Harvard University Press).

Bratich, J. Z. (2003) "Making Politics Reasonable: Conspiracism, Subjectification, and Governing through Styles of Thought", in J. Z. Bratich, J. Packer and C. McCarthy (eds.) *Foucault, Cultural Studies, and Governmentality* (Albany: State University of New York Press).

—— (2008) *Conspiracy Panics: Political Rationality and Popular Culture* (Albany: State University of New York Press).

Carey, J. W. (2009 [1989]) *Communication as Culture: Essays on Media and Society*, rev. edn. (New York: Routledge).

Carey, T. J., and D. R. Schmitt (2009 [2007]) *Witness to Roswell: Unmasking the Government's Biggest Cover-Up*, rev. and exp. edn. Edgar Mitchell (fore.) and George Noory (after.) (Franklin Lakes, NJ: Career Press).

Clinard, M., R. Quinney and J. Wildeman (1994) *Criminal Behavior Systems: A Typology* (Cincinnati: Anderson).

Cohen, S. (2002 [1972]) *Folk Devils and Moral Panics: The Creation of the Mods and Rockers*, 3rd edn. (London: Routledge).

Collins, J. and J. Jervis (2008) "Introduction", in J. Collins and J. Jervis (eds.) *Uncanny Modernity: Cultural Theories, Modern Anxieties* (New York: Palgrave Macmillan).

Conrad, P. and J. W. Schneider (1980) *Deviance and Medicalization* (St. Louis: Mosby).

Costello, B. J. (2006) "Cultural Relativism and the Study of Deviance", *Sociological Spectrum*, 26, 581–594.

Culler, J. (2000) "The Literary in Theory", in J. Butler, J. Guillory and K. Thomas (eds.) *What's Left of Theory? New Work on the Politics of Literary Theory* (New York: Routledge).

Davis, N. J. (1975) *Sociological Constructions of Deviance: Perspectives and Issues in the Field* (Dubuque, IA: William C. Brown).

Dean, J. (1998) *Aliens in America: Conspiracy Cultures from Outerspace to Cyberspace* (Ithaca, NY: Cornell University Press).

Debord, G. (1994 [1967]) *The Society of the Spectacle* (New York: Zone Books).

Denzin, N. K. (1992) *Symbolic Interactionism and Cultural Studies: The Politics of Interpretation* (Cambridge, MA: Blackwell).

—— (1995) *The Cinematic Society: The Voyeur's Gaze* (London: Sage).

Dolan, R. M. (2002 [2000]) *UFOs and the National Security State: Chronology of a Cover-Up 1941–1973*, rev. edn. (Charlottesville, VA: Hampton Roads).

—— (2009) *UFOs and the National Security State: The Cover-Up Exposed 1973–1991*, L. Moulton Howe (fore.) (Rochester, NY: Keyhole).

Dotter, D. (1997) "Introduction: The Scenario as Postmodern Interpretive Strategy", *Sociological Spectrum*, 17, 249–257.

—— (2002) "Creating Deviance: Scenarios of Stigmatization in Postmodern Media Culture", *Deviant Behavior*, 23, 419–448.

—— (2004) *Creating Deviance: An Interactionist Approach* (Walnut Creek, CA: AltaMira Press).

—— (2011) "Cultural Criminology and the Carnival of Deviance: An Interactionist Appreciation", in H. Peters and M. Dellwing (eds.) *Langweiliges Verbrechen. Warum KriminologInnen den Umgang mit Kriminalität interessanter finden als Kriminalität* (Wiesbaden: Springer).

Dotter, D. and J. B. Roebuck (1988) "The Labeling Approach Re-examined: Interactionism and the Components of Deviance", *Deviant Behavior*, 9, 19–32.

Douglas, J. D. (1967) *The Social Meanings of Suicide* (Princeton: Princeton University Press).

—— (ed.) (1984) *The Sociology of Deviance* (Boston: Allyn and Bacon).

Downes, D. and P. Rock (2007 [1982]) *Understanding Deviance: A Guide to the Sociology of Crime and Rule-Breaking*, 5th edn. (New York: Oxford University Press).

Durkheim, E. (1951 [1897]) *Suicide: A Study in Sociology* (New York: Free Press).

Faris, R. E. L. (1970) *Chicago Sociology: 1920–1932* (Chicago: University of Chicago Press).

Fenster, M. (2008 [1999]) *Conspiracy Theories: Secrecy and Power in American Culture*, rev. and updated edn. (Minneapolis: University of Minnesota Press).

Foucault, M. (1977) *Language, Counter-Memory, and Practice: Selected Essays and Interviews* (Ithaca, NY: Cornell University Press).

—— (1980) *Power/Knowledge: Selected Interviews and Other Writings 1972–1977* (New York: Pantheon Books).

——(1983) "Afterword: The Subject and Power", in M. Foucault *Beyond Structuralism and Hermeneutics*, H. L. Dreyfus and P. Rabinow, 2nd edn. (Chicago: University of Chicago Press).

Freud, S. (2003 [1919]) "The Uncanny", in Sigmund Freud *The Uncanny*, D. McLintock (tr.) and Hugh Haughton (intro.) (New York: Penguin Books).

Gergen, K. J. (2000 [1991]) *The Saturated Self: Dilemmas of Identity in Contemporary Life* (New York: Basic Books).

Goffman, E. (1986 [1963]) *Stigma: Notes on the Management of Spoiled Identity* (New York: Touchstone).

Goldberg, R. A. (2001) *Enemies Within: The Culture of Conspiracy in Modern America* (New Haven, CT: Yale University Press).

Goode, E. (2000) *Paranormal Beliefs: A Sociological Introduction* (Long Grove, IL: Waveland Press).

——(2002) "Does the Death of the Sociology of Deviance Make Sense?", *American Sociologist*, 33, 107–118.

—— (2003) "The MacGuffin That Refuses to Die: An Investigation into the Condition of the Sociology of Deviance", *Deviant Behavior*, 24, 507–533.

—— (2004a) "The 'Death' MacGuffin Redux: Comments on Best", *Deviant Behavior*, 25, 493–509.

—— (2004b) "Is the Sociology of Deviance Still Relevant?", *American Sociologist*, 35, 46–57.

—— (2006) "Is the Deviance Concept Still Relevant to Sociology?", *Sociological Spectrum*, 26, 547–558.

Goode, E. and D. A. Vail (2008) *Extreme Deviance* (Thousand Oaks, CA: Pine Forge Press).

Goode, E. and N. Ben-Yehuda (2009 [1994]) *Moral Panics: The Social Construction of Deviance*, 2nd edn. (Malden, MA: Wiley-Blackwell).

Grant, B. K. (2010) *Invasion of the Body Snatchers* (London: Palgrave Macmillan/ British Film Institute).

Hall, G. and C. Birchall (eds.) (2006) *New Cultural Studies: Adventures in Theory* (Athens: University of Georgia Press).

Hall, S. and T. Jefferson (eds.) (2006 [1975]) *Resistance through Rituals: Youth Subcultures in Post-war Britain*, 2nd edn. (London: Routledge).

Hebdige, D. (2002 [1979]) *Subculture: The Meaning of Style* (London: Routledge).

Hendershott, A. (2002) *The Politics of Deviance* (San Francisco: Encounter Books).

Hester, S. and P. Eglin (1992) *A Sociology of Crime* (London: Routledge).

Hofstadter, R. (1964) "The Paranoid Style in American Politics", *Harper's Magazine* (November), 77–86.

——(1979 [1964]) *The Paranoid Style in American Politics and Other Essay* (Chicago: University of Chicago Press).

Holstein, J. A. and G. Miller (eds.) (1993) *Reconsidering Social Constructionism: Debates in Social Problems Theory* (New Brunswick, NJ: Transaction).

Ibarra, P. R. and J. I. Kitsuse (1993) "Vernacular Constituents of Moral Discourse: An Interactionist Proposal for the Study of Social Problems", in J. A. Holstein and G. Miller (eds.) *Reconsidering Social Constructionism: Debates in Social Problems Theory* (New Brunswick, NJ: Transaction).

Jay, M. (1998) "The Uncanny Nineties", in M. Jay (ed.) *Cultural Semantics: Keywords of Our Time* (Amherst: University of Massachusetts Press).

Jenks, C. (2003) *Transgression* (New York: Routledge).

Jervis, J. (1999) *Transgressing the Modern: Explorations in the Western Experience of Otherness* (Malden, MA: Blackwell).

Jordan, G. and C. Weedon (1995) *Cultural Politics: Class, Gender, Race and the Postmodern World* (Oxford: Blackwell).

Katz, E. (1994) *The Film Encyclopedia*, 2nd edn. (New York: HarperCollins).

Kearney, R. (2003) *Strangers, Gods and Monsters: Interpreting Otherness* (London: Routledge).

Kellner, D. (1995) *Media Culture: Cultural Studies, Identity and Politics between the Modern and Postmodern* (London: Routledge).

Knight, P. (2000) *Conspiracy Culture: From Kennedy to the X Files* (London: Routledge).

—— (ed.) (2002a) *Conspiracy Nation: The Politics of Paranoia in Postwar America* (New York: New York University Press).

—— (2002b) "Introduction: A Nation of Conspiracy Theorists", in P. Knight (ed.) *Conspiracy Nation: The Politics of Paranoia in Postwar America* (New York: New York University Press).

Marcus, G. E. (ed.) (1999) *Paranoia within Reason: A Casebook of Conspiracy as Explanation* (Chicago: University of Chicago Press).

Matza, D. (2010 [1969]) *Becoming Deviant*, rev. edn. (New Brunswick: Transaction).

Melley, T. (2000) *Empire of Conspiracy: The Culture of Paranoia in Postwar America* (Ithaca, NY: Cornell University Press).

Miller, L. J. (1993) "Claims-Making from the Underside: Marginalization and Social Problems Analysis", in J. A. Holstein and G. Miller (eds.) *Reconsidering Social Constructionism: Debates in Social Problems Theory* (New Brunswick, NJ: Transaction).

Mills, C. W. (1943) "The Professional Ideology of Social Pathologists", *American Journal of Sociology*, 49, 165–180.

Presdee, M. (2001) *Cultural Criminology and the Carnival of Crime* (London: Routledge).

Rock, P. (1979) *The Making of Symbolic Interaction* (Totowa, NJ: Rowman and Littlefield).

Royle, N. (2003) *The Uncanny* (Manchester: Manchester University Press).

Rubington, E. and M. S. Weinberg (2010) *The Study of Social Problems: Seven Perspectives*, 7th edn. (New York: Oxford University Press).

Sagarin, E. (1975) *Deviants and Deviance: An Introduction to the Study of Disvalued People and Behavior* (New York: Praeger).

Salla, M. E. (2004) *Exopolitics: Political Implications of the Extraterrestrial Presence* (Tempe, AZ: Dandelion Books).

Schur, E. M. (1971) *Labeling Deviant Behavior: Its Sociological Implications* (New York: Harper & Row).

—— (1979) *Interpreting Deviance: A Sociological Introduction* (New York: Harper & Row).

—— (1980) *The Politics of Deviance: Stigma Contests and the Uses of Power* (Englewood Cliffs, NJ: Prentice Hall).

Spector, M. and J. I. Kitsuse (1987 [1977]) *Constructing Social Problems* (New York: Aldine de Gruyter).

Sumner, C. (1994) *The Sociology of Deviance: An Obituary* (New York: Continuum).

Surber, J. P. (1998) *Culture and Critique: An Introduction to the Critical Discourses of Cultural Studies* (Boulder, CO: Westview).

Sutherland, E. H. (1983 [1949]) *White Collar Crime: The Uncut Version* (New Haven, CT: Yale University Press).

Sutherland, E. H., D. R. Cressey and D. F. Luckenbill (1992) *Principles of Criminology*, 11th edn. (Dix Hills, NY: General Hall).

Taylor, I., P. Walton and J. Young (1973) *The New Criminology: For a Sociology of Deviance* (London: Routledge & Kegan Paul).

Thompson, K. (1998) *Moral Panics* (New York: Routledge).

Vidler, A. (1992) "Introduction", in A. Vidler (ed.) *The Architectural Uncanny: Essays in the Modern Unhomely* (Cambridge, MA: MIT Press).

Weber, E. (1999) *Apocalypses: Prophecies, Cults, and Millennial Beliefs through the Ages* (Cambridge, MA: Harvard University Press).

Webre, A. L. (2005) *Exopolitics: Politics, Government, and Law in the Universe* (Vancouver: Universe Books).

Young, A. (1996) *Imagining Crime: Textual Outlaws and Criminal Conversations* (London: Sage).

8
Religious Deviance

Robin D. Perrin

Introduction

There is no shortage of interesting hits when one conducts Google or Google Scholar searches of the key terms "Fringe Religion" or "New Religious Movements" and, most productively, "Cults". Some organizations, articles and books one encounters take a scholarly and objective look at fringe religion, while others – indeed the vast majority – are alarmist and conspiratorial. They warn of evil beliefs and leaders, "brainwashing", Islamist takeovers and the like. Fascinating stuff, indeed, and a clear reminder that religion *as* deviance is alive and well.

Yet, when I examine the table of contents of the vast array of deviance textbooks on my shelves, I find very little mention of religion as deviance. For example, the text I used most recently in my Sociology of Deviance course, *Constructions of Deviance* (Adler and Adler, 2012), is an edited collection of 47 articles on deviance, *none* of which examines religion as deviance. Likewise, a review of the table of contents of the journal *Deviant Behavior* suggests that religion is not high on anyone's list. Needless to say, there are exceptions. For example, Coates examines "Cult Commitment" in a recent article in *Deviant Behavior* (2012). On my own shelves I find a religion chapter in the deviance text *Social Deviance: Being, Behaving, and Branding*, but since it was co-authored by yours truly it hardly counts (Ward et al., 1994). Another exception is Erich Goode's text *Deviant Behavior* (2011), which includes a chapter on "Cognitive Deviance: Holding Unconventional Beliefs". Despite these exceptions, however, the overall picture is clear. Religion is rarely discussed by deviance scholars.

Sociologists who study deviance typically focus on two core questions: (1) What is deviance? and (2) How do we explain deviance? The same two questions can be asked about deviant religion: (1) What is deviant religion? and (2) How do we explain it? The answer to these questions depends on how one conceptualizes deviant behavior. For the *objectivist* (or *normativist*) deviance is behavior that violates a norm. Deviance is said to be "objectively given" because norms can presumably be identified and measured. From this perspective, deviant religious groups, or "cults", are non-normative, "new" religious groups. Objectivist theories focus on how and why cults form and who joins cults.

For the *subjectivist* (or *interactionist, constructionist, reactivist*), deviance is behavior so labeled. From this perspective, deviance is said to be "subjectively problematic" because norms are abstract and situational, and matter only to the degree that they influence reactions. In the end, it is reactions, rather than norms, that determine deviance categories. Deviant religions, therefore, are fringe religions defined as "cults" by others. Subjectivist theories focus not on etiology, but on explaining and understanding reactions.

These two sociological conceptions can be compared to the more popularized, *absolutist* conception, which suggests that deviance is behavior that is inherently bad. For the absolutist, the "cults" are inherently evil, cult leaders are manipulative and self-serving and believers are "brainwashed". In the end, we discover that deviance conceptions and theory can be easily applied to the study of fringe religion, and the results remind us that the so-called death of deviance has been greatly exaggerated.

Debating the death of deviance

Before we proceed, it is important to connect the present discussion on religion as deviance to the larger question of the death of deviance. As far as I can tell, the death of deviance debates, at least as it is articulated by Sumner (1994) and Hendershott (2002), begins with two implicit definitional assumptions, one of which I agree with, the other I do not: (1) some behaviors are inherently wrong, and (2) these are the deviant behaviors.

We sociologists are not without our passions and absolutes, and I am more than happy to share my list of absolutes with anyone who will listen. Mistreating someone because of the color of his or her skin is wrong. Abandoning an unwanted infant in a trash bin is wrong. Milking unsuspecting investors in a Ponzi scheme is wrong. I have a long list. Importantly, since I am not alone in my condemnation, at least at this time, and this place (the United States, in my case), these behaviors could quite reasonably be deemed "deviant behaviors". The important question, however, is *why* they are defined as such. To be sure, my belief that these things are inherently wrong is relevant because many people share my views, and this consensus ultimately shows itself in norms and reactions. However, to pretend that deviance exists apart from norms and reactions, as the aforementioned second assumption suggests, is to miss the point – or, at least, to miss the *sociological* point.

In an attempt to distinguish absolutist understandings of "wrong" from sociological understandings of "deviance", I sometimes use the example of racial discrimination with my students:

Perrin: "Is racial discrimination wrong?"
Students: (*Affirmative nods.*)
Perrin: "African Americans in the 1950s sitting in the back of the busses...excluded from all white schools. These things are wrong?"
Students: (*More affirmative nods.*)
Perrin: "We can we agree, then, that racial discrimination is wrong now? And it was wrong then?"
Students: "Yes."
Perrin: "Can we also agree that racial discrimination is deviant now?"
Students: "Yes."
Perrin: "But was racial discrimination 'deviant' in the 1950s South? Clearly, it was not. Indeed, in some parts of the country at least, it was the norm."

The point is this: Inherent wrongness is *not* a conception of deviance. For the sociologist, furthermore, it is uninteresting. The sociologist is interested in:

> how definitions of right and wrong are established and maintained, how collectivities in every society struggle over notions of what is to be demarcated as acceptable and unacceptable behavior, beliefs, and even physical traits; what and who will be stigmatized; what and who will be honored and respected, what and who will be ignored, accepted, tolerated, and condoned. (Goode, 2004, p. 46)

So, when Sumner (1994) and Hendershott (2002) lament the death of deviance, they appear to be remembering a day, before the inter-actionists/contructionists ruined it all, when right was right, wrong was wrong and there was little sociological reflection on such things. Sociologists "regarded identifying and stigmatizing deviant behavior as an indispensable process, allowing us to live by shared standards" (Hendershott, 2002, p. 4). They identified wrongs, tried to explain them and hoped that the knowledge would lead to a fix. I am not sure they are remembering this history correctly, but for now that is irrelevant. For these scholars, it would seem, inherent rights and wrongs determine "deviant behavior" and norms and reactions are largely irrelevant. Or, perhaps they are saying that norms and reactions *should* be largely irrelevant. For most of us who study such things, however, norms and reactions are precisely what make deviant behavior so fascinating.

Religion as deviance

What is deviant behavior? As stated in the introduction, two perspectives dominate sociological understandings: the *objectivist* (or normativist) conception and the *subjectivist* (or interactionist, constructionist, reactivist) conception (Ward et al., 1994). The *absolutist* conception, discussed earlier, is a popularized, "off the street", non-sociological understanding of deviance. However, as we see in the views of Hendershott (2002) given earlier, the absolutist conception remains relevant, at least for a minority of social scientists. For popularized conceptions of deviant religion (i.e., "cults"), furthermore, it is the dominant perspective and is therefore especially relevant for our discussion here.

Absolutist conception of fringe religion

For the absolutist, deviant behavior is immoral, harmful, sinister behavior. Deviance is "*intrinsic* to certain phenomenon; it dwells or resides *within* them" (Goode, 1997, p. 17, orginal emphasis). Deviance is an inherent moral standard – presumably a law of nature or God. Deviance exists apart from social and cultural context.

According to the absolutist, some religions, and some religious leaders, are seen as inherently evil and sinister. The cult is, by definition, a manipulative mind-control group dominated by an authoritarian leader who is preoccupied with growth and money, and who demands intense commitment from his followers. Cults exploit members psychologically and financially.

One way to demonstrate the absolutist conception is to simply ask people, "What is a cult?" I decided to do just that with three office staff colleagues at the university where I teach. I prefaced my question by saying that they did not have to come up with a sophisticated definition and that if they wanted they could just list some words that come to mind:

Person #1: "Mind control, manipulation, deception."
Person #2: "A small, radical group; witchcraft, satanic ritual, Jonestown (*although she could not remember the name*), KKK."
Person #3: (*who has been hearing all of this*): "Ok, it is small and radical...but doesn't it have to do with one's perspective?"

Note that the first person has employed the absolutist conception. Person #2 has avoided absolutist language, but the list she provides suggests that she too conceptualizes cults in absolutist terms. Person #3, on the other hand, brings sociology into the discussion, suggesting that it depends on "one's perspective".

Objectivist conception of fringe religion

The objectivist conception has dominated discussions of deviance from Durkheim until the mid-20th century. According to the objectivist conception, deviance is behavior that violates a norm. Since norms are the lone measuring rod, no deviance exists if no norms exist. For Robert Merton (1966), deviant behavior "refers to conduct that departs significantly from the norms set for people in their social statuses" (p. 805). For Albert Cohen (1955, p. 62), deviant behavior "violates institutionalized expectations – that is, expectations that are shared and recognized as legitimate within a social system".

Since norms are measurable, they serve as an objective standard against which behaviors can be compared. In this sense, deviance can be said to be "objectively given". Yet, to argue that deviance is "objectively given" is not to argue that inherent badness should be our definitional criteria. Indeed, the deviance heavy-hitters of the first half of the 20th century – Merton, Sutherland, Shaw, McKay, Cohen and others – were not absolutists. They were objectivists/normativists.

From this perspective, religion becomes deviance when it violates normative standards. Terms like "cult" or "sect" are used without prejudice and merely describe culturally deviant religions that are in a higher state of tension with established religious norms. This perspective, which traces its roots to Max Weber and his student Ernest Troeltsch, is perhaps most clearly articulated in the work of Stark and Bainbridge (1985). In any society, the culturally accepted religious mainstream is referred to as *church*. Church is religion in its most accepted, culture affirming, secularized form. *Sects* are splinter revival groups that attempt to return to the presumably lost ideals of the institutionalized and secularized church. Because sects challenge established norms, and sit in relative tension with surrounding society, they maintain a marginally deviant status. However, as revivals of established religion, sects are less culturally offensive than cults. *Cults* are religious innovation – "new" religion. Given the pejorative nature of the word cult in common parlance, many sociologists of religion will avoid the word cult altogether, and instead refer to the New Religious Movements (NRMs).

Looking at cults in this way can be disconcerting to students, most of whom understand fringe religion from an absolutist perspective. I will sometimes ask my classes, "What is the most famous cult of all time?" Of course when they hear the word "cult" they imagine something inherently sinister, or something they perceive to be inherently sinister, and they answer predictably; Jonestown, Heaven's Gate, the Moonies, Scientology and so on. Very few come up with the answer I have in my head: Christianity. Yet, according to the objectivist, Christianity most certainly began as a cult. "Beginning with the resurrection", writes Rodney Stark (1997, p. 44), "Christians were participants in a new religion, one that added far too much new culture to Judaism to be any long an internal sect movement".

Subjectivist conceptions of fringe religion

During the 1960s and 1970s an increasing number of deviance scholars began to question the objectivist conception. While not necessarily dismissing norms altogether, they nonetheless led us away from norms as the key to definitional clarity. For the subjectivists, also referred to as constructionists, interactionists or reactivists, societal reactions are the key. Early subjectivist John Kitsuse (1962, p. 253) argued, for example, that deviance is a result of the "responses of the conventional and conforming members of the society who identify and interpret behavior as deviant which sociologically transform persons into deviants". Likewise, for Howard Becker (1963, p. 9), deviance is not a "quality of the act a person commits, but rather a consequence of the application by others ... The deviant is one to whom that label has successfully been applied; deviant behavior is behavior that people so label". For Kai Erikson (1962), deviance is not *"inherent in* certain forms of behavior". Instead it is a property *"conferred upon"* some behavior and some people. "Sociologically, then, the critical variable in the study of deviance is the *social audience"* (p. 308, orginal emphasis). In arguing that deviance is "subjectively problematic" rather than "objectively given" (Rubington and Weinberg, 2007), the subjectivists shift deviance conceptions even further away from absolutism, bringing relatively trivial behaviors and conditions into play (e.g., smokers, physically handicapped, etc.).

From this perspective, religion becomes deviant when it is labeled as such. Norms matter only because they influence reactions. The subjectivist asks questions that are irrelevant, or at least uninteresting, to the objectivist or absolutist. Why is one religion labeled a cult, and its adherents labeled irrational, nuts or brainwashed, when another somehow manages to avoid the label? Whose interests are served? How did cult come to be seen as a four-letter word? To re-write the words of Erikson (1962, p. 308), as quoted earlier, cultism is not a property *inherent in* certain forms of religious behavior; it a property *conferred up* by some religious groups. Sociologically speaking, the critical variable in the study of cults is the *social audience*.

History is littered with relevant examples. Christianity was condemned as dangerous and conspiratorial for the first three centuries of its existence. Contemporary movements, such as the Mormons and Jehovah's Witnesses, were seen (or are seen?) as a threat to American society. More recently, Scientology has, arguably, become the most recognizable cult of the 21st century.

Deviance theories

Now that we have considered competing conceptions of deviant religion, it is time to turn to theory. How do we explain deviant religion? The answer to this question depends in large part on how we conceptualize deviance.

Absolutist theories of fringe religion

If, from an absolutist perspective, cults are inherently evil, and their badness is clear for all to see, how then do we explain their success? Why would anyone join? The answer depends, in part, on whose behavior we hope to explain. The behavior of the cult leader is perfectly understandable for the absolutist. Money and power are alluring, and most typically the absolutist assumes that the cult leader is after both. Or, perhaps he/she is crazy. Either way, he/she is up to no good!

The behavior of the adherent, on the other hand, is far more problematic. The costs of joining a deviant religion are great – time, money and the condemning judgment of others. The benefits, on the other hand, don't exist, at least not from an absolutist point of view. Since no rational or sane person would join a cult, the absolutist often turns to medicalized explanations.

According to Conrad and Schneider (1992, p. 35), "the medical model of deviance locates the source of deviant behavior within the individual, postulating a physiological, constitutional, organic, or, occasionally, psychogenic agent or condition that is assumed to cause the behavioral deviance". When absolutists argue that cult adherents are victims of "mind control", "coercive persuasion" or most dramatically, "brainwashing", they are essentially employing a medicalized explanation. And since the cult follower has not exercised free will in joining the cult, he/she cannot freely leave the cult. He/she has been "sucked in", "manipulated", "coerced", "seduced" or "hypnotized" by the cult leader (Enroth, 1977; Singer and Lalich, 1995).

Objectivist theories of fringe religion

For the objectivist, deviance is a *behavior* that violates a *norm*. Given the definitional reliance on behaviors and norms, it should come as no surprise that objectivist theories focus on etiology – on explaining behavior. The first half of the 20th century was dominated by these "why do they do it?" theories (e.g., Emile Durkheim, Robert Merton, Edwin Sutherland, etc.). This was, according to some in the death of deviance crowd, the heyday of deviance theory, when scholars ignored the question of how deviance categories are created and instead devoted their attention to explaining deviant behavior.

Objectivist theories of fringe religion likewise focus on etiology. At a micro level, the objectivist asks the same question the absolutist asks: "Why do people join cults?" Unlike the brainwashing arguments endorsed by absolutists, however, objectivist theorists generally assume that the cult convert is a rational, volitional actor; an "active, self-determining agent" and "author and negotiator" of the conversion experience (Machalek and Snow, 1993, p. 57).

Several empirical observations have influenced objectivist theory. Converts are disproportionately likely to be young, unmarried, middle-class and educated. They are generally unattached, have fewer "stakes in conformity" and are thus freer to participate in deviant religions (Barker, 1984; Snow and Machalek, 1984). As with the study of deviance more generally, there is a tradition of theory in relative deprivation that focuses on strain and stress in the life of the convert (Glock, 1964). Specific triggers, such as marital strain, the loss of a family member and the loss of a job, are not uncommon among cult converts (Snow and Machalek, 1984).

Deprivations and predispositions may be a necessary condition for conversion, but they are hardly sufficient. In the end, in fact, they explain very little. Interestingly, these same observations have driven deviance theory more generally. The disciples of Robert Merton, for example, were quick to abandon "pure" strain/relative deprivation theories in introducing learning/subcultural components to strain theory (Cloward and Ohlin, 1960; Cohen, 1955). Structural or pre-dispositional factors may predispose one toward deviance, but subcultural interactions ultimately explain the deviant career.

The same theoretical observations can be applied to the study of religion as deviance. We see this articulated most clearly in the widely cited work of John Lofland, who looked at the factors that explained conversion among the earliest followers of the Unification Church (i.e., the Moonies) in the United States (Lofland and Stark, 1965; Lofland, 1977). Lofland distinguishes between three *Predisposing Conditions* (tensions and outlooks that exist prior to contact with the group) and four *Situational Contingencies* (social interaction and attachments) that explain conversion to a deviant religious ideology. We might think of these things as a funnel, with each of the seven steps "filtering out" people at a rapid rate.

The first predisposing condition is *Tension*, which recognizes that the process that ultimately produces ideological change begins with a felt tension or dissatisfaction on the part of the actor. If we were to put this in the language of Durkheim or Merton, we might say that some people experience anomie or normlessness. In an attempt to relieve this tension, some people, but certainly not all, will have a *Religious Problem-Solving Perspective*. The idea here is that religion is only one of a number of ways an actor might seek to relieve a state of tension. *Religious Seekership* refers to the idea that the Moonie converts encountered by Lofland had all been seeking religious solutions for some time, but had grown disillusioned with mainstream religion.

The first Situational Contingency, *Turning Point*, refers to any of a number of specific disruptive events (e.g., dropping out of college, losing a job, making a big move) that push the recruit toward a conclusion that it is time for a big change. *Intragroup Affective Bonds* are especially important in the conversion process. Close personal attachments must form between the recruit and cult members if conversion is going to occur. *Weakened Extra-Cult Affective Bonds* refers to the necessity to neutralize, or perhaps even sever, relationships with family and friends outside the group. Compared to more mainstream conversions, neutralizing outside bonds is especially important in deviant conversions. Finally, total conversion – that is, full acceptance of the deviant ideology – occurs only after a prolonged time of *Intense Interaction*.

Objectivist theorists also explain fringe religion at a macro level. Here the question becomes, "Where do cults come from?" or "How do they form?" We begin with debates about the functional necessity of religion. For some, most notably Emily Durkheim (1958 [1895]), the moral and social integration functions of religion, along with the "ultimate questions" religion addresses, means that religion performs an indispensable function in society. Others contend that as societies progress and become more modernized, religion will be slowly discredited by the findings of science. These "secularization theorists" view religion as an endangered species, slowly withering away in the bright sun of modernization.

It is within the context of the secularization debate that we return to the question of cult formation. In their book *The Future of Religion*, Rodney Stark and William Sims Bainbridge (1984) argue that the existence of fringe religion reminds us of the limits of secularization theory. They begin by acknowledging that *institutions* secularize. That is to say, high-tension sects and cults tend to become low-tension churches over time. In the words of Weber, harisma is "routinized": "Prophets are followed by Popes, revolutionaries by administrators" (Berger, 1963, p. 127). As institutions secularize and become more this-worldly in focus, they struggle to offer answers to life's most compelling questions – the so-called ultimate question. The result of institutional secularization, however, "has never been the end of religion, but merely a shift in fortunes among religions as faiths that have become too worldly are supplanted by more vigorous and less worldly religions" (Stark and Bainbridge, 1985, p. 2). In other words, as institutions secularize they are replaced by new sects (revivals of traditional religion) and cults (new religious movements).

If we return our focus to the most deviant religions – the cults – we would anticipate that cults would arise when and where established religious institutions are the weakest. In the United States, for example, we would anticipate relatively more cults in the secularized west, and relatively fewer cults in the southern states of the Bible Belt. Stark and Bainbridge (1985) demonstrate that this is indeed what we find, with cults involvement rates highest in the "unchurched" regions of the United States, the Canadian west and Western Europe

An illustration will help make this point. I was born in Searcy, Arkansas, where there is a church on every street corner – more than enough options to serve its 23,000 residents. A very high percentage of Searcy residents are in church on Sunday morning, so if one wanted to start a new religious movement this might not be the best place to go. I currently live in Malibu, California, where only a handful of churches serve 13,000 residents. Outside the Christian university where I teach, I know very few people who attend church. While the residents of Malibu may not be attending church, however, this does not necessarily mean that they have stopped asking ultimate questions. It only means that Malibuites who continue to ask these questions are less likely to be finding answers in mainstream churches and sects. What we would expect to find, and in fact what we do find, is that Malibu is an especially fertile ground for new, fringe, belief systems (Stark and Bainbridge, 1985). The relative weakness of mainstream churches and sects has merely created a fertile ground for deviant religion.

Subjectivist theories of fringe religion

Recall that one's conception of deviance determines the kinds of theoretical questions that are asked. For the objectivist, deviance is a behavior that violates a norm. Since norms are "objectively given", there is no need to explain deviance categories. What needs to be explained, on the other hand, are behaviors. Objectivist theories are etiological in focus, attempting to answer the question, "why do people do it?" For the subjectivist, on the other hand, deviance is a label – a societal reaction. Norms and perceived absolutes might matter because they influence reactions, but they are definitionally irrelevant. No label, no deviance. Subjectivist theories, therefore, are largely uninterested in the behavior of individual actors. Rather, they seek to explain the creation and application of deviance definitions.

The death of deviance argument rests on the claim that when subjectivists shifted focus away from the behavior of deviants they effectively killed deviance. I would argue, however, that the subjectivists did not undo anything the objectivists had done. Subjectivists simply shifted the definitional and theoretical focus away from offenders and on to reactors and reactions.

Subjectivist theory returns our focus to the derogatory label "cult". How does a religious movement come to be seen as a cult? For the subjectivist, it has little to do with religious norms in a society, and everything to do with interests and claims-making. Claims-makers essentially compete for the right to define the boundaries of religion as deviant. Competing claims about the sinister nature of some religious ideologies will, according to Barker (1995, p. 289), "not be random, but significantly influenced according to their interests". Understanding and explaining cults, therefore, rests on understanding and explaining interests and reactions.

History reminds us that fringe religion is often seen as threatening to the religious and cultural mainstream. Jesus of Nazareth threatened Judaism. Martin Luther threatened the Catholic Church. John Wesley threatened the Church of England. In the United States in the late 1800s, the Mormons (who fled to Utah in an attempt to avoid persecution) and the Jehovah's Witnesses were persecuted because it was feared that they would have some detrimental effect on US society. In the United States during the mid-to-late 1900s, it was the Unification Church, the Hare Krishna and Scientology. Even more sensationalistic, the tragic deaths of adherents to the People's Temple (Jonestown), Branch Davidians and Heaven's Gate fueled public concerns about the sinister nature of fringe religion.

Interest Group Theories focus on the social, political and economic forces that ultimately lead to deviance definitions. "Interests" can come in various forms, but for our purposes it is perhaps sufficient to consider two broad categories of interests. Sometimes individuals or groups will have a financial/vested interest in the outcome of deviance negotiations. Other times, reactors are engaged in a purely moral crusade. They are, in the words of Howard Becker (1963), "moral entrepreneurs". Both are relevant in the discussion of fringe religion.

Who are the interest groups involved in the fringe religion debate? Referring specifically to the heightened concern over fringe religion during the 1970s, sociologists David Bromley and Anson Shupe (1981, p. 1) have written of the "Great American Cult Scare": "Anyone who has followed the newspapers for the past decade, or even for the past few years, knows that America is presently preoccupied with one of the bitterest and most significant religious conflicts of the twentieth century". Bromley and Shupe maintain that the perceived proliferation of cults and cult adherents was mostly a "hoax", a "scare in the truest sense of the word": "*There is no avalanche of rapidly growing cults.* In fact, there probably are no more such groups existing today than there have been at any other time in our recent history" (pp. 3–4, orginal emphasis). In the world of threats and fears, however, perceptions are everything.

The Anti-Cult Movement (ACM) offers perhaps the best starting point as we explain deviant religion from an interest group perspective. Sociologists began to refer to "the" ACM in the 1980s, when the cult scare was at its peak. The ACM, however, was never well defined and understood. It was never more than a loose coalition of parents, cult defectors, mental health professionals, deprogrammers and exit counselors and conservative Christians. According to Bromley and Shupe (1981), the movement's beginnings can be traced to concerned parents whose children joined deviant religious movements during the 1960s and 1970s. Many parents, confused by their children's conversions and fanatical commitment, were anxious to expose the cults in order to get their children back.

Barker (1995) maintains that for the most part, the groups and individuals involved in the ACM over the years have had relatively pure interests and are perhaps best described as moral entrepreneurs. That is, most people associated with the ACM worked tirelessly because they believed the cults represent a significant threat. They stood to gain nothing financially. Understandably, parents who felt they had lost their children to the cults wanted their children back and wanted to protect other families from having the same experiences. Defectors wanted the evil practices of the cults exposed. Christians wanted to save a world lost in sin.

Other times, however, individuals and groups do have a financial interest in the anti-cult cause. Deprogrammers, exit counselors, lawyers and expert witnesses in court cases typically charge handsomely for their services (Barker, 1995). During the height of the "cult scare", civil suits were not uncommon. Defectors provided first-hand accounts of the "atrocities" of the NRMs, and their claims about being "brainwashed" energized the ACM (Shupe, 2009). The ACM also found lawyers who argued that cults should pay for their deceptive and manipulative practices (Delgado, 1982). Finally, the research and writing of a few social scientists and mental health professionals gave scientific punch to allegations of cult brainwashing, and their expert testimony strengthened the legal case against NRMs (Anthony, 1990; Aronoff et al., 2000).

A second constituency important in the anti-cult movement is the mass media. The media do not necessarily have an anti-cult agenda, of course, but the tendency to report and exaggerate the sensationalist has often contributed to fears of fringe religion. In Britain during the 1970s, for example, parents who had generally interpreted their children's conversion experiences as positive suddenly became worried when they read media accounts (Beckford, 1983). According to Richardson (1983, p. 101), media accounts were especially superficial and misleading following the People's Temple (Jonestown) tragedy: "There was a failure to differentiate the groups: the Manson Cult and People's Temple were discussed in articles that also talked about the Hare Krishna, the Children of God, the Unification Church, and other groups. Major differences were not mentioned and any similarity was exploited".

Consider the following example from the highly regarded *Newsweek* (1993), following the Branch Davidian tragedy in 1993. This quote reminds us of the potential of media – even mainstream media – to create the impression that fringe religions are larger and more significant than they might actually be: "Waco is a wake-up call. If the cult watchers are to be believed, there are thousands of groups out there poised to snatch your body, control your mind, corrupt your soul ... Warning: do you know where your children are?" (p. 60).

Conclusion

In this chapter, I have tried to demonstrate that fringe religion can be conceptualized and explained in much the same way as deviant behavior is conceptualized and explained. The absolutist perspective, which dominates popularized understandings of "cults", suggests that the evil and destructive nature of deviant religion is self-evident. We sociologists, while certainly acknowledging the existence of inherent rights and wrongs, nonetheless reject absolutism as a *conception of deviance*. Societies create deviance categories, so conceptualizing religion *as* deviance is always norms and/or reactions.

As with the study of deviance more generally, two conceptions dominate sociological understanding of religion as deviance. The objectivist (or normative) perspective defines deviance as a behavior that violates a norm. The objectivist thus focuses on religious norms in society and conceptualizes the so-called cults as non-normative NRMs. Objectivist theories attempt to explain why NRMs form and why people join NRMs. The subjectivist (or interactionist, constructionist, reactivist), on the other hand, largely abandons norms, and instead defines deviance as a label. Subjectivists focus on reactions to fringe religion on the social construction of the "cult" label. Theory in this area attempts to understand and explain the competing interests involved in the social construction of "cults".

References

Adler, P. A. and P. Adler (2012) *Constructions of Deviance*, 7th edn. (Belmont, CA: Wadsworth).

Anthony, D. (1990) "Religious Movements and Brainwashing Litigation: Evaluating Key Testimony", in T. Robbins and D. Anthony (eds.) *In Gods We Trust: New Patterns of Religious Pluralism in the United States*, 2nd edn. (New Brunswick, NJ: Transaction).

Aronoff, J., S. J. Lynn and P. Malinoski (2000) "Are Cultic Environments Psychologically Harmful?", *Clinical Psychology Review*, 20, 91–111.

Barker, E. (1984) *The Making of a Moonie* (New York: Basil Blackwell).

—— (1995) "Presidential Address: The Scientific Study of Religion? You Must Be Joking!", *Journal for the Scientific Study of Religion*, 34, 287–310.

Becker, H. S. (1963) *Outsiders: Studies in the Sociology of Deviance* (New York: Free Press).

Beckford, J. (1983) "The Public Response to New Religious Movements in Britain", *Social Compass*, 21, 49–62.

Berger, P. (1963). *Invitation to Sociology* (New York: Doubleday).

Bromley, D. G. and A. Shupe Jr. (1981) *Strange Gods: The Great American Cult Scare* (Boston, MA: Beacon Press).

Cloward, R. and L. E. Ohlin (1960) *Delinquency and Opportunity: A Theory of Delinquent Gangs* (New York: Free Press).

Coates, D. D. (2012) "'Cult Commitment' from the Perspective of Former Members: Direct Rewards of Membership versus Dependency Inducing Practices", *Deviant Behavior*, 33, 168–184.

Cohen, A. K. (1955) *Delinquent Boys: The Subculture of the Gang* (New York: Free Press).

Conrad, P. and J. W. Schneider (1992) *Deviance and Medicalization: From Badness to Sickness* (St. Louis: C. V. Mosby).

Delgado, R. (1982) "Cults and Conversion: The Case for Informed Consent", *Georgia Law Review*, 16, 533–574.

Durkheim, E. (1958 [1895]) *The Rules of the Sociological Method* (Chicago: University of Chicago Press).

Enroth, R. (1977) *Youth, Brainwashing, and Extremist Cults* (Grand Rapids, MI: Zondervan).

Erikson, K. (1962) "Notes on the Sociology of Deviance", *Social Problems*, 9, 307–314.

Glock, C. Y. (1964) "The Role of Deprivation in the Origin and Evolution of Religious Groups", in R. Lee and M. Marty (eds.) *Religion and Social Conflict* (New York: Oxford University Press).

Goode, E. (1997) *Deviant Behavior*, 5th edn. (Upper Saddle River, NJ: Prentice Hall).

—— (2004) "Is the Sociology of Deviance Still Relevant", *The American Sociologist*, 35, 46–57.

—— (2011) *Deviant Behavior*, 9th edn. (Upper Saddle River, NJ: Prentice Hall).

Hendershott, A. (2002) *The Politics of Deviance* (San Francisco: Encounter Books).

Kitsuse, J. I. (1962) "Societal Reactions to Deviant Behavior: Problems with Theory and Method", *Social Problems*, 9, 247–257.

Lofland, J. (1977) *Doomsday Cult* (New York: Irvington).

Lofland, J. and R. Stark (1965) "Becoming a World Saver: A Theory of Religious Conversion", *American Sociological Review*, 30, 862–874.

Machalek, R. and D. A. Snow (1993) "Conversion to New Religious Movements", in D. Bromley and J. Hadden (eds.) *Religion and the Social Order, Part B* (Greenwich, CT: JAI Press).

Merton, R. K. (1966) "Social Problems and Sociological Theory", in R. K. Merton and R. Nisbet (eds.) *Contemporary Social Problems*, 2nd edn. (New York: Harcourt Brace and World).

Newsweek (1993) "Cultic America: A Tower of Babel", March 15, pp. 60–62.

Richardson, J. (1983) "New Religious Movements in the United States: A Review", *Social Compas*, 10, 85–110.

Rubington, E. and M. S. Weinberg (2007) *Deviance: The Interactionist Perspective,* 10th edn. (Boston: Allyn and Bacon).

Shupe, A. (2009) "The Nature of the New Religious Movements—Anticult 'Culture War' in Microcosm: The Church of Scientology versus the Cult Awareness Network", in James R. Lewis (ed.) *Scientology* (New York: Oxford University Press), pp. 269–281.

Singer, M. and J. Lalich (1995) *Cults in Our Midst: The Hidden Menace in Our Everyday Lives* (San Francisco: Jossey-Bass).

Snow, D. and R. Machalek (1984) "The Sociology of Conversion", *Annual Review of Sociology,* 10, 167–190.

Stark, R. (1997) *The Rise of Christianity* (San Francisco: HarperCollins).

Stark, R. and W. S. Bainbridge (1985) *The Future of Religion: Secularization, Revival, and Cult Formation* (Berkeley, CA: University of California Press).

Sumner, C. (1994) *The Sociology of Deviance: An Obituary* (Buckingham: Open University Press).

Ward, D., T. Carter and R. Perrin (1994) *Social Deviance: Being, Behaving, and Branding* (Boston, MA: Allyn and Bacon).

9

The New Moral Entrepreneurs
Atheist Activism as Scripted and Performed Political Deviance

Lori L. Fazzino, Michael Ian Borer and Mohammed Abdel Haq

Social media have become an arena for religious discussion, debate and downright vitriol (see Lovheim, 2007; Borer and Schafer, 2011). Anonymous comments can be made and left for others to find without the demands or accountability of face-to-face interaction. Imagine, for a moment, stumbling upon a Facebook page or Twitter feed filled with hateful and threatening comments such as "I'm gonna drop an anchor on your face!" or "#thatbitchisgoingtohell, and Satan is gonna rape her!!!"[1] How might a person react if those comments were written about a complete stranger? About one's friend? About one's family? Mark Ahlquist, a firefighter and engaged community member in Cranson, Rhode Island, did not have to imagine how he might react. These comments, and a slew of other equally damning ones, were directed at his teenage daughter, Jessica.

Jessica was a student at Cranson High School where a Christian prayer banner has hung in the west auditorium since 1963. In July 2010, the American Civil Liberties Union (ACLU) contacted the Cranson School District asking for the banner's removal, citing the display as a violation of the Establishment Clause Amendment I in the Constitution which states: "Government shall make no law respecting an establishment of religion, prohibiting Congress from favoring one religion over another".

---

[1] These are just two comments that were posted on Twitter and Facebook by classmates in response to Jessica Ahlquist's request to have a prayer banner removed from her high school. The full list can be found on the Blag Hag blog: http://freethoughtblogs.com/blaghag/2012/01/that-christian-compassion/.

The school board denied this request and in April 2011, the ACLU filed a lawsuit against the Cranson School Distinct in Rhode Island on behalf of the Ahlquist family (Schiedrop, 2012).

In January 2012, the US District Court for the District of Rhode Island made their ruling on 840 F. Supp. 2d 507 – Dist. Court, D. Rhode Island [2012], *Ahlquist v. Cranson* in favor of Mark Ahlquist. The school district removed the banner a few months later and agreed to pay the ACLU's $150,000 legal fees. Although the school district decided not to appeal the rule, town residents were outraged. Sixteen-year-old Jessica and her family became the focal point of that outrage. They were harassed by students, community members and even elected state officials. The day after the initial ruling was made, Representative Peter Polombo (R) publically called Jessica an "evil little thing" on local talk radio. Others publically denounced her, calling her names such as "witch" and "little snot" (Schiedrop, 2012). The Ahlquist's family home was vandalized and Jessica was repeatedly threatened with bodily harm, often needing a police escort to and from school. She was perceived and typified as a walking personification of evil and remains a prominent target for cyberbullying, continually vilified on the Internet. Much of the contempt stemmed not only from her actions against the overt religious symbolism in her public high school, it was also due to a label she had given herself: "atheist".

Jessica's story is not unique. Eighteen-year-old Max Nielsen is another atheist student who publically fought the unconstitutional inclusion of prayer at his high school commencement, and, like Jessica, was demonized for acting out of a moral obligation to protect the separation of church and state. Atheists have been a historically deviant and socially excluded population (Cimino and Smith, 2007; Smith and Cimino, 2012; Smith, 2013). The unprecedented rise of publically acknowledged and open atheism has had mixed effects on members of the so-called movement. Regardless, examples of atheist activism discussed herein show the difficult and potentially dangerous reality of challenging Christian hegemony in the United States. In what follows, we explore atheist activism in the United States as a form of "political deviance" that comprises "direct and explicit acts that either challenge the social order, or the abuse of power and morality by those in the centers" (Ben-Yehuda, 1990, p. 3). The politically deviant acts of atheist activists have helped them rebrand themselves as *new* moral entrepreneurs organizing and performing, individually and collectively, to achieve goals ranging from eliminating anti-atheist discrimination to the total eradication of religion in the public sphere.

Becker (1963) first used the term "moral entrepreneurs" to describe those in positions of power who enforce mainstream societal moralities and thereby label those who do not follow them as deviant offenders. Such a limited view of moral entrepreneurship unfortunately squelches the power out of the concept. We contend that moral entrepreneurs are countercultural, especially when we recognize that entrepreneurship is often about constructing new ideas and ideals. The new moral entrepreneur, then, is much more like Levi-Strauss's creative *bricoleur* than Becker's custodian of the status quo. As such, we conceptualize atheist activists as new moral entrepreneurs who engage in persuasive performances when attempting to counter stigmatized labels. In this sense, these new moral entrepreneurs necessarily contribute to atheism's potential rise in acceptance, or at least tolerance, by successfully circumventing the stigma associated with non-believers through changing cultural attitudes (see Benford and Hunt, 1992).

Employing a social constructionist approach to deviance demonstrates how a politically silenced and socially stigmatized population is able to mobilize and transform themselves into an embattled moral community. In turn, this analysis shows the utility of the term "deviance" for understanding social power dynamics in a pluralistic society that continues to see both new and old fronts emerge and re-emerge in the "culture wars".

Studying atheist activism as political deviance

This analysis relies on a combination of qualitative methods including participant observation, informal conversational interviews and textual analysis of documents from popular print news and social media sources. A significant portion of the data comes from public documents collected from a variety of offline and online sources. In the event we were unable to recall specific details or content, e-mails were sent to participants asking for further clarification. Computer-mediated communication allowed us to document specific ideas that were in question through e-mail correspondence, and in some cases, we received conference presentations. To obtain additional textual data, we visited the websites of visible atheist/secular organizations, followed blogs from well-known atheist activists, joined several atheist/secular Facebook groups and read books by prominent atheist authors, some of which were written by the individuals we interacted with. We followed current news stories and collected past news on American atheism by conducting a series of searches on computer databases such as Lexis/Nexis and search engines such as Google. The primary search terms that yielded the most usable information include "atheist stigma", "atheist campaigns", "atheist lawsuits" and "atheist activism".

Our data analysis relied on an inductive analytic approach. We printed field notes and textual data and used line by line and focused coding techniques. Our analysis was guided by Benford and Hunt's (1992) dramaturgical framework from which we focused on two thematic techniques: *scripting* and *performing*. Movement scripting relies on the ability of moral entrepreneurs to align their claims with the beliefs of potential advocates in an attempt to achieve a shared definition of the problem and promote viable solutions for solving it (ibid.; Loseke, 2005). The enactment of power occurs through various types of cultural, political and identity performances (Benford and Hunt, 1992). We identify the conceptual performance categories that emerged from our empirical data as political and cultural moral performances and moral identity performance.

Before we present our interpretations, we briefly discuss the labeling of atheism as a form of political, cultural and religious deviance. This is followed by a discussion of Christian hegemony and atheist stigmatization. The latter sections demonstrate the nuanced ways that atheist activists have sought to speak to power and establish themselves and their young movement as a legitimate political, cultural and religious voice within and across the contemporary American cultural landscape.

The social construction of atheists as deviants

Atheists have a long-standing history of being labeled as immoral, deviant and untrustworthy (Edgell et al., 2006; Cimino and Smith, 2011; Smith, 2013). The social and political marginalization of atheists dates back to classical Greek antiquity when the term *atheistos* was used to label those who denied the traditional religion of the Athenian state and has evolved alongside historical transformations in all subsequent periods of societal evolution (McGrath, 2006). Labeling approaches to deviance argue that definitions of "deviant" are socially constructed and assigned; deviance is not an inherent characteristic of behavior (Becker, 1963; Erickson, 1966). According to Becker (1963, p. 9), "The deviant is one to whom the label has successfully been applied". Applying the label and getting it to stick, however, is a matter of social power. Conrad and Schneider (1980, p. 17) state that "the power to define and construct reality is linked intimately to the structure of power in a society at a given historical period... constructions of deviance are linked closely to the dominant social control institutions in society". Despite grand claims about the secularization of Western societies, atheists have had very little, if any, social power to construct deviant labels or to defend against those applied to them in the United States (see Borer, 2010). The social construction of atheists as deviants in early American history was a result of norms stemming from a Puritan ideology of "sheer religious absolutism" and the role of legal authorities was to uphold a "universal law of morality" (Erikson, 1966, p. 187). The Bible was the primary source for Puritan legal structures; all behavior believed to oppose the Puritan ethos was defined as a moral transgression and perpetrators were labeled "deviants" – an identity that required public punishment (ibid.). Goode and Ben-Yehuda (2009) suggest that all industrialized pluralistic societies that experience rapid social change often have an increased risk for value conflicts to arise that require moral enterprises to defend. Individuals who reject religion, therefore, engage in "dissident behavior [that is] perceived as a threat to the normative society" (Mizruchi, 1983, p. 11). Atheists – due to their worldview and not necessarily by their actions – were, and continue to be, perceived as a threat to the dominant and dominating moral order.

Moral campaigning has been an effective method for protecting the moral order by constructing and maintaining social and symbolic boundaries between "us" and "them" (Goode and Ben-Yehuda, 2009). According to Best (1995), moral campaigning is the work of moral entre-preneurs who attempt to define deviance, drawing on cultural typifi-cations of good and evil to frame particular beliefs, behaviors and/or people as dangerous and/or immoral. Constructing deviant categories requires claims-makers to conceptually link typifications of social "evils" with moral claims, accomplished through evoking anger, outrage and fear by presenting only the most severe cases and/or exaggerating malig-nant threats to core cultural values. Successful emotional manipulation can create a "moral panic" among a concerned audience (Cohen, 1972). Moral panics prey upon already existing fears and rely on dramatized presumptions instead of empirical facts, which keep public audiences on continued alert (Bivens, 2008).

The "Red Scare" is a poignant example of a contemporary moral panic that ensued from successful moral campaigning of political claims-makers against atheism. Discrepant religious worldviews supported American democracy and Soviet communism in the post–World War II era. Communist leaders viewed religion as delusive and irrelevant and sought to reject it, while the establishment of Christo-centric religion amalgamated Christian and political ideals in the United States (Bates, 2004). When conflicts between the United States and the USSR erupted, a moral crusade against Soviet policy was launched, driven by the insidious force of Cold War rhetoric (e.g., "godless communism") that parallelized communism and atheism – two distinct ideologies that are, at best, tenuously related.

Moral claims-makers were successful in cultivating anticommunist fears by promoting religion as the ideological foundation for American values, intertwining religious faith with national purpose (Bates, 2004). Hence, the inclusion of the phrases "One Nation Under God" to the Pledge of Allegiance and "In God We Trust" to American currency in 1954 and 1957, respectively, solidified the belief that the United States was founded as a Christian nation (Barb, 2011). The corollary of establishing nationalism as a "quasi-religion" shows how antidemocratic and antireligious codes, when used in tandem, become discursive typifications of anti-Americanism responsible for revitalizing previous claims that irreligion is a social problem by constructing atheists as a national threat (see Alexander, 2001).

Typifications depend on processes of meaning-making where objects, events and individuals are organized into various cognitive categories. How categorizations are understood is contingent upon the meaning that is assigned to them that, in turn, influences action (Loseke, 2005). Creating perceptions of atheists as nihilistic, immoral and dangerous based on the absence of faith requires claims-makers to construct a definitive connection between religion and morality and present their claims *as if* they were inherently true. The Christo-centric undertones of the dominant American cultural code can be understood through Douglas's (1966) analysis of the binary logic of "purity" and "pollution". Purity, in the national community, is signified through the embodiment of "good" where displays of religious belief are markers of patriotism and morality. Despite having freedom of religion – which arguably includes freedom from religion – the absence of faith is a form of pollution that correlates "evil" with immorality, immorality with godlessness, all of which are synonymous with anti-Americanism. Cultural membership in American social life relies largely on religious belief as a symbolic boundary that reinforces and perpetuates the deviant status of atheists as "moral others" in civil society (Edgell et al., 2006).

Christian hegemony, religious oppression and anti-atheist discrimination

Protestant themes are deeply embedded in the cultural narrative of Western societies, evidenced by the emergence of a "civil religion" that relies on a generic "God" for national protection (Bellah, 1967). Though civil religion is *supposed to be* a cultural resource for uniting individuals with different worldviews under the same banner of "universal" and "transcendent" values, it still tends to be dominated by Christian hegemony in the United States. Adams (2007) defines Christian hegemony as:

> a religious worldview that publically affirms Christian observances, holy days, and sacred spaces at the expense of those who are not Christian and within a culture that normalizes Christian values as intrinsic to an explicitly American public and political way of life. Christian norms are termed *hegemonic* in that they depend only on "business as usual." (p. 253, emphasis in original)

The systematic discrimination of non-belief is a strong indicator for the existence of Christian privilege, a conceptual term used in the same manner as white privilege, privileging religion instead of race. When one group is privileged over another, oppression ensues. We use the term "oppression" to mean "the unjust exercise of power by a dominant group over a subordinate group" (Mansbridge, 2001, p. 2). The nascent scholarship on American atheism, as well as multiple secular publications, are beginning to elucidate the hierarchal system of domination and subordination between religion and non-belief that has been largely ignored (see Barb, 2011; Cimino and Smith, 2011; Jacoby, 2004).

The hegemonic influence of religious power is best understood by how it influences public perceptions about particular social groups (e.g., atheists, women, LGBT communities). Findings from the *American Mosaic Project Survey* (2003) show the success of claims-making in the moral crusade against atheism. Almost 40 percent of Americans ranked atheists as being the group most likely not to share their vision of American society, while almost 48 percent of Americans would disapprove if their child wanted to marry an atheist (Hartmann et al., 2003). In 2006, a study of American attitudes toward atheists furnished similar results to the Minnesota study, claiming atheists are the least trusted group in the United States and are perceived as not being part of the American vision (Edgell et al., 2006). There are, however, several studies relying on a sample of atheist respondents that offer a portrait of non-believers that suggest atheists have a clear sense of values, a strong commitment to civic participation, are politically involved and hold strong beliefs about contemporary social issues (Abdel Haq, 2013; Hunsberger and Altemeyer, 2006; Zuckerman, 2009).

The vast discrepancy between these findings strongly supports the idea that atheists suffer from successful labeling and stigmatization. Adding further insult to injury, findings from two studies that suggest that "immoral" atheists may have a stronger sense of social justice and be more ethical compared to their "moral" religious counterparts. Concerning contemporary social issues, Zuckerman (2009) and Abdel Haq (2013) posit atheists as (1) less prejudiced, close-minded and authoritarian; (2) less socially supportive of the Iraq War/invasion, the death penalty and torture; and (3) more socially supportive of gender equality, women's rights, gay marriage, LGBTQ rights, assisted suicide and marijuana legalization, compared to Americans with theistic beliefs. The disparity between the image of atheism by others and the reality of lived atheism is evidence of the success of deviant labeling by Christo-centric moral entrepreneurs.

The stigmatization of non-belief is a salient experience for many atheists who are keenly aware of their "deviant" status in the United States (Smith and Cimino, 2012; Smith, 2013). Recent findings from Hammer et al. (2012) identify 29 *different* types of perceived anti-atheist discrimination. Secular intolerance forces many non-believers to either remain "in the closet" or to try and manage the stress that is associated with disclosing and negotiating their deviant status. The hypocrisy of unreciprocated tolerance is a source of stress, anxiety and frustration (ibid.). Because Christianity in particular, and God(s)-related worldviews in general, occupies a privileged status in the United States, the symbolic boundaries between powerful believers and powerless non-believers make anti-atheist discrimination an inescapable experience for those with a salient atheist identity.

The scripting of atheist activism

According to Loseke (2005, p. 14), "a social problem does not exist until it is defined as such". Defining social problems relies on the use of "frames" or what Goffman (1974, p. 21) refers to as "schematas of interpretation" that help individuals "locate, perceive, identify, and label" events and experiences. Core-framing tasks require individuals to define various aspects of a condition. Framing processes generate collective action frames, described by Benford and Snow (2000, p. 614) as "action-oriented sets of beliefs and meanings that inspire and legitimate the activities and campaigns of a social movement organization". Casting the roles of victims, villains and heroes (creating a set of *dramatis personae*) and developing a vocabulary of motive (providing dialogue and direction) occurs via framing processes (Benford and Hunt, 1992). The end product of such processes help define the problem and align actions often in response to a cultural trauma, which Alexander (2001, p. 1) defines as "a horrendous event that leaves indelible marks upon the consciousness of members of a collectivity, and changes their identity fundamentally and irrevocably". We show how the horrendous events of 9/11 lead to both increased stigmatization and increased recognition of atheist activism through the active scripting.

Interpreting political threat as political opportunity

Christian nationalism is a political ideology underscored by "dominionism" that claims Christians have God-given authority and a divine right to rule. It was a major mobilizer of the Evangelical movement facilitating the emergence of the New Christian Right and Moral Majority in the 1970s and the Christian Coalition in 1989 (Goldberg, 2007). Explicit incorporation of Christianity in political institutions perpetuated conservatives' role as moral gate-keepers of American values. They amplified the war on secularism that discounted the logics of rationality and science as weapons belonging to a supposedly scheming liberal elite (ibid.). Former President George H. W. Bush's 1987 declaration, "I don't know that atheists should be considered as citizens, nor should they be considered patriots. This is one nation under God!" is a blatant expression of secular intolerance. It exemplifies "strategic marginalization", a central political strategy that creates stigmatized identities to justify social exclusion and hinder civic participation (Jasper, 2010).

The beginning of the 21st century was marked by the presidential victory of George W. Bush in 2000. During his presidential campaign, Bush was a desirable candidate to Christian voters, promising to reinstate Christian morality to the White House and declaring Jesus as the world's most important political philosopher. The strong inclusion of Christian themes during the Bush/Cheney campaign indicated that governmental politics would continue to be heavily influenced by fundamentalist Christianity. The 2001 Faith-Based Initiatives Program proposed creating abstinence education in schools, opposing abortion rights, blocking access to birth control and promoted the inclusion of creationism in public school textbook, signaling a clear departure from the Constitutional amendment separating church and state (Jacoby, 2004; Niose, 2012).

Infusing public policy with religious ideology is a continual reminder of the spurious relationship between democracy and faith for many atheists; political lobbying for conservative policies underscored by

Christian Fundamentalism was more than troubling. Ideological dangers of radical extremism are rooted in absolutist and essentialist terms that project simplistic and often dichotomous views of how society operates (Ben-Yehuda, 2006). According to atheist activist and author Susan Jacoby (2004, p. 356), "The problem, of course, is not religion, of whatever brand, as a spiritual force but religion melded with political ideology and political power". Transforming American secular government into a Christian theocracy was perceived as a political threat and interpreted as a foreboding reality. This transformation, however, provided an opportunity for atheists as the government became an explicit and formidable "villain" for atheists to rally against.

Interpreting ideological threat as political opportunity

The physical dangers of religious fundamentalism were crystallized by the 9/11 events, when a group of Islamic terrorists enacted their extremist beliefs. Terrorism is a political performance of symbolic action with moral reference. It creates political instability by exposing vulnerabilities in national security, social instability by sowing chaos, fear and distrust and moral instability by provoking inexorable responses that incite institutional distrust among citizens (Alexander et al., 2006, pp. 93–94). President Bush's response to 9/11 was constructed using the Christian rhetoric, drawing on religious themes of good versus evil to promote America's "war on terror" as a moral campaign, not against religious fundamentalism, but rather against a "sacred evil" (Smelser, 2004). *New York Times* op-ed columnist David Brooks (2003) claims that recovering from periods of inconceivable trauma, such as 9/11, people seek meaning through understandings of a world that reflects God's will, arguing against scientific interpretations in favor of meanings rooted in moral judgments, questioning only if the moral vision is of "righteous rule". Jacoby (2004) criticizes Brooks, arguing that individual perceptions of morality are inconsequential in the absence of power; the 9/11 attacks may have been motivated by subjective morality, but they were mobilized by power. Herein lies the problem when institutional authorities allow their personal moral compass to influence political policy. Some citizens are inevitably left out of the dominant vision.

Cognitive liberation, framing and 9/11

Sadly it has taken this terrible act of terrorism to kick start the resurgence of atheism and to motivate us to organize. No longer can reasonable people sit on the sidelines and allow the ridiculous ideas

of religion to corrupt our society without criticism. No longer can bad
ideas and beliefs get a pass.

– Staks Rosch, Philadelphia Coalition of Reason

Most contemporary social movements arise from identity conflicts and
struggles over meanings and values (Buechler, 2000). Atheist conten-
tions emerge out of collective history of cultural and moral imperialism,
specifically in the United States where religionists systematically impose
theistic cultural and moral belief systems on non-theists. With a long-
standing history of political and cultural invisibility, despite a few minor
attempts in the early 20th century (e.g., the Ethical Culture Society, the
development of the Humanist Manifestos I and II), atheists have failed
to develop the organizational infrastructure, obtain and utilize resources
and garner social support necessary to mobilize real collective action,
consistently confronting a closed political opportunity structure despite
an open democratic system (McAdam, 1982).

Atheist author David Niose claims the political climate post-9/11
was the wake-up call secular Americans, like former Westboro Baptist
Church member Nathan Phelps, needed. His turn to atheism was not
immediate. He struggled with anger and faith for many years after his
defection. During his talk at the 2013 Secular Student Alliance convention, Phelps recalled the precise moment his identity was transformed:

> Then one sunny September morning, the illusion of a personal god
> that I tried so hard to believe in exploded over the skies of Manhattan.
> Even as the ashes and ruin of this horrific act [of] blind faith settled
> over New York, Washington, and Pennsylvania, I watched people
> across America scrambling to that same irrational altar for their
> answers. In the fierce storm of emotion that rolled across this country,
> one realization rose to the surface of my mind in blinding clarity:
> certainly this mechanism of unassailable blind faith is one of the
> greatest risks mankind faces today.

Compounded by confusion, the events *of* and political response *to*
9/11 generated a "moral shock" among many atheists. Moral shocks
occur "when an event or situation raises such a sense of outrage in
people that they become inclined toward political action, even in the
absence of a network" (Jasper and Poulsen, 1995, p. 498). The moral
shock of 9/11 facilitated "cognitive liberation" – "a shift in consciousness based on a sense of injustice and obligations to act" – among early
movement entrepreneur whose published writings provided foundational scripts (Futrell, 2003, p. 359). Sam Harris temporarily suspended

his doctoral studies in 2001 and began writing *The End of Faith* on "the morning after seeing the trade towers bombed with jet fuel and airline passengers"; Richard Dawkins "became the patriarch of anti-theistic activism" in his 2006 publication *The God Delusion*; and Christopher Hitchens wrote a severe critique of religion in his 2007 publication *God Is Not Great* (Tarico, 2012).

Despite the substantial ideological fragmentation that exists among atheist activists, their collective status as deviant minority outsiders is realized and mobilized through a master "injustice" frame. Dawkins, Harris and Hitchens started a strident anti-religion campaign that rests on two claims: (1) religion is a set of untrue "fairy tales" that are (2) inherently dangerous and destructive to society; claims that are amplified by an aggressive and unapologetic approach. The message positing the dangers of religion characterizes a new era of secular activism. Following Kituse (1980, p. 3), we describe atheists "who have been culturally defined and categorized, stigmatized, morally degraded, and social segregated [and who] engage in the politics of producing social problems when they declare their presence openly and without apology to claim the rights of citizenship" as embattled activists. Stigmatized atheists become "embattled" when they frame conditions as opportunity and/or threat and script "resistance identities" to mobilize on individual and/or collective levels (see Cimino and Smith, 2007). Labeled within the movement as "firebrand atheists", embattled activists have successfully constructed a contentious collective action script rooted in counter-hegemonic ideals that enables them to assert their political character and challenge religious power (see McAnulla, 2012). Table 9.1 details a collective action

Table 9.1 Five points of "firebrand" atheism

1. Tell the truth as often as possible.
   - Religion is a lie – all of it
   - Gods are false – all of them
   - Respect is earned, and religion hasn't earned any. Belief does not warrant respect.
2. Dont't feign respect for the unrespectable.
3. Don't accept inequality (privilege) as acceptable, even if it is the norm.
4. If someone claims to be offended by the truth, it's because they are used to privilege and inequality. Do not let "I'm offended by your words" silence you. Clarify that it's their beliefs, not the people, with which you take issue.
5. If someone tries to limit freedom using religion, do points 1–4, only louder.

Source: READY, AIM, FIREBRAND! IN DEFENSE OF HARDLINE ATHEISM-David silverman, student secular Alliance Convention, 2013.

script detailed in the five points of the "firebrand atheism" presented by David Silverman, president of American Atheists.

The dynamics of atheist embattlement are apparently in the framing contests between the Religious Right and firebrand atheists regarding 9/11. In the days following the attacks, religious leaders Jerry Falwell and Pat Robertson publically stated, "I really believe that the pagans...the abortionists...the feminists...the gays, and the lesbians...the ACLU, People for the American Way, all of them who have tried *secularizing* America. I point the finger in their face and say 'you helped this happen'" (Goldberg, 2007, p. 8; our emphasis). The formation of a group's standpoint is contingent upon a shared awareness *of* and collective struggle *against* the dominant oppressor. Notable increases in civic solidarity and American pride reaffirmed the boundaries of civic inclusion based on the religious character assigned to the attacks. This once again excluded atheists. Negotiating the politics of belonging was crucial for the formation of a distinctive atheist "standpoint" and has mobilized the collective action of "active atheists...who participate in atheist activism or are members of atheist communities or organizations" (LeDrew, 2013, p. 1).[2]

Embattled atheists draw on both their standpoint and emotions to speak out against Christian hegemony. Atheist activist Greta Christina makes this point:

I'm angry about 9/11, and I'm angry that Jerry Falwell blamed 9/11 on pagans, abortionists, feminists, gays and lesbians, the ACLU, and the People For the American Way. I'm angry that the theology of a wrathful God exacting revenge against pagans and abortionists by sending radical Muslims to blow up a building full of secretaries and investment bankers...this was a theology held by a powerful, widely-respected religious leader with millions of followers. (Freethought Blogs, 2007)

Transforming *I* into *we* provides situated knowledge from the atheist scripts that justifies "boundary" or "adversarial" framing and empowers the stigmatized community. At the 2013 Secular Student Alliance convention, David Silverman expressed, "Theists liking us is not the objective. Equality is the objective. If the theists love us because we

---

[2] Our use of atheist standpoint is synonymous with Smith and Cimino's (2012) concept "atheist consciousness".

acquiesce to inequality, we fail. If they hate us because we demand equality and achieve it, we succeed". It is our contention that through atheists' scripts, irreligious deviants are transformed into empowered moral entrepreneurs who, by directly challenging perceived religious authority and demanding civic equality, engage in a necessary form of political deviance.

Performing atheist activism

The idea that human beings are social actors who perform roles is a cornerstone of the dramatist (Burke, 1945) and dramaturgical (Goffman, 1959) perspectives. We are not, however, only role-takers. We are also role-makers. That is, people do not merely follow the roles given by others based on already existing meanings alone. We also purposefully create and manipulate roles and meanings, especially when faced by the oppressive forces that threaten our political, cultural and religious well-being and worldviews. Atheist activists have recently begun performing deviant roles in order to thwart the persistent marginalization. Benford and Hunt (1992, p. 38) define "scripts" as emergent guides for collective consciousness and interactions that are sufficiently judicious to provide cues for behavior when unexpected events occur. Those scripts are, however, flexible enough to permit improvisation. The improvisation of scripting is a type of performance that, of course, leads to other performance. We will show how atheist activists have performed improvised scripts as means for staking a claim – or perhaps a stake – in the dominant discourse of American civic culture.

Political moral performances

Denial of participation in organizations such as the Boy Scouts of America, legal statutes in seven states against atheists right to hold public office, legal oaths be sworn on the Christian bible and the ubiquitous cultural, political and social endorsements of theism are just a few of the many ways atheists cannot participate as fully fledged citizens in American civic life. Reversing the civic exclusion of atheists from the public sphere is a primary goal of political performances, evident through constant political interventions of secular groups, including outright atheist groups, at the local and national levels.

In 2002, several secular organizations came together to form the Secular Coalition for America (SCA). Since then, SCA has become visibly involved in asserting their presence in political matters. Founder Herb Silverman notes, "The Secular Coalition for America has lobbyists in Washington. Our mission is to increase the visibility of and respect for nontheistic viewpoints and to protect the secular character of our government. It is an uphill battle, but we are moving in the right direction" (*Washington Post*, 2011). One political performance by the SCA urged members of the House Armed Services Committee to allow nontheistic military chaplains into the Chaplain Corps of the Armed Forces. SCA pointed out the fact that although atheists are more numerous than Hindus, Muslims and Jews in the military, all of whom have chaplains, atheists do not have a single chaplain. Atheists' attempts to be part of the Chaplain Corps of the Armed Forces support Benford and Hunt's (1992) dramaturgical approach of creating the image of a "respectable figure" to strengthen the movement and perform as a moral entrepreneur.

Atheists' political civic engagement extends to filing lawsuits to stop symbolic displays of Christian hegemony, as we saw with Jessica Ahlquist in Rhode Island. When the twin towers at the Worlds Trade Center collapsed on 9/11, two intersecting steel beams from the building were found crossing one another. They were seen as iconic to Father Brian Jordan, a Franciscan monk, who ministered to clearing that area after the attacks and blessed the cross at a ceremony. Shortly afterward, the cross was put on display at the 9/11 Memorial and Museum. A group of atheists filed a lawsuit to stop the display of the cross. US District Judge Deborah Batts dismissed the lawsuit contending that the cross "helps demonstrate how those at ground zero coped with the devastation they witnessed during the rescue and recovery effort" (Neumeister, 2013). She went on to say that the steel cross could be viewed as a secular symbol. Apparently this was part of her own improvised performance, which was imbued with more power than the performance of the disgruntled and disrespected atheists.

Other lawsuits filed by American Atheists involved the department of Internal Revenue Service for preferential treatment to religious groups. The legal battle was sparked by "Pulpit Freedom Sunday", an initiative spearheaded by Jim Garlow, the pastor of the Skyline mega church in Lemon Grove, California. The initiative called on 1,500 pastors to ignore their tax exempt status and endorse a presidential candidate two months before the 2012 presidential elections (Mehta, 2012a). The argument presented by American Atheists focused on discrimination against atheists, since churches have a tax exempt status and a fundraising advantage in that they do not have to disclose the names of donors who contribute more than $5,000, a privilege not extended to secular organizations such as American Atheists (ibid.). Though these lawsuits have been, for the most part, unsuccessful, they have provided symbolic platforms for political performances.

Moral identity performances

> They called me a rebel. For years, I wore that name with shame until I realized that confronted with the god of my father, rebellion is the only moral option.
>
> – Nathan Phelps

Firebrand atheists reject feelings of shame associated with their stigmatized status and attempt to re-appropriate their deviant label onto religious antagonists, explicitly "condemning their condemners" (Sykes and Matza, 1957). Embattled atheist and gay rights activist Greta Christina encourages atheist activists to use the LGBT movement as a model for their movement. As an identity movement, the struggle for LGBT equality was about civic inclusion and political/cultural recognition; challenging cultural hegemony parallels challenging religious hegemony. Atheists have appropriated a number of tactical strategies into their repertoires.

The deviant status of atheists often makes it difficult to exit the closet. Discursive strategies such as "coming out" and the valorization of "pride" are an integral part of embattled activism. Atheist Pride Day (June 6) encourages explicit visibility of non-belief to improve public perceptions of atheism and all non-theistic identities. Students from the Atheists, Humanists, Agnostics student organization at the University of Wisconsin, Madison, organized the first atheist pride parade in 2013. According to director Chris Calvey, "The goal is to improve the public perception of atheism. We aren't interested in attacking anyone; rather, the parade is a celebration of our own identity. We want to show that atheists come from all walks of life, and that we are nothing to be afraid of" (Erickson, 2013).

A devastating tornado struck the city of Moore, Oklahoma, on May 21, 2013, killing 24 people, injuring at least 337 people and devouring over a thousand houses (Magee, 2013). Many residents fled their homes and managed to escape the catastrophe. Rebecca Vitsmun was among those who fled the city, narrowly escaping the havoc, then coming back to a home that no longer existed. The next day, media outlets broadcasted the devastation and interviewed some of the tornado victims. Vitsmun was interviewed by CNN's news anchor Wolf Blitzer. The interview started out as a typical tornado victim's interview, but then took a sudden turn when Blitzer asked, "You've gotta thank the Lord, right?"

Vitsmun, carrying her 19-month-old son, replied graciously with a smile and a slight tilt of the head, "I'm actually an atheist" (ibid.). Rebecca's courage to disclose her atheism on national television struck a chord with many non-believers. The interview "went viral" and was viewed on YouTube hundreds of thousands of times in less than three weeks (ibid.).

Vitsmun's performance was a perfect example of all the necessary components for a successful act. Not only that she adapted to unforeseen circumstances, she had self-control over her facial expressions and presented an image of loyalty to outsiders. This dramaturgical circumspection can exist only if the actor possessed dramaturgical discipline and loyalty (Benford and Hunt, 1992; Goffman, 1959). Moreover, the presentation of Vitsmun as a mother carrying a baby created an image of a "respectable figure", countering the stereotypically negative and deviant images associated with atheists in the United States.

On the other side of the story was Blitzer's question, which was an attempt to concretize the pervasive Christian privilege by implying that "thanking the Lord" is a normative and expected behavior. Christian hegemony relies heavily on constructing a social reality in a manner accepted as common sense (Blumenfeld, 2006). In addition, Blitzer's question supports the idea that the language we use structures reality and can be manipulated to exclude and oppress others (Dobratz et al., 2012, p. 82). Vitsmun's response created a dialectical performance that involves discussion, reasoning and dialogue as a method for arriving at the "truth". Yet those in power can still manipulate such performances so that the outcome is in favor of the Christian majority (p. 96).

Atheists' awareness of their deviant social location encourages them to use scripts that extend membership to all forms of non-believers and select liberal religions. The collaboration of many secular organizations in the United States led to the creation of the Reason Rally on March 24, 2012. Tens of thousands of atheists, non-believers and some believers gathered in the National Mall for a day-long event of speakers and comedy to advance secular principles. The event was publicized as friendly, benevolent and inclusive. This well-intentioned atmosphere and comic performances refuted the stereotypical "angry atheist" image.

Cultural moral performances

Firebrand atheists enact cultural moral performances by engaging in consciousness-raising via billboard campaigns and bus/train ads in public spaces with tension-raising, attention-grabbing messages such as "Are you good without God? Millions are", "Don't believe in God? You are not alone" and "Millions of Americans are good without God". Most of these ads are timed to pop up around Christmas. Atheists realize that there is a fine balance between what may be perceived as attacking Christmas and raising consciousness, which explains their endorsement of the holiday, yet rejecting the mythical origins in some of their ads. For example, American Atheist purchased a Christmas billboard in New York City in December 2012. The billboard read "Keep the Merry! Dump the Myth!", suggesting that Americans should keep traditions such as Santa Clause, but get rid of beliefs similar to the Immaculate Conception and the subsequent virgin birth. This falls in line with Benford and Hunt's (1992) suggestion that for a successful performance the actors must find a balance between appearing sincere but not so much as to become over-involved. Furthermore, all forms of activism shouldn't ignore the audience's interpretation as they could risk getting labeled as "extreme" (ibid.). In the case of keeping "the merry" or the Santa Clause tradition, atheists are willing to compromise to accommodate to their audience. Atheist billboard and bus campaigns have shown to be a successful tactic of cultural moral performance. Figure 9.1 illustrates how trends in searching the term "atheist" have increased with various firebrand performances. The top line represents changes in the number of times the term atheist has been searched since 2005. The bottom line represents the "floor" – how many times the word atheist is searched without explicit references to atheism in the press.

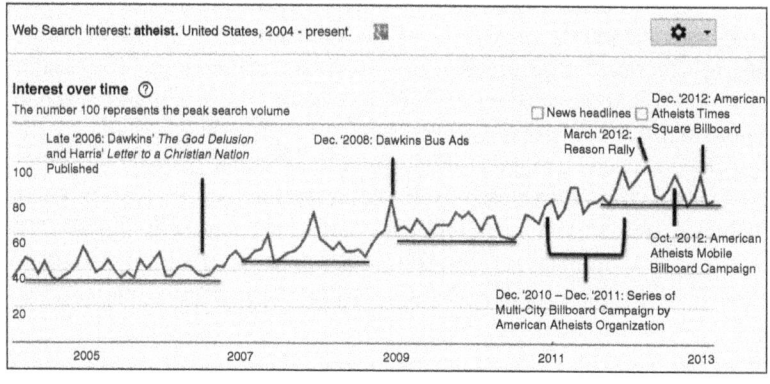

Figure 9.1   Web search interest in "atheist", 2004–2013
Source: Google Trends.

Every time a new floor is established, increases in Google searches of the term "atheist" indicate a new "norm", thus producing a new trend. The continued floor increases over time are indicative of the normalization of atheist activism in the United States.[3]

Unfortunately, even when atheists compromise and are attentive to their audience, they can still be perceived as offensive by some. For example, the Shenandoah Area Secular Humanists in Virginia put up a display alongside a Nativity scene in front of the Warren County courthouse. The sign read, "With reason and compassion as our guide, let us work together to produce a world in which peace, prosperity, freedom, and happiness are shared by all". The sign was vandalized twice. On December 16, 2012, it was spray-painted and then again, five days later, on December 21, 2012, it was set on fire (Mehta, 2012b). Although the sign was an attempt at an inclusive performance, the audience can sometimes disrupt the performance. The ability to re-appropriate and re-interpret the meanings of performances goes beyond the performer once it reaches an audience, which further demonstrates the malleability of moral order and deviant labels.

The case of atheist activism and future studies of political deviance

We have discussed how atheist activism in the United States has emerged as a form of political deviance. Regardless of the subjective nature of what is considered "deviant", we argue that deviance is more than a relative concept. Rather, it should be understood as not only a label used and applied to others by those with social power, but also as something which is enacted *as* a form of power (see Foucault, 1980). The conscious-raising strategies of groups like the American Atheists and the Secular Coalition for America advertise the message of atheism in an extremely visible manner drawing media attention through public lawsuits, opportunities to engage in stigma transformation by public displays of philanthropy and cultural expressions of resistance such as atheist campaigns on buses, trains, stationary billboards and most recently, mobile billboards. These campaigns often trigger strong reactions from citizens. A consequence of secular *consciousness*-raising is the likelihood of secular

---

[3] The full version of David Silverman's talk about Firebrand atheism regarding the normalization of atheism can be found on YouTube at: http://youtu.be/qw3XGegH8dE.

conflict-raising between theists and non-theists. As such, scripting and performing deviance by a historically marginalized population are forms of empowerment.

The study of deviance provides scholars with several useful tools for analytically examining the formation, emergence and behaviors of current and new cultural populations, such as movements like Occupy. Applying a dramaturgical lens takes us a step further, not only showing how deviance is socially constructed, but also how performances shape deviant labels, as in the case with "hactivists" in the Anonymous movement who justify their "deviant" actions by constructing governmental entities as the villains of societal progress. Finally, political deviance offers a conceptual tool for studying deviant heroes. How do activists like Mahatma Gandhi and Martin Luther King Jr., who were deviantized in their respective eras, become movement heroes responsible for facilitating widespread social change? Applying the lens of political deviance can help scholars understand what may motivate the actions of governmental whistleblowers who risk their safety and freedom in order to uncover political corruption.

Are firebrand atheists like Richard Dawkins, Sam Harris and David Silverman deviant heroes? Although we argue that they are "morally driven rebels" who have emerged as "agents of justice and social change", only time will tell (Wolf and Zuckerman, 2012, p. 639). For now, we can safely say that both atheist activists and less publicly vocal atheists continue to feel oppressed by Christian hegemony and privilege. The actions of social marginalization have put them squarely in the realm of political deviance because of their beliefs, or non-beliefs, depending on which side of Pascal's wager you stand and who stands with you.

References

Abdel Haq, M. (2013) "The Collective Consciousness of Atheism: How Do Atheists Social and Political Frameworks Differ from Protestants", Master's thesis (California State University, Fullerton).

Adams, M. (2007) *Teaching Diversity for Social Justice* (New York: Routledge).

Alexander, J. C. (2001) "Toward a Sociology of Evil", in M. P. Lara (ed.) *Rethinking Evil* (Berkeley: University of California Press).

Alexander, J. C., B. Giesen and J. L. Mast (2006) *Social Performance: Symbolic Action, Cultural Pragmatics, and Ritual* (Cambridge: Cambridge University Press).

Barb, A. (2011) "An Atheistic America Is a Contradiction in Terms: Religion, Civic Belonging, and Collective Identity in the United States", *European Journal of American Studies*, 1, 1–18.

Bates, S. (2004) "Godless Communism and Its Legacies", *Society*, 41, 29–33.

Becker, H. S. (1963) *Outsider: Studies in the Sociology of Deviance* (New York: Free Press).

Bellah, R. (1967) "Civil Religion in America", *Daedalus*, 96, 1–21.

Benford, R. D. and D. A. Snow (2000) "Framing Processes and Social Movements: An Overview and Assessment", *Annual Review of Sociology*, 26, 611–639.

Benford, R. D. and S. A. Hunt (1992) "Dramaturgy and Social Movements: The Social Construction and Communication of Power", *Sociological Inquiry*, 62, 36–55.

Ben-Yehuda, N. (1990) *The Politics and Morality of Deviance: Moral Panics, Drug Abuse, Deviant Science, and Reversed Stigmatization* (Albany: State University of New York Press).

—— (2006) "Contextualizing Deviance within Social Change and Stability, Morality, and Power", *Sociological Spectrum*, 26, 559–580.

Best, J. (1995) *Images of Issues: Typifying Contemporary Social Problems* (New Brunswick: Transaction).

Bivens, J. C. (2008) *Religion of Fear* (New York: Oxford University Press).

Blumenfeld, W. (2006) "Christian Privilege and the Promotion of 'Secular' and Not-So 'Secular' Mainline Christianity in Public Schooling and in the Larger Society", *Equity & Excellence in Education*, 39, 195–210.

Borer, M. I. (2010) "The New Atheism and the Secularization Thesis", in A. Amarasingam (ed.) *Religion and the New Atheism: A Critical Appraisal* (Boston: Brill).

Borer, M. I. and T. Schafer (2011) "Culture War Confessionals: Conflicting Accounts of Christianity, Violence, and Mixed Martial Arts", *Journal of Media and Religion*, 10, 165–184.

Brooks, D. (2003) "Kicking the Secularist Habit", *The Atlantic*, http://www.theatlantic.com/magazine/archive/2003/03/kicking-the-secularist-habit/302680/, date accessed May 13, 2013.

Buechler, S. M. (2000) *Social Movements in Advanced Capitalism* (New York: Oxford University Press).

Burke, K. (1945) *A Grammar of Motives* (New York: Prentice Hall).

Christina, G. (2007) "Atheist and Anger", Freethought Blogs, http://gretachristina.typepad.com/greta_christinas_weblog/2007/10/atheists-and-an.html, date accessed March 6, 2013.

Cimino, R. and C. Smith (2007) "Secular Humanism and Atheism beyond Progressive Secularism", *Sociology of Religion*, 68, 407–424.

—— (2011) "The New Atheism and the Formation of the Imagined Secular Community", *Journal of Media and Religion*, 10, 24–38.

Cohen, S. (1972) *Folk Devils and Moral Panics: The Creation of the Mods and the Rockers* (New York: MacGibbon and Kee).

Conrad, P. and J. W. Schneider (1980) *Deviance and Medicalization: From Badness to Sickness* (St. Louis: V. Mosby).

Dobratz, B., L. Waldner and T. Buzzell (2012) *Power, Politics and Society: An Introduction to Political Sociology* (New York: Allyn and Bacon).

Douglas, M. (1966) *Purity and Danger: An Analysis of Concepts of Pollution and Taboo* (New York: Routledge).

Edgell, P., J. Gerteis and D. Hartmann (2006) "Atheist as 'Other': Moral Boundaries and Cultural Membership in America", *American Sociological Review*, 71, 211–234.

Erickson, D. (2013) "In the Spirit: Atheist Pride Parade Perhaps the First in the Country", *Wisconsin State Journal*, http://host.madison.com/lifestyles/faith-and-values/religion/in-the-spirit-atheist-pride-parade-perhaps-the-first-in/article_9f7f64b2-875e-11e2-b470-001a4bcf887a.html, date accessed May 13, 2013.

Erickson, K. T. (1966) *Wayward Puritans: A Study in the Sociology of Deviance* (New York: John Wiley & Sons).

Foucault, M. (1980) *Power/Knowledge: Selected Interviews and Other Writings 1972–1977* (New York: Pantheon Books).

Futrell, R. (2003) "Framing Processes, Cognitive Liberation, and NIMBY Protest in the U.S. Chemical-Weapons Disposal Conflict", *Sociological Inquiry*, 73, 359–386.

Goffman, E. (1959) *Presentation of Self in Everyday Life* (New York: Anchor).

——— (1974) *Frame Analysis: An Essay on the Organization of the Experience* (New York: Harper Colophon).

Goldberg, M. (2007) *Kingdom Coming: The Rise of Christian Nationalism* (New York: W. W. Norton).

Goode, E. and N. Ben-Yehuda (2009) *Moral Panics: The Social Construction of Deviance*, 2nd edn. (Oxford: Wiley-Blackwell).

Hammer, J. H., R. T. Cragun, K. Hwang and J. M. Smith (2012) "Forms, Frequency, and Correlates of Perceived Anti-atheist Discrimination", *Secularism and Nonreligion*, 1, 43–67.

Hartmann, D., J. Gerteis and P. Edgell (2003) "American Mosaic Project Survey, Inter-university Consortium for Political and Social Research", http://thedata.harvard.edu/dvn/dv/icpsr/faces/study/StudyPage.xhtml?globalId=hdl:1902.2/28821, date accessed June 29, 2013.

Hunsberger, B. E. and B. Altemeyer (2006) *Atheists: A Groundbreaking Study of America's Non-believers* (New York: Prometheus Books).

Jacoby, S. (2004) *Freethinkers: A History of American Secularism* (New York: Metropolitan Books).

Jasper, J. M. (2010) "Strategic Marginalizations and Emotional Marginalities: The Dilemma of Stigmatized Identities", in D. Singharoy (ed.) *Surviving against Odds: The Marginalized in a Globalizing World* (New Dehli: Manohar).

Jasper, J. M. and J. D. Poulsen (1995) "Recruiting Strangers and Friends: Moral Shocks and Social Networks in Animal Rights and Anti-Nuclear Protests", *Social Problems*, 42, 493–512.

Kituse, J. I. (1980) "Coming Out All Over: Deviants and the Politics of Social Problems", *Social Problems*, 28, 1–13.

LeDrew, S. (2013) "Discovering Atheism: Heterogeneity in Trajectories to Atheist Identity and Activism", *Sociology of Religion*, 74, 1–23.

Loseke, D. R. (2005) *Thinking about Social Problems*, 2nd edn. (New Brunswick: Aldine Transaction).

Lovheim, M. (2007) "Virtually Boundless?: Youth Negotiating Tradition in Cyberspace", in N. Ammerman (ed.) *Everyday Religion: Observing Modern Religious Lives: Observing Modern Religious Lives* (New York: Oxford University Press).

Magee, B. (2013) "Atheists Give $10,000 to Oklahoma Tornado Victim Rebecca Vitsmun after CNN Appearance", *American Humanist Association*, http://www.americanhumanist.org/news/details/2013–05-atheists-give-10000-to-oklahoma-tornado-victim-rebec, date accessed May 30, 2013.

Mansbridge, J. (2001) "The Making of Oppositional Consciousness", in J. Mansbridge and A. Morris (eds.) *Oppositional Consciousness: The Subjective Roots of Social Protest* (Chicago: University of Chicago Press).

McAdam, D. (1982) *Political Process and the Development of Black Insurgency, 1930–1970* (Chicago: University of Chicago Press).

McAnulla, S. (2012) "Radical Atheism and Religious Power: New Atheist Politics", *Approaching Religion*, 2, 87–99.

McGrath, A. (2006) *The Twilight of Atheism: The Rise and Fall of Disbelief in the Modern World* (New York: Random House).

Mehta, H. (2012a) "American Atheist Is Suing the IRS, Claiming That It Gives Preferential Treatment to Religious Groups", *Patheos Blog*, http://www.patheos.com/blogs/friendlyatheist/2012/12/20/american-atheists-is-suing-the-irs-claiming-that-it-gives-preferential-treatment-to-religious-groups/, date accessed March 15, 2013.

—— (2012b) "Inoffensive Atheist Sign Gets Vandalized in Virginia; It Was Spraypainted and Burned", *Patheos Blog*, http://www.patheos.com/blogs/friendlyatheist/2012/12/28/inoffensive-atheist-sign-gets-vandalized-in-virginia-it-was-spraypainted-and-burned/, date accessed March 15, 2013.

Mizruchi, E. H. (1983) *Regulating Society: Marginality and Social Control in Historical Perspective* (New York: Free Press).

Neumeister, L. (2013) "NY Judge Tosses Lawsuit over Sept. 11 Steel Cross", Associated Press, http://bigstory.ap.org/article/ny-judge-tosses-lawsuit-over-sept-11-steel-cross, date accessed April 10, 2013.

Niose, D. (2012) *Nonbeliever Nation: The Rise of Secular Americans* (New York: Palgrave Macmillan).

Rosch, S. (n.d.) "9/11 and the Rise of New Atheism", *Examiner*, http://www.examiner.com/article/9-11-and-the-rise-of-new-atheism, date accessed April 10, 2013.

Schiedrop, M. (2012) "Ahlquist: Fight over Mural, Despite Harassment, Threats, 'Worth It'", *Cranson Patch*, http://cranston.patch.com/articles/ahlquist-fight-over-mural-despite-harassment [sic]-threats-worth-it, date accessed October 17, 2012.

Silverman, H. (2011) "Why Do Americans Still Hate Atheists? Herb Silverman Explains", http://live.washingtonpost.com/why-do-americans-hate-atheists-herb-silverman.html, date accessed March 3, 2013.

Smelser, N. (2004) "Epilouge: September 11, 2001, as Cultural Trauma", in J. C. Alexander, R. Eyerman, B. Giesen, N. Smelser and P. Sztompka (eds.) *Cultural Trauma and Collective Identity* (Berkley: University of California Press).

Smith, C. and R. Cimino (2012) "Atheism Unbound: The Role of New Media in the Formation of a Secularist Identity", *Secularism and Nonreligion*, 1, 17–31.

Smith, J. M. (2011) "Becoming an Atheist in America: Constructing Identity and Meaning from the Rejection of Theism", *Sociology of Religion*, 72, 215–237.

—— (2013) "Creating a Godless Community: The Collective Identity Work of Contemporary American Atheists", *Journal for the Scientific Study of Religion*, 52, 80–99.

Sykes, G. M. and D. Matza (1957) "Techniques of Neutralization: A Theory of Delinquency", *American Sociological Review*, 22, 664–670.

Tarico, V. (2012) "Should Atheists Slam Religion or Show Respect?", *Alternet*, http://www.alternet.org/story/155278/should_atheists_slam_religion_or_show_respect, date accessed October 13, 2012.

Wolf, B. and P. Zuckerman (2012) "Deviant Heroes: Nonconformist as Agents of Justice and Social Change", *Deviant Behavior*, 33, 639–654.

Zuckerman, P. (2009) "Atheism, Secularity, and Well-Being: How the Findings of Social Science Counter Negative Stereotypes and Assumptions", *Sociology Compass*, 3, 949–971.

10

The School-to-Prison Pipeline and the "Death of Deviance" in the American Public School System

Scott Wm. Bowman

Introduction

In 1994, the US Congress passed the "Gun Free Schools Act", requiring states to enforce "zero tolerance" expulsion of students specifically for firearms found on school property (Advancement Project, 2005). As a result, states not only determined that this was a worthwhile effort for protecting youth enrolled in schools, but also that this approach could (and should) be expanded to incorporate other forms of behavior and other, more formal forms of discipline. Moreover, a lack of clearly defined punishment(s) for zero tolerance activities allowed for the social and criminological construction of implementing a myriad of sanctions for a wide variety of behaviors (Skiba and Knesting, 2001). While there have been numerous social and political instances that have influenced the overall growth of "zero tolerance" policies in schools and the growth of the "school-to-prison pipeline" type of punishments (e.g., the growth of gang violence in the early 1990s), it can be argued that no single instance holds greater influence on these policies than the Columbine school shooting.

In 1999, two young men named Dylan Klebold and Eric Harris went into Columbine High School in Littleton, Colorado, armed with semi-automatic weapons and explosive devices, and killed 15 people – including teachers, students and themselves – and injured an additional 21 people (Cullen, 2009). While there had been both school shootings and significant youth-related gun violence in prior years, the country had never witnessed a level of teen violence of that magnitude – particularly taking place within a school. For the general public, it was a shocking, horrifying incident. For school administrators and politicians, it was the culmination of the types of zero tolerance policies that had been established years prior. Furthermore, regardless of the pathology of the offenders, two things were made certain in the subsequent discourse: (1) *any* child (regardless of age) was capable of carrying out this type of violent act, as children today were deemed more violent, predatory and unpredictable than at any other point in history; and (2) our schools were ill-prepared for not only this type of attack, but also addressing these predatory, violent children preventively and proactively.

As a result of increased fears of youth violence and a perceived inability of school districts to enforce effective discipline, a zero tolerance philosophy was further implemented to include "trivial conduct, much of which is subjectively labeled as 'disrespect', 'disobedience', and 'disruption'" (Advancement Project, 2005, p. 15). More specifically, a formal, rational system of zero tolerance school enforcement has produced the contemporary, accompanying "school-to-prison pipeline". While much has been written and examined regarding both the zero tolerance policies and the resulting school-to-prison pipeline, little has been written on the manner in which these policies and sanctions have come to exist. Moreover, pointing to reactionary factors such as the increasing use of drugs and violence in schools explains in part the reactionary desire to adjust existing policies; however, it does not address the specific manner in which the policies and punishments were formed and the apparent theoretical force(s) behind this particular manner of change.

In order to effectively examine the contemporary application of zero tolerance policies within American schools and how these policies have produced a school-to-prison pipeline, I present a theoretical foundation to direct and inform this examination. The theoretical foundation for this chapter comes from the pre-eminent sociologist Max Weber, who has been examined and analyzed for not only his construction of legal decision making (Gerth and Mills, 1946; Inverarity et al., 1983) and bureaucratic organization (Gordon, 2009; Weber, 1947), but also the constructive interpretation of punishment application(s) from a Weberian perspective (Garland, 1990).

After a brief biography of Max Weber, zero tolerance policies are presented and analyzed according to Weberian legal perspectives. Next, the punitive school-to-prison pipeline sanctions that often accompany zero tolerance policies are explained and analyzed according to Weberian constructions of punishment. Finally, a cumulative presentation of the issue is examined according to the effects from an overarching, Weberian perspective. Using Max Weber as a theoretical foundation, I argue in this chapter that the growth of a formal, rational process of both criminalizing school behaviors through the practice of constructing formal, legal precedents and the formalizing of rational, consistent punishments has resulted in the "death of deviance" for many American youth. In other words, instead of seeing the "death of deviance" in terms in which it is usually understood, here it refers to the formal criminalization of behaviors traditionally treated informally as non-criminal deviance. In American public schools there is little "deviance" left in the sense of informally disapproved, informally sanctioned behavior that is, in the end, formally tolerated as a part of growing up; instead, the legal-formal response drives itself deep down into the school system, turning "deviants" into criminals. The result is that school administrators are structurally bound to enforce consistent, yet emotionless regulations and punishments that socially construct youth in schools as formal, legal "juvenile delinquents."

Max Weber

Max Weber (1864–1920) is considered one of the pre-eminent scholars on the subjects of organizations, legal decision making and the expansion of bureaucracy. Though this work focuses primarily on the interpretations of laws and punishments, Weber is equally (if not more) relevant to the influences of political, historical and economic thought, where MacRae (1974, p. 34) suggests, "he can be thought of as lawyer, historian, economist, philosopher, political scientist, as well as sociologist". Weber's far-reaching knowledge can be exemplified by the positions he held during his earliest teaching experiences as professor of law, political economics and economics (Gerth and Mills, 1946; Greenwood and Lawrence, 2005).

Weber experienced personal struggles during the early part of his career and was granted paid leave from his university (Gerth and Mills, 1946); this allowed him to construct an immersed study in a variety of subjects and incorporate a variety of scholarly disciplines. From this experience, he wrote numerous essays, especially over his early academic years – none more arguably famous than his 1906 text "The Protestant Work Ethic and the Spirit of Capitalism" (1930) that was largely influenced during his time in the United States (Greenwood and Lawrence, 2005).

In the final years of his life, he was active in creating and supporting the growing discipline of sociology. Though his canonization in the field of sociology (he is often referred to as "the father of modern sociology") came posthumously, he clearly provided the foundation for not only the direct study of law, politics and economics, but also the interpretive study of fields such as criminal justice and punishment. For the purposes of this chapter, the primary focus is on Weber's construction of formal, rational legal decision making and the Weberian interpretation of punishment.

The "zero tolerance" legislation of schools

Prior to establishing a presence in the American education system, the principles and practices of zero tolerance legislation were associated with the "war on drugs." During the early 1980s, the Reagan-era narratives of drug use as a criminological issue and subsequent get-tough, zero tolerance policies (often constructed in the form of "codes of conduct") that accompanied this belief produced harsh, unwavering and non-discretionary laws such as mandatory minimum legislation. According to Skriba and Rausch (2006), the term "zero tolerance" became a widely adopted philosophy that mandated pre-determined, non-discretionary sanctions – regardless of the gravity of the circumstance, any mitigating circumstances or any desired counter-decision to the zero tolerance policies. These policies were implemented according to the perception that there were both student-based activities that were dangerous and/ or detrimental to daily school functioning and that pre-emptive policies would act as a deterrent to other students. Moreover, these policies were established and implemented as a reaction to the perceived actions of violent, delinquent teens, despite the fact that statistics on juvenile delinquency contradicted the need for these types of policies. Aull (2012) indicates:

> Policymakers imported this attitude to public schools during the 1990s in response to the widespread perception that juvenile violence was increasing and school officials needed to take desperate measures to address this problem ... It turns out that the public's fears were misguided – statistics show violent crime among juveniles was in decline just as the zero tolerance movement was picking up steam. (pp. 182–183)

In large part due to the inconsistencies between the original construction of zero tolerance policies and the comparatively minimal amount of violent, dangerous and delinquent activities that were actually taking place throughout American public schools, zero tolerance policies evolved into the policing (both formal and informal) of micro-level behaviors and actions, having more to do with social control and less to do with delinquency.

In addition, the traditional practices of administratively interpreted behaviors and actions were replaced with the formal legislation of conduct, as well as the formal incorporation of the juvenile justice system (e.g., Safety/School Resource Officers) as the co-agents of public school social control. For example, the American Psychological Association Zero Tolerance Task Force (2008) presented a clear example of the shift from the original philosophy to a more formal and unforgiving system, where "a 10-year-old girl found a small knife in her lunchbox placed there by the mother for cutting an apple" (p. 852). Even though she immediately turned in the knife to her teacher, she was expelled for possessing a weapon. These types of behavior-based infractions have increased dramatically during the growth of zero tolerance policy implementation, where it has been estimated that between 79 and 94 percent of public schools have implemented a zero tolerance policy for at least one infraction (Heaviside et al., 1998). In addition, it is of significant consequence that there are clear racial/ethnic, gendered and socioeconomic implications associated with zero tolerance policies. For example, research from the Advancement Project (2007) indicates that while white students were suspended at a rate of 4.8 per 100,000, blacks (15 per 100,000), Latinos (6.8 per 100,000) and (Native Americans 7.9 per 100,000) were comparatively overrepresented. Moreover, the intersection of gender and socioeconomic status (specifically living in disadvantaged neighborhoods) further exacerbates the disproportionalities (Advancement Project, 2005; Skiba and Rausch, 2006).

Through the construction and enforcement of codes of conduct, school administrators and agents of the juvenile justice system have produced a system that seeks to control minor (documented) behaviors. For example, the State of Texas can send a student to a "Disciplinary Alternative Education Program" (depending on the school district) for "offenses that range from fighting and gang activity to disrupting class, using profanity, playing a prank (e.g., throwing a tennis ball in the hallway and narrowly missing another student [a case in Texas]), misusing a school parking decal, inadvertently bringing a prescription or over-the-counter drug to school or doodling in class (when the drawing contains a weapon)" (Texas Appleseed, 2007, p. 19). These examples are an indication of policy implementation that reaches beyond the initial fears of school violence into micro-level opportunities for formal, social control. Moreover, they demonstrate a markedly different approach compared to previous generations. Prior to the zero tolerance practices, the "code of conduct" was established in a very different manner with a very different purpose. Robbins (1956), in an article titled "A Code of Ethics is Born", describes a process by which a student won a contest by submitting her code of ethics. This code included unspecific content such as "loyalty", "honesty", "respect", "manners" and "responsibility" (pp. 82–83). There were no specific regulations presented, nor was there any attempt to establish social control over particular diminutive behaviors. Instead, the student's submitted code of ethics encouraged positive behaviors. Subsequent to the early growth of conduct regulation, the rules and regulations have increased substantially and have become increasingly micro-managing.

Specifically over the past two decades, there has been a paradigmatic shift in the manner that disciplinary policies and procedures are implemented within the American educational system. The growth of the behaviors that are included in the contemporary code of conduct severely limit the opportunity for students to be "deviant" (as opposed to "delinquent"), thus formalizing behaviors (e.g., fighting, classroom disruption) under specific rules of social control. Within this model, the inevitable result leads to the "school-to-prison pipeline" (which is discussed in detail later).

Finally, it is noteworthy that there is no scholarly research that correlates the use of zero tolerance policies to their intended outcomes. According to the American Psychological Association Zero Tolerance Task Force (2008), one of the three primary considerations for the effectiveness of zero tolerance policies is: have zero tolerance policies made schools safer and more effective in handling disciplinary issues? According to their findings, (a) school violence has either remained steady or decreased slightly; (b) the consistency of zero tolerance implementation has not been demonstrated; (c) zero tolerance regulations have produced a less satisfactory school climate; and (d) zero tolerance regulations have not demonstrated a deterrence effect on students. In light of the deficiencies of zero tolerance policies, an examination of its implementation and sustainability should be considered.

Weber, legal decision making and "zero tolerance"

As it pertains to the subject of the contemporary construction of zero tolerance policies, the incorporation of Weber's writings on "rationality" is the beginnings of a theoretical correlation. Weber's initial view of rationality was that it was a unifying theme that effectively described modernization within Western society (Cockerham et al., 1993). More specifically, Trubek (1972, p. 727) suggests that Weber's rationality within a legal context is the measure of a system that is "capable of formulating, promulgating, and applying universal rules". According to Sterling and Moore (1987, pp. 67–68), "Weber was the first modern social theorist to develop a comprehensive approach to sociology of law through an analysis of the internal forms of legal thought, rather than the actual content of the law and the efficacy of law in assuring order and predictability in social behavior." Initially, Weber suggests that an action can be deemed as either "instrumentally rational" or "value-rational" (Callinicos, 1999). Whereas instrumental rationalization is determined by the expectations of *means* for the attainment of rationally calculated actions, value rationalization is determined by a conscious belief in the ethical or aesthetic, rationally calculated *ends* of actions (ibid.). Of the two forms, Weber believed that instrumental rationalization would be the pre-eminent form of social, economic and legal construction in a modern society.

Within the contextualization of instrumental rationalization, Weber argued that there are two major, dichotomous archetypes of rationalization – rationality/irrationality and formal/substantive (Inverarity et al., 1983; Sterling and Moore, 1987). The first archetype (rationality/irrationality) addresses the presence/absence of logical, legal decision making. For Weber, the primary presumption of this archetype is that modern societies will inevitably move away from irrational, illogical legal decision making and will seek a more rational, logical, legal decision-making process. The second archetype (formal/substantive) addresses the presence/absence of predictable, legal decision making. Again, Weber's primary presumption of this archetype is that modern societies will inevitably move away from more substantive, unpredictable legal decision making and seek a more formal, predictable, formal, legal decision-making process. While Weber believed that these typologies were consistent with legal decision making, he did not believe that they were mutually exclusive. Instead, he believed that there would be a dominant typology for legal decision making that included elements of other typologies. Moreover, Weber believed that the combination of archetypes would produce four unique, legal decision-making modes: (1) substantive irrational; (2) formal irrational; (3) substantive rational; and (4) formal rational – with these modes (in order of presentation) demonstrating a sociological (yet non-exclusive) "evolution" of legal decision making (Inverarity et al., 1983).

In a substantive irrational mode, legal decision-making would be neither formal nor rational, subject to "case-by-case decision making on basis of insight of charismatic judge" (Inverarity et al., 1983, p. 105). In a formal irrational mode, legal decision making would be formal; however, it would lack rationality. Inverarity, Lauderdale, and Feld (1983) suggest "specialized legal procedures are used, but decisions are not derived from general rules but are determined by supernatural forces" (p. 105). Also, a substantive rational mode suggests that there is the presence of a logical, rational decision-making process; however, there is no formal, predictable process. Here, Inverarity et al. imply that "cases decided by applying rules from some extralegal source, e.g. religion, ideology, economic expediency, science" (ibid.). Finally, in a formal rational legal decision-making process, there is the presence of both formal and rational procedures. The example provided by Inverarity et al. indicates "cases are decided by applying logically consistent abstract rules that are independent of moral, religious, and other normative criteria", where "general rules require that all cases of the same nature be treated equally" (ibid.). For the purposes of examining the establishment of zero tolerance policies within the American public school system, the modes of substantive rationality and formal rationality are considered.

According to Ritzer and Walczak (1988, p. 4), "the conflict between formal and substantive rationality may be descriptive of the current relation between (formal) rationalization and professionalization (a specific case of professionalization)". What Ritzer and Walczak are suggesting is that in a substantive rational, legal decision-making setting, professional people are led by social values in order to make a rational decision that is a means to an end (p. 4). Conversely, the attempted shift toward a more formal rational, legal decision-making process (and the consistently unwavering rules and regulations associated with it) produces conflict between social values and bureaucratic practices. While Ritzer and Walczak are examining this conflict for the medical profession, the argument is made that a similar conflict has arisen within the field of public education.

As indicated earlier, early American public school systems implemented a more substantive rational form of addressing legal decision making within the school system. Also, schools were autonomously guided by the philosophy of the administrative staff, substantively regarding how to address school violations. Professionals (teachers, principals, etc.) were provided the opportunity to implement logical rules within both the classroom and within the school itself, where a measure of substantive "social values" were both allowable and encouraged. For example, if two students got into a fight in the halls of a school, there was a formal, logical rule regarding the act of fighting in schools. If the regulatory process were irrational, a teacher might suggest that the student who has broken the rule of fighting was "the first to throw a punch" on some days, while deciding that the student who "lost the fight" had broken the rule on other days. Yet, since the regulatory system was rational, it was clear that the regulation associated with fighting was wrong, regardless of circumstances. However, the substantive nature of the professionalized school system allowed for a teacher's or administrator's "social values" to determine the manner in which the violation of the regulation would be addressed. During this period of the American public school system, a teacher with a clear knowledge of the formal violation to the fighting rule could simply yell "break it up!", "could send the students to their next class" or "could decide to send them to the administrative office". Moreover, the administrator could additionally decide their professional, "social-value"-driven decision on how to address the violated regulation, with similar choices as previously mentioned. More important, professionals were empowered to determine (substantively) whether or not a student was a "delinquent" or a "deviant", simply through a substantive decision-making process.

Alternatively, the contemporary American public school system has relinquished much of its autonomy for a more bureaucratic, formal rational system of student regulation. In previous school systems, neither state governments nor formal policing agencies were directly and specifically involved in the administration of the disciplinary process. However, Congress passed the "Gun Free Schools Act" in 1994 (Advancement Project, 2005) not only requiring states to enforce "zero tolerance" expulsion of students specifically for firearms found on school property, but also simultaneously inaugurating the paradigmatic shift to a more formal, legal practice of legislation. The underlying implication by the federal government was that the substantive rational practices, the informal professionalism and the social values were in need of a more formal rational process – explicitly the paradigmatic shift in legal decision making and increased bureaucracy that Weber believed would inevitably take place. Returning to the example of the state of Texas, one year after the passage of the "Gun Free Schools Act", the legislature passed "the state's first set of regulations specifying the range of disciplinary measures that schools could imposed for different types of offenses" (Texas Appleseed, 2007, p. 17). According to the Texas Appleseed report, the provisions listed have been amended nearly every legislative session, with mandate rules and corresponding disciplines for a list of specific serious offenses, and provide the school *districts* "wide discretion" for disciplinary measures for other violations to the student Code of Conduct (ibid.).

The growth of the formal rational legislation produced four noteworthy shifts in the legislation of behavior in American public schools. First, where historical professionals in American public schools were empowered to make social value assessments of delinquent and/or deviant situations as they arose, contemporary teachers and administrators (no longer "professionals") are subjected to the bureaucratic legislation of the state and federal government (and subsequently the school districts) in unrelenting support of the principles of formal rational legislative decision making. The result is that federal, state and district-based rules and regulations are placed not only upon the students, but also upon the teachers and administrators as a means of constructing an emotionless, passionless, "iron cage" of modern, educational rationalism (Tiryakian, 1981). Second, the increase in school-based bureaucratic rules and regulations fundamentally increases the need for a bureaucratic system of regulation enforcement and implementation. Clearly, the federal government recognized this need, as they provided substantial funding for School/Safety Resource Officers (SROs) to be placed in schools and school districts throughout the country. The SROs ensure that the formal rational regulations are not only enforced toward students in a consistent manner, but also ensure that the school's professionals adhere to a newly constructed formal rational buy-in. More specifically, the SRO ensures that the federal, state and district "iron cage" remains tightly shut, with no structural use for substantive alternatives. Third, the formal rational process seemingly became the guiding principle for all future school-based, decision making. Regardless of the effectiveness of the policies, the "romanticism" of a more formal rational school system produced additional rules (e.g., the "wide discretion", as described in the Texas Appleseed [2007] report) that would systematically fall into a similar type of zero tolerance regulation. The numerous examples provided by various studies on the subject of zero tolerance policies and the school-to-prison pipeline indicated student suspensions and expulsions for a variety of non-violent, micro-managed behaviors that were either formally, rationally regulated within the code of conduct or were interpreted through a broad, formal rational regulation to include general behaviors. Finally, the growth of formal rational regulations largely eliminated the possibility for student misbehavior to be treated informally. The American public school system places most of the formally regulated behaviors into two distinct, rational categories – "conformists" or "rule breakers." For example, yesterday's "deviant" student who "slept in class" was a "class clown", or even "questioned the teacher's information" are all today "student disruption" – a formal, rational, documented and regulated behavior (formally or informally in the Code of Conduct) that *must* result in the corresponding legal construction of a "delinquent" and the unwavering enforcement of the appropriate punitive sanctions. This has produced a school setting where there is no room for deviant behaviors that cannot be categorically formulated as either a conforming behavior or a formal, delinquent behavior and where kids can no longer make the types of mistakes that were correctable (or even developmentally acceptable) a generation prior.

This section addresses the formal rational process of behavior legislation; the accompanying issue to this death of deviance is the manner in which the punishment is administered in conjunction with the newly created/augmented delinquent behavior. While the formation of formal rational regulations in the school system are described here as constructing the "death of deviance", there is still a possibility that the accompanying punishments could (theoretically) allow for sanctions that are more wide-ranging. The next section examines the punitive sanctions in greater detail.

The punitive sanctions constructing the school-to-prison pipeline

Within the contemporary American public school system, zero tolerance regulations and the growth of the "school-to-prison pipeline" go hand-in-hand. Though this has been taken for granted within the general examination of the phenomenon, school-based zero tolerance policies did not have to fundamentally incorporate unusually punitive sanctions; nor could they be implemented outside of the school system itself. The school-to-prison pipeline has been loosely defined as the problematic outcome of zero tolerance (and other) policies that have placed school-aged children into the formal juvenile justice system – including a (potential) financial responsibility to the courts, the establishment of a formal, legal delinquency record and an unwavering removal from either the formal school day or removal from the school itself. More specifically, the contemporary school-to-prison pipeline demonstrates "the shift of school discipline for trivial incidents from principal's offices to police stations and courtrooms" (Advancement Project, 2005, p. 12). The shift as suggested by the Advancement Project is noteworthy for three reasons. First, school discipline was traditionally implemented within the school. Whether the form of discipline involved simply removing the student from the classroom for a temporary period of time or implementing a more serious form of corporal punishment, the decision involved a measure of discretion amongst teachers and school administrators. Even with the enactment of social contract based, codes of conduct, interpretations of behavioral severity and the accompanying punitive decision making remained discretionary (Robbins, 1956). Clearly in the contemporary era of "zero tolerance" policies and punishments, discretion has been all-but-removed from the decision-making process. Second, behavioral "mistakes" were an expected aspect of child development, where individual deviant/delinquent acts were constructed neither as symptomatic nor as unforgivable. Currently, the smallest behavioral infractions, including such offenses as "classroom disruption", would have been considered the previous generation's "class clown". Third, with the general exception of students' more severe behaviors, there traditionally remained a "restorative" aspect to the larger procedure of school punishments, where expulsions and suspensions were reserved for the most egregious acts and the remainder of punishments – including corporal punishment – consequently resulted in the student being returned to their schools, classrooms and peers. While early schools arguably did not have the same types of serious violence that exist in the contemporary American public school setting, these types of delinquent/deviant acts still remain comparatively rare. Conversely, most of the "zero tolerance" policies are geared more toward formally punishing "deviant" behavior as opposed to true delinquent/criminal activity, with more serious delinquent behaviors often resulting in automatic referrals or statutorial exclusions to either the juvenile or the adult court.

Unmistakably, the school-to-prison pipeline is descendant from the implementation of widespread zero tolerance policies and the growth of the juvenile justice system's role in enforcement. The beginning of the process of punishment has been the remarkable growth of the presence of SROs in public schools throughout the United States. In addition, there are schools that have increasing technological surveillance for the purposes of policy enforcement, metal detectors and canine units; however, the most prevalent aspect of enforcement comes specifically from the substantial increases of SROs in or assigned to American public schools. The result is a dramatic increase in the number of schools that have SROs and the manner in which they operate. Gonzalez (2011, p. 288) indicates that "forty-one states require schools to report students to law enforcement for various misbehaviors on campus", suggesting that SROs are an integral aspect of the American public school system. SROs in public schools were largely funded by the US Department of

Justice (with $60 million dollars) and the Safe Schools Initiative Program (granting an additional $19.5 million dollars) in order to help assist with enforcing the issues associated with the narratives of zero tolerance policies. As would be expected, with (minimally) $80 million dollars of SRO funding, the growth of SRO institutions was unprecedented in schools throughout the United States. For example, school districts in cities such as Houston, Los Angeles, Baltimore and Miami not only have their own police departments, but also have the same or more powers (such as increased, on-campus search and seizure rights) than their local police counterparts (Advancement Project, 2005). Moreover, Gonzalez (2011, p. 288) explains that "the New York Police Department's School Safety Division is larger than the entire police forces of the District of Columbia, Detroit, Boston, and Las Vegas". The result of the increased presence of formal, legal agents of social control is not only a fundamental increase in the number of students who will have an adversarial interaction with a formal agent of the juvenile justice system, but will also suffer the accompanying formal punishment associated with the delinquent act. Research supports these assertions, with not only increased levels of in-school suspensions, out-of-school suspensions and expulsions, but also increased juvenile court referrals for in-school behaviors and actions – many of which would have been addressed within the school system a generation ago.

Unmistakably, the SROs were not positioned in public schools to act as an informal buffer between delinquent students and school administrators. Instead, they were brought in shortly after the historical implementation of zero tolerance policies to further formalize the enforcement of the policies. Logically, the formal, rational zero tolerance policies that were implemented needed the accompaniment of zero tolerance punishments. Essentially, neither the formal, rational or consistent system of zero tolerance regulations that were established within American public schools could be complemented by punitive sanctions that were informal and inconsistent, nor could informal, inconsistent punishments establish (in theory) an effective deterrence doctrine (Beccaria, 2011). Through Garland's (1990) interpretation of Weber, the justification(s) for this punitive process are examined here.

Weber, punishment and the school-to-prison pipeline

While much of Weber's work has been analyzed according to the legal constructions associated with a formal, rational process, scholars such as David Garland (1990) have suggested that an additional analysis of

Weberian theory can be applied to the implementation of punishments. It is important to note, as Garland does in his landmark work, that Weber did not establish an explicit theory of punishment in a particular scholarly manner (p. 178). Instead, Garland's work attempts to correlate the core Weberian tenets of rationalization and bureaucratization to an understanding of both historical and contemporary punishment.

Similar to the application of Weberian theory to legal constructs, the examination of punishments is associated with a formal rational structure. Garland (1990) suggests:

> The move from traditional or affective practices to rationalized forms of action is seen by Weber ... as a distinctly modernizing development, in which social practices become better informed, more efficient, and more self-consciously adapted towards specific objectives. In consequence, social practices and institutions become more instrumentally effective, but at the same time they become less emotionally compelling or meaningful to their human agents. (p. 179)

However, unlike the formal rational processes of legal decision making, the process for the implementation and enforcement of punishments must acquiesce to the centralized, bureaucratic demands and expectations. The established bureaucracy of the federal government, state government and school district leaders not only hold the centralized authority to construct the school-based regulations within a Code of Conduct, but are also authorized to establish the corresponding penalties. Purposely, the SROs (as well as the teachers and administrators) become inextricably charged with activating the punitive process when deemed necessary within the formal rational setting for which they hold no control. Garland writes of this process, describing a situation in which:

> over the course of the last 200 years, the localized, *ad hoc*, and frequently makeshift penal arrangements of previous periods have given way to a professionalized, administrative infrastructure which commands significant tax-funded budgets, large numbers of career personnel, an extensive network of institutions and agencies, and a range of technical knowledges and social science discourses. (p. 180)

In the specific case of the American public school system, the previous years of makeshift (substantive formal and professional) arrangements for punishment have given way to an infrastructure that incorporates a network of agencies that were previously absent and a justification for punishments that are deeply rooted in the sociology, child development, psychology and most importantly *political science* literatures. Moreover, the national co-funding of public education has elicited a tax-funded system of SROs that bring knowledge to the American public system that was otherwise unknown. Included in this knowledge is the "handling" of delinquents, the formal processing of students into the juvenile justice system within the school setting and the incorporation of the "extensive network of institutions and agencies" to include (but not limited to) (a) the juvenile court system; (b) juvenile probation; (c) community service agencies; (d) diversion programs such as teen courts; and (e) potentially therapeutic services. Each of these examples that were traditionally designed for relatively serious juvenile delinquent offenders, have now become an integral element toward constructing a contemporary school-to-prison pipeline that can seek punishment for fundamental non-conformity. In addition, the construction of the contemporary school-to-prison pipeline – much like the construction of zero tolerance policy implementation – is constructed in a "passionless, routinized, matter-of-fact kind of way" (p. 183). While the emotional, passionate response(s) have been removed from the decision-making process formation through zero tolerance policies, the SROs, juvenile judges, juvenile probation officers and other agents of the juvenile justice system are emotionlessly and passionlessly completing the work set forth by the bureaucratic agencies that administer both school and juvenile justice-based policies and punishments.

There are three significant results from the shift to a formal system of punishments that can seemingly produce enough juvenile "delinquents" that the process has been labeled as a school-to-prison pipeline. First, the shift to more formal rational processes of school-based punishment has created a system that is much less accessible to the public and much more socially secretive (Garland, 1990, pp. 186–187). In the case of the contemporary American public school system, this often includes the parents. The explanation is two-fold. First, since zero tolerance policies are either already documented (more severe) or subject to interpretation (less severe), there is little need for parental involvement in the process. In a historical setting, the punishment phase of a substantive formal process would and/or could involve a parent/administrator discourse, where there would be a mutually constructed punishment that would be formal (in the fact that a punishment was to take place), yet could be substantive according to the manner in which it was implemented (by parent, administrator or both). Within the contemporary setting, the punishments are either pre-determined or non-negotiable within the context of "zero tolerance", leaving the parent's role in the punitive process as merely an informed afterthought. According to Garland, "The extent that the role of the public – or even of those who claim to represent them – has been diminished, the role of the expert has been correspondingly increased and, in the same movement, technical knowledge and diagnoses have displaced...moral evaluation and condemnatory judgment" (p. 187). Therefore, a parent with a desire to punish a student will be secondary (and possibly even shared) compared to the responsibilities of the juvenile court, the student's probation officer or some diversion program. Second, the punishments associated with a more formal system indirectly, yet fundamentally, support the disproportionate racial/ethnic, gendered and socioeconomic outcomes. When these disproportionalities appear as outcomes of formal, consistent and emotionless punitive sanctions, implementers of the school-to-prison pipeline can suggest that the process is a "student structured" that has been produced from a systematic approach. Alternatively, the research suggests that punitive sanctions are not nearly as routinized as indicated in the literature. Third, a system of punishment that is rooted in zero tolerance policies and interpretive Codes of Conduct *cannot* formally and rationally allow for informally handled "deviants" within a school-to-prison pipeline. The aforementioned "technical knowledge" that is associated with a myriad of behaviors and actions that produce a school-to-prison system must be primarily reinforcing a dichotomous construct of "student conformists" or "student delinquents". Seemingly, because a deviant's behaviors can neither be ignored within the environment of conforming students, nor can it be labeled as deviant without a policy to address both decision making and punishments, the non-conforming behavior must be labeled as formally, rationally delinquent with an applicably addressed punishment. In effect, there is no room for "deviants" within the school punitive system.

Schools and the death of deviance

In 1994, Colin Sumner made the claim that the sociology of deviance "had died". More specifically, he was suggesting that the larger relevance of "deviance" within the larger field of sociology had become increasingly inconsequential. Erich Goode (2002) explains Sumner's main point(s) in this manner:

> It starts with the assumption that the ruling elite follows the ideas and research of the academy very closely and makes use of those ideas to maintain hegemony…But with the dawn of the modern age and a correspondingly more sophisticated and diverse public, a simple characteristic of wrongdoers as degenerates became less and less plausible and, therefore, less effective as an instrument of social control. (p. 110)

Similar to Goode's assessment of Sumner (1994), the social construction of the contemporary school-to-prison pipeline has deconstructed the general label of "wrongdoers" to fit a more "sophisticated" ideology. While the surface narrative has been that of an effective form of social control, the fundamental construct of a more formal rational school structure of zero tolerance regulations has resulted in several problematic outcomes for youth that fall into the punishments that reinforce the school-to-prison pipeline:

1. The process of youth development has shifted from an emotional, physiological process to a (falsely) presumed ideology of formal, rational children. It appears that part of this process is directly associated with the growth of the role of the juvenile justice system and its correlation to the construction of the larger contemporary education system. In the contemporary American public school system, students as young as elementary school are presumed to have formed rational, logical minds to correspond to the Code of Conduct, as well as a rational, logical understanding with every implication associated with the accompanying punitive sanctions. Fundamental deterrence research suggests that fully functioning rational adults do not accurately weigh the certainly, severity and celerity of punishments as they relate to committing criminal acts (Schaub, Jr., 2004; Williams and Gibbs, 1981); however, we have a higher expectation for children through zero tolerance policies. This is problematic for the perceived development of students and their rudimentary ability to be inquisitive, mistake-prone beings.
2. According to a Weberian analysis, the "iron cage of modern rationalism" indicates that once formal, rational policies and punishments are implemented, it is considerably difficult to return to a decision-making process that is individualized, emotive and specialized.

Moreover, a formal rational system in the "iron cage of modern rationalism" inexorably suggests that there will be additional formal, rational laws and punishments that youth will face. Not only does the "iron cage of modern rationalism" suggest that the educational system is locked into its own formal, rational system of laws and punishments, but also the subsequent growth of the system must be forged in more laws and punishments, followed by more laws and punishments. The laws and punishments associated with the school-to-prison pipeline already indicate this, as ongoing behaviors will remain under drastic scrutiny to the point where deviance no longer remains and is regulated with additional laws and punishments. More specifically, a system is created where formal, rational laws and punishments feed upon themselves, further formalizing, further regulating and further punishing.

3. Whether formal or informal, rational, structured punishments must remain with the child as a function of the juvenile justice system. Where informal legal systems and punishments can remain undocumented, a formal, rational system that refers youth to the formal court system inevitably produces a documented outcome that remains with the child. The effects of this process can be both formal and informal. In a marginal sense, a formal charge and punishment can follow the student throughout their education, directly influencing how the school and/or safety resource officer interacts with the student, as well as having a direct influence on being viewed as a "repeat offender" for future offenses. On the other hand, a more serious charge could influence their ability to enter college, find gainful employment, or many of the additional factors that currently effect felons re-entering society.

4. Because youth in schools have little recourse within the educational system, the processes and procedures that are used to enforce the formal, rational laws will remain largely unchecked. For example, Fourth Amendment ("search and seizure") laws are clear for most Americans. Police must generally have probable cause and/or the individual's permission before conducting a search of automobiles, homes or personal property. This is dramatically different for youth in schools, where most fourth amendment protections are waived. This quasi-violation of fourth amendment rights has often been explained as necessary in order to protect students from violence or delinquency in schools; however, it is a fundamental violation nonetheless. Students are often subjected to searches of lockers, personal property (e.g., backpacks) and automobiles on campus property with

no recourse. As a result, additional legal and punitive sanctions that are deemed necessary to preserve school safety can be implemented by either schools or legislators with little recourse of opposition.

5. It establishes the "death of deviance" via formal social control and eliminates isolated incidents of informally handled "deviant" activity. Because of the process of implementing formal legal and punitive practices, youth are no longer provided the opportunity to "make mistakes", to "learn" or to have emotional reactions to life circumstances that are age-appropriate. Youth who "throw tantrums", who engage in school fights or simply disrupt classes are neither constructed as simply "deviant" for their acts, nor are their acts constructed as isolated ones for the purpose of social reintegration. For example, a 16-year-old student in Florida conducted an amateur science experiment in 2013 without school supervision that resulted in a small explosion though caused no damage and did not harm anyone (Welsh, 2013). In a historical school setting, both the student and the student's act would have been labeled as "deviant" and would have been addressed by the school's principal or dean of discipline, resulting in a punishment that was deemed appropriate by the respective decision maker. However, in this instance, the student was immediately expelled from her school (according to the school's formal "code of conduct" regulations) and faced felony charges that would have resulted in "up to five years in prison." As an alternative outcome, she served a 10-day suspension, enrolled into a different school, and was placed in a diversion program. It is noteworthy that both the original punishment and the alternative punishment were both formal and legal and were devoid of any potential alternate, informal consequence. In this example, not only was this young girl never provided the opportunity to be "constructed" as a deviant, but her actions cannot be constructed as an individual "deviant act". The formality of the process unavoidably labels her as a delinquent, regardless of the diversion-based outcome.

Conclusion

On the basis of the arguments made in this chapter, there are several issues that are essential to addressing zero tolerance policies, the school-to-prison pipeline and the manner in which they interact within a formal, rational school setting. One significant aspect that is included in this analysis is the possibility of the return of student deviance in the contemporary, American public school system. The conclusion to this chapter is unique, in that there is normally a suggestion for a policy implication or an optimistic assessment of future possibilities for an issue. Under ideal circumstances, the suggestion for restorative justice-type practices would be a more ideal and viable alternative, as it (theoretically) holds the offender accountable while simultaneously restoring their social (and educational) status (Gonzalez, 2011). In addition, it could constrain the wide-ranging practices of zero tolerance regulation and subsequently diminish the effects of the school-to-prison pipeline.

Unfortunately, it would seem that the "iron cage" of modern rationalism will endure and informally treated deviance in America's public schools will remain dead for the foreseeable future. I am cautiously pessimistic, as recent changes to the death penalty, life imprisonment without parole and the age of automatic culpability have been demonstrated as a means for challenging the current belief system of rational logical youth. However, and as previously stated, Weber's purpose of writing about the "iron cage" was to suggest that increasing forms of formal rational decision making would accumulate increasingly more forms of formal rational decision making. It would seem that the death of deviance is presumably in the hands of those bureaucratic agencies that have thrived, constructed knowledge and bolstered formal rational decision making at the expense of minor-level juvenile offenders. The alternative hope for the resurrection of deviance as a substantive alternative to the current system of zero tolerance policies and the school-to-prison pipeline within the American public school system seems to lie in the continued elucidation of the wide-ranging and long-lasting effects of the current arrangement.

References

Advancement Project (2005) *Education on Lockdown: The Schoolhouse to Jailhouse Track* (Washington, DC: Advancement Project).
—— (2007) *Youth Speak Out on the School-to-Prison Pipeline* (Washington, DC: Advancement Project).
American Psychological Association Zero Tolerance Task Force (2008) "Are Zero Tolerance Policies Effective in the Schools? An Evidentiary Review and Recommendations", *American Psychologist*, 63 (9), 852–862.
Aull IV, E. H. (2012) "Zero Tolerance, Frivolous Juvenile Court Referrals, and the School-to-Prison Pipeline: Using Arbitration as a Screening-Out Method to Help Plug the Pipeline", *Ohio State Journal on Dispute Resolution*, 27, 179–206.
Beccaria, C. (2011) *On Crimes and Punishments* (Piscataway, NJ: Transaction).
Callinicos, A. T. (1999). *Social Theory: A Historical Introduction* (New York: New York University Press).

Cockerham, W. C., T. Abel and G. Lüschen (1993) "Max Weber, Formal Rationality, and Health Lifestyles", *The Sociological Quarterly*, 34 (3), 413–428.

Cullen, D. (2009) *Columbine* (New York: Hachette Book Group).

Garland, D. (1990) *Punishment and Modern Society: A Study in Social Theory* (Chicago, IL: University of Chicago Press).

Gerth, H. H. and C. W. Mills (1946) *From Max Weber: Essays in Sociology* (New York: Oxford University Press).

Gonzalez, T. (2011) "Keeping Kids in Schools: Restorative Justice, Punitive Discipline, and the School to Prison Pipeline", *Journal of Law and Education*, 41 (2), 281–335.

Goode, E. (2002) "Does the Death of the Sociology of Deviance Claim Make Sense?", *The American Sociologist*, 33 (3), 107–118.

Gordon, V. (2009) "Early Twentieth Century Management Theories and Models That Shaped Twenty-First Century Leadership", *Journal of Philosophy & History of Education*, 59, 67–70.

Greenwood, R. and T. B. Lawrence (2005) "The Iron Cage in the Information Age: The Legacy and Relevance of Max Weber for Organizational Studies", Editorial, *Organization Studies*, 26 (4), 493–499.

Heaviside, S., C. Rowand, C. Williams and E. Farris (1998) *Violence and Discipline Problems in U.S. Public Schools: 1996–97* (NCES 98–030) (Washington, DC: US Department of Education, National Center for Education Statistics).

Inverarity, J. M., P. Lauderdale and B. Feld (1983) *Law and Society: Sociological Perspectives on Criminal Law* (Boston, MA: Little, Brown).

MacRae, D. G. (1974) *Weber* (London: Fontana Collins).

Ritzer, G. and D. Walczak (1988) "Rationalization and the Deprofessionalization of Physicians", *Social Forces*, 67 (1), 1–22.

Robbins, B. B. (1956). "A Code of Ethics Is Born". *The Clearing House*, 31 (2), 80–83.

Schaub, Jr., G. (2004) "Deterrence, Compellence, and Prospect Theory", *Political Psychology*, 25 (3), 389–411.

Skiba, R. J. and K. Knesting (2001) "Zero Tolerance, Zero Evidence: An Analysis of School Disciplinary Practice", in R. J. Skiba and G. G. Noam (eds.) *New Directions for Youth Development (No. 92: Zero Tolerance: Can Suspension and Expulsion Keep Schools Safe?)* (San Francisco: Jossey-Bass).

Skiba, R. J. and R. L. Rausch (2006) "Zero Tolerance, Suspension, and Expulsion: Questions of Equity and Effectiveness", in C. M. Evertson and C. S. Weinstein (eds.) *Handbook of Classroom Management: Research, Practice, and Contemporary Issues* (Mahwah, NJ: Erlbaum).

Sterling, J. S. and W. E. Moore (1987) "Weber's Analysis of Legal Rationalization: A Critique and Constructive Modification", *Sociological Forum*, 2 (1), 67–89.

Sumner, C. (1994) *The Sociology of Deviance: An Obituary* (Buckingham, UK: Open University Press).

Texas Appleseed (2007) *Texas' School to Prison Pipeline – Dropout to Incarceration: The Impact of School Discipline and Zero Tolerance* (Austin, TX: Texas Appleseed).

Tiryakian, E. A. (1981) "The Sociological Import of a Metaphor: Tracking the Source of Max Weber's 'Iron Cage'", *Sociological Forum*, 51 (1), 27–33.

Trubek, D. M. (1972) "Max Weber on the Law and the Rise of Capitalism", *The Yale Law Journal*, 82 (1), 1–50.

Weber, M. (1930) *The Protestant Ethic and the Spirit of Capitalism*, T. Parsons (trans.) (London: Unwin University Press).

—— (1947) *The Theory of Social and Economic Organization*, A. N. Henderson and Talcott Parsons (trans.) (New York: Free Press).

Welsh, J. (2013) "16-Year-Old Florida Honor Student Charged with Two Felonies for Doing a Science Experiment", *Business Insider*, http://www.businessinsider. com/kiera-wilmot-arrested-for-science-explosion-2013–5, date accessed May 2, 2013.

Williams, K. R. and J. P. Gibbs (1981) "Deterrence and Knowledge of Statutory Penalties", *The Sociological Quarterly*, 22 (4), 591–606.

11

For These People It Is Almost Too Late

German Citizenship Education, Islam and the Construction of Normativity and Deviance

Jessica A. Brown

Introduction

Following the post-Holocaust and post-colonial eras, models of nation-hood grounded in racial and ethnic exclusionism have declined in popularity, while a concurrent multiculturalist trend led many Western immigrant-receiving nations to assert (or at least pay lip service to) the desirability of fostering cultural, racial and religious diversity. Although multiculturalism has itself increasingly come under attack, nativists now find it difficult to argue that outsiders should be excluded merely because they are racially or culturally *different* (Koopmans et al., 2006; Goldberg, 2009). Instead, advocates of restrictive immigration policies will often isolate one group (quite often the largest, most visible or newest migrant group) and make assertions for why that group *in particular* is uniquely problematic. Such speakers will often simultaneously single out other migrant populations for praise as "model minorities", a tactic that both insulates the speaker from charges of xenophobia and provides "proof" that successful integration is possible for outsiders with the right values or attributes (Espiritu, 2007). Nativists thus increasingly class outsiders into two groups, those who are merely *different*, and thus acceptable, and those who are in some way *deviant*, and thus are not.

When charges of deviance are leveled at migrant groups, these often center around suspicions of crime (Melossi, 2000; Goode and Ben-Yehuda, 2009). However, as this chapter shows, forms of behavioral or ideological deviance thought to preclude cultural integration, or pose threats to social unity, are of concern as well. In Western immigrant-receiving nations Muslim migrants have increasingly been singled out as the "significant Other": the most salient and threatening outside group and the group against whom conceptions of both "deviant" and normative citizenship come to be defined (Triandafyllidou, 2001).[1] The focus of this chapter is to contribute to the literature on Muslim exclusion in Western immigrant-receiving states by examining the presence and use of deviant definitions of Muslim immigrants in Germany, and to explore how deviance theories can be used to understand nativist responses to immigration and vice versa. I examine the extent to which Muslim migrants are stigmatized, either as potential criminals or as carriers of deviant cultural values, within programs and state-interventions specifically aimed at integrating them into German society. Three constellations of behaviors and ideologies were used to label this population: violence, sexism and adherence to an insular and collectivist orientation, and these behaviors were also used to articulate distinctions between "good" or assimilable outsiders, and "bad", unassimilable ones. Finally, insofar as the primary utility of the deviant is often his or her ability to create a sense of solidarity among members of the in-group (Erikson, 1966), this chapter concludes, the role of deviance helps national groups forge a sense of collective identity in the face of demographic and cultural transition.

Muslims in Germany and Western Europe

Despite its status as a major post-war labor importer and its generous asylum policies, Germany clung to a notion of itself as a *Volksnation* long after other Western countries, like the United States, had abandoned

---

[1] One exception to this has tended to be the United States where Hispanics are still the primary target of anti-immigrant discourses. The deviance of Latino migrants is generally established by labeling them as criminals (due to actual or assumed illegal entry and work) or as "welfare cheats" suspected of abusing state services (Calavita, 1996). Migrants may also be framed as disloyal outsiders whose perceived failure to assimilate linguistically is held as evidence of divided cultural or national loyalties (Zolberg and Long, 1999). However, proposed legal changes aimed at extending citizenship to undocumented immigrants may help destigmatize Latinos, while persistent nativist Islamophobia, fueled by events like 9/11 and the Boston Marathon bombing, will likely continue to generate backlash against American Muslims. Given this, it is not improbable that this group could eventually come to replace Hispanics in the position of America's "significant Other".

their own ethnically restrictive naturalization laws (Brubaker, 1992). Beginning in the 1990s, Germany began to implement a series of legal changes which dramatically opened the possibilities of full citizenship to immigrants and their descendants; people still tellingly referred to as *Ausländer* (foreigners) even though many were second- or third-generation German-born (BMI, 2008). This change in the concept of "Germanness", from something carried in the blood to something that can be achieved through a process of naturalization, has required a significant renegotiation of national identity.

Although they hail from a diversity of national, ethnic and class backgrounds and follow a range of interpretations of Islam,[2] "Muslims" tend to be discursively lumped into a singular ethno-religious category and, as such, they are the largest and most problematized minority group in both Germany and in most of its Western European neighbor states (Fekete, 2006). Anti-Muslim nativism is evident among both German elites and the population at large. In 2010, banker and center-left politician Thilo Sarrazin published a bestselling book, *Deutschland Schafft Sich Ab* (Germany Does Away with Itself), arguing that Muslim migrants' high birth rates and adherence to fundamentalist ideologies would eventually cause the collapse of Germany's democratic government. That same year Bavaria's Governor Horst Seehofer stated that since immigrants from cultures such as "Turkey and the Arabic countries" found it too difficult to integrate, Germany did not "need any more immigrants from (these) cultures" (Focus Online, 2010). Other political and media elites have advocated for an exclusionary liberalism wherein the acceptance of Muslim migrants would be predicated on their demonstrated willingness to adopt a German *Leitkultur* (leading culture) grounded in values such as non-violence, gender egalitarianism and religious pluralism (Pautz, 2005).

These discourses both reflect and shape public opinion. Survey data indicate that Germans tend to hold more negative attitudes toward Muslims than do their European neighbors: whereas 62 percent of Dutch and 56 percent of French respondents reported having "positive feelings" toward Muslims, only about a third of Germans reported the same. Germans were also less likely to believe that Islam could "fit in

---

[2] About 63 percent of German Muslims are of full or partial Turkish descent. The second largest subgroup (13.6 percent) comes from Southeastern European nations such as Bosnia, Bulgaria and Albania. All together the German Muslim community consists of about 4 million individuals from 40 different countries (Haug et al., 2009).

well" with Western culture and were more likely to support restrictions on Muslim or minority group religious practice. To the question "what comes to mind when you hear the word 'Islam'?", the most common answers listed by German respondents were "the oppression of women", "fanaticism", "willingness to engage in violence" and "social insularity" (Pollack et al., 2010).

Germany has adopted a range of policies aimed at screening for, or reforming, such forms of deviance among members of its immigrant population. To combat fears of radicalization in German mosques, it has instituted programs aimed at training "pro-integration" Imams at public universities and seminaries (Brandt and Popp, 2010). As in other European nations like France and Belgium, Germany has also passed laws restricting Muslim women's ability to cover: half of German states (*Länder*) now forbid female civil servants or public school teachers from wearing the headscarf (*Kopftuch*), arguing it prevents them from "representing" German values like gender equality (Rottman and Ferree, 2008). A federal law, passed in 2005, instituted a series of nation-wide mandatory 30-hour "orientation courses" to teach foreign residents and prospective citizens about German laws, culture and social norms.[3] The government has also set aside additional funding for the creation of voluntary, local-level "integration projects", like computer or sport classes for migrant youth, aimed at combating poverty and social insularity (BAMF, 2005). In 2006, the German state of Baden-Württemberg began instituting an interview schedule specifically for Muslim naturalization applicants with questions meant to ascertain their views on things like democratic governance, gender equality and religious or political violence (Die Zeit, 2006). Federally standardized citizenship and orientation course tests, instituted in 2008 and 2009, respectively, likewise require test takers to demonstrate knowledge of laws forbidding practices most commonly ascribed to German Muslims: including forced marriage, polygamy, honor crimes and the use of threats or violence to solve disputes (BAMF, 2011).

---

[3] After the end of this research, orientation courses were increased in length to 60 hours. Any foreign resident wishing to reside in Germany is required to take an Integration course sequence (which consists of at least 600 hours of language instruction followed by the orientation course itself) either as a prerequisite for a permanent residency permit or as a condition of receiving state benefits. Foreign residents who have attended school or university in Germany are exempted from mandatory course attendance as they are perceived to have attended a "comparable education program". Those wishing to naturalize can do so after a shorter waiting period (seven years instead of eight) upon successful course completion (BAMF, 2012).

Methodology

This chapter uses both original and existing research to examine deviance framing in these kinds of citizenship training programs and integration initiatives. The data come from several sources. The predominant one is original ethnographic and interview research conducted in the German city of Frankfurt am Main and its suburbs in 2006–2007. Ethnographic data comes from participant observation as a "student" in five different 30-hour orientation classes (total classroom time = 150 hours) offered by different course purveyors in the Frankfurt area.[4] Classes consisted of 15–25 adult students from a diversity of national, ethnic and religious backgrounds, both genders and ages ranging from young adults to retirees. Commensurate with the overall population demographics, Turks, Middle Easterners or students from other majority Muslim sending nations (such as Bosnia-Herzegovina) usually made up between one-third to one-half of each class, with other students coming from a range of majority non-Muslim nations throughout Africa, Asia, Latin America and the former Soviet Bloc countries.

In addition to participant observation, I conducted semi-structured interviews with teachers (n = 15), integration project developers and administrators (n = 30) and local policy makers (n = 6) engaged in various aspects of the integration project (total n = 51). Interview subjects were selected by contacting area language schools and integration projects, and by asking all interviewees to suggest other potential contacts.[5] All subjects have been given pseudonyms that reflect their preferred form of address (either first name or the more traditional and formal "Herr" or "Frau" and surname).

Data are also drawn from a basic content analysis of naturalization tests: including the standardized orientation course and naturalization tests

---

[4] Originally, I approached all of the seven orientation course purveyors currently operating in the city for permission to sit in on a course; only one outright refused my request (for unspecified reasons), another had no courses that fit my schedule.

[5] I was able to meet my goal of interviewing at least one teacher from each of the area schools offering courses, and interview subjects themselves represented a mix of ages, both genders, and included people from both immigrant and non-immigrant backgrounds. However, because of the voluntary nature of participation and the limited geographical area from which subjects were recruited, I cannot claim to represent the opinions of integration course teachers or project workers as a population.

administered at the federal level to all migrants, and one state-level test that was briefly administered *exclusively* to Muslim migrants by Baden-Württemberg (the state discontinued this so-called *Muslimtest* several weeks after initiating it due negative publicity [Jähn, 2006]). Content analysis was also performed on each of the three textbooks approved by the BAMF (Federal Agency for Immigration and Refugees) for use in orientation classes during the time of data collection. These include *30 Stunden Deutschland* (Germany in 30 Hours; Klett, 2005), *Orientierungskurs: Geschichte, Institutionen, Leben in Deutschland* (Orientation Course: History, Institutions, and Life in Germany; Langenscheidt, 2005) and *Zur Orientierung: Deutschland in 30 Stunden* (For Orientation: Germany in 30 Hours; Hueber, 2006).

Respondents' views of Muslim migrants

All interview respondents were questioned as to whether, in their experience working with migrants as teachers, integration project developers or policymakers "there were particular groups of immigrants who, due to factors like age, gender, educational, religious, or cultural background, found it more difficult to integrate than others". A follow-up question asked was: "Some people in politics or the media say Muslim immigrants have a harder time integrating, do you think this is true?" All respondents agreed that there was a tendency in German politics and media to present Muslim migrants as more problematic or difficult to integrate than non-Muslim migrants. About 50 percent (25 respondents) believed this characterization of Muslims was unfair or inaccurate, while a substantial minority of 40 percent (20) agreed with it to some extent (the remaining 10 percent didn't answer or didn't know). About half of this second group qualified these statements by asserting that problems were generally caused only by a subset of migrants: those who were *Islamist* (Islamic fundamentalist) or who had come from rural or impoverished communities where levels of education were lower.[6] However, about 25 percent of the total sample argued that there was something unique to the "Islamic religion" or "culture" as a whole that prevented many or all Muslim migrants from being successfully incorporated into a Western democracy.

---

[6] This distinction would include the majority of the original "guest workers" since these were mostly low or semi-skilled laborers, often from rural villages, who were recruited to fill post-war jobs in industry, agriculture and the construction trades.

Negative attitudes toward Muslims among members of this sample were much less visible than those observed among the general population by Pollack and his colleagues (2010). This is not a surprising finding, given that all respondents in this sample shared characteristics that have been observed to correlate with lower levels of anti-immigrant hostility: all were university educated, urban and had significant contact with immigrants due to their professions (EUMC, 2005). However, as this sample draws from one specific population – individuals who work directly with migrants, located in one particular German city – the goal is not to argue that these opinions are representative of overall German attitudes toward Muslims, or even the attitudes of integration services people as a whole. Instead, the intent is to explore how individuals who view Muslims as particularly problematic justify these attitudes through framings of deviance. The analysis of course materials and tests also explores the extent to which similar frames are reflected in official texts.

When Muslim migrants were framed as deviant, this tended to be justified through arguments that, compared to Germans or other migrants, they were more violent, sexist and socially insular (prone to self-segregation) or collectivist (prone to privilege the interests of their religious or ethnic group over those of the German state or community as a whole). These frames were most apparent in private interviews, although each was sometimes echoed in orientation course classroom interactions and in standardized or official materials.

Violence

One of the primary ways that Muslims are deviantized is through associations with violent crime – a frame that, in these discourses, included both terrorism and gender-based violence. The aforementioned Baden-Württemberg naturalization interview, nicknamed the "*Muslimtest*" by German press, featured 30 questions, half of which probed test takers on their attitudes toward political, religious or domestic violence. Applicants were questioned on whether they believed "a man should be allowed to lock his wife or daughter in the house to keep her from bringing shame to the family," if they thought it was acceptable for husbands "to beat disobedient wives" and how they personally viewed men who murdered sexually transgressive female relatives in the name of "restoring family honor". Test administrators were also instructed to ask applicants whether they thought the 9/11 hijackers were "terrorists or freedom fighters" and what they would do if they discovered a friend was "planning a terrorist attack". As a follow-up to questions on terrorism, administrators were told to remind test takers of a statement issued by the Central Council of German Muslims (*Zentralrat der Muslime in Deutschland*) which proclaimed that cooperation with police in such matters was an "Islamic religious obligation and not an act of betrayal" (Die Zeit, 2006).

While the "*Muslimtest*" was eventually abandoned in the face of public backlash, including an unsuccessful attempt by Green and Left (*Linkspartei*) politicians to pass a federal measure barring Baden Württemberg from continuing to use it (Jähn, 2006), the labeling of Muslims as potentially violent did remain evident in some classroom interactions and course materials. Non-violence as a value was stressed in all course textbooks and usually presented as a neutral good: something "all people" or "all societies" should work toward. However, some classroom interactions explicitly framed Muslim migrants as deficient in this respect. The most striking example of this came during a unit on religious diversity in one of the orientation courses I observed. The instructor, whom I call Eliza, asked a student to read textbook *30 Stunden Deutschland*'s inclusively worded statement on the subject aloud: "Wars have been, and continue to be, fought and crimes committed in the name of various religions. Most believers characterize this behavior as an example of the misuse of faith. However, critics of religion argue that there is a tendency toward fanaticism and cruelty present in all religions" (Langenscheidt, 2005, p. 24.). When the student had finished, however, Eliza provided her own more pointed opinion:

Eliza: "Unfortunately in history we see many wars in the name of God. War can never be holy, murder can never be holy, but unfortunately it is the case that in Islam there is this tendency. This tendency is primarily in Islam."

Petya (an Orthodox Christian student from Bulgaria, attempting to defend her Muslim classmates): "But such people misread the Koran!"

Eliza: "Hitler also said the Jews were bad. He took that from the Old Testament. He misinterpreted the Bible and with that justification he did these things. That is sick! It is always sick! Here we have Christians and Muslims together. Must we fight each other? Do we have to make war against each other?"

Students: "Nein!" (*A few laugh and playfully pantomime stabbing or choking a non-coreligionist neighbor.*)

Eliza: "No religious person should kill. Killing is always wrong."

Salime (Turkey): "The Koran says there should always be respect for other people, that we should understand others."

Eliza (interrupting): "But everyone interprets it differently! Everyone takes something different away from it ... People want to do good things, but when they misunderstand religion they end up doing bad things instead. And everyone interprets religion differently!"

While the textbook did not specifically target Islam in its discussion of the dangers of violent religiosity, Eliza nonetheless used the exercise to communicate her own view that Islam, and its followers, were more prone to violence. This drew protests from both Christians and Muslims in her class, but these didn't sway Eliza's negative opinion – nor did her allusions to Germany's *own* problematic history of violent religious intolerance or her assertion that Hitler's violent anti-Semitism was inspired by *Christian* scripture.

Next to the "terrorist" was the threatening outsider, the "domestic abuser" or the "honor criminal". Much media and political attention has been paid to incidences of so-called honor crimes in European migrant communities: wherein women who violate community sexual norms are beaten or killed in order to restore their families' social standing. While inextricably linked with Islam in the European imagination, concepts like "honor" and "provocation" are common justifications for violent crimes against women across religious groups and throughout the world (Welchman and Hossain, 2006). Moreover, as Katherine Ewing (2008) notes, the perception that this practice is endemic among Muslims is encouraged by the tendency, among both press and law enforcement, to label *any* domestic abuse in these communities as "honor violence" – thus selectively ascribing cultural motivations to crimes that, when committed by members of the native-born majority or other immigrant groups, are framed as evidence of personal, not cultural deviance.

Nevertheless, "honor violence" and "forced marriage", a corollary practice wherein parents compel children (usually daughters) to marry against their will, were a focus in some materials and classes. Two of the three course textbooks included specific information reminding readers that, in Germany, individuals had the right to choose their own spouses and that families could not use violence or threats of violence to change those decisions. For example, *Orientierungskurs* featured a section called "Questions for the Germans" in which fictional migrants asked, and got answers to, questions about life in their new country. Among them:

Question: "My daughter refuses to marry the man that I have chosen for her and is meeting secretly with another. Someone must do something to restore our family's honor. Why should I be punished for this?"

Answer: *In Germany we do not recognize the principle of "family honor". We value life and individual rights.* (Langenscheidt, 2005, p. 49)

In textbook passages like this one, deviance is marked by implicit comparisons between European societies, which "value life and individual rights" and Islamic societies, which, the reader is left to assume, do not. Given that these are presented in a format that implies that they are frequently asked questions from typical migrants, readers may also assume that practices like honor violence are far more common in Muslim communities than they actually are.

Instructors also reminded students that forced marriage and honor violence were not acceptable in Europe in three of the five classes observed. Often this was done in such a way as to make clear invidious comparisons between "Western" and Muslim societies. For example, in her class, instructor Jutta urged students to read a memoir, *We Are Your Daughters, Not Your Honor* (Wir sind eure Töchter, nicht eure Ehre), by a Turkish-German woman who had fled her abusive natal family after being forced into marriage and threatened with violence if she refused :

Jutta: "In some cultures, there is this idea of honor (*Ehre*) and men feel their honor is located in the sexual purity of women in their families. This is also a double standard, because men can do what they like and they get to make decisions for women instead of women getting to make them for themselves. Have any of you read the book *We are Your Daughters, Not Your Honor?* I recommend you all read it. Here in Europe, women go [out] alone, and sometimes unpleasant things happen to them, but they have choice and freedom". (Cileli, 2006)

Jutta's problematization of Muslim culture was less overt than Eliza's repeated assertions that violence is "primarily a problem in Islam". However, Jutta's framing of sexual double standards as if these were exclusively non-European phenomena, her recommendation that students read a memoir about a Turkish-German woman's escape from arranged marriage, and her comparisons between cultures "where men feel their honor is located in the sexual purity of women" and Europe "where women have choice and freedom" implicitly single out migrants and, particularly Muslim migrants, as carriers of deviant, anti-Western values and practices.

Sexism

Fears of honor violence in Muslim communities are closely related to generalized fears of Muslims as problematically sexist in more global terms. Almost all respondents who agreed that Muslims were particularly poorly suited for life in Germany referenced gender practice in their explanations. For these participants, while the differences that separated Germans and other migrant groups could be overcome, the gendered norms and practices unique to the Muslim culture or religion slowed or precluded their successful integration. As instructor Herr Kremer argued:

> We can't transform these people into democratic citizens. There is no hope. People who have been here 20 years, and I have met such people, when they are Muslims it is very hard to make them accept a constitutional democracy. This is because Islam brings along with it its own judicial and legal system ... A while ago I had some women from Turkey in my class and to them women's rights were not important. I tried to explain to them that in Germany our constitutional values are as important as religion, but for these people it is almost too late. (Interview, June 25, 2007)

For this respondent, while other migrant groups did not arrive in Germany holding loyalties to another "judicial and legal system", Muslims did, and it was this belief that kept them from understanding or accepting "women's rights" and other constitutionally enshrined values. Drawing on a similar perception of Muslims as sexist, another respondent explained:

> People out of the Middle Eastern countries have a limited conception of what democracy is. They think democracy means "I can do whatever I want". They don't understand the concept of duties and responsibilities. Muslims come here and say "ah, I don't have to send my daughter to school", but that's wrong. (Interview, March 5, 2007)

In addition to being a recurrent theme among respondents, policy interventions and orientation course materials focused on addressing deviant gender practices. Sexism was a major focus of Baden-Württemberg's *Muslimtest* (Die Zeit, 2006) and the standardized citizenship and orientation course exams adopted shortly afterward also contain questions testing applicants' understanding of the illegality of forced marriage, honor violence, polygamy and discrimination on the basis of sex (BAMF, 2011). Lessons on gender equality were also well integrated into orientation course materials. As with non-violence, most official course materials emphasized this topic in such a way as to avoid stigmatizing any one group (the question on forced marriage and honor violence quoted from *Orientierungskurs* earlier is an exception). However, the focus on this topic did communicate the assumption that gender equality would be a "new idea" for class participants. For example, in one book students were asked to look at pictures of German women engaging in various kinds of paid work and discuss how things were different in their own home countries (Klett, 2005, pp. 46–48). In fact, in both of the classes that opted to use this exercise, all students said that women-working-for-pay was a "common" and "normal" practice in their own native countries as well. Other lessons asked students to indicate agreement or disagreement with statements like: "My daughter does not need school. She will marry later and have children, and she doesn't need school for that" (p. 25); "The role of the man is to speak for his family in public" (Langenscheidt, 2005, p. 17); or "Women must not hold the same kinds of jobs as men" (Hueber, 2006, p. 5). Instructors emphasized these lessons by explaining that there were correct and incorrect answers to each of these questions.

Even when the textbooks did not single out Muslims as *the* problematic group, teachers' own opinions on the subject sometimes bled into classroom interactions. In both her class and in our interview, Jutta repeatedly bemoaned the fact that "certain cultures" still placed a lower value on women. During the interview, she was open and candid about her feeling that it was really "Muslim culture" where this was an issue (March 2, 2007). Lessons in her class, which featured a diverse group of students from China, Eastern Europe, Latin America and the Middle East (as well as one US observer), still targeted this same group but usually more obliquely. The aforementioned lecture in which Jutta contrasted cultures where men "control the sexual purity of women" with those where "women have choice and freedom" was one example. Another came during an anecdote that she told in class (and repeated during our interview) about a former student who, despite having seven daughters, continued to have children in the hopes of having a boy. "Muslim men have to have their son," she told students while shaking her head sadly. Although Jutta's association of Islam with misogyny was not unusual, one could have drawn similar examples of the devaluation of girls and women from every nation represented in her diverse classroom: from

China's "lost generation" of abandoned girls to the persistent pay and job discrimination that still constrains women throughout Europe and North America. That *these* examples of sexism were not used to label entire populations of people from those countries in the same way is reflective of the subjective assignation of deviance to one particularly problematized group.

One of the most contentious sites of struggle around immigration and gender practice in Western Europe is the tradition, observed by some Muslim women, of covering their hair or (more rarely) all or part of their faces and bodies. While the French government's decision to enforce state secularism by forbidding Muslim girls from wearing headscarves in school received significant international attention, Germany has also passed headscarf bans—albeit at the state level and in a more piecemeal fashion (Rottman and Ferree, 2008; Joppke, 2009). Despite its focal role in integration debates, two-thirds of self-identified Muslim women in my classes did not wear a headscarf (*Kopftuch*). This figure seems to reflect general practice: about 70 percent of German Muslim women report that they "never wear a headscarf" (Haug et al., 2009). Research on German Muslims who do cover indicates that reasons for doing so vary widely by individual, but none said that it was meant either as a statement of female subordination or a refusal to integrate (ibid.; see also Read and Bartkowski, 2000).

Nevertheless, respondents who expressed discomfort with the practice generally assumed that the scarf was evidence of "anti-Western" values. During her interview, language school supervisor Frau Heller spoke with dismay about one of her instructors: a Muslim woman who persisted in covering her hair even after she (Heller) had told her it set a "bad example" of both sexist practice and "non-integration" for female students (Interview, July 5, 2007). Frau Heller then suggested that *I* interview the instructor and encouraged *me* to try to convince her to "take the scarf off". The instructor declined to be interviewed. Instructor Frau Köhler opined that the headscarf was both a sign of "hostility" toward German values and a means of abusing the generosity of the welfare state. "I think it's a tactic", she said. "I think there's a real hostility behind it. Also some of them do it so they won't be able to get a job. They think 'if I stay jobless, I will be able to keep collecting unemployment'" (Interview, April 17, 2007). A third subject, Frau Ebke, spoke of her frustration with women who chose to veil not only their hair, but also all or part of their faces, explaining that this practice was itself antithetical to democracy. "We must be engaged with and in conversation with each other. That's how democracy works," she explained. "You cannot work and talk with someone and trust them when you cannot see their face" (Interview, May 14, 2007).

For these respondents, veiling or covering was a signal for a range of deviant attitudes and behaviors. Both Frau Heller and Frau Köhler felt that the practice functioned as a kind of oppositional political stance: a communication of the wearer's rejection of gender equality and general noncompliance with the goals of the integration project. This same interpretation of covering has been used to justify headscarf or veil restrictions in most countries that have enacted or considered them (Joppke, 2009). Frau Ebke's argument, that veiling precluded the "trust" and "communication" necessary for civic participation, takes this common argument one step further by positing that the veiled woman is not merely hostile to democracy, she is fully incapable of practicing it. This same viewpoint would be partially echoed by French president Nicolas Sarkozy in 2010, when he defended a move to ban facial veiling in public areas arguing that "citizenship has to be lived with an uncovered face" (Davies, 2010).

Finally, for Frau Köhler, covering also signaled the wearer's rejection of yet another Western norm: that of individual self-sufficiency. Frau Köhler's concern that covered women made strategic use of discrimination and headscarf bans to abuse unemployment assistance was significant in that, while deviance frames in nativist discourses, both in European Union nations and in the United States, often mobilize the image of the "immigrant welfare cheat" (Yoo, 2008; Eurostat, 2011), Frau Köhler was the only person in this particular sample to even mention the issue. These findings are in line with others which show that, while "social benefit abuse" is cited as a top concern when Germans are asked about immigration more broadly (Boeri, 2009; European Commission, 2011), questions about Muslim migration are more likely to elicit concerns about violence, women's rights, religious fanaticism or self-segregation (Pollack et al., 2010).

Insularity and collectivism

Although not as common as complaints about violence and sexism, a final framing of deviance came in the form of concerns that Muslim migrants had on the inappropriate orientation toward the German national community or government as a whole. For these respondents, Muslim migrants were either too "insular" (prone to self-segregation, and reluctant to engage, either socially or culturally, with mainstream German society) or, alternately, too "collectivist" (problematically oriented toward, or over-concerned with, the welfare and interests of their own subgroup). "Insularity" is among concerns commonly cited by survey respondents (Pollack et al., 2010; European Commission, 2011). A great deal of German press and political attention has also been paid to the tendency of immigrants to self-segregate, or be segregated, into "parallel societies" (*Parallelgesellschaften*). Whether this separation is presented as a voluntary choice on the part of migrants, a forced response to exclusion and discrimination, or a combination of the two, however, depends on the point of view of the speaker (see Koopmans et al., 2005).

These critiques of Muslim migrants have well-documented historical parallels. Accusations of "clannishness" and "insularity" were commonly leveled against Jews in Europe and the United States both before and after World War II (Levinson and Sanford, 1944; Chebel d'Appollonia, 2012). Germany's post-war "Guest workers" from Turkey and Southern and Eastern Europe were initially discouraged from assimilating, in the hope that this would assure they would eventually leave, and later accused of being "reclusive" and "refusing to integrate" when it became clear that many intended to stay (Koopmans et al., 2006). American ethnic and religious minorities ranging from the earliest German colonists to today's Latino migrants have all faced the same dilemma of finding themselves alternately shut out of the mainstream and then criticized for a perceived disinterest in joining (Portes and Rumbaut, 2006). Closely related to charges of insularity is the fear that foreigners represent a kind of "fifth column" by clinging to sending nation, ethnic or religious group loyalties that preclude them from developing a true allegiance to the host nation and its values (Chebel d'Appollonia, 2012).

The issue of reclusivity and refusal to integrate came up frequently in interviews. For instance, language teacher Grete brought up the topic of *Parallelgesellschaften* in her interview, arguing that the segregation of migrants was largely self-imposed:

> *Grete*: "Most foreigners here are Turkish and they can be very withdrawn, very isolated. I've often noticed that some of the Turkish women who show up for our course, this is the first time they've ever been out of their house (*laughs to indicate some comical exaggeration*) even though they've lived here for 10 years!"
>
> *Me*: "Is this primarily a problem among the Turks?"
>
> *Grete*: "Primarily. It's probably a problem with a lot of them, but primarily with the Turks. That's what I've seen. It's not so much a problem with other Europeans, because of the culture. With the

Turks, it's Islam and there's this fear: 'we'll lose our children! We'll lose our religion!' It's brainwashing. And so there is this drive to stay isolated. It's probably not just the Turks, you'd find it among others, like the Pakistanis, but yes, I am certain these parallel societies exist." (Interview, December 9, 2006))

For Grete, "parallel societies" existed because of Islam and a kind of protectionist "brainwashing". "Turks" and "others" refused to engage German culture because their beliefs were threatened by contact with the outside world. Other subjects shared this concern and all instructors routinely urged students to work on making friends with Germans rather than just "spending all their time with people from their own countries". Two instructors, Jutta and a woman I call Frau Boklova, lectured students on being open to marrying, or allowing their children to marry, outside their ethnic and religious groups as well. Building relationships with native-born citizens is a useful way of both developing language skills and ameliorating isolation, but such interactions also indicated that instructors were trying to urge immigrants to resist, in Grete's words, the "drive to stay isolated".

A corollary to the assumption that migrants chose segregation was the belief that Muslims demonstrated a problematically Eastern "collectivist" orientation, rather than an acceptably Western "individualist" one. The view that the cultures of North America and Western Europe are more "individualist" in approach has some support in scholarship. However, within nativist discourses, "outsiders" are commonly collapsed into a single, de-individualized "collective", sharing one monolithic ideology and set of objectives. This view of Other as having a kind of "hive-mind" operates in stark contrast to the insider's perception of his or her own social group, which is understood to be populated by diverse individuals with different beliefs, loyalties and interests.

As Ulrich, an older man who was a party official for a local branch of the CDU (Christian Democratic Union: Germany's largest center-right party) explained, it was exactly this kind of "collectivism" that made Muslims either unwilling or unable to integrate in Germany. "The real issue is between Christianity and Islam", he stated candidly. "Islam is a very different mindset from that of Christianity. With the French, the Portuguese, the Americans, it's not a problem, we all have the same mentality."

Me: "What about the Jews in Germany?"
Ulrich: "No, they're the same as us, no problem."

Me: "But they aren't Christian."
Ulrich: "Yes, but the *mentality* is the same." (Interview, October 11, 2006)

Confused, I asked Ulrich about other non-Christian migrant groups, such as Chinese Buddhists or Indian Hindus. Ulrich was increasingly frustrated by my inability to grasp what was, for him, an obvious distinction and he stressed that these people were also "no problem", because, while they were different from Germans, their basic values and "mentalities" were still congruent. Finally, Ulrich elucidated what he believed it was that set Muslims and non-Muslims apart:

> The difference in the German mentality versus the Islamic mentality is the value placed on individualism. Here everyone just looks out for themselves: the emphasis is on the individual. In the Islamic system, the emphasis is on the collective. One acts for the benefit of the collective and also for the benefit of the religion. Everything else is secondary to them. (Interview, October 11, 2006)

Like many other speakers, Ulrich drew a distinction between groups who were merely different, like Americans, Jews and the Chinese, and those whose oppositional mentality crossed the line into deviance. For him, the problem was that Muslims did not function as "individuals" in pursuit of separate and self-interested goals in the same way "non-Muslims" did, but rather subsumed everything to the "benefit of the collective" and the "benefit of the religion".

Of course, this idea of the foreigner as collectivist or "hive-minded" is really threatening only when coupled with the assumption that their interests are antithetical to those of the native-born. The fear that Muslims placed their religious loyalties over loyalties to the host country and its civic values came across in Ulrich's comment, "everything else is secondary to them" and also in statements by other subjects. Herr Kremer, for example, expressed this view when asserting that Muslims could not be taught to "accept a constitutional democracy" both because Islam provided a competing "judicial and legal system" and because such people could never understand a government that placed "constitutional values" on par with religious ones (Interview June 25, 2007). The question from the Baden-Württemberg *Muslimtest* which probed applicants on whether they would go to the police if they discovered a friend or acquaintance was "planning a terrorist attack" (and then sought to reassure them that it was not a "betrayal" of their religion if they did so) provides another example of this same fear of divided loyalty. Within this particular faming of deviance, it is implicitly understand that, while Westerners could hold multiple value sets simultaneously (as Christians and German citizens both, for example), Islam functioned as a "total identity" that precluded this kind of ideological complexity.

Conclusion

No respondent in this study argued that continued immigration was unnecessary or even undesirable for Germany, which is not surprising given the characteristics of people in the sample. However, 40 percent agreed that Germany's largest demographic group of immigrants faced more problems with integration than did other migrants, and a quarter of respondents ascribed this to deviant traits they believed were inherent to the group's culture or belief system as a whole. Similar framings of Muslim deviance, some implicit and some quite explicit, were also present in standardized integration materials.

The continued stereotyping of Muslim minorities as violent, sexist, reclusive or disloyal represents a threat to successful integration, especially when it occurs within the context of social projects meant to orient migrants to their new communities and prepare them for eventual citizenship. Applying such labels risks fueling feelings of alienation and persecution among members of the out-group, encourages the development of oppositional identities among minority group members and aggravates the existing social distance between newcomers and the native-born (Becker, 1963; Portes and Rumbaut, 2006). This social distance, in turn, perpetuates the "parallel communities" that come to serve as "proof" of the problematic ideologies of Muslim migrants.

However, as scholars have noted, assignations of deviance routinely work at cross-purposes to their purported goal of reducing negative behaviors (Becker, 1963). Instead, one of the primary utilities of deviance is the role it plays in the formation and maintenance of the in-group itself: allowing members to develop "a tighter bond of solidarity than existed earlier" (Erikson, 1966, p. 4) both by defining the boundaries of normative membership and by giving insiders the pleasurable opportunity to "wax indignant in common" (Durkheim, 1960, p. 102). By ascribing negative traits to outsiders (such as violence, sexism, authoritarian fundamentalism and social insularity), members simultaneously lay claim to the inverse of these traits (tolerance, egalitarianism, democratic rationality and civic engagement) as features of group identity. Drawing distinctions between immigrants who are "acceptably different" and those who are "unacceptably deviant" helps reinforce the idea that exclusion is not driven by xenophobia but is rather a result of the host nation's understandable desire to protect itself from crime, violence and social balkanization. This ability to use the out-group as a tool to re-draw boundaries, justify discrimination and maintain a positive sense of self in the face of demographic upheaval suggests that deviantization is not an occasional and unfortunate by-product of the citizen-making process, but rather a central component of it. If so, this would predict that deviance labeling will become especially important to, and frequent in, societies undergoing any crisis of self-definition. Since immigration is the most common precipitant of such a crisis in modern states, this also indicates that theories of deviance should be accorded a more central role in helping social scientists understand host societies' responses to immigration.

References

30 Stunden Deutschland (2005) *Materialen Für Den Orientierungskurs* (Stuttgart: Ernst Klett Sprachen).

BAMF (2005) "Wege Zur Einbürgerung: Wie Werde Ich Deutsche-wie Werde Ich Deutscher?", *Ministry for Immigration and Asylum* (Nürnberg).

—— (2011) "Einbürgerungstest/Orientierungskurstest", *BAMF Online-Testcenter*, http://www.bamf.de/DE/Einbuergerung/OnlineTestcenter/online-testcenter-node.html, date accessed January 18, 2011.

—— (2012) "Integrationskurs-Was Ist Das?", Nürnberg: Federal Agency for Immigration and Refugees, http://www.bamf.de/DE/Willkommen/DeutschLernen/Integrationskurse/integrationskurse-node.html.

Becker, H. (1963) *Outsiders: Studies in the Sociology of Deviance* (New York: Free Press).

BMI (2008) "Migration and Integration: Residence Law and Policy on Migration and Integration in Germany", *Federal Ministry of the Interior* (Berlin).

Boeri, T. (2009) "Immigration to the Land of Redistribution", May 5. LSE "Europe in Question" Discussion Paper Series. The London School of Economics and Political Science, http://www2.lse.ac.uk/europeanInstitute/LEQS/LEQSPaper5Boeri5.pdf.

Brandt, A. and M. Popp (2010) "Imams Made in Germany: Will Efforts to Train Homegrown Muslim Leaders Fail?", *Der Spiegel Online*, http://www.spiegel.de/international/germany/imams-made-in-germany-will-efforts-to-train-homegrown-muslim-leaders-fail-a-717512-3.html., date accessed September 16, 2010.

Brubaker, R. (1992) *Citizenship and Nationhood in France and Germany* (Cambridge, MA: Harvard University Press).

Calavita, K. (1996) "The New Politics of Immigration: Balanced Budget Conservatism and the Symbolism of Proposition 187", *Social Problems*, 43 (3), 284–305.

Chebel d'Appollonia, A. (2012) *Frontiers of Fear: Immigration and Insecurity in the United States and Europe* (Ithaca and London: Cornell University Press).

Cileli, S. (2006) *Wir Sind Eure Töchter, Nicht Eure Ehre* (Munich: Blanvalet Verlag).

Davies, L. (2010) "Nicolas Sarkozy's Cabinet Approves Bill to Ban Full Islamic Veil", *The Guardian*, sec. World News, http://www.guardian.co.uk/world/2010/may/19/nicolas-sarkozy-defends-veil-ban., date accessed May 19, 2010.

Deutschland in 30 Stunden (2006) *Zur Orientierung*, 2nd edn. (Ismaning: Max Hueber Verlag).

Die Zeit (2006) "Integration: 30 Fragen Für Den Pass", *Zeit Online*, sec. Politik: Deutschland, http://www.zeit.de/online/2006/02/gesinnungstest/seite-1., date accessed January 11, 2006.

Durkheim, E. (1960) *The Division of Labor in Society*, G. Simpson (trans.) (Glencoe, IL: Free Press).

Erikson, Kai T. (1966) *Wayward Puritans: A Study in the Sociology of Deviance* (New York and Sydney: John Wiley & Sons).

Espiritu, Y. L. (2007) *Asian American Women and Men: Labor, Laws and Love*. 2nd edn. (Lanham: Rowman & Littlefield).

EUMC (2005) "Majorities' Attitudes toward Minorities: Key Findings from the Eurobarometer and the European Social Survey", *European Monitoring Centre on Racism and Xenophobia*, http://fra.europa.eu/sites/default/files/fra_uploads/146-EB2005-summary.pdf.

European Commission (2011) "Qualitative Eurobarameter: Migrant Integration", *European Commission*, http://ec.europa.eu/public_opinion/archives/quali/ql_5969_migrant_En.pdf.

Eurostat (2011) "Migrants in Europe: A Statistical Portrait of the First and Second Generation", *European Commission* (Luxemburg).

Ewing, K. P. (2008) *Stolen Honor: Stigmatizing Muslim Men in Berlin* (Stanford CA: Stanford University Press).

Fekete, L. (2006) "Enlightened Fundamentalism? Immigration, Feminism and the Right", *Race & Class*, 48 (2), 1–22.

Focus Online (2010) "Horst Seehofer: Kampfansage an Schmarotzer und Zuwanderer", *Focus*, October 9, 2010.

Goldberg, D. T. (2009) *The Threat of Race: Reflections on Racial Neoliberalism* (Malden, MA: Wiley-Blackwell).

Goode, E. and N. Ben-Yehuda (2009) *Moral Panics: The Social Construction of Deviance*, 2nd edn. (Malden, MA: Blackwell).

Haug, S., S. Müssig and A. Stichs (2009) "Muslimisches Leben in Deutschland", BAMF (Federal Agency for Immigration and Refugees), www.bamf.de/SharedDocs/Anlagen/DE/Downloads/Infothek/Sonstige/muslimisches-leben-kurzfassung-deutsch.html?nn=1366152.

Jähn, C. (2006) "Kein Muslimtest Mehr", *Zeit Online*, sec. Integration. http://www.zeit.de/online/2006/04/bundestag_fragebogen, date accessed January 19, 2006.

Joppke, C. (2009) *Veil: Mirror of Identity* (Cambridge: Polity Press).

Koopmans, R., P. Statham, M. Giugni and F. Passy (2006) *Contested Citizenship: Immigration and Cultural Diversity in Europe* (Minneapolis: University of Minneasota Press).

Levinson, D. J. and R. N. Sanford (1944) "A Scale for the Measurement of Anti-semitism", *The Journal of Psychology: Interdisciplinary and Applied*, 17 (2), 339–370.

Melossi, D. (2000) "The Other in New Europe: Migrations, Deviance, and Social Control", in *Criminal Policy in Transition* (Oxford and Portland: Hart).

Pautz, H. (2005) "The Politics of Identity in Germany: The Leitkultur Debate", *Race & Class*, 46 (4), 39–52.

Pollack, D., N. Friedrichs, O. Müller, G. Rosta and A. Yendell (2010) "Wahrnehmung Und Akzeptanz Religiöser Vielfalt: Eine Bevölkerungsumfrage in Fünf Europäischen Länder", *Westfälische Wilhelms-Universität Münster,* http:// www.uni-muenster.de/Religion-und-Politik/aktuelles/2010/dez/PM_Studie_ Religioese_Vielfalt_in_Europa.html.

Portes, A, and R. Rumbaut (2006) *Immigrant America: A Portrait,* 3rd edn. (Berkeley and Los Angeles: University of California Press).

Read, J. G. and J. P. Bartkowski (2000) "To Veil or Not to Veil? A Case Study of Identity Negotiation among Muslim Women in Austin, Texas", *Gender & Society,* 14 (3), 395–417.

Rottman, S. B. and M. Marx Ferree (2008) "Citizenship and Intersectionality: German Feminist Debates about Headscarf and Anti-discrimination Laws", *Social Politics,* 15 (4), 481–513.

Triandafyllidou, A. (2001) *Immigrants and National Identity in Europe* (London: Routledge).

Welchman, L. and S. Hossain (2006) *Honour: Crimes, Paradigms and Violence against Women* (London: Zed Books).

Yoo, G. (2008) "Immigrants and Welfare: Policy Constructions of Deservingness", *Journal of Immigrant & Refugee Studies,* 6 (4), 490–507.

Zolberg, A. and L. W. Long (1999) "Why Islam Is Like Spanish: Cultural Incorporation in the United States and Europe", *Politics & Society,* 27 (1), 5–38.

12

The Mass Killer's Search for Validation through Infamy, Media Attention and Transcendence

Jennifer Lynn Murray

Introduction

This chapter examines the mass killer's fractured self-concept. The emergence of a mass killer involves the interplay of psychological and sociological factors. By examining the personal histories of many multiple murderers, a common theme of severe psychological and social developmental interruption emerges. Derailed identity-formation and psychosocial development is a characteristic shared by all of the killers in this study. I contend that certain pre-dispositional factors result in the killer having a pathologically fragmented identity, which is the catalyst for fantasy progression. As a result of such impediment, the killer becomes consumed with one or more fantasy themes, which ultimately underlie his crimes. Fantasies may include imagined reactions of peers, or the general public's reaction and imagined media attention. These fantasies commonly portray a transcendent image, which resolves, transforms or otherwise alters the meaning of the mass killing. These fantasy themes are an impetus for homicide. The analytical importance of these fantasies points to a *transcendent fantasy theory* of mass killing.

The presence of public labeling that would impose negative definitions of self on the killers is somewhat weak in most cases, thus relegating deviance theory to a limited role in explaining the construction of the mass killer. Nevertheless, Lonnie Athens's (1997) earlier sociological writing on killers underscores the significance of early life trauma in certain types of social situations in forging the fragmentation of self – a factor clearly at work in the career of the mass killer.

Ethnographic content analysis is used to identify common themes expressed through mass media accounts of the mass shootings of Dylan Klebold and Eric Harris (Columbine High School), Seung Hui Cho

(Virginia Tech), George Sodini (LA Fitness) and Joseph Stack (IRS). Source materials for this analysis include: artifacts generated by the offenders prior to commission of their crimes (e.g., diaries, manifestos, blogs, drawings, photographs and videotapes); official findings of governmental review panels; sheriff reports; other public documents; survivor, witness and/or family accounts; news reports; and previous work conducted by other academics. The resultant themes include managing one's fractured identity; transcendence from social obscurity; re-claiming one's masculinity, pride and power; the reaction fantasy; infamy and media attention; the glorification of infamy; seeking revenge; and realizing hubristic desires for attention, reaction and public infamy.

Although the presence of public labeling by *significant others* does not appear prominent, the role of the *generalized other* in terms of the mass media is a key sociological contribution to this analysis. Mass killers frequently use media materials such as video recordings, Web blogs, and handwritten journals to record their plans. The killers not only map out the logistics of the assault, but also use their records as a platform to vent their frustrations, to project real or imagined personal failings onto others and to offer some self-righteous justification for their crime. In doing so, the killers unwittingly paint a portrait revealing their true, maladjusted nature. Creating videos and journals of their vengeful plans appears to give these perpetrators a sense of power and control and justification while fantasizing their revenge.

Managing the fractured identity

Mass killers attach violent meanings to their negative social experiences. "Our past significant social experiences are like 'voices' that stay in our thoughts and go wherever we go, lying 'far beneath our normal level of conscious awareness'" (Athens, 1997, pp. 130 and 139; Rhodes, 1999, p. 83). Together, these voices of past experiences form an amalgam of past social experiences. "It is from this internal repository that a killer generates 'hidden sources of emotions' such as 'fear, anger and hate'" (Rhodes, 1999, pp. 83 and 275). Over time, the potential mass killer develops a fractured self, arising from this distorted conceptualization through which he finds justification for his violent acts.

The self must account for both "conformity and individuality" (Rhodes, 1999, p. 274). If our past social experiences are fragmented – that is, if there is dissonant internal dialogue – then formation of the self is neither completed nor clear. This dissonance causes one to become a riddle to himself or herself, resulting in a contradictory, divided self (ibid.). For mass killers, it is the distorted subconscious dialogue that forms inaccurate perceptions of themselves and society. Ultimately, the killer's self-concept is at odds with his understanding of individuality and social conformity.

Despite such emotional handicaps, many mass killers desperately try to fit into society and their immediate social groups, be it at school or at work. Being unable to achieve a solid sense of who they are – beyond others' definitions of them as misfit or loser – many mass killers give up on conventional means of recognition. In serial killer Ted Bundy's quest for identity, he became a man of many disguises – always putting on a dynamic and charismatic performance (Hickey, 2010). In truth, Bundy saw himself as worthless and a nobody (ibid.). He admitted to his inadequacies in an interview given after his capture and conviction: "I didn't know what made people want to be friends. I didn't know what made people attractive to one another. I didn't know what underlay social interactions" (Michaud and Anesworth, 1983, p. 68). Ill-equipped to make any real social or emotional connections, Bundy created facades in order to blend in with the right groups (Hickey, 2010). Bundy failed, though, in maintaining whatever persona he adopted, and thereby failed to maintain the social connections that gave him self-validation.

In their work on the "Fractured Identity Syndrome" of serial killers, Holmes and Holmes (1999) apply two of Goffman's (1963) concepts of *virtual social identity* and *actual social identity* to the developmental process of serial killers. The virtual social identity is the result of one's self-regulation that society sees and the actual social identity" is "who the person really is, and who the individual knows himself or herself to be" (Holmes and Holmes, 1999, p. 266). It is this fractured internally recognized identity that serial and mass killers constantly wrestle with in an attempt to mask their true self from the public gaze.

Transcendence from social obscurity

According to Athens (1995, p. 579), "people with highly reprobative selves on the horizon may well conclude that it is far better to be known for something bad than not to be known for anything at all". Seung Hui Cho, the (23-year-old) Virginia Tech shooter who killed 32 people, injured 17 others and then committed suicide, exhibited this behavior. He saw himself as invisible to his peers and society, yet he was incapable of fitting in and made little attempt to do so. In class, Cho would sometimes sign his name and identify himself as "question mark" (Virginia Tech Review Panel Report, 2007, p. 42). Cho would often show up in class wearing "reflector" sunglasses and a "hat pulled down to obscure his face" (p. 42). One could say, psychologically, that his attempt at disguise was nothing but a passive-aggressive form of antagonism, a way to draw more attention to himself as a misfit. It is this duality of conformity and individuality that the mass killer cannot achieve, and they simply can neither deny nor escape their fragmented identity and relentless self-talk, which creates a sustained internal crisis.

Artifacts such as blogs, essays, manifestos and videotapes left by some mass killers prior to their massacres speak in very tangible terms of their incompleteness, their inability to cope, their unsatisfactory social experiences and the self-aggrandizement intended to mask their true image of themselves as misfit or loser. For example, the Columbine shooter Eric Harris ponders his complete lack of any real self-identity: "I always try to be different, but I always end up copying someone else. I try to be a mixture of different things and styles but when I step out of myself I end up looking like others or others THINK I am copying" (Shepard, 1999a, Handwritten Journal Entries, A Columbine Site). At the same time, his journal writing espouses his false sense of superiority:

> No one is worthy of shit unless I say they are, I feel like GOD and I wish I was, having everyone being OFFICIALLY lower than me. I already know that I am higher than almost anyone in the fucking world in terms of universal intelligence and where we stand in the universe compared to the rest of the UNIV. (Ibid.)

The killer's narratives attest that both conformity and individuality are unachievable, and there is a recognition of oneself as being incomplete or enigmatic. This self-definition does not happen overnight – some document well their many attempts to reinvent themselves in order to fit in. When multiple attempts have failed to build a unified self, it plays out further in full detail under the strain of a socially obscure life that's no longer worth living. On April 20, 1999, the "Columbine Killers", Eric Harris (18 years old) and Dillon Klebold (17 years old) "dressed in black trench coats and draped with 95 explosive devices and ammunition, walked through their high school in Littleton, Colorado" (Hickey, 2013, p. 120) and killed 15 people, including themselves, and injured 23. Their homicidal rampage gave them a new sense of themselves as having power over people who have wronged them and gave their lives a purpose. Their year of planning and fantasizing about the massacre temporarily made them feel good. They were going to show everyone how superhuman they were and transcend this uncomfortable world in a destructive and commanding way.

Many mass killers will plod along with their injured and splintered self for years until the last final blow – such as the loss of a job, home, partner or money – shatters them completely. Their final violent transcendent fantasies, that they have enough will to create, will sustain them temporarily while plotting their revenge and infamy. During this period of planning a massacre, the self may actually feel more unified than ever before. Like Seung Hui Cho, their new rancorous self may even be derived from previous read-about experiences of infamous mass killers. There could be a kinship developed with other mass killers' defiant acts, especially if it appears that they have suffered similarly to them. Cho (15 years old at the time) wrote a disturbing paper for his English class vividly recounting his thoughts about "suicide and homicide", and he indicated that he "wanted to repeat Columbine" (Virginia Tech Review Panel Report, 2007, p. 35). Cho deeply identified with the Columbine shooters, Harris and Klebold. He openly expressed admiration for the Columbine Killers' "martyrdom" and for their ability to "stand up" to those who had mistreated them (ibid.).

Reclaiming masculinity, pride and power

Reclaiming masculinity, pride and power seems to be at the heart of many vengeful mass killings. This theme especially appears very relevant to high school and college campus shootings. In fact, males have committed nearly all school shootings: "masculinity" is at the forefront and perhaps "the single greatest risk factor in school violence" (Kimmel and Mahler, 2003, p. 1442). It is the risk of falling prey to a form of "cultural marginalization" structured around "criteria for adequate gender performance, specifically the enactment of codes of masculinity". This is more about "the fear that heterosexuals have, that others" might incorrectly "perceive them as gay", than it is about actually being gay (pp. 1445–1446).

If one appears different, or weird, and does not measure up to the norms of hegemonic masculinity, one becomes a prime target for harassment. Studies show that many school shooters, prior to carrying out their massacres, were "gay-baited" for inadequate gender performance (Kimmel and Mahler, 2003, p. 1445). Dylan Klebold, one of the Columbine killers, for example, was constantly "gay-baited" by "being pushed into lockers, grabbed in the corridors and cafeteria and harassed with homophobic slurs" (Levin and Madfis, 2009, p. 1231).

School shooters overwhelmingly tend to be isolated, social outcasts who are repeatedly "physically bullied, teased, humiliated, or ignored by their schoolmates" (Levin and Madfis, 2009, p. 1231). In his book *Comprehending Columbine* (2007), Larkin says that bullying is perpetuated by peer elite groups such as athletes, in the protection of their own social advantage and appearance. Kimmel and Maher (2003) and Newman et al. (2004) have noted the function of school shootings as an acting out of a distorted masculine gender role (Levin and Madfis, 2009). Commonly, school rampage shootings, including those at Columbine, are "retaliatory violence by the victims of physical and/or psychological violence" (Giroux, 2009, p. 227). Thus, a final catastrophic show of force redeems the continually humiliated, ignored or emasculated teen.

In some cases, "it could be argued that these boys are not psychopathological deviants but rather over-conformists to a particular normative construction of masculinity, a construction that defines violence as a legitimate response to a perceived humiliation" (Kimmel and Mahler, 2003, p. 1440). Here again, one can trace predispositions or stressors reflecting the shooter's social or psychological maladjustment. Often with school shooters, the catalyst is some sort of final humiliation (e.g., rejection by a girl, loss of academic standing, ostracism from a community of peers or lack of social integration generally, or even a major illness) (Levin and Madfis, 2009; Madfis and Arford, 2008; Vossekuil et al., 2004).

Columbine was one such place that tragically failed its students (Tonso, 2009). This failure likely was due to a lack of awareness by teachers and administrators, rather than intentional oversight. Today, unlike 20 or so years ago, anti-bullying efforts receive significant attention among school administrators, school resource officers, teachers, parents and the students themselves. The Columbine incident illustrates the dangers in failing to identify, and thus letting flourish, a culture where "some [children] are [perceived as] more worthy than others, and those ... who for whatever reason, would not or could not conform to the dominant mode, deserve predation, get what they deserve and have no claim to dignity" (Larkin, 2007, p. 120).

According to Tonso (2009, p. 1276), this "*systemic subordination ... allowed things to not only get out of hand, but also to remain that way*". The perpetuation of such a culture ultimately led Harris and Klebold to a very dark place of vengeance and vigilantism. Believing they could not get help or attention from school authorities or their own parents, the boys sought to reclaim their power and pride by assuming the identity of a hyper-masculine, violent anti-hero.

As discussed earlier, it is common for some victims of bullying to retreat into a fantasized world of revenge, as a means to reclaim their personal power. The fantasy provides a temporary sanctuary and way of rebuilding a stronger provisional self that is able to cope. Unfortunately, for some of these victims, the provisional self they conceive is not always constructive. Moreover, they do not inhibit acting on such fantasies. This, of course, was the case of the Columbine shooters. Tonso (2009) explains how the provisional selves, re-created by Harris and Klebold, were the product of the boys' psychological derailment:

> With the notion of supremacy, being better than others, more capable and more in power, the two shooters hoped to take over the empowered high ground from those currently in favor at Columbine and to subjugate students in ascendance or destroy the school. Through complicated mental gymnastics, the Columbine shooters developed a way to think of themselves as people with a righteous mission, people who were not subjugated victims of an unjust system but who could instead engage another identity. (p. 1277)

On "Judgment Day", as they called it, Harris and Klebold stormed their high school in Littleton, Colorado. The boys' goal was to kill hundreds, but the explosives they placed throughout the school, thankfully, did not go off. Five secret, self-made videotapes discovered after the assault revealed the boys' scorn for and anger toward their peer group. The tapes detailed the boys' plans to punish all who had mistreated them.

The reaction fantasy: infamy and media attention

In Western culture today, tragedy is sensationalized by the media (Altheide and Snow, 1979). It translates into "viewership, Nielsen points and market share", which is reflected in larger advertising revenues (Larkin, 2009, p. 1322). The media tend to be biased in their coverage of murder cases, deeming certain cases newsworthy because of the number of fatalities or the horrifically exceptional nature of the incidents.

For example, school shootings tend to receive more coverage than the far more common familicides which make up the largest sub-category of mass killing, comprising 28 percent of such homicides (Fox and Levin, 2005). "The family annihilator is someone who feels alone, anomic, and helpless, (who) launches a campaign of violence typically against those who share his home" (Holmes and Holmes, 2001, p. 85). The Columbine and the Virginia Tech massacres are examples in the extreme. Both incidents had all the ingredients for a good news story – an element of disbelief in the likelihood of such an enormous tragedy, the numbers of innocent and defenseless young victims slain or critically injured and a large and gory crime scene. News media outlets went on a feeding frenzy, "oftentimes compet[ing] with police and emergency medical services for space" and opportunity to interview survivors (Larkin, 2009, p. 1322).

The killer, being aware of and influenced by pop culture, sometimes consciously takes media attention into account when plotting his or her crime. For some killers, the extent of media attention seems closely related to which and how many victims are targeted (Larkin, 2009). For example, the Columbine shooters wanted to "create a nightmare so devastating and apocalyptic that the entire world would shudder at their power" (Cullin, 2004, p. 1). Cho also wanted to be included among the notorious ranks of Harris and Klebold, so much so that Cho had the macabre forethought to chainshut the doors of Norris Hall. This act turned Norris Hall into a slaughterhouse, limiting escape routes for victims and delaying the police tactical units from storming the building.

Media and emotion: the effects of broadcasting – real and fictional violence

In his article "The Columbine Shootings and the Discourse of Fear", David Altheide (2009, p. 1355) discusses how "school shootings are very rare", but very commonly feared events. Altheide explains that the elevated sense of danger is partly driven by media reports of such comparatively rare yet sensational homicides. The media are "the most powerful resource for public definitions in our age", and the media have the means to elicit powerful emotional responses – fear, insecurity and hyper-vigilance – from audiences (ibid.). In doing so, the media create an environment where individuals reactively cede their liberty in exchange for an aura of safety (ibid.). Whether or not commercial media intentionally manipulate public perception to favor a political agenda of increased social control, there is an amoral motivation for these corporate conglomerates.

Imagining the aftermath

The media's depiction and characterization of violence – and audiences' reinforcement in accepting the commodity without question – creates for some viewers the perception that utter destruction is an acceptable alternative route to power and infamous status. An aspect of both suicidal (and homicidal) ideation is imagining the aftermath. Fantasizing the aftermath, and how family and community will perceive it, is closely tied to power and infamy fantasies. Individuals may speculate how friends, family or co-workers will react or feel. Some suicidal individuals imagine how their death will hurt those people whom they perceive as having no idea or understanding of their internal turmoil. A common theme involves imagining those people tearfully saying that they wish they had treated the suicidal individual better. This sort of passive aggression fits the "intro-punitive" nature of a suicide victim (Fox and Levin, 1998, p. 439). They turn their anger inward by viewing themselves as "worthless" and blame themselves for their perceived "failures in life", but they do not physically harm anyone (ibid.).

Homicidal individuals, in contrast, might fantasize about wanting society to see them as powerful, clever and superior for pulling off a massacre and making (in their view) oppressive people pay. This difference fits the homicidal individual's pattern of externalizing anger and blame (Fox and Levin, 1998). The mass killer never sees himself at fault (ibid.). Regardless, in both cases, the desire to hurt or seek revenge (as expressed through reaction fantasies) is considered an important warning sign and an important piece to their planning fantasy stage (Rudd et al., 2006).

What's in an exit line?

Killers put much forethought not only into the mechanical planning of mass homicide, but also into delivering an exit line. Exit lines are meant to be another lasting form of revenge that are often rehearsed and fantasized about profusely. This message is an attempt to impress upon the public just how clever and powerful the killer is. In addition, some exit lines are a catch-phrase to secure infamy and media attention. Moreover, exit lines often make known exactly where or on whom the killer directs his anger and why.

Exit lines can be delivered in person – anytime during the mass killing, or often just before a killer commits suicide at the end of the mass killing – or in a blog, manifesto or in video or series thereof. For example, the Columbine killers took the latter approach by making a videotape on April 20, 1999, just 30 minutes prior to their attack. In the self-made video tape, Eric Harris and Dylan Klebold are recording their goodbyes.

Eric: "Say it now."
Dylan: "Hey mom. Gotta go. It's about a half an hour before our little
        judgment day. I just wanted to apologize to you guys for any

crap this might instigate as far as (*inaudible*) or something. Just know I'm going to a better place. I didn't like life too much and I know I'll be happy wherever the fuck I go. So I'm gone. Good-bye. Reb ... "

Eric: "Yea ... Everyone I love, I'm really sorry about all this. I know my mom and dad will be just like ... just fucking shocked beyond belief. I'm sorry, all right. I can't help it."

Dylan: (*interrupts*) "We did what we had to do." (Shepard, 1999b, Video Tape Transcripts, A Columbine Site)

Also, several days earlier, Eric Harris had written in his diary about his plans to "leave a lasting impression on the world" (Healey, July 6, 2006, *Time*). Rather than expressing remorse, the boys' parting words are an attempt to justify the mass homicide and secure infamy for themselves.

Mass murderer George Hennard (35 years old) who, in October of 1991, rammed his pickup truck right through a large plate glass window into a crowded Luby's Cafeteria in Killeen, Texas, was known for his intense and delusional "hatred of women" (Ramsland, 2005, p. 46). The attack occurred at lunchtime and resulted in the deaths of 23 people and the injury of 19 others. While shooting at the Luby's Cafeteria patrons, Hennard shouted: "Wait till those fuckin' women in Belton, Texas see this! I wonder if they think it was worth it!" (Fox and Levin, 2005, p. 231; Hightower, 1991). Although Hennard was shooting at both sexes in the restaurant that day, his words demonstrated a deep-seated hatred and fixation of revenge toward women.

Other exit lines reveal the killer's more amorphous targets – getting back at an institution. Andrew Joseph Stack III (53 years old) vehemently held an irrational belief that the government was wrongful and unjust toward him. On February 18, 2010, Stack made an unsuccessful attempt at mass homicide. His target was the Internal Revenue Service office in the Echelon office complex in Austin, Texas. The building housed other state and federal agencies and, therefore, made a perfect target for a killer with a grievance against the "system." At 9:56 a.m. local time, Stack crashed his Piper Dakota airplane into the building, killing himself and one Internal Revenue Service manager and injuring 13 others. Stack's final words left in his manifesto clearly exposed his hatred for the government and the IRS: "Well, Mr. Big Brother IRS man, let's try something different; take my pound of flesh and sleep well" (FOXNews.com, February 18, 2010).

What is clear from these examples is that, on some level, the mass killers believe they are making a powerful impression and effecting change – as